T5-CQA-929

Each Other

an introduction to interpersonal communication

John R. Bittner
The University of North Carolina at Chapel Hill

Prentice-Hall, Inc., Englewood Cliffs, N.J. 07632

Bittner, John R., (date)
  Each other.

  Bibliography: p.
  Includes index.
  1. Interpersonal communication. 2. Success.
I. Title.
BF637.C45B573 1983   153.6   82–14981
ISBN 0-13-222190-X

For

DENISE

Editorial/Production Supervision: Barbara Kelly Kittle
Interior and Cover Design: Janet Schmid
Page Layout: Gail Cocker
Cover Photograph: © The Bez Box
Aquisitions Editor: Stephen Dalphin
Manufacturing Buyer: Ron Chapman

Chapter opening photo credits: chapter 3, from the MGM release "The Sunshine Boys",
copyright © 1975 Metro-Goldwyn-Mayer, Inc.; chapter 4, Courtesy of Children's Television Workshop; chapter 5, Courtesy Kragen & Co., Los Angeles, CA; chapter 6, Courtesy
Spelling-Goldberg Productions; chapter 7, Copyright © Walt Disney Productions;
chapter 8, Courtesy of Twentieth Century Fox. © 1971, 1982 Twentieth Century-Fox
Film Corp., All Rights Reserved; chapter 9, © Lorimar Productions.

Printed in the United States of America
10 9 8 7 6 5 4 3 2 1

ISBN 0-13-222190-X

Prentice-Hall International, Inc., London
Prentice-Hall of Australia Pty. Limited, Sydney
Editora Prentice-Hall do Brasil, Ltda., Rio de Janeiro
Prentice-Hall of Canada Inc., Toronto
Prentice-Hall of India Private Limited, New Delhi
Prentice-Hall of Japan, Inc., Tokyo
Prentice-Hall of Southeast Asia Pte. Ltd., Singapore
Whitehall Books Limited, Wellington, New Zealand

Contents

Introduction

Introduction

One Monday morning, a student with whom I had become close friends came into my office to chat. During a conversation about campus life, she mentioned she had had a "super" weekend because of a very enjoyable date. When I asked her what was so special about the date, she replied, "We went for a long walk, looked at the stars, then went back to the sorority house and talked."

I didn't think much about the student's comments until two weeks later when she dropped by the office again. This time she told me the relationship with her new boyfriend was progressing and that she was very happy. I inquired what was so special about this person. She replied "We have such good talks; I really enjoy our good talks."

While talking with her further, I found that they had often repeated the same kind of date as when they first met. They would go for a long walk, then go back to the sorority house and talk. Whether or not the relationship had progressed past talking was not important. What was important was that she was putting such a premium on the conversations, "the talks" that they had.

Interpersonal communication had become the precious jewel of the relationship, the important part of the togetherness they were sharing. It was something that she valued higher than any other part of the relationship, at least at that point in its development.

I thought about other students with whom I had chatted about their dates, campus weekends, or other personal relation-

> *Talk is by far the most accessible of pleasures. It costs nothing in money, it is all profit, it completes our education, founds and fosters our friendships, and can be enjoyed at any age and in almost any state of health.*
>
> **Robert Louis Stevenson**

ships they wanted to share. I thought about the students who had said somewhat jokingly, but with more seriousness than they would admit, that they really did not care for the people they were dating or that they just went out to have a good time. Many were disappointed with their relationships, disenchanted with their peers. One student exclaimed, "I even read the *Joy of Sex* and things still haven't improved."

I thought back to the student who had put such a value on the talks she had with her date. Perhaps the students who were disenchanted had really read the wrong book. Perhaps what they should have read was a book on interpersonal communication. I thought of how many dating relationships break down or never even develop because the people are unskilled in effective interpersonal communication. They either don't understand or cannot fully appreciate good listening, good conversation, or the other factors that play an important part in good interpersonal communication.

> **The brain is to think.**
> **The mouth is to talk**
> **In that order.**
>
> **Robert Half**

The student came to mind again a few months later when I read an article by psychologist Phillip G. Zimbardo. Zimbardo was talking about "the age of indifference," in which it is the devil's strategy to trivialize human existence and isolate us from one another while creating the illusion that time pressures, work demands, or economic anxieties are responsible for our being strangers. Zimbardo talked about a handsome and successful television director who had problems dating women after the fifth date. After the first five outings, his "preprogrammed script for entertaining his date" would run out, and the whole relationship would sour when the director had to be himself. Zimbardo pointed out that like many of his peers, the director had not learned how to be intimate, how to be close with another person, and how to make disclosures about his past, his fears, his frustrations, and his future plans. In essence, the director had never learned to reveal the private self that existed behind the "public facade." Such disclosure would presuppose trust, which would in turn be nourished by sharing, something which would give substance and meaning to an intimate relationship. Unlike the student who had learned how to develop a relationship based on mutual communication, the director was only communicating a make-believe image. Even then, he couldn't carry the image beyond the first five meetings. Without good interpersonal communication, the relationship could not exist.

Our perspective of people, of events, and perhaps even of governments changes when interpersonal communication plays a part. Diplomatic shuttle missions would be banished if nations did not think a special quality could exist when two people discussed face to face. The rich rewards of interpersonal contact cannot be duplicated in a diplomatic memo, through a television screen, or through pomp and circumstance. Only interpersonal communication—people-to-people contact—can create a sensitivity to the myriad of emotions involved in making major world decisions. When we realize that the fate of millions of people can hinge on the effective interpersonal communication skills of two leaders, we realize that interpersonal communication may very well be more important than the workings of giant political systems or complex media operations.[1]

An orchestra leader friend wanted to instill an appreciation of music in young children. As the conductor of a children's symphony, he devised a way to break down the interpersonal distance that often existed between the orchestra and the audience. What he devised was to have members of the orchestra actually step down from the stage, walk into the audience, and talk to the children. This action opened up an entire new appreciation of symphonic music for the children. When the symphony played again, it played more than mere sounds. The sounds were made by people, people the children knew on an interpersonal basis.

The idea of close contact with an orchestra was not something new. In the sixteenth and seventeenth centuries, small chamber orchestras played in the homes of wealthy industrialists and plantation owners. But as the wind instruments became louder, the "auditoriums" began to expand in size, and the interpersonal distance became greater and greater. What the orchestra leader did was to shrink the distance so that the music became a personal experience for the audience once again.

If interpersonal communication is something special, yet something that has been diminishing, do we actually communicate less than we did on an interpersonal basis, and if so, why?

A perspective on answering that question was posed by James D. Robinson III, while he was serving as Chairman of the American Express Company.[2] In a speech to the American Advertising Federation, Robinson pointed out the paradox of communication in an information society. We operate in a media environment with attention spans determined by ten- and thirty-second commercials, and we expect communication, whether interpersonal or not, to be in the same neat packages.

Robinson pointed out that we have reached a point in the 1980s at which the public demands ever-increasing amounts of information, yet has dwindling time and patience to absorb it. He speculated we are becoming "fast-fact junkies." We are mastering the art of the "buzz-word," the short descriptive phrase that will capture headlines. Many business leaders, unable to operate and discuss complex issues in such a compressed, "fast-fact junkie," "buzz-word" world, shy away altogether from being interviewed by reporters. Moreover, management, sensing that employees are consuming information and forming opinions based on this condensed information, hesitate even to communicate with them. Robinson offers the opinion that we are at a dangerous point of divergence. "We are talking *at* each other instead of *to* each other. That is not communication; it is monologue. Effective communication runs in both directions. We must improve the ways in which we *listen* to our publics, and then respond to what we hear."

If the mass media are responsible for compressing information and consequently for affecting the way we consume communication, then we should consider the role that two forms of mass media

The whole problem of life is to understand one another.

Woodrow Wilson

—computers and telephones—might play in our ability to communicate with each other.

James Robinson's perspectives came to mind recently while I was driving to school. On that drive, I passed a large billboard with a picture of a smiling farmer advertising hybrid corn. After passing the billboard morning after morning, I almost began to depend on the farmer's bright smile to start my day. After all, he was the first person I was able to look at after stumbling out the door half awake into the wee hours of the morning. Somehow, no matter how dreary the weather, the farmer's bright smile always kept things in perspective. I thought how feed sales representatives probably enjoyed calling on such a farmer. His bright smile obviously showed a positive outlook on life. Without uttering a word, each morning the farmer's smile would say "Have a great day."

Then one morning, the billboard changed. Our bright smiling farmer was replaced with an advertisement for the local telephone company. Reading "around town and out of town," the advertisement showed a large telephone with mock wheels speeding down an interstate highway. The billboard left an unmistakable suggestion: Use the telephone, it's much less expensive than face-to-face communication. But the words "around town" bothered me most. The cost of gasoline, the rush of society, and the demands on people's time all meant that business associates across town, or even people who live nearby, would be reached quicker and less expensively by the telephone.

At the same time, I thought about an advertisement for a famous airline company. It talked about how important it was for an executive to be comfortable while traveling 3000 miles for a business meeting. I also thought how important it was for that executive to have good interpersonal-communication skills. It was so important, in fact, that a corporation would invest tens of thousands of dollars in that executive's salary and a few more thousand to fly that person half way around the world for a face-to-face meeting with another executive. They could have met much less expensively, *yet not as productively*, over the telephone. Anyone who lacked good interpersonal-communication skills would not have been sent on the trip, and even more importantly, would not have reached a high-level position in the company.

It made me stop and consider that with the increased cost of travel and the surge of new technology, interpersonal face-to-face communication was fast becoming a limited resource. As a limited resource, it would become more valuable. Obviously, a business executive could accomplish much by using the telephone. But when that person appeared at the office of a client or at the home of a customer, the meaning and importance of the visit and the communication which took place would carry much greater value than it had in the past.

While interpersonal communication is vital in corporate settings, from selling corn to meeting with international executives, we should also not forget its importance in the home and our daily interactions with family members. Again, technology is and will continue to affect those interactions.

In the same article in which Phillip Zimbardo talked about the television director's having trouble on his fifth date, he also alluded to the effect of home computers on family relationships. Any parent whose son or daughter has been bitten by the computer bug can understand Zimbardo's comment that many people are becoming part of a new subculture in which "hackers"—people who spend excessive amounts of time with computers—will have a profound affect on any American family. Zimbardo pointed out that

> hackers spend long hours at night or early in the morning, when "down time" is shorter, playing with their programs and sending messages via electronic bulletin boards to hacker associates seated at terminals a few feet away. Fascination with the computer becomes an addiction, and as with most addictions, the "substance" that gets abused is human relationships.[3]

Zimbardo goes on to suggest that the "hacker mentality" can end up putting people at the bottom of a priority stack.

Whether or not technology will interfere with interpersonal communication so much that relationships will disintegrate, and we will become a society interacting electronically with special languages, is open to speculation. In any case, however, in this age of technology, in which fast facts, buzz words, and hackers are part of everyday life, good interpersonal communication is perhaps more important than it has ever been.

It is with this in mind that I approach the subject of interpersonal communication. The text talks about interpersonal communication in the family, at work, at school, and elsewhere. It also examines such concepts as language, nonverbal communication, our self-concepts, and our ability to listen to what others may be communicating to us.

I hope you enjoy the chapters which follow. I have attempted to avoid using academic jargon, and when new terms do appear, I have tried to explain them so that they are easy to understand. I have also attempted to use examples to which all of us can relate. I hope that when you finish the book, you will have gained a new appreciation for interpersonal communication.

I am reminded of the student who rode a charter boat off the southern California coast to watch whales migrating from Alaska. She said of the experience, "It was an encounter of substance." Effective interpersonal communication creates encounters of substance with meaning, a foundation, something of lasting value rather than fleeting appeal. It helps to create true communication in which two people join ideas, thoughts, and feelings in an interactive experience that is rewarding and beneficial to both.

An encounter of substance is like a fine jewel, to be prized, appreciated, and nurtured. Encounters of substance build relationships, develop trust, instill credibility, and create an atmosphere for mutual exchange which can continue to improve the value of future interpersonal relationships. Encounters of substance are what this book is all about.

SOCIAL SKILLS 100: PREVENT DEFENSE

WASHINGTON — Now that summer vacation is almost here, we'd like to suggest a new fall-term elective be set up for high school and college students: Social Skills 100.

We recommend this course because we've met a number of social misfits at patio cookouts lately. Most of them have been men just recently out of college.

Of course, it's always been easier to laugh at the social misadventures of others rather than at our own. We recently observed a handsome 22-year-old friend telephone a female classmate whom he'd been eyeing for months. The resulting conversation left him demoralized for weeks.

After the fellow mumbled, "Is Susie there?" he overheard her roommates plot their reply. First, he was told that "Susie" was already at the movies. When he foolishly inquired how long she'd be gone, he heard a deafening chorus of "Forever!" in the background.

But everyone has his or her own horror stories about dating and other social misfortunes.

What these memorable experiences prove is that men and women should polish their social skills before leaving school. Otherwise, they may find themselves, as millions do now, living alone and friendless in a singles apartment.

It's no fun trying to meet members of the opposite sex after college graduation. One can take the afterwork-drinks routine, make blind dates with a friend's roommate or check out "personal ads" in the back of the New York Review of Books. But these avenues don't always have the markings of long-term relationships.

Two recent university studies indicate, as we've already suspected, that men are increasingly more intimidated by dating than women. One study by Hal Arkowitz at the University of Arizona has revealed that male college students are definitely more troubled by their role than women are by theirs.

Though not every man is bothered by recent social changes, many men don't know who's in charge anymore. On one hand, some believe women still expect them to initiate social activities; on the other, they're often incapable of doing so. Consequently, many a fellow spends his Friday evenings at home, fretting by the telephone.

While the older generation may snicker at today's slow learners, they should understand that the sexual revolution of the last 10 to 15 years is by no means complete.

Not surprisingly, some undergraduate men are owning up to their troubles and seeking psychological assistance before leaving school. Campus counseling centers and community hot lines are reporting a lively business.

To help young men reduce their anxiety, Arkowitz and other doctors are trying to expose their patients to "dating-like situations." Patients practice initiating dates and social conversation in prearranged exchange with members of the opposite sex.

It's indeed a sad day for romance when Americans have to enroll in dating clinics. Yet, because many need such help and can't afford costly psychologists, schools may want to fill the gap.

For some, a course in social skills, as ludicrous as it may sound, might nip the problem in the bud. We'd like to see a course that includes everything from telephoning techniques to hints for talking with total strangers. Video cameras might be used to record exercises in interaction. Students could then see how silly they sound when describing an appendectomy or playing the "who-you-know game."

Men would also learn to stop boring women with irrelevant conversation. Or, at least, do more than grunt between slugs of beer. Women we know are tired of being good listeners. They don't appreciate doing "support work" in cocktail conversation such as, "That's right, dear," or "Oh, what a good point Jim."

Such a course would have multiple benefits. Often times men who have trouble with women are no better in developing friendships with other guys.

A social skills class won't guarantee that all men and women will someday feel comfortable asking each other out for the evening. Both sexes would, however, benefit from actively pursuing a more cooperative social spirit.

Social self-confidence is nothing to laugh about. But if we don't offer young men and women an opportunity to develop it, our country could foster more loners who try to kill a president for a movie star's attention. And we don't need any more of them.

Here and Now by Glen Shearer. Copyright © Field Enterprises, Inc. Courtesy of Field Newspaper Syndicate.

chapter one

Getting Started: Approaches and Perspectives

PREVIEW   *After completing this chapter, we should be able to:*

Trace the development of human communication and language.

Develop our own definition of communication.

List three types of communication.

Understand intrapersonal communication.

Understand interpersonal communication.

Describe the role of physical and semantic noise in interpersonal communication.

Explain fields of experience, homophily, and heterophily.

Distinguish the factors which differentiate mass communication from intrapersonal and interpersonal communication.

Understand the common ground between all three types of communication.

Distinguish the different approaches to studying interpersonal communication.

Describe the interpersonal needs of inclusion, control, and affection.

To begin our discussion of interpersonal communication, let's venture back in time to the dawn of our prehistoric ancestors, those first humans to emerge from caves and begin reacting to each other and their environment. Archeologists, who refer to this era as the Ramapithecus Age, tell us that these creatures resembled apes more than humans. They did, however, possess the basic senses of sight, hearing, touch, smell, and taste. As the central nervous system developed, they began to acquire basic tools necessary for communication.

The Development of Human Communication

The cave dwellers of prehistoric times could tell the difference between pleasurable and unpleasurable experiences. Although at first their perceptions were rudimentary, such as the difference between the chill of a blizzard or the pleasure of a warm fire, they gradually refined their ability to perceive other experiences. This development of a more sophisticated brain and central nervous system ultimately aided in satisfying their basic needs: sex to increase their numbers, light to see, air to breathe, food to eat, water to drink, sleep to strengthen, and shelter to protect them from the environment. By 300,000 B.C., the nervous system and brain as well as the genetic features began to resemble those of present-day humans.

The Development of Language

Some 200,000 years later, the fundamentals of language emerged. Prior to this time, humans communicated mostly through touch. Researchers have debated even to this day whether language developed through learning or instinct. Recent experiments conducted under the eye of retired Harvard University psychologist B. F. Skinner put two white male pigeons, whimsically named Jack and Jill, in Plexiglas cubicles.[1] The pigeons were taught to both recognize and to press keys that had colors or symbols on them. If they hit the right keys, they were rewarded with grain. It wasn't long before the two pigeons actually began to converse with each other by depressing keys. The pigeons grew increasingly sophisticated in their communication until they were able to both initiate a conversation and reward each other through conditioning techniques. From this experiment, the Harvard team

IN SCIENCE

Scientists begin to question grammatical competence of apes

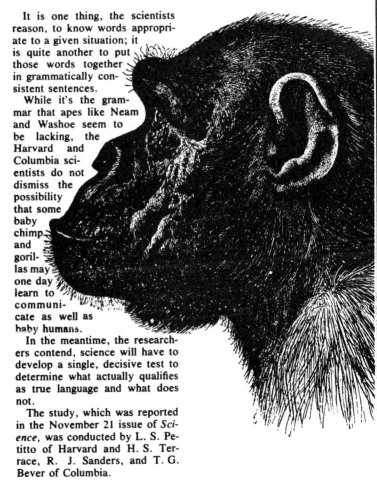

In recent months, Washoe, Sarah, Lena, Koko, and a handful of other chimpanzees and gorillas have been breaking down what scientists had long considered the most formidable barrier between human beings and the lower primates: the ability to communicate in words.

Although physical limitations restrict the apes' ability to speak, most who have been trained to communicate with their human captors are able to learn a vast vocabulary in American Sign Language or other "artificial" dialects.

So impressive have been the apes' linguistic achievements that one of the researchers working with primates at the University of Oklahoma recently proclaimed, "Language is no longer the exclusive domain of man."

Now, however, a group of scientists from Columbia and Harvard Universities are beginning to question the grammatical competence of apes.

With the help of their own talking monkey, Neam Chimpsky, the researchers have concluded that ape utterances only superficially resemble human sentences. Upon close observation, the scientists say, the ape phrases are proving to be nothing more than "unstructured combinations" of signals.

It is one thing, the scientists reason, to know words appropriate to a given situation; it is quite another to put those words together in grammatically consistent sentences.

While it's the grammar that apes like Neam and Washoe seem to be lacking, the Harvard and Columbia scientists do not dismiss the possibility that some baby chimp and gorillas may one day learn to communicate as well as baby humans.

In the meantime, the researchers contend, science will have to develop a single, decisive test to determine what actually qualifies as true language and what does not.

The study, which was reported in the November 21 issue of *Science*, was conducted by L. S. Petitto of Harvard and H. S. Terrace, R. J. Sanders, and T. G. Bever of Columbia.

(*The Chronicle of Higher Education*, December 3, 1979.)

suggested that behavioral conditioning, "not some unique characteristic of the brain," enables pigeons, chimps, and humans to learn and participate in symbolic conversation.

At Columbia University, another research team was dealing with chimpanzees, and came to somewhat similar conclusions. A chimp named Nim had learned 125 word signs and almost 20,000 phrases which seemed to follow the rules of grammar used by humans.[2] But when scientists started to look more closely at Nim, they found that his "conversation" was initiated by prompting. Rather than his using anything resembling instinct, they felt the chimp had been taught to use words in sequence because he understood a reward would follow.[3] Yet there are those who disagree with exactly how Nim learned language. When a scientific journal reported on Nim's language abilities, other researchers who claimed to have taught chimpanzees to place words in meaningful order strongly disagreed with the findings. But they blamed the Columbia researchers for causing the chimp to learn the language by conditioning, not the chimp's inability to compose grammatically correct sentences or to communicate with humans by using our own language.

Regardless of which idea we accept, we do know that about 7000 B.C., humans began to communicate with *pictographs*, which were wall etchings on the insides of caves and temples (Figure 1-1). Even today, these pictographs remain vivid messages of what life and religious beliefs were like for our ancestors. We know that between 3000 and 2000 B.C. pictographs became highly stylized. The first symbols came into existence, and primitive alphabets of 600 characters were developed. Our

FIGURE 1-1

Cave paintings found in Lascaux, France. Early forms of human communication included pictographs, which were wall etchings on the insides of caves and temples. Today, these images provide an important clue to discovering how our system of communication developed and the role of symbols and language in human interaction. (*Peter Buckley*)

ancestors began to record sociocultural events, attitudes, values, and habits on the walls of caves, on animal skins, and on the bark of trees. From these records, we can even trace the development of their moral codes.

We now know that as society develops, communication is a key factor in the rapid growth of learning. It's also the medium through which people can exchange symbols and thus propagate that learning at a much faster rate. Along with a system of production to create goods and services, a system of defense to protect against intruders, and a method of member replacement sufficient to counteract disease and other elements, a system of communication develops social control and maintains order in society. Even today, these basic functional requirements are fulfilled, though the methods may be more sophisticated and efficient.

But this is not a history book. We want to concentrate our attention on contemporary uses of interpersonal communication, on the system of communication we use to talk to each other in everyday life.

To better understand this system of communication, let's define what it is. When we have that definition, we can begin to understand interpersonal communication.

Toward Defining "Communication"

What is the definition of communication? Do not be surprised if one does not automatically come to mind. Even scholars disagree on an acceptable definition.

Transmitting Information We frequently answer the question using the term *transmit*. Yet if we transmit something, are we communicating? Consider the person who stands on a hilltop and shouts across the valley to hear the echo. Is that person communicating? Consider the football coach who comes off the sidelines to yell at a referee. Certainly the football coach is transmitting information. But is he communicating? Consider the student who tells her roommate to clean up the room. She has transmitted information; but two days later, the room remains a mess. Again, people are all transmitting information. But did communication take place?

Transferring Information Another term students frequently use to define communication is *transfer*. Stop again and consider the examples used in the previous paragraph. Is the person who stands on the hilltop shouting across the valley to hear the echo transferring information? Certainly that person is transmitting, but does transfer take place if no one hears the shouting? What occurs if someone on the other side of the hilltop shouts back with an answer? Does communication take place? Now let's consider the roommate. What if the roommate heard the request but was too busy to clean up the room and did not res-

FIGURE 1-2

Public speaking is one example of human communication. Although many speakers transmit information, information transfer and transaction does not always take place. (*Irene Springer*)

pond? Was information transferred? Did communication take place? And what about the football coach? What if the referee refuses to change the call after the coach yells from the sidelines? A transfer of information took place, but did communication take place? What about a person who delivers a speech? (Figure 1–2).

Transaction   Still a third word which frequently crops up in a definition of communication is *transact*. What happens during transaction? Transaction means not only that information has been sent and received, but that some additional information has been *sent back* as a form of *feedback* (Figure 1–3). For example, we might suggest that if the person yelling across the valley heard a reply, then decided to yell back again, transaction had taken place. If the roommate had at least acknowledged she heard the request to clean up the room, even though she didn't clean it, is that a transaction? And what if the referee refuses to change the call but nevertheless has a healthy argument with the football coach? Is this a transaction?

Dictionary Examines Communication The first definition of *communicate* (Figure 1–4) in the dictionary states that it is "To make known; impart; transmit." All three of our examples—the person shouting from the hilltop, the roommate, and the football coach—made known, imparted, and transmitted information. The dictionary next defines *communicate* as "To have an interchange, as of thoughts or ideas." The latter definition is perhaps closest to the word *trans-action* and certainly *transfer*. If you're talking with your instructor about a grade on an examination, you're probably having an interchange of thoughts or ideas. If you're participating in a class discussion, you're having an interchange of thoughts or ideas.

com•mu•ni•ca•tion

1. To make known; impart; transmit. 2. To have an interchange, as of thoughts or ideas. 3. Something communicated. 4. A system of sending and receiving messages, as by telephone, television, or computer. 5. A connection. 6. A channel or conduit for information. 7. Movement of messages from sender to receiver.

FIGURE 1-4

Apply the definition of communication to your own experiences with interpersonal communication. Think of different people with whom you interact and ask yourself: How does the definition of communication fit my own skill and behavior in interpersonal communication? (*Irene Springer*)

Educators Define Communication

How have other writers defined this elusive term? Some define communication as "the process of creating meaning."[4] Others define communication as "a dynamic process in which man consciously or unconsciously effects the cognitions of another through materials or agencies used in symbolic ways."[5] Still others stress the importance of viewing communication as "an act of sharing, rather than as something someone does to someone else."[6]

All of the definitions we have just discussed fit in some way into our examples. The person standing on the hilltop obviously gave some meaning to the words that he was shouting across the valley. Perhaps he was shouting "I love you," "Help!" or merely "Hello there." Definite meanings would be expressed in all of those words. Certainly the roommate who wanted the mess cleaned up and the football coach who wanted the play changed were also creating meaning, if not for the person receiving their communication, then certainly in their own minds when they transmitted it. And there is little doubt we are correct when we call communication a dynamic process which "consciously or unconsciously" affects others. We have all had experiences in which we both consciously made an effort to communicate to someone, and unconsciously communicated something entirely different than what we had intended. On the other hand, we might have difficulty agreeing with the football coach if we define communication as "an act of sharing, rather than . . . something someone does to someone else."

We can see how difficult it is to arrive at a single definition of communication. No one definition seems to encompass every facet and type of communication. Yet all of them are correct. "It's a dynamic process."

If you started this section expecting to pick out a specific definition, I hope you are not too disappointed. I have deliberately avoided prescribing a definition because it is more important for you to work at your own definition (Figure 1–5). Look at the different concepts we have explored and arrange them to fit what your own experience with communication is or has been. Examine how you might define communication in different situations, how different rules of good communication you already perceive might affect your definition. By exploring all of these approaches, I hope you will discover that communication, and especially interpersonal communication, is truly a dynamic, ever-changing process.

Types of Communication

Moving from our analysis of the term communication, we now examine the *process* of communication. We begin by studying a communication model and the three types of communication important to our study in this text: intrapersonal, interpersonal, and mass communication. These three types of

FIGURE 1-5

Develop your own definition of COMMUNICATION. Here are some words to help you begin.

Transmit
Transact
Transfer
Interact
Interchange
Irreversible
Information
Receiver
Connection
Channel
Messages
Interactive
Symbols
Sender
Passage
Meaning
Words
Face-to-Face
Unconscious
Conscious
Intention
Dynamic
Ideas
Coder

communication are directly interrelated with each other; one is not necessarily exclusive of the next. An understanding of all three is critical to an awareness of the role of human communication in society.

Using a Communication Model

Different communication models serve as our guides to the communicative process. They enable us to examine it from different perspectives. As with definitions for communication, all communication models are workable.

Another way to think of a communication model is as a stop-action picture of the communicative process. When we take a photograph of something, we stop the action. Similarly, when we use a communication model, we capture it for a moment to study it. For this book, we define a communication model as a stop-action picture of the communication process. Let's now develop our model (Figure 1–6) to understand the different types of communication.

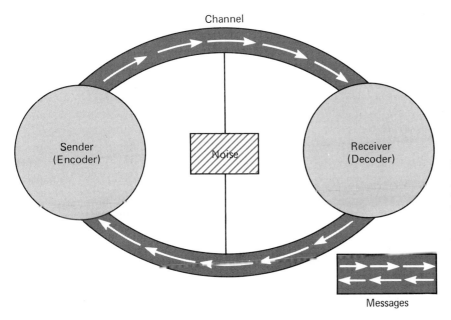

FIGURE 1-6

A model of communication can be viewed as a stop-action picture of the communication process. Keep in mind, however, that effective interpersonal communication is a dynamic process where messages are continually being exchanged by sender and reciver.

Intrapersonal Communication: Communication Within Ourselves

We began this chapter with a discussion about prehistoric humans interacting with their environment. Much of that communication was intrapersonal communication—communication within oneself. Each human commu-

'Ears' and 'eyes' in your skin

You're piloting a supersonic airplane and you're confronted with an emergency. You need all of the information you can get in a hurry to make a critical decision. Your eyes are rapidly scanning the dials and your headset is absorbing a clattering of audio input.

Why not relieve the overburdened channels by taking some of the information through the skin? For some kinds of messages the skin offers a valuable supplement to the ears and eyes, contends Prof. Frank A. Geldard of Princeton University. It has a receptive surface about a thousand times greater than the retina. It is derived from tissue similar to that of the ear drum. . . .

Bell Telephone Laboratories devised for him an instrument for leading speech sounds into an electromechanical transducer actuating the skin. This piezoelectric unit, called a teletactor, was applied to the fingers. After 28 half-hour training periods, the feeler could learn to judge with about 75 percent accuracy which one of 10 short sentences had been delivered to the skin. In another experiment, Gault found that after 30 hours of practice single words could be recognized in about half the time.

(Source: A.J. Snikder, "'Ears' and 'eyes' in your Skin," Science Digest 61 (June, 1967), pp. 17–76)

FIGURE 1–7

nicated with other people but not in the highly developed form of symbolic language that we use today. A grunt or a knock on the head may have been the equivalent of saying, "Would you like to spend the evening together?" or "I love you." But even before the knocks and the grunts, the environment created the first forms of communication. Cave dwellers perhaps awoke on a clear morning, blinked at the sunlight, touched the warm rays of sun on a stone, and felt the cold breeze against their faces. If it rained, they sought shelter. If it snowed, they sought warmth. If it became too hot, they went inside the shaded cave and cooled off. This process of sunlight entering the eye and communicating brightness to a central nervous system, the tactile sense organs of the skin (Figure 1–7) detecting warmth on a rock or a cold breeze, and the decisions to go inside to seek shelter were all forms of communication taking place within the individuals. Most of the communication took place between the sense organs and the central nervous systems: an electrochemical action of the body. The sense organs detect and send information; the central nervous system processes it. In our communication model, such action would be described by the components of the sender and the encoder. We process such information every day, although we've probably never stopped long enough to think about it. Let's start thinking about it now by considering some of the common applications of intrapersonal communication.

We can view the process of intrapersonal communication most clearly by examining how we use our central nervous system and our senses to adapt to reality in our lives (Figure 1–8). First, let's discover how we adapt biologically to our environment.[7] While studying this adaption, remember: Although we may make personal decisions to exist within the environment, we do not make these decisions in a vacuum, away from the concerns of other people. For example, each Sunday morning, the head of the household goes outside to pick the paper off the front walk where the delivery girl always deposits it—under the limb of a large apple tree. And each Sunday morning, half awake, the head of the household invariably stands up and hits that tree limb. Connecting one's head with a tree limb sends an immediate impulse to the brain which is encoded. Intrapersonal communication definitely takes place.

The head of the household has a number of ways to adapt to the environment and avoid colliding with the apple tree. The person might ask the papergirl to place the paper on the porch. But that request could delay the papergirl's schedule perhaps two minutes. It could also prompt the rest of her customers to request the same kind of service. So that idea is discarded for a more realistic one: cutting the limb off the apple tree. Yet all of the neighbors have commented on how beautiful the street looks when the apple blossoms are in full bloom. Finally, the decision is made to simply be more careful. But as you can see, that decision and consequential adaptation to the environment was made with full consideration of other people and other relationships. In other words, we integrate our biological functions with those of others in order to survive in our environment.

Practical Applications of Intrapersonal Communication

Let's examine some of the more common forms of intrapersonal communication and how they affect our behavior.

Adapting to Stress Consider how we adapt to stress. Stress can be one of the most damaging influences on the biological makeup of the body, to say nothing of its affect on our ability to communicate interpersonally. Stress is a stimulus just like hitting your head on an apple tree. And any stimulus causes one or more reactions. We may have a headache under extreme stress. We may sweat under extreme stress. All of these are biological reactions our bodies are making to signal us that we are overloading our sensory systems.

How do we adapt to stress? By adapting biologically, we may decide to overeat. Yet overeating may produce just the opposite effect we desire, especially if a stress-prone digestive system can't handle that much food. We may decide to overdrink, but find the consequences of the local pub worse than the cure. We may also lie awake with a case of insomnia while trying to solve a stressful problem and pay for that wakefulness the next day. As we can see, these negative biological adaptations can cause more stress, not less.

We might be much better off to try positive adaptions to stress. Physical exercise tends to prepare the body for stressful situations and creates in some people a tension-relieving mechanism. Under a doctor's care, we might develop a jogging program or a strenuous exercise program (Figure 1–9). Some form of relaxation may also help us to alleviate stress. Sit-

In the blink of an eye, virtually all visual stimulus is cut off from the brain. Under normal conditions, a person blinks every few seconds. But despite all those interruptions, the world looks normal to most people. In contrast, when the lights in a room are switched off momentarily, or when people voluntarily blink their eyes, they experience a pronounced visual effect—the world goes temporarily black.

Why does involuntary eye blinking go unnoticed?

Frances C. Volkmann, of the department of psychology at Smith College, and Lorrin A. Riggs and Robert K. Moore, of the Hunter Laboratory of Psychology at Brown University, have tried to answer that question.

Their conclusion is that the brain generates an "inhibitory signal" that accompanies the blink, thus diminishing its effect.

By using a special technique to stimulate the retina through the back of the eyeball, the scientists were able to observe how this so-called neural inhibitory mechanism contributes to the "continuity of vision." Details of their study were published in the February 22 issue of *Science* magazine.

(*From the* Chronicle of Higher Education *and the February 22, 1981 issue of Science*)

FIGURE 1–8

FIGURE 1–9

Under careful supervision and doctor's care, strenuous exercise programs are being utilized by some as a way of coping with stress. The body's internal mechanisms which adapt to our environment through intrapersonal communication function to help us overcome obstacles in our daily lives. © 1979 Universal City Studios, Inc.

Change your thoughts and you change your world.

Norman Vincent Peale

ting quietly in pleasant surroundings or going for a walk in the park or the country are all ways of alleviating stress. Cutting down on the amount we eat and cutting back or stopping the intake of caffeine or other stimulants may also be solutions to handling stress. All of the solutions are biological adaptations to our environment using our own personal encoding system.

One of the most recently acclaimed methods of handling stress through intrapersonal communication is biofeedback. You've probably heard about it or read about it in popular magazines or scholarly journals. Among other things, a machine is used to help monitor one's own body stresses. Then through a system of trained relaxation, using everything from relaxing muscles to imagining relaxing scenes, people are able to minimize reactions to stressful responses. Biofeedback has even been used to help students control anxiety during examinations.

Using Memory Memory is another form of intrapersonal communication with a practical application. It actually involves retrieving and encoding information stored in our brains. Remembering not to bump into the tree limb is an example of our memory helping us to biologically adapt to our environment.

When we are trying to remember something, we know, for example, that associating it with something else can help us increase our memory potential. Let's assume you go to a party and meet someone whose name you'd very much like to remember. You would either like to ask that person out for a date or be asked out for a date by that person at some future time. You've decided that remembering that person's name is the first step in being able to strike up a conversation. Suppose the person's name is Heather. Perhaps at some time in the past, you've met another person named Heather. Stop for a moment and mentally compare the qualities of that Heather with the Heather you just met. There may be many or no similarities, but you are forming an association with previous information. In short, you're "hanging" new information on old information. The new information is then stored, and the recall is aided by your earlier experience. If you've never met a Heather before, you can help your memory with other associations. A friend of the author likes to remember names by rhyming them with other familiar words. For example, Heather might be rhymed with feather. If Heather happens to be a very petite person, you might say to yourself, "There's Heather; she's light as a feather." Another person I know likes to visualize an image to remember a name. In this instance, she may create the image of a girl named Heather riding a white horse. Another friend easily remembers everyone she meets named Sarah, because she always thinks of a Sarah as sitting on the seat of a covered wagon. Although these associations may seem humorous and have no relationship to the people we may meet, they are simply ways to aid memory and stimulate the process of intrapersonal communication. By using them, we're helping our encoding systems by improving our memories.

> *A strong memory is generally coupled with an informed judgment.*
>
> **Montaigne**

Adapting to Physical Things

Intrapersonal communication also helps us to integrate with our physical environment. Physical environments are different from biological environments. Whereas the former is concerned with our ability to process information directly associated with our bodily functions, such as overcoming stress, the latter concerns our ability to deal with the physical things with which we come in direct contact. Asking directions on how to get around a collapsed bridge in the road would be one example. Now let's see how intrapersonal communication helps us through interpersonal adaptation.

Adapting to Individuals

Intrapersonal communication is the foundation for interpersonally adapting to other people. We process all kinds of stimuli when we communicate with other people. Using that *intra*personal processing to communicate *inter*personally is one of the most important functions of our *internal* body-processing systems. For example, many psychologists feel that to successfully manage worry, stress, and anxiety, we must share our problems and communicate with others. Other research suggests that the least damage from stressful situations is done to people who discharge their fears through interpersonal relations.[8] Throughout this text, I talk about how to successfully interact through interpersonal communication. And we find that intrapersonal communication is the first step toward that successful interaction.

Adapting to Groups Another function of intrapersonal communication is to help us adapt to group relationships, again by using the same internal message-processing systems. Suppose you're sitting around the family dinner table, talking with your family about someone with whom you are in love or perhaps about your college finances. As you sit there, you're constantly processing information received from the other members of your family. Even though you may not be talking to them directly, you are listening, making judgments, and sorting out the various bits of communications being sent to you.

Perhaps you are at a party at your living unit. You are continually processing information in order to associate with the group. Perhaps there is a bowl of popcorn and you'd very much like to have the last handful remaining in the bowl. Yet, you consider how the other members of the group might feel and how conspicuous you would be to go over and grab that last morsel. You're using intrapersonal communication to adapt to the group.

Do you live with roommates? If you do, your behavior adapts to the group, and things you say and do are in a different context than if you were living alone. Participating in group discussions, hanging pictures on the wall, and putting a plant on a windowsill are all forms of adapting to the sociocultural group of which you're a part. We examine these group situations in more depth in the chapter on small-group communication.

In conclusion, we should remember that intrapersonal communication is the most basic form of communication: communication within ourselves. Essentially, it encodes information from our environment and helps us to adapt to that environment, whether it be biological, physical, interpersonal, or sociocultural. It is an integral part of all other kinds of communication. In fact, interpersonal and mass communication cannot exist without it. Let's discover why by discussing these next two kinds of communication.

Interpersonal Communication

In his book *Interpersonal Communication: Survey and Studies*, Dean Barnlund defines interpersonal communication as being "concerned with the investigation of relatively informal social situations in which persons in face-to-face encounters sustain focused interaction through the reciprocal exchange of verbal and nonverbal cues."[9] Another definition is offered by Fred Jandt, who defines interpersonal communication as "the academic study of how values and self-identity are developed through face-to-face interaction."[10] Many of the ideas encompassed in both of these definitions are dealt with in detail in later chapters in this text. We examine Barnlund's "social situations" in our discussion about interpersonal communication in small groups. We also look at how his "nonverbal cues" affect interpersonal communication. Jandt mentions "self-identity." In the next chapter, we discuss how our own self-identities are developed and how they play an important part in interpersonal communication.

If we apply interpersonal communication to our communication model, we add a *receiver* and a *decoder*. We also add a *medium* of communication which in this case is the human voice.

To better understand these components, suppose Jim is walking to work this morning, and coming toward him is someone he would like to ask to a party. He begins to think (intrapersonal communication). How will I start the conversation? What will I say to get her to stop and talk to me? After she does what will my first words be? What will her response be? Will I be embarrassed? Will she say yes or no? How will I react if she says yes? Finally, when she is close to Jim, he slows down his walk, looks toward her, and says, "Sally, do you have a second?" And Sally replies, "Sure, Jim, how are you doing this morning?"

At this point, interpersonal communication has occurred. Jim has encoded information, communicated it through the medium of the human voice to Sally, and Sally has replied. Sally has also decoded information. She may have been thinking, "Gee, there's Jim. I wonder if he'll stop and talk? I wonder where he got that sharp new sweater?"

By Sally's responding to Jim's question, we see another component of our communication model—*feedback*. And we have also seen a reversal of our original communication model, because when Sally spoke to Jim, she became the sender while Jim became the receiver.

Once again we see that interpersonal communication is a very *dynamic* process. Each person participating in the conversation switches roles back and forth between being sender and receiver, all the while providing feedback to the other person.

The Role of Noise in Interpersonal Communication

Another component of our communication model that is important to understand is the concept of noise. For our purposes, we describe two kinds of communication noise—semantic and physical.

Physical Noise   Physical noise is concerned with sounds which may interrupt the communcation process. If a truck goes by when Sally and Jim are speaking and they do not hear each other, that would be an example of physical noise. Perhaps it starts to rain and they need to interrupt the conversation to take cover. That would also be physical noise.

Semantic Noise   On the other hand, Sally may say something that Jim does not understand, something in which the meanings of words become confused. That is an example of semantic noise.

For example, when Jim asked Sally to go to the party, she may have replied, "Jim, I would love to. You are so sweet." Sally may have meant her reply to be a form of superficial response similar to "that sounds neat." Yet by being conditioned to hear and use the word "love" only in the romantic sense, Jim may have gasped slightly at Sally's comment.

In review, we've learned that interpersonal communication is face-to-face communication in which at least two people are participating. It is a process in which roles are interchanged between the sender and receiver with each receiving feedback from the other. The process, however, can be broken up by noise, be it physical or semantic.

S haring with Each Other

At this point, we want to add an additional component to our communication model—the *field of experience.*

Fields of Experience Fields of experience (Figure 1–10) are abstract concepts necessary before effective interpersonal communication can take place. For example, if Sally were unaware of a Saturday night party, Jim would have had to inform her. In this case, Jim's field of experience would not have overlapped Sally's. Yet they *did* have things in common. They had obviously met someplace before and perhaps they even took a class together. These experiences would be common references that would aid them in processing both intrapersonal

FIGURE 1–10

Overlapping "fields of experience" facilitate effective interpersonal communication. The process of overlapping those fields of experience is the responsibility of all persons involved in a communicative exchange. This sharing process, also referred to as "homophily," opens up channels of communication and creates a mutual awareness of each other's ideas, opinions, references, feelings, emotions, and other factors which have an effect on interpersonal communication. (*Based on W. Schramm, "How Communication Works," in* Process and Effects of Mass Communication, ed. Wilbur Schramm, Urbana: University of Illinois Press, 1955, pp. 4, 6, 7, 8)

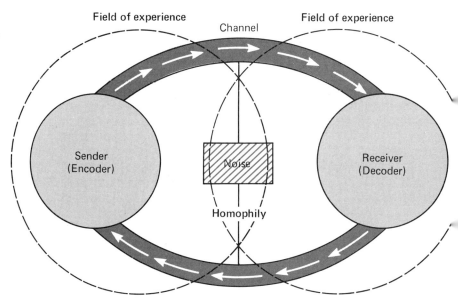

Field of experience   Channel   Field of experience

Sender (Encoder)   Noise   Receiver (Decoder)

Homophily

Getting Started: Approaches and Perspectives

and interpersonal communication. When such fields of experience overlap, effective interpersonal communication can take place.

Homophily   Another term that can be applied to our communication model is *homophily*. Homophily is concerned with where fields of experience *overlap*, that point at which two people communicating have things in common (Figure 1–11) with each other. Studies show that communication has an opportunity to succeed much more readily when considerable homophily exists between a sender and receiver.[11] Let us examine this concept in more detail.

Imagine that you have just received a B on an examination, and you feel you want to know more about the questions you missed. You make an appointment with the instructor to go over the test. What do you both have in common that will have a bearing on your conversation? First and foremost is the course itself, which you take and she teaches, and second is the examination, which you took and she authored. These, then, become the basis for your conversation. In effect, it was this commonality, this overlap of fields of experience, that brought you to communicate with the instructor in the first place.

Or suppose you have had a hard day of classes and decide to go to the student union for a snack. Upon entering the lunch area,

ATTITUDE

Doesn't think like me:	1	2	3	4	5	6	7	:Thinks like me
Behaves like me:	1	2	3	4	5	6	7	:Doesn't behave like me
Similar to me:	1	2	3	4	5	6	7	:Different from me
Unlike me:	1	2	3	4	5	6	7	:Like me

BACKGROUND

From social class similar to mine:	1	2	3	4	5	6	7	:From social class different from mine
Economic situation different from mine:	1	2	3	4	5	6	7	:Economic situation like mine
Status like mine:	1	2	3	4	5	6	7	:Status different from mine
Background different from mine:	1	2	3	4	5	6	7	:Background similar to mine

VALUE

Morals unlike mine:	1	2	3	4	5	6	7	:Morals like mine
Sexual attitudes unlike mine:	1	2	3	4	5	6	7	:Sexual attitudes like mine
Shares my values:	1	2	3	4	5	6	7	:Doesn't share my values
Treats people like I do:	1	2	3	4	5	6	7	:Doesn't treat people like I do

APPEARANCE

Looks similar to me:	1	2	3	4	5	6	7	:Looks different from me
Different size than I am:	1	2	3	4	5	6	7	:Same size I am
Appearance like mine:	1	2	3	4	5	6	7	:Appearance unlike mine
Doesn't resemble me:	1	2	3	4	5	6	7	:Resembles me

FIGURE 1–11

One way of further examining the concept of homophily is to divide it into common attitudes, background, values, and appearance. With a friend or acquaintance, and using the scale above, rate numerically the perceived homophily existing between you and the other person. You might ask that person to do the same, then compare the results of your ratings. (J.C. McCroskey, V.P. Richmond, and J.A. Daly, "The Development of a Measure of Perceived Homophily in Interpersonal Communication," Human Communication Research, 1(1975) 324–332. Published by permission of Transaction, Inc. from HUMAN COMMUNICATION RESEARCH, Vol. 1, Copyright © 1975 by The International Communication Association)

WHEN
YOU GOT sick
I KNEW IT WAS
A BAD OMEN...

NOW I'M SICK
TOO!!!

you see another student you know from class. You remember from one of the class discussions that this person liked hiking and camping. You also enjoy hiking and camping. You decide to go over and ask if he minds if you sit down and chat. Because you perceive a similarity of enjoying hiking between the two of you, you initiate the conversation. From this beginning, you may learn even more about each other and discover other things you have in common, or where your fields of experience overlap.

Some things people have in common may have little or no bearing on the communication process. That you are the same sex as someone with whom you are communicating may have very little bearing on the success of the conversation. If you are lost and ask a police officer for directions, the fact that the police officer is male or female may not get you where you want to go.

Heterophily   Yet dissimilarities may also play a part in communication patterns. Such dissimilarities are referred to as *heterophily*. Imagine that you are asked out on a date, and the initial homophily creates a very positive atmosphere to start the evening's conversation. You like the same food, the same restaurants, and the same music. But you have very different ideas about religion, sex, and politics. As the evening progresses, although you are polite to each other, the differences between you start to play a more important role in your interpersonal relationship than the similarities. Perhaps you decide the differences are so great that encountering each other again would simply be unpleasant. On the other hand, you may seek to use the things you do have in common to try to develop some type of on-going relationship.

One sign of a good communicator is the ability to adapt to the different degrees of homophily and heterophily. Both are operative in any communicative interaction. Being able to recognize when each exists and the importance they play in communication interaction is an important step in good interpersonal interaction.

Before leaving our discussion of interpersonal communication, we should point out that we have only briefly talked about the *message* portion of our communication model. Later in this book, when we discuss language, we examine the kinds of messages that people receive and the role messages play in good interpersonal communication. Let's now turn our discussion to the third type of communication, mass communication.

Mass Communication

Five factors differentiate mass communication from intrapersonal and interpersonal communication: the presence of a mass medium, a gatekeeper, physical distance, limited sensory channels, and delayed feedback.[12] Let's examine each of these concepts in greater detail.

First, the presence of a mass medium *helps* carry the

message between a sender and a receiver. Assume that you are running for class president. Campaigning interpersonally, you will meet and speak face-to-face with other students you would like to vote for you. Yet you would also like to communicate with students through a mass medium, such as the student newspaper. This time, instead of the human voice carrying your message, the newspaper carries it. Applying this example to our communication model, we see that you are still considered the sender of the message, and other students are considered the receivers. You encode information to be sent to the students, while the students decode the information and form an opinion about you. The advantage of mass communication is that you reach a larger number of people. The disadvantage is that you cannot immediately react to the feedback they provide and thus alter your message. If you say the wrong thing, you might not be able to alter your message until the next edition of the newspaper. And if you aren't on good terms with a reporter, you might never be able to alter your message.

The second distinguishing factor between mass communication and interpersonal communication is the presence of a *gatekeeper*. In mass communication, a gatekeeper is anyone who controls the flow of information via a mass medium.

In mass communication, gatekeepers can take on many different forms. They may be reporters, television camerapersons, newspaper photographers, and a host of other people. Gatekeepers can also be institutions, those collective bodies of people making decisions which affect what we read, see, and hear via the mass media. A television network is an example of a gatekeeper organization. It is important to understand that distinction. Many people assume that a network commentator is the sender of communication, and the audience is the receiver. But the network is actually the gatekeeper, whereas the people the network *reports about* are senders of communication.

We should also keep in mind that gatekeepers both expand and shrink our informational environment. We can understand these two concepts by using an example of a debate at the United Nations. Because we are not present at the United Nations and thus do not have direct access to the debate, the gatekeeper in the form of a reporter expands our informational environment. On the other hand, the same gatekeeper also shrinks our informational environment because he or she determines what information we will *not* receive. The same principle can work in interpersonal communication, especially when interpersonal communication operates within an organization. We learn later in this text how interpersonal communication networks operate within a corporation.

Physical distance is another factor distinguishing mass communication from interpersonal communication. With interpersonal communication, the people conversing are in direct proximity to each other. In mass communication, considerable distance, even thousands of miles, can separate sender and receiver. Later in this book, when we talk about nonverbal communication, we discuss the advantages and disadvantages of being in direct proximity.

This lack of direct proximity leads us to still another factor distinguishing types of communication: limited numbers of sensory channels available during mass communication. When one individual is in direct proximity to another, all of the senses can take part in the communication process. Suppose Doug meets Cynthia at a party. They might shake hands (touch), smile at each other (sight), detect each other's perfume or lotion (smell), listen to each other talk (hear), and if they happen to kiss each other hello, even permit taste to take part in the sensory process. In fact, a major lipstick manufacturer created an advertising campaign for fruit-scented lipsticks, capitalizing on the role taste plays in a relationship. Yet with mass communication, Doug might see and hear Sally on television, but smell, taste, and touch would not be able to be used as sensory indicators in the communication linking the two together.

Still another difference between mass communication and interpersonal communication is the presence of delayed feedback. If you do not like what the mayor of your town said on the evening news, you *cannot* say "Wait a minute, I have a better idea" and expect the mayor to stop speaking and acknowledge your presence. The best you can do is to write a letter, make a phone call, or perhaps send a telegram. All of your actions would be examples of delayed feedback.

In spite of their differences, intrapersonal, interpersonal, and mass communication share similarities with one building upon and complementing the other. We now look at this common communicative ground.

Common Ground Between Types of Communication

As we stated earlier, intrapersonal communication is the foundation of all communication. We process information through our central nervous systems and then verbalize our intended messages to other people. Imagine you are reading a magazine and see an advertisement for a popular recording artist's newest tape. You think about buying the tape, but you are not sure if you will like all of the songs and therefore question whether it is worth the money. So you seek the advice of a friend, an *opinion leader*, someone who influences your decisions, attitudes, and behavior. Perhaps your friend collects tapes and keeps abreast of the latest releases. Or perhaps you enjoy the same kind of music as your friend and therefore trust his or her judgment. Your friend tells you the first song is great but the others are terrible. Based on this advice, you decide not to buy the record. Your decision involved all three types of communication—intrapersonal communication, as you read the advertisement; mass communication, because you received the advertisement through a mass medium; and interpersonal communication, because you sought an opinion from your friend.

Approaches to Understanding Interpersonal Communication

In the paragraphs to follow, we consider different ways of looking at interpersonal communication.[13] As we examine different approaches to interpersonal communication, keep in mind that all have important contributions to make, but some can be applied more readily to a particular interpersonal encounter than others. Interpersonal communication that takes place between you and a bank teller, for example, is much different from interpersonal communication that takes place between you and someone you love. Moveover, you probably will not have the *time to develop* much of a relationship with the bank teller, whereas you make the time to develop that relationship with someone you love.

Interpersonal Situations Let's begin by examining interpersonal communication from the perspective of different situations; this is aptly called the *situational* approach (Figure 1–12). Note that you should *not* analyze every interpersonal encounter based on

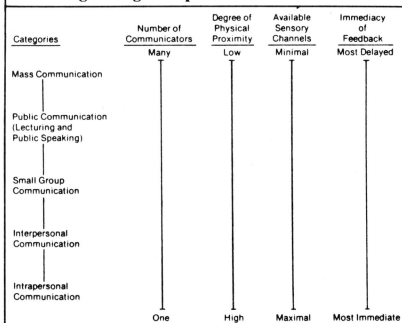

A Set of Categories Frequently Employed in the Situational Approach to Distinguishing Interpersonal Communication

Categories	Number of Communicators	Degree of Physical Proximity	Available Sensory Channels	Immediacy of Feedback
	Many	Low	Minimal	Most Delayed
Mass Communication				
Public Communication (Lecturing and Public Speaking)				
Small Group Communication				
Interpersonal Communication				
Intrapersonal Communication				
	One	High	Maximal	Most Immediate

FIGURE 1–12

(G.R. Miller, "The Current Status of Theory and Research in Interpersonal Communication," Human Communication Research, 4(1978) 164–178. Published by permission of Transaction, Inc. from HUMAN COMMUNICATION RESEARCH, Vol. 4, Copyright © 1978 by The International Communication Association)

the given situation within which it occurs. But situations *can* be and often are important. Consider the following scenario:

The president of a company has just commissioned a new executive meeting room to be built, located adjacent to the president's office. The president wants the room to be large enough for comfort and to have two windows so that regardless of where people sit, they can see outside. The president also wants the table to be round but only large enough to seat four people, because more people, the president feels, inhibit interpersonal communication. Finally the room is completed and the first meeting is held. The president invites three vice presidents to sit at the table for a discussion about the budget. Everyone has an equal chance to talk, and each vice president spends an approximately equal amount of time supporting his or her own division's request for funding. Each feels equally important since no one can be considered at the "head" of the round table. If one vice president notices something out the window, they can all look. When the meeting is over, the president is delighted.

If we examine the interpersonal communication which took place in the new meeting room, we might consider it successful. The president made all the necessary arrangements to see that a good interpersonal atmosphere existed: the round table, the two windows, the amount of equal interaction between the vice presidents, and the successful conclusion of the task, which was the completion of the budget.

We can help improve our own communication competency by approaching interpersonal communication from the situational perspective. Again, remember that it is but one approach. After a meeting, an evening with a date, a discussion with the bank teller, or a conversation with a friend in class, we could take a few moments to analyze how well we used our knowledge of interpersonal communication. Was each interpersonal situation successful? How can we improve a similar interpersonal encounter? We might anticipate who we will meet during the next twenty-four hours and plan how we will participate in each interpersonal situation. Yet although approaching interpersonal communication from a situational perspective is important, it also has its liabilities. Let's return to our discussion of the president's new meeting room.

If we were to assume that every time people had the opportunity to interact equally, that the table is round, that there are two windows, and that the goal of the meting is achieved that successful interpersonal communication takes place, we would be sadly mistaken. What would have happened if the goal had been reached, but one of the vice presidents had been rudely insulted by the other two? What would have happened if two of the vice presidents had talked continually while the third vice president never got a word in edgewise? What would have happened if the president had not permitted the vice presidents to take part in the decision-making process? Moreover, what would have happened if one of the vice presidents received a job offer from another company and a new vice president entered the picture? Situational perspectives are important, but they do have limitations in studying interpersonal communication.

For example, the situational approach does not permit us to understand the development of communicative interaction over more than a short period of time. We do not know what effect on the organization the exiting vice president will have when he or she talks to coworkers. Or suppose one vice president's division is not funded. We do not know what pattern future communication will take when that executive vows at the next meeting to get that division funded or else. In fact, the next meeting may turn into a fireworks display instead of a congenial gathering. And yet the fireworks were really fused in the first meeting, which we might have thought was relatively successful.

In studying interpersonal communication, do not hesitate to analyze each interpersonal situation. On the other hand, keep in mind that interpersonal communication is a dynamic process. Relationships change, perceptions of people change, and everything which happens in one encounter can affect subsequent encounters.

| Interpersonal | Our example of the vice president who was not able |

Interpersonal Communication as a Developmental Process

Our example of the vice president who was not able to say anything, or who was rudely insulted, or who accepted the new job even though the president's "perfect" meeting room was used leads us to view interpersonal communication as more than situational.

We realize that one communicative encounter can affect others. For instance, people who decide to marry usually have had reasonably good experiences communicating interpersonally. We could say that they have had a succession of good interpersonal "situations." Yet perhaps months or even years after the ceremony, these situations may become bad examples of interpersonal communication. What has happened is that the relationship between the two individuals has changed, and perhaps neither has the skill to replace bad interpersonal encounters with the good encounters of their courtship days. Sometimes it takes a marriage counselor to explain where the relationship broke down and how, if possible, it can be rebuilt. The reason for this is that the counselor can look at the entire history of the relationship, that is, its development (Figure 1–13), and not just a set of disconnected interpersonal situations.

Similarly, although group discussions within a corporation may enable the company to meet its goals, relationships between employees may actually be deteriorating. This condition develops to the point that one day, the goals are not met because the tension and animosity between employees makes it impossible for people to communicate with each other. Obviously an inept administrator felt everything was fine because he or she examined the organization in terms of short-range goals which were being met by a succession of interpersonal situations. What the administrator failed to do was monitor the interpersonal communication

---

THINKING DEVELOPMENTALLY

Every manager has discovered — sometimes quite rudely—that there is more to managing than simply knowing the job inside and out. Being an effective manager also requires facility with skills much like those employed by guidance counselors. They are masters of the helping skills, and managers with technical ability would do well to scrutinize the *modus operandi* of counselors to sharpen their own people skills.

What benefits can a manager expect to reap by taking a few tips from the guidance field? To answer that question, consider what guidance counselors do. They help individuals grasp information about themselves, about a particular situation, and about the relationship between the two. They encourage their clients to think developmentally (over periods of time) and ultimately to mobilize their capacities.

Office and plant managers easily fit into this scheme for working with and understanding people. Employees are the "clients," the office or plant is the "situation," and the time is *now*.

(*Supervisory Management*, 26, May, 1981)

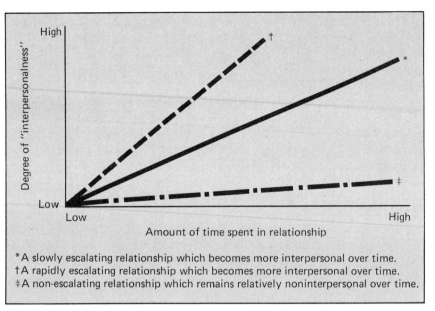

* A slowly escalating relationship which becomes more interpersonal over time.
† A rapidly escalating relationship which becomes more interpersonal over time.
‡ A non-escalating relationship which remains relatively noninterpersonal over time.

FIGURE 1-13

(G.R. Miller, "The Current Status of Theory and Research in Interpersonal Communication," Human Communication Research, 4(1978) 164–178. Published by permission of Transaction, Inc. from HUMAN COMMUNICATION RESEARCH, Vol. 4, Copyright © 1978 by The International Communication Association)

developing between the workers over the long term. Thus, we can see the importance of examining interpersonal communication from the perspective of the developmental process rather than merely from isolated, disconnected situations. Nevertheless, situations are still important, and we should be prepared to anticipate and participate in them, using all of our knowledge about good interpersonal communication.

Professors Charles Berger and Richard Calabrese present us with one possible perspective on interpersonal communication as a developmental process.[14] Keep in mind that these are *possible stages.* Berger and Calabrese label the first stage of an interpersonal transaction the *entry phase.* During this portion of the interpersonal interaction, the communication is somewhat structured. Two people might begin by exchanging greetings, engaging in small talk, saying the polite things appropriate for a particular situation such as talking about the weather. Berger and Calabrese offer the second phase of interpersonal interaction as the *personal phase.* Here discussion might stress more personal issues, such as attitudes and beliefs. In this phase people disclose information about themselves that they would not disclose during the entry phase. Communication is less constrained by politeness and appropriateness and becomes spontaneous. The rules of courtesy on what to say are relaxed. They might ask such questions as "How long have you been dating each other?" or "How do you feel about close relationships?" These questions might be inappropriate to ask the first time they meet.

Berger and Calabrese's third and final phase of interpersonal interaction is called the *exit phase.* Here the people involved might make a decision as to whether or not to continue their relationship. In the case of a marriage, divorce would certainly be an example of an exit phase. Similarly, the vice president's resignation to pursue another job would also be an exit phase.

Let's examine how these phases produce a developmental relationship in the context of a sorority or fraternity party. At the beginning of the evening, new acquaintances operate in the entry phase. That phase is replaced by the personal phase as the party progresses. Finally, the evening closes on the exit phase. Keep in mind that a relationship may have different parameters and different time frames around it. This is so because we actually define what we mean by a relationship and how interpersonal communication plays a part. What is important in looking at interpersonal communication from the developmental perspective is to be aware of how a relationship moves from the entry phase to the exit phase. Furthermore, an interpersonal relationship can progress through many more stages, and even the three we discussed here can be broken down into many subphases. We'll learn more about interpersonal communication as a developmental process in the chapter on relationships.

Interpersonal Communication as Rules of Behavior

In the entry phase of our developmental-perspective approach, we talked about people exchanging greetings and saying polite and appropriate words to each other. These "appropriate words" are part of the rules-of-behavior approach to understanding interpersonal communication. Seriously violating social rules or norms may hinder interpersonal communication. Conversely, following the rules and norms can enhance it. Again, remember that rules change within different situations. Nothing is absolute.

Let's assume it's the first day of classes, and you have just arrived on campus to meet your roommate. Your initial greeting is tempered by certain appropriate rules of behavior common to society. Upon meeting your roommate for the first time, you do not exclaim, "I wish you took as much care keeping this room clean as I will. I would never permit my clothes to lay around like you do." Chances are that if you greeted your roommate in such a fashion, you might find yourself sleeping in the hall. Even later in the semester when you ask your roommate to help keep the room clean, you will hopefully use a suggestion phrased, "Could we work together to help keep the room clean?" which will promote a much better relationship. Certain rules of behavior and norms exist within our society, and adhering to them helps us in our interpersonal relationships. Many relationships break down because people lose track of some of these basic rules and common courtesy until the relationship, whether it be working, friendship, or marriage, begins to disintegrate.

Interpersonal Communication as Laws of Behavior

Still another way to approach interpersonal communication is to examine various laws which describe behavior. A word of warning is in order, however, when we start talking about laws. Human communication is a complex, dynamic process which varies over time. Laws, on the other hand, are fixed and inflexible, and do not readily lend themselves to studying something as complex as interpersonal communication.[15] For example, we know that because of intrapersonal communication, when we look directly into the sun, our eyes blink. We could assume that unless we are blind, virtually *every time* we look into the sun our eyes will blink. We could say that such behavior is part of the laws which govern intrapersonal communication. Similarly, we could say that if our heads are underwater, we cannot breathe. It would be difficult to find a person who could disprove that law. But when we leave the biological functions of the body and move toward the psychological functions, we have difficulty applying laws with any consistency. If you meet a new friend and say to that person, "I love you," you do not know for certain whether the person will respond with, "I love you, too." Too many unknowns are inherent in this type of a relationship to call such a reaction a law of human behavior. Thus we can see that although there are certain biological laws which govern our relationships with the environment, trying to apply laws of human behavior to every situation in the realm of human communication is just not feasible.

Common Ground among Approaches to Interpersonal Communication

Just as there is considerable common ground among types of communication, there is also considerable common ground among approaches to interpersonal communication. Throughout this book we use examples of various interpersonal situations, developing relationships, rules of behavior, and even rules of law affecting interpersonal communication. All are useful in helping us to understand interpersonal interaction.

Assume that you are appearing for a job interview. You meet the interviewer and discuss your employment background. After the interview, the interviewer suggests that you meet the next day for lunch. You are pleased. You have made a good first impression. You appear for lunch the next day, the discussion goes well, and you are offered the job.

Applying our different approaches to your experience with the job interviewer, we can see that you had two distinct *situations:*[16] the first interview and the later luncheon interview. Both situations were related to each other. If you had not performed well in the first interview, you might not have had an opportunity to have a second. One situation thus developed from the other. Moreover, you undoubtedly followed certain rules of interpersonal behavior in these interviews. The luncheon interview, for example, probably dealt with more personal issues than the first interview, such as where you went to college, your hobbies and interests, and even your family. In the first interview such personal discussions might have been inappropriate, depending on how the interview progressed. Moreover, there were undoubtedly certain "laws" which were also operating. If you dressed too warmly, you might have perspired and become uncomfortable, which in turn would have affected your ability to stay alert.

We can see from our example that we can approach interpersonal communication from many different perspectives. Not all of the perspectives are interrelated in every interpersonal encounter, yet all of them might play a part.

Interpersonal Needs

We began our text talking about the student who placed a premium on her evenings out with a friend because they had such good conversations. She wisely saw these conversations as a prerequisite to a good relationship. We talked about the importance of interpersonal communication in a working situation and how goals could be accomplished in direct face-to-face interaction that could not be accomplished over long distances. All of these examples reflect certain *needs* that interpersonal communication helps to fulfill. Before moving on to Chapter 2 and discussing how our self-concepts, or how we feel about ourselves, affect interpersonal communication, we will look more closely at these needs.

William Schultz, a noted author and scholar, specifies three primary needs that interpersonal communication can help to fulfill: *inclusion, control,* and *affection.*[17]

Inclusion   Schultz states that inclusion

... has to do with interacting with people, with attention, acknowledgement, being known, prominence, recognition, prestige, status, and fame; with identity, individuality, understanding, interest, commitment, and participation. It is unlike affection in that it does not involve strong emotional attachments to individual persons. It is unlike control in that the preoccupation is with prominence, not dominance.[18]

We can examine our own lives and find numerous examples of inclusion (Figure 1–14). Our desire to have friends is one example. Wanting to be popular is a natural desire, and when we first enter a new class or first ar-

FIGURE 1-14

Our everyday lives are filled with situations which call for the need of "inclusion."
children engaged in a shared task is one example. Inclusion is important to self-
concept, a key to effective interpersonal communication. *(Ken Karp)*

rive at school, we seek out new friends. Perhaps we go out of our way to invite another person to have lunch with us. Or perhaps we take a few
moments each day after class to interact with a classmate. Perhaps we even
join a club to acquire friends with interests similar to ours. When we
associate with these club members, our fields of experience immediately
overlap, and homophily is present at the very beginning of our relationships
because we have things in common. Thus, we probably find that conversation with other club members is much easier than it is with total strangers.

A conversation indicative of inclusion might occur
between two students preparing to study:

> *"We need to get together and study for the exam."*
> *"I agree. Let's include John and Christin since they seem to understand*
>   *some of the tougher concepts."*
> *"Good idea. I'll invite them, or would you like to?"*

Notice how the conversation not only talked about bringing other people
together to study, but also was sensitive to the two people talking, as expressed in the phrase, "Good idea. I'll invite them, or would you like to?"

Different degrees of inclusion can be found in dif-
ferent people. Introverted people who do not seek inclusion are said to be
undersocial, or are sometimes called outcasts. This does not mean the need
does not exist, just that it is not fulfilled. Feelings of worthlessness and
depression can result from extreme undersocial behavior. The opposite ex-

treme is being *oversocial.* An oversocial individual is constantly overcompensating in an effort to belong. Joining every club on campus, wanting to be "in on everything," and trying to steal the show or attract attention all the time are characteristics of the oversocial person. The person who is comfortable in any social situation including being alone is said to be *social.* This is the well-adjusted person, who fits in well, who has a positive self-concept, and who can relate well to others in a relaxed atmosphere.

Extreme failure to fulfill the inclusion need can result in serious psychological problems. School counselors deal with such problems regularly. The student who is rejected by a fraternity or sorority may lapse into a serious state of depression. When new "inclusive" relationships develop, the individual again adjusts to new people and begins to again function properly in relating to others. If the person has likened acceptance into the organization as being the equivalent to either total inclusion or total exclusion, and if things do not turn out as planned, depression or even psychosomatic illnesses can occur. Some schools are sensitive enough to explain before such things as fraternity or sorority rush or pledging begins that it is not the end of the world if a person does not pledge or is not invited to join a Greek organization.

All of our actions are means of satisfying the need for inclusion. If we develop and use methods of effective interpersonal communication, inclusion not only becomes easier but deeper, more broad-based, and has the ability to feed upon itself.

Control The *control* need specified by Schultz does not necessarily mean controlling other people. Control is a range of behavior that varies from strong or total control to no control. It can shift from controlling others to being controlled by others. For example, at certain times and under certain conditions, we may want strong control of others. If we were a vice president responsible for helping a company overcome its financial difficulties, then when we discuss problems with groups of employees, we need the employees' understanding of our being in control of the situation. This does not mean that a dictatorial attitude will produce results. But if we are not in control, we will not be able to successfully direct the measures to get the company back in good health.

Now imagine we are serving as a consultant to the company. Although we will give advice on how to solve the problem, we will not be responsible for making sure the job gets done. In this case, we need some control over the situation to be able to convince management that certain steps need to be taken, but we won't need absolute control, as we would if we were the vice president.

Let's go one step further and suppose we're a company supervisor and our division is losing money. We might welcome any help offered, whether from the vice president or the consultant. When we talked with these two people, therefore, we would do most of the listening and therefore would not need control over the situation.

Whatever natural right men have to freedom and independency, it is manifest that some men have a natural ascendency over others.

Greville

The military is one organization in which the extremes of control operate every day. We know that a sergeant is in a "strong-control" position over a private, and that a captain is in a strong-control position over a sergeant. This does not mean that every time a sergeant talks to a private that the sergeant is issuing orders, or that the same relationship exists between the captain and the sergeant. What it means is that as interpersonal communication takes place between the two, there is little doubt who is in control. Some highly structured corporations with a "chain-of-command" atmosphere also leave no doubt as to what type of control exists.

Let's analyze conversation patterns between a controller and a person being controlled. First of all, the person in control may do more talking than the person being controlled. Statements such as, "I'd like you to have this assignment completed before noon" or "We need this order ready by tomorrow" are typical of controlling interaction. The reply, "I'll have it ready" or "Yes, of course" would be typical of the person being controlled. Where less control exists, the conversation might be more like: "Do you think we can get this order ready by tomorrow?" followed by "I'll do my best. Do you mind lending a hand?"

Another way to understand the control function is through the terms abdicrat, autocrat, democrat, and psychopath. These terms are psychological bases for understanding the control need.

The *abdicrat* is a submissive individual. His or her control need is best fulfilled by being controlled, not by controlling others. In a company, this individual enjoys being supervised and might not normally seek positions which demand supervisory abilities and skills. In some cases, these people could be said to "know their limitations and accept them." In other cases in which deep-seated fears of failure might exist, we could say the individuals lack confidence in their ability.

At the other extreme is the *autocrat* who basically mistrusts those around him or her. This person's decisions may be dogmatic, based on his or her insecurity to maintain control. In organizations, such individuals may limit the amount of feedback they receive from subordinates, fearful that the information may be critical of their judgments.

The ideal level of control is to function as a *democrat*. To do so does not mean that we relinquish control, that someone else is in charge, or that decisions, even unpopular ones, are not made. What it does mean is that we have the ability to understand the feelings and desires of others and, whenever possible, to make decisions which take those feelings into consideration. A person must be capable and secure and have a positive self-concept to operate as a democrat. Organizations which possess such talent are fortunate. More importantly, the manner in which such individuals are able to relate and talk with other people in the organization can make a great difference in the organization's success.

The quality that best sums up the control need in interpersonal relations is *self-respect*. Schultz points out:

the flavor of control is transmitted by behavior involving influence, leadership, power, coercion, authority, accomplishment, intellectual superiority, high achievement, and independence, as well as dependency (for decision making), rebellion, resistance, and submission. It differs from inclusion behavior in that it does not require prominence ... control behavior differs from affection behavior in that it has to do with power relations rather than emotional closeness.[19]

Affection　The final need Schultz describes is for *affection.*
Affection is a much more emotional relationship than that which exists in either inclusion or control. When affection is involved, such terms as love, infatuation, and intimacy are used to describe the relationship. All people need affection, although the degree to which they need it depends on the individual and his or her background.

We all know that different people seek affection in different ways. For example, people can be *underpersonal* and relate very superficially to others. This type of individual shies away from close relationships. Various reasons account for such behavior, such as a broken relationship that left unpleasant emotional scars or an unhappy childhood. Another level of affection can be the other extreme, the overpersonal. The *overpersonal* individual is just that—overbearing in social relationships. We have all heard the phrase "he trys too hard" or "she trys too hard" at being liked. Such behavior is indicative of the overpersonal person who may even resort to deviousness in attempting to gain affection. Ideally, a person can be classified as *personal* when he or she has satisfactory relationships centering around affection. The personal individual is sensitive to other people's feelings, has the ability to "give people room to breathe," and does not crowd a relationship. Of course, matching one's own needs for affection to those of a partner is not always easy, and the needs themselves aren't constant.

In our relationships with each other, the key to successful interpersonal interaction is to strike the proper balance between all three types of interpersonal needs and then to operate as a normal person within each type. But that is easier said than done. The mere pressures of everyday life create some deviance from the norm. And different situations and different developing relationships all affect how we fulfill these three needs. A healthy interpersonal relationship is one sensitive to other people's needs as well as to the range of feelings and emotions which are associated with those needs.

SUMMARY

As we conclude our introductory chapter, we want to emphasize once again that interpersonal communication is a dynamic process. Although we use communication models to stop the communication process so we may analyze it, that does not mean that the process itself is static. Although we talk about understanding interpersonal communication by examining interpersonal situations, developing relationships, rules, and laws, this does not mean that each is a separate entity. All are related to each other, sharing common characteristics. Similarly, different types of communication overlap. For instance, intrapersonal communication is present every time interpersonal communication takes place. Moreover, how we react to communication from the mass media may be directly determined by the interpersonal communication in which we may take part while discussing the content of those media messages. And finally, all of our different interpersonal needs are interrelated and function as a unit.

Many categories, models, concepts, needs, and approaches to interpersonal communication exist in addition to those we have discussed. Books on communication theory, psychology, sociology, and a host of other disciplines offer still more perspectives to the field. But we have laid the groundwork to help you begin to *relate* to interpersonal communcation, to begin thinking about it, and most importantly, to become sensitive to it so that you may enhance the way you interact with others.

OPPORTUNITIES FOR FURTHER LEARNING

BITTNER, J. R., *Mass Communication* (3rd ed). Englewood Cliffs, N.J.: Prentice-Hall, Inc., 1983.

BORMANN, E. G., *Communication Theory.* New York: Holt, Rinehart & Winston, 1980.

CIVIKLY, J. M., *Contexts of Communication.* New York: Holt, Rinehart & Winston, 1981.

DANCE, F. E., *Human Communication Theory: Comparative Essays.* New York: Harper & Row, Pub., 1982.

DeVITO, J. A., *Communicology: An Introduction to the Study of Communication* (2nd ed). New York: Harper & Row, Pub., 1982.

EAKINS, B. W. and R. G. EAKINS, *Sex Differences in Human Communication.* Boston: Houghton Mifflin Company, 1978.

FRISBY, J., *Seeing: Illusion, Brain and Mind.* Oxford: Oxford University Press, 1979.

GREEN, E. and A. GREEN, *Beyond Biofeedback.* New York: Delacorte Press, 1977.

GRUNEBERG, M. M. and P. MORRIS, eds., *Aspects of Memory.* London: Methuen and Co., Ltd., 1978.

HAYAKAWA, S. I., *Through the Communication Barrier: On Speaking, Listening, Understanding.* New York: Harper & Row, Pub., 1979.

JOHANNESEN, R. L., *Ethics in Human Communication.* Prospect Heights, IL: Waveland Press, Inc., 1975.

KARLINS, M. and L. M. ANDREWS, *Biofeedback: Turning on the Power of Your Mind.* Philadelphia: Lippincott, 1972.

LORAYNE, H. and J. LUCAS, *The Memory Book.* New York: Ballentine, 1974.

MacKENZIE, N., *Dreams and Dreaming.* New York: Vanguard, 1965.

MATSON, F., *The Human Connection.* New York: McGraw-Hill, 1979.

MORTENSEN, C. D., *Basic Readings in Communication Theory* (2nd ed.). New York: Harper & Row, Pub., 1979.

NORMAN, J., *Ancestral Voices*. New York: Four Winds Press, 1975.

PERKINS, D. H., *The Minds Best Work*. Cambridge: Harvard University Press, 1981.

RYCROFT, C., *The Innocence of Dreams*. New York: Pantheon, 1979.

THOMSON, D. S., *Language*. New York: Time-Life Books, 1975.

TOMPKINS, P. K., *Communication as Action: An Introduction to Rhetoric and Communication*. Belmont, CA: Wadsworth, 1982.

WEINHOLD, B. and L. ELLIOTT, *Transpersonal Communication: How to Establish Contact with Yourself and Others*. Englewood Cliffs, NJ: Prentice-Hall—Spectrum Books, 1978.

WILSON, E. O., *On Human Nature*. Cambridge: Harvard University Press, 1978.

chapter two

Understanding Self-Concept

PREVIEW   *After completing this chapter, we should be able to:*

List the building blocks of self-concept.
Explain positive and negative stroking.
Compare the three ego states: adult, parent, and child.
Understand the everyday forces which can affect our self-concepts.
Discuss impression management, and how we present our self-concepts to others.
Explain how we can deal with shyness.
Distinguish between assertive and abrasive interaction.
Give examples of "bypass statements."
Describe the role of self-disclosure.

When famed baseball catcher Yogi Berra first approached the gate of Yankee Stadium in 1947, he must have been awed about the challenges before him. He certainly didn't look like an athlete. Short and squatty, he was anything but the picture of the famous Major-League hitters of the day. Around the League the bench jockeys would laugh at his walk. When Berra threw the ball, it was anyone's guess where it would end up. Once he hit a second-base umpire in the head with a wild throw. Another wild throw landed in the chest of the pitcher. For Yogi, however, the laughs, the mistakes, and the continual sighs of disgust from players and coaches didn't stop his determination to be good at baseball. Instead, he studied the competition, watched the rival batters, and spent extra hours in the batting cage until he knew his and their every weakness. When his career ended, he had played with fourteen pennant-winning teams, had hit 358 home runs, had set eighteen World-Series records, and was voted the League's most-valuable player.[1]

Undoubtedly, if Yogi Berra had not worked to improve or had not accepted his limitations and worked within them, he would have never achieved success. And his self-concept when he hit the umpire and pitcher with wild throws was undoubtedly different than it was after he logged pennant-winning games and most-valuable player awards.

As senders of communication, we constantly go through life transmitting messages to others. Sometimes our messages show on our faces; sometimes we speak them; other times we communicate by the way we dress. Although we may consciously create messages to derive a certain effect, many times the messages we communicate are unintentional. And we communicate them because we cannot help ourselves. Sometimes the messages may reflect positively on us, such as our positive attitudes' contagiously rubbing off on everyone around us. Other times we may be pessimistic and negative in our feelings. At these times, we become individuals to be avoided. Unfortunately, as we learned in Chapter 1, our need for inclusion makes this avoidance a very negative experience, which can make us even more pessimistic.

The messages we communicate, intentionally or un-

Doubt whom you will, but never yourself.

Christian Bovee

Understanding Self-Concept

intentionally, are directly connected to the way we feel about ourselves. The way we intrapersonally process to answer to "Who am I?" can influence how we present ourselves to others.

Parts of our self-concept are related to our pasts and the influences that people and things we encountered early in life had upon our personal and social development. Still other parts of our self-concept are derived from things present—obtaining rewards and accomplishments from our jobs, doing well in school, and receiving positive feedback from people who are important to us. In many ways we can help alter our self-concept. We can work hard to perfect our skills, which can improve our job or school performances.

As we begin to examine the building blocks of self-concept and gain an understanding of how we send messages, try to think about how your own self-concept was formed. What things from your past and what things about your present have an important influence on the way you feel about your self? What has an important influence in answering your question, "Who am I?"

The Building Blocks of Self-Concept

If we wanted to draw a model of self-concept, we might show a picture of a large building. We could then liken every brick or block of that building to a specific quality we possess which contributes to our self-concept. We will now examine some of these building blocks which affect how we relate to other people.

Values *Values* can be defined as broad-based qualities of the individual self that are important and that affect behavior.[2] Different scholars have broken down values into categories. What the categories are is not as important as the importance individuals place on them. Let's consider some of the most basic values: aesthetic, humanitarian, intellectual, material, power, and religious.[3]

One way to study values is to look at a value hierarchy.[4] Consider which of the values just listed you place high in your life. People who place aesthetic values high tend to examine the world in terms of beauty. They may be interested in art and music. Or if this value is especially high in their personal value hierarchy, they might even be professional artists or musicians. A person who feels humanitarian values are very important (Figure 2–1) might be what we have heard called "people-oriented." The love of people and caring for them would be very important to this individual. When making a career choice based on such a value structure, this person might become a social worker or consider work in a medically related field.

FIGURE 2-1

Personal values, which are the building blocks of self-concept, are divided into different categories, one of which can be labeled "humanitarian." Strong humanitarian values may influence career choices that permit considerable interpersonal contact, such as nursing. (*Carmine L. Galasso*)

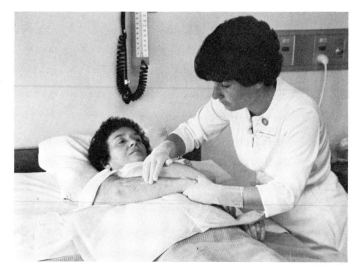

Two values which are closely related are material and power. Material values stress material things. Wanting to possess the nicer things of life is not uncommon in any society. For people who place a very high value on material things, their personal income might be the most important aspect of their job. This type of individual might choose a less desirable job that pays more rather than a job he or she would enjoy doing that pays less. Power or prestige is another common value in society. In Chapter 1, we discussed that control is one of the important interpersonal needs. People with high power values tend to seek positions of control in their lives. Perhaps they function best as administrators, supervisors, or politicians.

Religious values stress the importance of a supernatural being in guiding one's life. In very religious societies, entire populations may hold this value very high. We've heard the phrase "traditional values" used in some political campaigns; these are often religious values. People who hold values of religion extremely high may find satisfaction in a career with close ties to a church or synagogue.

It's easily possible for all of these values to operate within the same individual. Let's suppose that having a corporate executive position is a very positive concept in your plan of life. You also enjoy making enough money to be comfortable and to help a family or person close to you enjoy nice material things. At the same time you retain a deep interest in your place of religious worship, you readily volunteer your time for charitable causes to help the less fortunate, and you thoroughly enjoy art and music. All of these values can thus operate at the same time, although some influence our behavior more than others. They do so because we tend to rank our values in order of importance to our lives. What values do you hold most important? How do they reflect on your relationships with other people? In what ways do they influence how you choose your friends?

Attitudes   Just as values support our self-concept, so do *attitudes.* One way to look at attitudes is to think of them as subparts of values. Another way is to think of them as more narrowly defined than values. Still another approach is to consider them as "support mechanisms" for values. The latter is true especially when we begin to interact with other people. Our attitudes often reflect our values. For example, your attitude about a politician might be that you will vote for him because he is a good man. Or perhaps you'll vote for the politician because she supports aid to nations suffering from famine. Or you'll vote for her because she believes in creating jobs for depressed areas. All of these attitudes can refine other values, as expressed in their statements, "Big business is not harmful (material)" or "Authority is necessary for society to function (power)." Yet people who hold material or power values important may or may not have these same attitudes. Again, attitudes are more narrowly defined than values.

Beliefs   Closely related to attitudes are *beliefs.*[5] In fact, some people argue that there is little distinction between the two, and trying to separate them merely causes confusion and artificial divisions that do not exist or are not necessary.[6] Nevertheless, on the assumption that discussing them separately might help you to understand how your own beliefs and attitudes fit into and support your self-concept, we feel it's important to distinguish between them. We begin by acknowledging that beliefs, like attitudes and values, have a hierarchy of importance to us, and we hold some stronger than others.

Basic Beliefs   Some of our most closely held beliefs are those we acquired as we were growing up. Our parents played a large role in developing many of those beliefs. Some of these may be: "My family is very supportive of me," or "I believe the farm I grew up on was a good place to raise children." Other basic beliefs might include: "I believe my mother was a good woman," or "I believe my father was a good man." In each case, the belief is central to our own sense of being. Still other beliefs might be: "If I am in trouble, I can count on my brother or sister," or "If I am in trouble, I can count on my parents." All are basic beliefs of which we do not seek continual confirmation, which are not easily changed, and which have been positively reinforced over time.

How we relate to other people in interpersonal communication can depend very heavily on our beliefs. The fact that our parents were very supportive might give us a sense of self-confidence and an ability to meet others with a positive sense of well-being. Perhaps we have a close friend or loved one who provides us with "inner strength." Communicating with this individual is easy and "supportive." The basic beliefs we hold are actually part of the answer to "Who am I?" Of all our beliefs, these are the most central to our lives. Even if we don't live on a farm (or never want to), the fact that we once held certain beliefs close to us means they play a part in our self-concepts and our relationships to others.

Yet these basic beliefs can be changed, although not easily. Perhaps an unhappy childhood can be "sorted out" within oneself, and corresponding behavior adjusted to compensate for current relationships with others.

Peripheral Beliefs Branching out from our basic beliefs are peripheral beliefs. The dividing line between the two is hazy, yet there. For example, if you believe strongly that your best friend would help you in a time of need, you may have no doubt in your mind that this belief is absolute. It is basic. You cannot imagine anything which would make you believe differently. On the other hand, if you believe you dislike chocolate cake, you may be less willing to say that particular belief is absolute. A good piece of chocolate cake might be the only thing standing in the way of your changing your mind. This type of belief would be peripheral.

In between basic and peripheral beliefs are those which have various degrees of changeability and influence over the way we behave and interact with other people. Beliefs about birth control, gun control, wilderness preservation, and aid to foreign countries are examples of such beliefs.

Remember, we have separated values, attitudes, and beliefs in order to gain a clearer understanding of our self-concept. The distinctions between the three seem to lie in the degree of commitment to certain values, attitudes, and beliefs and the role that each plays in a given communicative encounter.

Self-Concept: Interpersonal Interactions

It is not possible to go through life without having our values, attitudes, and beliefs challenged, altered, or in some cases, drastically changed. We all meet people who have ideas different from ours. We meet people who argue with us, who both intentionally and unintentionally deceive us, and who simply do not see all things the way we do. Some of these challenges to our basic ways of thinking can be very healthy. Other challenges may cause considerable internal strife and make us stop and consider our own worth or our abilities to work or reason. This is especially true when we encounter *challenges to values, attitudes, and beliefs about ourselves.* Herein lies the relationship to self-concept. The beliefs we hold about politics, social issues, and even other people can be challenged without too much internal damage. But when we have the very important answers to "Who am I?" challenged, we face a crisis in our self-concept. And how we identify our self-concept affects how we interact in interpersonal communication. Because no values, attitudes, or beliefs are closer or more important to us than the ones we hold about ourselves, we need to understand more about how they affect our lives.

THIS WILL MAKE YOU FEEL BETTER

If you sometimes get discouraged, consider this fellow: He dropped out of grade school. Ran a country store. Went broke. Took 15 years to pay off his bills. Took a wife. Unhappy marriage. Ran for House. Lost twice. Ran for Senate. Lost twice. Delivered speech that became a classic. Audience indifferent. Attacked daily by the press and despised by half the country. Despite all this, imagine how many people all over the world have been inspired by this awkward, rumpled, brooding man who signed his name simply, A. Lincoln.

(© *United Technologies Corporation, 1981)*

Maintaining Our Self-Concept

To maintain our self-concept, we need to understand that challenge to our value-attitude-belief structure is something we will always face and something we should take for granted.[7]

Challenges to Our Beliefs In the cliché "Life is a series of challenges." we find an analogy to our belief structure which could be worded "Life is a series of challenges to our beliefs." Once we accept the fact that we will be continually challenged in minor and major ways, we can handle these challenges better. No one would be surprised if we were discussing politics at a social gathering and someone disagreed with us. It is natural to disagree about politics. Moreover, the way in which people disagreed would vary considerably. We might encounter a polite friend who would temper his or her comments with statements such as:

"That's an interesting opinion, I wonder what would happen if . . . ?"
"I see some strong points in your argument; however, perhaps we should begin to . . ."

Neither of the comments are particularly threatening or would bother us much if we did not place such importance on our political beliefs that they were rigid and inflexible.

Now consider how we might react if the comments were less polite. What if the other person had said:

"That view doesn't show much intelligence."
"I cannot believe any intelligent person would think that way."
"A view like that could get us into war tomorrow."

The comments now become more personal. They not only refute us but also imply a deficiency in our worth. Comments such as these are not uncommon; we have all met the individual who is extremely candid and forthright regardless of how his or her comments are taken.

Now consider how we would react if we were faced with the same type of person's challenging beliefs about ourselves:

"I think your approach to life is rather silly."
"Your values are worthless."
"I cannot stand people like you who place any importance on material things."

If we were close to the person making these statements, if we respected that person's opinion, or if we were in love with the person, and he or she made such statements directly opposed to our own values, attitudes, and beliefs, it could very well shatter our self-confidence. At the very least we would be

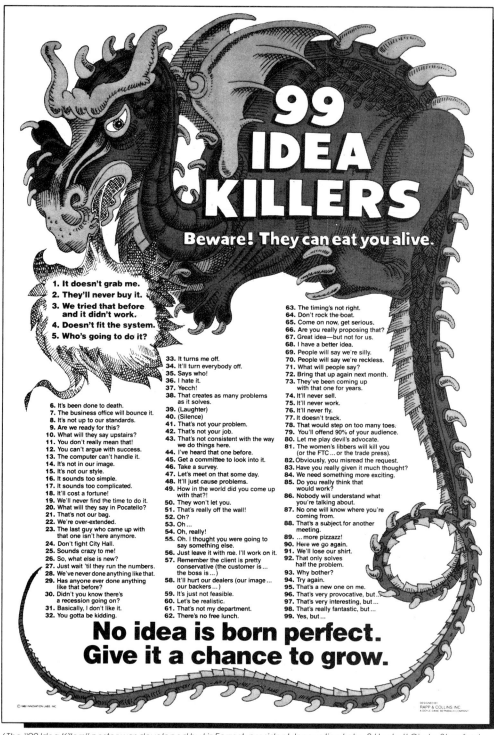

No idea is born perfect.
Give it a chance to grow.

(The "99 Idea Killers" poster was developed by Liz Forrest, president, Innovation Labs, 3 Hackett Circle, Stamford, CT., and Stan Rapp, president, Rapp & Collins, 475 Park Avenue South, New York, NY.)

faced with realigning our thoughts to either agree and change our self-concept, or disagree and attempt to protect our self-concept.

These dilemmas that we all face are attempts at maintaining congruity for our self-concept. Out of this grows our self-confidence. When we develop intimate relationships with people, we are much more likely to encounter communication dealing with these personal beliefs. When serious dilemmas exist, we might decide that instead of changing our self-concepts, we will draw away from the person, end a relationship, undergo counseling, or undertake a host of other actions to protect and maintain our self-concept.[8]

Now let's examine two other ways to approach these inevitable encounters. The approaches deal with how people interact with each other. Understanding interactions will, again, help us to better understand ourselves and how we both intentionally or unintentionally send and receive communication from others.

Stroking Why are we concerned about maintaining our self-concept? We're concerned because support for our actions and egos is a necessary part of life. Moreover, this support is the foundation of positive relationships with other people. And these relationships, as we learned in Chapter 1, fulfill the interpersonal need of inclusion. Support for our egos actually starts from the day we are born. At this point the support is almost entirely of touch, that of baby to mother and father. Later, as we begin to develop the ability to use language, we seek support through interpersonal communication using symbols. A smile, words, phrases, and sentences all form modes of support (Figure 2–2). Psychologists refer to this supportive process as *stroking*.[9]

FIGURE 2-2

Support for our egos starts when we are born. Positive "stroking" is important to a well-developed self-concept. Interpersonal communication in a positive, supportive atmosphere contributes to self esteem. As we mature and begin to use language, words play an increasingly important role in stroking. (*Kenneth P. Davis*)

Stroking occurs in transactions, or the process of exchanging messages, with other people and can include all types of human communication, from verbal to nonverbal. A pat on the shoulder accompanied by supportive words is an example of each. Many of us seek stroking in every day life to confirm what we say and do.[10] One way to look at stroking is to consider it as the product of interpersonal communication. We have a need to be stroked, therefore we enter into interpersonal transactions that will be "payed off" in strokes. Naturally, it is more pleasant to receive positive than negative strokes. We may choose our friends and acquaintances because they are supportive of our attitudes, values, and beliefs (self-concept). We may avoid people who do not stroke us positively. Yet some people who continually endure verbal and sometimes physical abuse in a relationship could be said to prefer negative stroking rather than no stroking at all.

What helps to determine our self-concept and the self-concept we tend to protect is the kind of stroking with which we grew up.[11] If we feel positive about ourselves, then chances are that we have received positive strokes during our formative years which have helped build a positive self-concept. If we have had many negative experiences, our self-concept may be negative.

It's possible to have a positive self-concept in one area of our lives and a negative self-concept in another, even though some relationship will exist between the two. A friend of mine is a very successful business executive. As head of a growing and prosperous company, he oozes self-confidence anytime he talks about his business. On the other hand, his driving, unrelenting style has caused the breakup of two of his marriages, and when he discusses his personal life, his conversation is filled with self-doubt. His business life has been filled with positive stroking, his personal life with negative stroking.

Stroking determines not only how we feel about ourselves but also how we relate to other people. One way to categorize these perceptions of ourselves and others is to use what psychologists refer to as the "I'm OK, you're OK" relationships.

The most basic relationship is one in which the communicator has a positive self-concept and the same perception of the person with whom he or she is communicating. In this instance, both communicators are engaged in positively stroking each other. Each communicator "is OK," and even disagreement is rational.

An alternative relationship is for one communicator to have been stroked negatively to the point that he or she forms an "I'm *not* OK" self-concept. When this occurs, interpersonal communication becomes difficult and hindered. The communicator, in striving to achieve a consistent "I'm not OK" position in life, tends to put himself or herself down continually. Sometimes this can take the form of continually making excuses for oneself. A secretary who worked for the author had an "I'm not OK" self-concept at work. Part of this self-concept had developed from a previous job

Understanding Self-Concept

because her boss thought she could never do anything right. As a result, any time she received criticism in her new job, her old "I'm not OK" self would surface, and she would continally say, "Oh, I'm such a jerk." Finally, I grew tired of hearing that comment. In the process of finding out why she always used the phrase, the story of her past employment surfaced. After my deliberate effort to compliment her for her work and to gently and supportively offer constructive criticism when it was needed, she began to stop using the phrase. Gradually, she developed an "I'm OK" self-concept in her working situation. In short, she gained her self-confidence back.

Because both communicators can have an "I'm OK" or "I'm not OK" self-concept, the possible combinations of interpersonal transactions can include:

I'm OK, you're OK;

I'm OK, you're not OK;

I'm not OK, you're OK;

I'm not OK, you're not OK.

Of all four possible combinations, the first is the healthiest whereas the last is the least healthy. We should not look at the possible combinations of relationships as being rigid. Even within the same conversation we can fluctuate between different postures about ourselves and other people. For the most part, however, our most consistent posture will determine how we interact with other people. And because we need to interact with other people, it's important to consider our own-self-concept. In what areas of our lives can we say "I'm OK"? In what areas do we say, "I'm not OK"? What about people with whom we interact? Do we perceive them as being OK or not OK? Are our perceptions justified? Can we provide stroking to other people which will improve their own self-concept?

U nderstanding Our Different Selves

The psychiatrist and proponent of transactional analysis, Eric Berne, developed an interesting approach to understanding human interaction. At the core of his approach is what he called the *ego state*.[12] In the simplest terms, there are three types of ego states which are, according to Berne, present in every individual. To better understand these three types in relation to what we have already been discussing about self-concept, think of them as different self-concepts which we possess and relate to at any given time.

Adult State   The ideal state is the adult state which we possess when we act as normal people with normal interactions with other people. This is the ego state of the well-adjusted person, the rational thinker. The adult state is important to us to be able to make rational choices about our daily lives. For example, in any given day, we encounter all kinds of situations which necessitate an adult approach. If a teacher hands back an examination with an F, we might want to just sit down and cry. Another side of us might want to stand up and say "This examination was ridiculous, and you are hereby ordered to prepare another one and assign me a better grade." Chances are neither approach will accomplish anything, will not communicate our feelings to the teacher, help us find out why we did poorly on the exam, or show us how to improve on the next one. The rational, adult decision would be to make an appointment with the instructor, listen to explanations of why we answered questions incorrectly, and learn how to prepare for the next exam. In the same sense, the instructor should listen to our explanations without telling us to get out of the office before we end up in the dean's office. Nor would we expect the instructor to break down and cry because we didn't measure up to certain expectations. For the meeting to be productive, both parties need to function as rational adults. Now let's examine what alternatives to this rational meeting might take place.

Parent State   Another ego state Berne suggests is the parent state. In this state, we tend to be very directive in our communication and behavior, much as a parent reacting to a young child. All of us enter parent states from time to time (Figure 2–3). The child scolding a pet is acting in the parent state. This state is illustrated by very specific actions and statements, often "commanding" in nature. "Don't do this" or "Do this" are examples of our parent states. There is nothing unusual about being in the parent state except that at times it is certainly less effective than the adult state. It is especially ineffective when we are communicating with someone who doesn't perceive himself or herself as being in a child state, and consequently reacts very negatively to parental communication.

Consider two workers on the assembly line. Both perceive each other as being of equal status and ability within the company and at the jobs they perform. One day, when a defective part passes before them, one says to the other, "Make sure you grab that part off the line. I don't want to see it get past your station." The reaction of the other worker is, "Who are you telling me how to do my job?!" Clearly the "parental communication" was inappropriate. Had the first worker's statements been more reflective of the "adult" ego state, such as by saying "We may have a defective part coming by," the reaction of the second worker may have been quite different.

But the parent state is not necessarily a negative state. Certain situations exist in which a superior/subordinate relationship is expected and accepted. The supervisor, the sergeant, the chief executive, the department chairperson are all, because of their "managerial" positions, faced with being perceived as "parent" figures, at least in terms of their

The Saturday Evening POST

March 20, 1954 — *15¢*

New York's Communist Cop
By CRAIG THOMPSON

THIS IS ON ME
By Bob Hope

FIGURE 2–3

One of the classic covers of *The Saturday Evening Post* presented four examples of the "parent state." Both adults and children can fall into the parent state from time to time. Parent states are sometimes recognizable by very directive language, such as "Don't do this" or "Do this." (*Reprinted from* The Saturday Evening Post © *1954 The Curtis Publishing Company*)

authority. Whether they treat people under them as being associated with the "child" state depends on the particular communicative style of the administrator.

　　We can see now that if we said to our instructor, "This examination is ridiculous, and you are hereby ordered to prepare another one and assign me a better grade," we would be acting in a parent state when an adult state would meet the needs of the situation much better.

Child State   Our examples of sitting down and crying when we received the F on the examination or our instructor's crying because we did not meet certain expectations are indicative of the child state. Although the child state is most prevalent in early childhood, we take some of this child ego state into our adult lives. Again, this is not necessarily a negative quality. Obviously, if we never acted silly, childlike, or just "let ourselves go" and had fun, life might be rather dull. But to adhere to the child state when an adult, rational state would be more beneficial is something else.

To acquire and maintain self-concepts which permit us to interact on an interpersonal basis with other people, we need to constantly work at achieving the *proper balance* between these three ego states. In essence, we can't continually act like children any more than we can continually order people around.

Camouflaging Our Different "Selves"

Even though our ego states may function inwardly, we may not always project the same ego states outwardly. Consider the following conversation:

MANAGER (parent):   *This work is inferior. You are capable of much higher quality and you can turn out more work per hour than you have in the past. I do not expect to see this sloppy performance again or you will be fired.*

EMPLOYEE (child):   *Yes, I agree. It will not happen again under any circumstances.*

There is little doubt in this conversation about the roles adhered to by the manager and the employee. A parent-child interaction is taking place. More diplomatic interaction might be achieved if the manager would tone his or her comments and attempt to camouflage his or her true feelings. Yet not clearly stating exactly what is expected of the employee could have greater repercussions. Let's examine the interchange again:

MANAGER (adult):   *Standards have slipped somewhat this week. Some previous production records show we might be able to improve output if we work at it. I hope we can see some improvement. Is there anything I can do to help?*

EMPLOYEE (adult):   *I realize it has been an off week. Let me examine the schedule and see what I can do to get back to normal output. By next week, we should see some changes.*

> *Man is not naturally a cynic; he wants pitifully to believe, in himself, in his future, in his community and in the nation in which he is a part.*
>
> *Louis Bromfield*

Certainly the interchange was much more adult to adult. However, do the manager and the employee "internally" feel, and consequently will they later act, in the same way as the conversation indicates? Does the manager internally still feel "parent" while outwardly communicating "adult"? Next week when the employee is fired, it might come as a total shock and crushing blow to his or her self-concept. For an explanation, the manager might say, "I warned you last week, and you did not meet my expectations." The problem was that the manager internally felt a certain way, but externally communicated something entirely different.

This example of the inward feeling versus outward communication is what we can call deceptive communication. Deceptive communication *may* or *may not* be intentional. As we are using it here *does not* necessarily mean deceitful, cunning, or with malice. Some supervisors who simply cannot communicate what is expected of employees and continually speak in vague generalities may be unconsciously guilty of deceptive communication. And work situations are not the only arenas in which such deceptive communication takes place. Within the family, in relationships between lovers, and in everyday interpersonal encounters even with the bank teller, we often fail to achieve the proper balance between what we inwardly feel and what we outwardly express. Considering that our true selves can range anywhere between parent and child or can assume a multitude of combinations in between, and that communication can be direct or deceptive, we can begin to see how many different combinations of interpersonal interactions can take place. Remember that "deceptive" communication is not necessarily deliberate nor should it be considered bad. Any kind of diplomatic communication can be deceptive or camouflaged. Also, camouflaged communication is sometimes necessary to achieve a goal. If we know a worker will react negatively to parent-oriented communication, then we might want to camouflage our statements and lessen the "command" approach in order to achieve a more positive result.

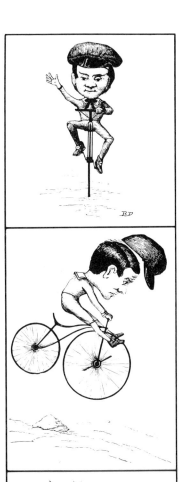

Everyday Forces Affecting Self-Concept

How do some of the everyday events in life which we all face affect our self-concept? In many ways these events can cause us to perceive ourselves as being "not OK" when we are, or to react as parents or children when we might very well be able to function as adults. As you read the examples which follow, think of how things you face daily might affect your self-concept. Starting to think about how you feel about yourself and *why* you feel the way you do is the first step towards effective interpersonal communication.

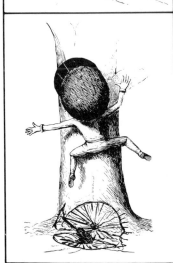

Changing Residences Each day, the things that are part of our routine schedule are supportive of our self-concept. Many times we take these for granted until they are removed, especially if this happens all at once. For example, each time we see someone we perceive as feeling positive towards us, this event subconsciously instills self-confidence. We see a teacher we respect and who we know respects us because of the work we have done in classes. We see friends we know like us and who want to be with us. Our self-concept is also supported by our ability to maneuver through the many "signs" of everyday living. In other words, we know what route to take to get to the doctor's office. We know where the little bakery is, the bookstore, or the restaurant where we can relax and enjoy familiar company. In short, the people with whom we interact and the things we do all support our self-concept.

When we leave familiar surroundings, such as by moving to a new town, arriving at a new school, or even visiting a foreign country, we are stripped of many of these supporting blocks. We know, for instance, that our good reputation may not have followed us to a new town. We must also renegotiate the geography. Our self-confidence in being able to find familiar places must be rebuilt. We do not know where the little bakery is, the bookstore, or the restaurant where we can get away and relax. In a foreign country these situations are compounded because of the added cultural obstacles which play havoc with our self-concept. Maneuvering around a new town can be doubly difficult because not only can we not read the road signs, but we also cannot ask for directions unless we find someone who speaks our language. Reading the menu in a restaurant or even using the telephone can be a harrowing experience. The director of an American university's international exchange program tells the somewhat amusing story of students who come to a foreign country and spend their first month eating at McDonald's because it is familiar to them and they can read the menu. But the director also points out that spending time in a foreign country is one of the best ways to build a strong self-concept. As one student who returned from a semester abroad said, "After living abroad, exploring new places and meeting new people in my own country was easy. I felt confident to go anywhere and meet anyone."

FIGURE 2-4

New schools can be especially challenging to one's self-concept. The support system and friends which were part of our self esteem are left behind, and we're forced to make new friends and develop new support systems. (*Ken Karp*)

A New School Attending a new school, (Figure 2–4) can create the same challenges to our self-concepts. Many times we leave our friends, our family, and the people we know respect us and want to be with us. Although we all talk about the "excitement of college," and the "opportunities to meet new friends," inside we are faced with tremendous and very natural self-doubts: "Will I be able to make new friends?" "Will I be able to find the room where my class meets?" "Will my clothes fit in?" All of these self-doubts usually cease to be of serious concern within a few weeks after classes begin, but during our early adjustment period, our self-concepts may be a bit shaky. And since, as we have learned, how we interact with other people depends on our self-concept, we may find the first few weeks of school a bit shaky.

The Social Fraternity or Sorority Deans and counselors point out that another rough time for our self-concept occurs if we decide to go through the procedure towards pledging a fraternity or sorority. Called "rushing," the normally week-long period challenges self-concepts to the core, and there are documented cases of suicide directly linked to people's not being invited to join the fraternity or sorority of their choice. This was especially true during times when our society placed great importance on joining these institutions, and one was not "in" if one did not pledge. It took an extremely strong and healthy self-concept to overcome such peer challenges. Interestingly, at some of the more liberal colleges and universities during the Vietnam War era, it almost became a stigma to belong to such an "establishment" as a fraternity or sorority.

Some schools compound this inherent jolt to our self-concepts of having our peers judge whether or not we are worthy of being a "Zeta-Zeta" by scheduling rush for either the first week of school or even the week before school starts. Let's list some of the challenges our self-concept may run into in this situation.

First, we are in a new environment; we don't know our way around or how we will fit in. Second, we don't know anyone or we know only a very few people. The support of family and friends is not there. Third, people don't know us. The reputation we worked hard to build back home didn't follow us. We are reduced from being perhaps the star of high school to being just another face in the college crowd. Because we feel so alone, the need for inclusion, as we learned earlier, is tremendous.

Along comes a method of inclusion—belonging to a sorority or fraternity. But in order to belong, we must, figuratively speaking, pass inspection before total strangers who give us approximately fifteen minutes to prove ourselves worthy. The inspection is not entirely one-sided, however, because we are also deciding whether or not we would like to become a member. As rush week progresses, the inspection periods lengthen, and both we and our prospective sororities or fraternities narrow down our membership choices. Finally, we are either included or rejected. Whatever the outcome, it has been an enormous trial for our self-concept.

Whatever ignominy or disgrace we have incurred, it is almost always in our power to reestablish our reputation.

La Rochefoucauld

Loneliness   Being alone in an otherwise empty apartment on Friday or Saturday night, knowing about a dance we did not attend, or being excluded from a particular group can all lower our self-esteems. Inclusion, a basic interpersonal need discussed earlier, crawls into our lives at any hour of the day or night. When we are not included, we grope for an explanation. We challenge our perceptions of ourselves and others. We read hidden and inaccurate messages into other people's actions. Too many times we equate being alone with not being liked. And the more we avoid being included, the more we are excluded. The viscious circle continues. The most important thing to remember when we're feeling lonely is that our basic desire for inclusion may be artificially inflating our loneliness and the lack of self-confidence it instills.

Scholastic Achievement   In scholastic achievement alone, college presents ample opportunities to evaluate and reevaluate our ability to learn. At the same time, we experience an evaluation of our self-concepts, that part of us which perceives us as being intelligent and "above average." But keeping a strong self-concept in the face of constant intellectual challenges can be difficult. Some troublesome times exist, and it helps to know when to expect them.

One of the first challenges occurs early in the first term when we face our first quiz or exam. In highly selective schools, the entering students come from high schools where they may have ranked in the top of their classes and were accustomed to achieving A's and B's. However, they find that all of the other students on campus are also accustomed to achieving A's and B's. Unfortunately, not everyone can receive A's and B's. Thus, as instructors curve exams, the student who perceived himself or herself as an A student may suddenly score well below the class average. The self-concept of being above average is suddenly shattered, and the illusion of the high-school grades and the support they provided disappears. Most students successfully adjust to the new intellectual environment by either accepting themselves as being average, or realizing they will need to work much harder for their A's and B's to restore their academic records and self-confidence.   Our examples of how everyday events affect our self-concepts are by no means exhaustive. The important thing is to begin to become sensitive to those events. If we have this ability, we can then evaluate the way we feel about ourselves at any given time and in any given situation. When our self-concepts are challenged, we can stop and analyze the events which are affecting them. In some cases, we may be able to change the events. At the very least, we can prevent them from negatively affecting our ability to participate in good interpersonal communication.

Presenting Our Self-Concept to Others

Up to this point, our discussions have centered on what self-concept is all about. Now we turn our attention towards how we present our self-concept to others. We will move from intrapersonal communication and how we "internally" think about ourselves to interpersonal communication and how we interact with others.

Impression Management: The Concept

Sociologist Erving Goffman offers an interesting way to look at the manner in which we interact with others.[13] Most of us have been to a play and have watched the actors fulfill different roles as they interacted with each other. Have you ever stopped to consider that we may fulfill "roles" as we interact with people in everyday life? Goffman thinks we do and offers the theatre as an analogy to human interaction. To play a part in Goffman's theory, imagine a scene which involves you and another person. Let's assume this other person has just answered an ad to share an apartment with you. You're about to meet this prospective roommate for the first time and know that what you say, what you are wearing, and your facial expressions will all leave an impression. If we use Goffman's approach, you begin playing a scene, just as an actor plays a scene.[14] You won't be as deliberate or as dramatic as an actor portraying a character, but you still want to leave an impression. Perhaps you want to show that you are very concerned about neatness. As a result, you make sure you are clean and neat when you meet the person in order to nonverbally say, "I want you to be as neat as me." After a few moments, you might relate a story about a previous roommate who was not neat and what an unpleasant strain it placed on the relationship. You also smile, hoping the person will smile back and acknowledge a mutual desire to be friendly.

In our example, you chose to present yourself in a certain way to another person. You acted and even told a story in order to do so. Even though the actions seemed spontaneous, you were trying to make the other person acknowledge the "self" you were presenting. Perhaps the other person agreed with you that neatness was important. Perhaps he or she had also had a messy roommate and told you a story to which you both could relate. At that time, both of you would be participating in what Goffman calls *impression management*.

If we accept Goffman's approach to understanding interpersonal communication, we can easily see how we present a certain self and maintain a certain impression for many different types of interpersonal encounters. Sometimes we do this with our clothes. For example, a college professor may want to maintain an image of authority or credibility with her students. To do this, the professor has acquired a substantial wardrobe of dark suits she wears to class. On weekends, she wears jeans. One Saturday, she is working in the garden. Without taking the time to change, she makes a quick trip to the store where she runs into one of her students. The student comments on how unusual it is to see the professor wearing jeans. The professor, trying to maintain her image, enters immediately into impression management by saying, "I have been working in the garden this morning and ran out of seeds." Instead of simply admitting to the student that she liked to relax on Saturdays, she felt self-conscious about being in jeans in front of a student—a person within whose presence she wanted to

53

maintain a "managed impression." When she saw the student, she quickly engaged in impression management to explain her behavior.

As another example, suppose we are doing especially well in a course. As a result, we make a conscious effort to be prepared each day and retain a good impression in the instructor's eyes. In essence, we structure our behavior to continue the impression we have worked so hard to achieve.

We even participate in impression management with the tone of our voice. In a work situation, when we speak to our supervisors, the tone of our voice might be one of a responsible, energetic, and competent person who is straightforward and enthusiastic. We structure the pitch, speed, volume, and inflection of our voice in order to achieve this "managed impression."

Like the person meeting a prospective roommate, our dress often reflects impression management (Figure 2-5). A maker of popular blue jeans sews a patch on the rear waistband which shows the brand name, length, and waist size of the jeans. When discussing impression management with a junior high-school student recently, he pointed out that students in his school always leave the patch sewn to the jeans to make sure others know they are wearing this authentic brand of jeans. However, because many of the students always want to appear to be slim, he told us that they take a pen to this patch and neatly cross out their waist size!

In some cases, we just want to be neat without too much concern over what we wear. If we are working on a building crew as a carpenter, whether we wear blue jeans or white carpenter's pants probably won't make much difference on the impression we leave with our boss. Yet sometimes what we wear can be very significant. For years, employees of the International Business Machines Corporation (IBM) were considered as those who wore blue suits, long-sleeved white shirts, and conservative ties.

FIGURE 2-5

Dress is one form of impression management. The clothes we wear are often chosen to reflect an image we want to convey to others. An "executive" dress is appropriate in many settings, and the use of a coat or jacket by either sex is a basic part of some middle and upper level management settings.
(Irene Springer)

Impression management, this time at the corporate level, reflected a certain image at IBM. We see the same type of impression management on a larger authoritative scale in organizations requiring uniforms, from the military to medicine.

Impression Management and Self-Concept

Such impression management, whether self-imposed or imposed by others, directly affects not only the way we present ourselves to others but also the impressions we maintain for ourselves. Some law-enforcement agencies have conducted research on how police officers' uniforms affected self-images. In one community, the traditional police uniform was changed to gray slacks, blue blazers, white shirts, and blue ties. Immediately, the public saw the officers as easier to approach and more receptive to their concerns. What was not foreseen was the change in self-image the new uniform created for the officers. They felt less effective and in some cases even fearful of dealing with the public without the traditional police uniform. As a result of the officers' self-perceptions and their desire to present themselves as more authoritative, especially in such high tension crime situations as robberies and murders, the uniform was reinstated for certain officers (Figure 2–6). Other officers dealing with the public in more noncrime situations, such as marital disputes and community safety workshops, retained the blazer attire.

All of these concepts contribute to the way in which we present ourselves to others. When we meet other people, we adapt to the situations. We assume the "roles" we want to play on those particular "stages" and those roles become the "selves" we establish for those particular encounters. Perhaps one role is simply to present ourselves as nice people. Or perhaps we're negotiating a raise in pay or entering into a dispute over a grade on an exam and we want to define our "selves" more asser-

> *Faith in our own powers and confidence in our individual methods are essential to success.*
>
> *Roderick Stevens*

FIGURE 2–6
Police uniforms are as much a part of the self-concept of the officer as the image they present to other people. Uniforms have this dual purpose of influencing others as well as managing the impression and contributing to the self-concept of the wearer. (*Marc Anderson*)

tively. Our interpersonal communication skills and our ability to correctly perceive what is taking place in each interpersonal encounter will determine how well we react and interact with other people.

Although we have used Goffman's marriage of impression management with the theatre to explain how we play different roles when presenting ourselves to others, we should not make the mistake of thinking that every time we meet someone, the situation demands contrived and deliberate kinds of behavior. Although some of our behavior is deliberate, many of the roles that we play, we play subconsciously.

Dealing with Shyness

For some people, participating in any kind of interpersonal communication is a painful experience. They are shy and withdrawn, not wanting to seek out others. As a result, they are often excluded from the social relationships others enjoy. In some rare cases, this shyness is learned through positive reinforcement. But in most cases, it occurs as a result of having been painfully rebuked when dealing with others.

In some ways everyone is shy. We all don't plunge head-on into every interpersonal encounter. Testing the waters of a relationship by gradually participating in self-disclosure is a form of shyness. We do not want to immediately bare our self-concepts and risk having them negatively stroked.

Problems arise when our hesitancy to interact with others reaches abnormal stages. We avoid other people. We avoid making friends. We avoid inclusion to the point of what some call a phobia. Sometimes shyness is caused by having a low self-concept. We may feel very different and inferior to other people and reason that if we interact with others, they will sense our inferiority. In other cases, we may simply lack the conversational skills necessary to feel confident about interacting with other people.

Overcoming shyness is not always easy, but it can be accomplished. Various approaches can help people overcome the inhibitions to interpersonal encounters that shyness creates. For example, some people need to work on developing good listening skills. Because approximately half of our communication is spent listening to the other person, the shy person who learns to listen attentively has something with which to react. As a result, he or she can accurately respond to the other person's conversation, and the other person can accurately respond back. When an individual does not listen carefully, his or her response to the conversation may be incorrect. That incorrect response may totally confuse the entire conversation, resulting in no conversation. For the shy person, this silence is the same as disapproval. And as we said earlier, disapproval most likely caused the person's shy behavior in the first place. It reinforces it now. Think about people who are always talking. Many times they are so afraid of the negative stroking perceived from silence that they monopolize the conversation to keep it going.

Changing elements in our nonverbal communication can help us overcome shyness. We can change our posture from dejected slumps to alert, positive, straight-shouldered stances. Instead of standing with our arms crossed, we can let them fall more openly by our sides. We can move closer to an individual and express more intimate communicative styles. One research study examined the actual distance people stood from each other while carrying on a conversation.[15] By first using a test to measure shyness, they split a group into two parts: very shy and less shy. They found that the very shy people preferred to be approximately eight inches further away from the person to whom they were talking than did the less shy people. When the opposite sex was involved, this distance increased to twelve inches. Practicing such other nonverbal communication skills as developing eye contact, touching, and nodding can formulate less shy modes of communicative behavior. As we practice these skills, we can gradually begin to redefine our self-concepts from being shy to being open.

Other methods of overcoming shyness included helping the individual to develop a positive self-concept. Sometimes this involves asking ourselves simply, "What are we afraid of?" When we cannot come up with an answer, or when we do and successfully realize what hinders our conversation and deal with it, we are on the road to more open and responsive communication.

B ecoming Assertive

In recent years, increased attention has been given to our ability to be more assertive in our daily relations with other people. Some of this has been the result of increased professional status for women who have, especially in the male-dominated corporate atmosphere, been perceived as less effective and competent than males simply because they weren't as assertive. In some cases, women have had to learn assertive behavior in order to achieve their deserved recognition and rewards in the competitive working world. The assertiveness movement has also uncovered many men who experience the same shyness and inhibitions towards supervisors as women. As a result, both men and women in professional atmospheres, in family life, and in everyday dealings with people are realizing the value of developing an assertive personality.

Assertive, It is important to realize and understand that asser-
Not Abrasive tive behavior is not aggressive, abrasive, or agitating
behavior. In fact, many people who have learned to be assertive report less of a need to be aggressive and pushy. Much like a safety valve, assertive behavior releases discomfort and pressure before it can climb to the level of anger and conflict. Suppose you find that the coat

you just bought has a blemish in the fabric. Feeling sheepish that you didn't notice the blemish, you decide to wear the coat anyway. You later change your mind and decide to return the coat. The clerk at the store suggests that you have worn the coat too long for you to receive a refund. You are upset, and enter into a heated discussion with the clerk who finally refers you to the manager. Another heated exchange occurs because the manager feels obligated to support the clerk's decision. Had you clearly stated you were unhappy with the coat and returned it when you first noticed the blemish, your assertive behavior would have avoided the heated exchange with the clerk. Perhaps you are eating in a restaurant, and you want your water glass refilled. The glasses are small and do not hold much liquid. Finally, you catch the waiter or waitress and ask for more water. Later you want another refill, and again you wait for a waitress or waiter. Near the end of the meal, you want the glass refilled again. By now, you are disgusted by the lack of attention and voice that disgust loudly. Had you clearly stated at the beginning of the meal that you were thirsty and would like the water glass kept filled, you would not have had to complain about the service.

Naturally, there is a thin line between being assertive and being aggressive. It takes diplomacy and tact not to cross over the line. When we have achieved the ability to say what we want and state our requests clearly, we can avoid crossing the line because we avoid misunderstandings. Otherwise, we will only build up frustration, which will eventually be released in an unpleasant way.

He who when called upon to speak a disagreeable truth, tells it boldly and has done, is both bolder and milder than he who nibbles in a low voice and never ceases nibbling.

Lavater

Understanding Self-Concept

SUPERVISOR QUESTIONNAIRE

Characterize your impression of the employee's behavior in
various situations by using the following number scale:

Never or Rarely	Seldom	Sometimes	Usually	Almost Always or Always
-1-	-2-	-3-	-4-	-5-

_____ 1. Others may take advantage of him/her because he/she finds it difficult to refuse requests.

_____ 2. A reluctance to express his/her ideas hampers effectiveness on the job.

_____ 3. Downgrades his/her own work or attempts to offer excuses for his/her work even though it hasn't been criticized.

_____ 4. Seems to prefer giving other people the upper hand in a discussion rather than challenging their opinions or data.

_____ 5. During a performance review, he/she receives criticism without comment.

_____ 6. If he/she were genuinely overloaded with work in comparison to peers, he/she would try to complete the assignments alone regardless of the sacrifices required.

_____ 7. If you were treating him/her unfairly, he/she would do nothing, but wait for you to explain your intention.

_____ 8. Able to discuss someone's criticism of him/her openly and constructively.

_____ 9. If a friend made an unreasonable request, he/she would refuse in a manner that would allow him/her to retain the person's full friendship.

_____ 10. Actively seeks more information about an assignment if he/she did not completely understand original instructions.

_____ 11. If informed of declining performance during a performance review, he/she would ask for more specific information or examples of how his/her performance had declined and seek suggestions for improvement.

_____ 12. Asks favors of other people when necessary but does not "wear out his/her welcome."

_____ 13. If he/she had a "personality conflict" with his/her office mate, he/she may suggest a meeting between them and perhaps with their supervisor to iron out their differences and solve the conflict.

_____ 14. In group meetings, he/she expresses ideas freely without dominating others.

_____ 15. May "fly off the handle" if he/she loses an argument.

_____ 16. Complains when he/she is unhappy in a work situation, before seeking ways to improve the situation.

_____ 17. Steps in and makes decisions for others, without consulting them, even if the principal person is available for consultation.

_____ 18. Reluctant to admit an error, regardless of how small the mistake may be.

_____ 19. If informed of a perceived decline in performance, he/she offers a series of excuses or tries to blame others.

_____ 20. Acts as if he/she "knows it all."

_____ 21. Once he/she has drafted a letter or memo, he/she firmly resists making significant changes and acts as if he/she resents the suggestions for change.

This assertiveness questionnaire is employed as an evaluation instrument for assertiveness training programs in organizations. Take the test and evaluate yourself. (_T.K. Meier and J.P. Pulichene, "Evaluating the Effectiveness of Assertiveness Training,"_ Training and Development Journal, _February, 1980_)

Asking for What We Want Just like waiting for the waiter or waitress to fill the water glass, clearly asking for something we want is one way to be assertive without being abrasive. This does not mean that you should spill your feelings all over the place just to prove that you are unintimidated. That's being abrasive. But at the same time, do not be vague. Many parents become extremely frustrated in disciplining their children because they fail to state precisely what behavior they wish. Instead, they participate in *word bypass*, or deceptive behavior we talked about earlier. Examine the following *bypass statements*, and then examine what behavior is really desired. The problem is that the desired behavior is not verbalized:

BYPASS STATEMENT	WISHED BEHAVIOR
"Perhaps we shouldn't play with the pots and pans so much."	The parent wants the child to stop banging the pots and pans because the noise is giving the parent a headache.
"What do you think Marsha's parents feel about the two of you seeing each other so much?"	The parent does not want the relationship to become annoying, since the son is practically living at Marsha's house.
"Well, we'll certainly be glad to meet all the girls you date at college. I'll bet you really play the field. That's the way to enjoy college!"	The parent does not want to experience an unwanted pregnancy in the family.

We are all guilty of hiding our true feelings from others. Consider the following examples, this time from a working situation:

BYPASS STATEMENT	WISHED BEHAVIOR
"I imagine these orders could be completed fairly fast if you worked at it."	The supervisor expects the orders to be filled in no later than thirty minutes.
"We have a lot of territories that are doing quite well this year: Atlanta, Tucson, Salt Lake City, Houston, Denver, Indianapolis, and Baltimore."	The manager is dissatisfied with the account executive's progress and expects a specific dollar amount of improvement by the end of the month.
"We had an employee in our Columbus store who was fired because he was continually talking to the sales clerks."	If you do not stop talking to the sales clerks, you will be fired.

Again, how could the supervisor have more clearly expressed his or her feelings? Sooner or later, we may all be in a position in which other employees

What the Professor Really Means

By J. Timothy Petersik

What he or she said	What it means
You'll be using one of the leading textbooks in this field.	I used it as a grad student.
If you follow these few simple rules, you'll do fine in the course.	If you don't need any sleep, you'll do fine in the course.
The *gist* of what the author is saying is what's most important.	I don't understand the details either.
Various authorities agree that. . . .	My hunch is that. . . .
The answer to your question is beyond the scope of this class.	I don't know.
You'll have to see me during my office hours for a thorough answer to your question.	I don't know.
In answer to your question, you must recognize that there are several disparate points of view.	I *really* don't know.
Today we are going to discuss a most important topic.	Today we are going to discuss my dissertation.
Unfortunately, we haven't the time to consider all of the people who made contributions to this field.	I disagree with what roughly half of the people in this field have said.
We can continue this discussion outside of class.	1. I'm tired of this—let's quit. 2. You're winning the argument—let's quit.
Today we'll let a member of the class lead the discussion. It will be a good educational experience.	I stayed out too late last night and didn't have time to prepare a lecture.
Any questions?	I'm ready to let you go.
The implications of this study are clear.	I don't know what it means, either, but there'll be a question about it on the test.
The test will be 50-question multiple choice.	The test will be 60-question multiple guess, plus three short-answer questions (1,000 words or more) and no one will score above 75 per cent.
The test scores were generally good.	Some of you managed a B.
The test scores were a little below my expectations.	Where was the party last night?
Some of you could have done better.	Everyone flunked.
Before we begin the lecture for today, are there any questions about the previous material?	Has anyone opened the book yet?
According to my sources. . . .	According to the guy who taught this class last year. . . .
It's been very rewarding to teach this class.	I hope they find someone else to teach it next year.

J. Timothy Petersik teaches in the psychology department at Southeast Missouri State University

(The Chronicle of Higher Education, *April 27, 1981*)

THE UNSPOKEN MESSAGE

SAID: I've outgrown this job. No future here.
UNSAID: I can't stand the management of the company. They're out to get me.

● ● ●

SAID: We're sorry to lose you, Charlie. You've been a good worker.
UNSAID: It's about time you woke up. We thought you'd be out of here months ago.

● ● ●

SAID: I think you have a nice background—lots of different experiences.
UNSAID: Why'd this guy move around so much? Must be flaky.

● ● ●

SAID: I was responsible for a 45% increase in profits at the Jones Company.
UNSAID: What about the other 35 guys in sales?

● ● ●

SAID: Charlie is one hell of a guy. You should be happy to have him on your team.
UNSAID: Better with you than with us.

● ● ●

SAID: This job is perfect for me—I can handle it.
UNSAID: Well, maybe it gives me time to find a better one.

● ● ●

SAID: It's our policy to start all our young tigers at the same salary.
UNSAID: . . . and work them as long as we can before they go elsewhere.

(Advertising Age, January 1, 1979. Copyright 1979 by Crain Communications, Inc.)

(Case Currents, February, 1980. Used by permission of Thomas W. Pratt and Paul H. Schneiter, Brigham Young University)

work under us. How we state our desires will have a direct effect on the level of performance we receive from those employees.

Handling Negative Stroking   One of the greatest benefits of assertive behavior is the ability to protect ourselves from negative stroking. We discussed how negative stroking can lower our self-concept. We can counteract that negative stroking with assertive rebuttals. Following are examples of negative stroking and some possible assertive replies:

NEGATIVE STROKING	ASSERTIVE REPLY
"Do you honestly think you have any chance of succeeding?"	"I certainly do, or I would not be attempting the task."
"If I were you, I would not take that course. I almost flunked it."	"You are not me, and I will not predict my own success based upon yours."
"Do you really feel comfortable wearing that outfit?"	"Yes I do. Moreover, I consider myself an individual not manipulated by clothes."
"There you go again."	"No, there *you* go again."
"That is a stupid idea."	"Few ideas are truly stupid. The people who do not understand them are."

These examples are clearly more direct than we encounter in every conversation. But we can encounter negative stroking in more subtle ways. Moreover, depending on our self-concept, what is negative stroking for one person may not be negative stroking for another. You know when you have been negatively stroked because you feel intimidated, hurt, and uncomfortable. Right at that moment is when to formulate an assertive reply to restore your self-concept within the conversation. But again, I am reminded of my friend who had just finished a training program on assertive behavior. I asked her if she considered the program a success. "Oh, undoubtedly," she replied. "I have exercised my assertive behavior five times in the last twenty-four hours and have lost five friends in the process!" Assertive behavior, if not tempered with the ability to be sensitive to other people's thoughts and feelings, can backfire. An assertive comment *can* inadvertently say to another person, "That was a rude, stupid comment." Such a message can provoke even nastier comments, which demand even more assertive behavior until interpersonal communication breaks down entirely. Thus, we must continually interact with others by supporting their self-concepts while protecting our own.

S elf-Disclosure

An important part of presenting ourselves to others centers around how much information we should divulge and how much we should withhold. Called self-disclosure, it is often a significant part of interpersonal communication.[16] For example, two people passing the time in a grocery line may comment on the checker's progress. If one says, "It sure takes a long time to get through this line" and the other person agrees with, "It sure does" both have disclosed to each other that neither likes waiting in line. Self-disclosure, yes, but not much is revealed.

Yet at other times, more intimate information may be disclosed. Two lovers, a married couple, or two close friends are much more apt to disclose information to each other than two workers in a mill.

Self-Disclosure as Support for Self-Concept   Earlier we discussed the process of stroking and how our self-concepts receive positive reinforcement from others.[17] Our continual need for this positive reinforcement (stroking) in order for our self-concept to grow and strengthen is well established. By disclosing information about ourselves—the things we hold close, our values, attitudes, and beliefs—we continually "test the waters" to see how other people are reacting to our self-concept. The more we disclose about ourselves, the more we can be supported by others. Disclosing very intimate things about ourselves and having those things reinforced can have a powerful influence on our self-concept. Thus, support for our own self-concept is one reason for self-disclosure.

Humbleness is always grace; always dignity.

James Russell Lowell

The most difficult thing in life is to know yourself.

Thales

A relationship in which self-disclosure can occur in an unthreatened environment is inherently valuable for the self-concepts of all parties involved. Psychologist Carl Rogers offers a prescription for effective interpersonal communication when he defines the characteristics of such a "helping relationship":

1. The communicators are perceived by one another as trustworthy, as consistently dependable.
2. They express their separate selves unambiguously.
3. They possess positive attitudes and warmth and caring for the other.
4. A partner in a helping relationship keeps his (her) own separate identity.
5. A partner permits the other to do the same.
6. The helping relationship is marked by empathy. (The communicator attempts to understand the feelings of the other.)
7. The helper accepts the various facets of the other's experience as communicated by the other.
8. The partners in a relationship respond with sufficient sensitivity to allay threat.
9. They are able to free themselves from the threat of evaluation from the other.
10. Each communicator recognizes that the other is changing and is flexible enough to permit the other to change.[18]

Roger's ten characteristics are the ideal, and not every relationship or every interpersonal encounter can meet all of them. Nevertheless, these characteristics are good foundations upon which to base improvement of our own skills at interacting with each other.

Avoiding Self-Disclosure Self-disclosure also carries with it a risk. It's the risk that instead of having our self-concept reinforced, we may have them shot down. And the deeper we reveal things about ourselves, the deeper the "hurt" if our qualities are not accepted positively.[19] The old saying "We always hurt the ones we love" could be rewritten to say "We *can* always hurt the ones we love" because two people in love frequently disclose a great deal of information about themselves. Each is thus very vulnerable to the other's discretion to either positively or negatively judge that disclosure.

In some cases, the risk of self-disclosure can be traced back to early childhood when we existed in a virtually positive environment. As we grew, we began to receive negative reinforcement in the form of scolding for doing or saying things that did not correspond to the kind of people our parents expected us to be. Other relatives or friends may have also provided negative reinforcement. We might have changed our behavior and, consequently, our selves because of this scolding, accepting that we could get along fine by not saying bad words at dinner or by not throwing temper tantrums at bedtime. Yet we could have surpressed certain feelings, allowing them to remain part of our selves but not discussing them with anyone. Such things as secret fears, fantasies, or other highly personal feelings we still may not reveal to other people, regardless of how close we are to the person.

In Chapter 1, we talked about *control* as a basic interpersonal need.[20] The threat of losing control over a person or situation is another reason to avoid self-disclosure. By disclosing too much about ourselves, we become vulnerable to attack. When this attack weakens our self-concept, it can interfere with our ability to be in charge of a relationship.

Still another reason for avoiding self-disclosure is very personal—the fear of revealing our true self-concept, *not* to others but to *ourselves.* We can try just as hard to keep our own true self-concept from ourselves as we do from others. And few experiences can be more jolting to our self-esteems than to examine our true characteristics. Under the supervision of a physician, therapy sessions in which we delve deeply into our true "selves," sometimes referred to as primal therapy, become necessary to begin healing mentally ill individuals. But on a less serious note, we can all be guilty of simply not admitting the truth to ourselves about ourselves.

When Self-Disclosure Occurs

Self-disclosure can occur at different times during interpersonal communication. In Chapter 1, we talked about viewing interpersonal communication as a developmental process.[21] Research has taught us that we tend to disclose things about ourselves at different points in a relationship, as that relationship develops.[22] You may disclose your views on politics on the first date, but you may not talk about your inner fantasies about making love. Such disclosures would occur much later in a relationship, if at all. Moreover, we tend to disclose negative things, if at all, much later. Part of our reason for disclosing positive things is the concept of impression management we talked about earlier. We want to be liked, respected, and to make a positive impression when we first meet people. Thus, we stress our positive qualities. As a relationship develops into what Carl Rogers calls a "helping relationship," we may feel less threatened by disclosing negative information.

Who Listens to Self-Disclosure?

Although the length of time we have been in a relationship determines the intimacy of our disclosures, the person listening to our disclosures also plays a part in what we will reveal about ourselves.[23] Think of a characteristic about yourself. Would you tell a stranger about it? If the characteristic is highly intimate, you probably would not. But would you tell a friend about it? Again, the level of intimacy would determine your answer. Select any number of things about yourself and then ask to which of the following people you

Sincerity resembles a
spice. Too much repels
you and too little
leaves you wanting.

Bill Copeland

would disclose this information: a stranger, an acquaintance, a parent, a friend, a spouse or someone equally as close. The more intimate the information you are disclosing, the more intimate a relationship you would have with the person receiving the disclosure.

Rules for Self-Disclosure In Chapter 1, we talked about the "rules approach" to interpersonal communication. If we want to examine self-disclosure from the perspective of certain rules existing in our society, then research suggests that we must be careful to time our self-disclosures. Ill-timed disclosures can result in others' perceiving us as maladjusted.[24] This is especially true during very intimate communication. Our social norms dictate certain expected rules of behavior, and our violating those rules suggests that we do not know how to interact in socially acceptable ways. In one research study, it was found that we are better off not to disclose anything about ourselves than to disclose intimate information too early in a relationship. Such communication between two people attracted to each other might result in one person's abruptly ending an evening with the statement, "Let's not rush things."

SUMMARY

Who am I? We discussed the answer to this question as we investigated self-concept and its role in interpersonal communication. At the foundation of self-concept are its building blocks, our values, attitudes, and beliefs—including basic beliefs and peripheral beliefs—and our ability to understand and apply these interpersonal interactions. To maintain our self-concept, we need to understand challenges to our beliefs and how to handle criticism. We need to understand the importance of both receiving and giving what psychologists call "stroking"—the positive and negative reinforcement we all encounter in interacting with others. Stroking determines not only how we feel about ourselves but how we relate to others.

Even though we use interpersonal communication every day, we may not interact each day from the same perspective of our "selves." Sometimes we may communicate from our adult states, at others from our parent states, and still others from our child states. Good interaction among mature adults is accomplished in the adult state, yet both parent and child states can creep into our conversations and interfere with this communication process.

A common force affecting our self-concept is a change of residence. We leave behind the people and things which have helped build our self-concept, and we enter emotionally naked into new settings. A new school with new students and new teachers can also affect our self-concept. Our reputations are left behind, and we must begin anew to develop supportive relationships. Joining a social fraternity or sorority can

Understanding Self-Concept

be a traumatic experience for many people because of the emphasis many societies artificially place on "belonging" and our own interpersonal needs of inclusion. Loneliness is really a form of self-concept reduction which can make us feel rejected or unwanted.

In presenting ourselves to others, we discussed what sociologist Erving Goffman refers to as impression management. We also talked about what shyness means and how in some cases assertive behavior can overcome shyness. While engaging in assertive behavior, there is a thin line between being assertive and being abrasive. The latter can alienate others.

Self-disclosure in interpersonal communication is necessary to permit two peoples' fields of experience to overlap and nurture human interaction.

OPPORTUNITIES FOR FURTHER LEARNING

BOWER, S. A. and G. H. BOWER, *Asserting Yourself: A Practical Guide for Positive Change.* Reading, MA: Addison-Wesley, 1976.

DYER, W. W., *Your Erroneous Zones.* New York: Funk & Wagnalls, 1976.

DYER, W. W., *Pulling Your Own Strings.* New York: Avon, 1977.

DYER, W. W., *The Sky's the Limit.* New York: Simon & Schuster, 1980.

FENSTERHEIM, H. and J. BAER, *Don't Say Yes When You Want to Say No.* New York: Dell Publishing Co., Inc., 1975.

FENSTERHEIM, H. and J. BAER, *Stop Running Scared!* New York: Rawson-Wade Pubs., Inc., 1977.

FRIDAY, N., *My Mother My Self.* New York: Delacorte Press, 1977.

GARNER, A., *Conversationally Speaking.* New York: McGraw-Hill, 1981.

HARRIS, T. A., *I'm OK. You're OK.* New York: Harper & Row., Pub., 1967.

MATSON, K., *The Psychology Today Omnibook of Personal Development.* New York: Morrow, 1977.

MAY, R., *The Meaning of Anxiety.* New York: W. W. Norton & Co., Inc., 1977.

NARCISCO, J. and D. BURKETT, *Declare Yourself: Discovering the Me in Relationships.* Englewood Cliffs, NJ: Prentice-Hall—Spectrum Books, 1975.

PHELPS, S. and N. AUSTIN, *The Assertive Woman.* Fredericksburg, VA: BookCrafters, 1975.

ROGERS, C., *Carl Rogers on Personal Power.* New York: Delacorte Press, 1977.

SMITH, M. J., *When I Say No, I Feel Guilty.* New York: Dial Press, 1975.

TIGER, L., *Optimism: The Biology of Hope.* New York: Simon & Schuster, 1979.

TUAN, Y., *Landscapes of Fear.* New York: Pantheon, 1979.

WALSH, R. N. and F. VAUGHAN, *Beyond Ego: Transpersonal Dimensions in Psychology.* Los Angeles: J. P. Tarcher, Inc., 1980.

YGLESIAS, H., *Starting Early, Anew, Over, and Late.* New York: Rawson-Wade Pub., Inc., 1978.

ZIMBARDO, P. G., *Shyness.* Reading, Mass: Addison-Wesley, 1977.

ZIMBARDO, P. G. and S. RADL, *The Shy Child.* New York: McGraw-Hill, 1981.

chapter three

Listening

PREVIEW   *After completing this chapter, we should be able to:*

Explain the approaches to understanding listening.
List and describe the steps to good listening.
Distinguish between selective perception, selective exposure, and selective retention.
Describe how stereotyping, source credibility, and cultural obstacles can interfere with good listening.
Explain what it means to switch listening styles.
Explain how misreading communicator styles can affect listening.
Discuss how the brain's right and left hemispheres affect listening.
Explain the role of feedback in the listening process.

I think the most important thing I've learned is to listen. So often a problem will start to be laid out and I immediately feel "I have an answer for that! I have a solution. . . ." And the problem still hasn't really been laid out.

I have to keep reminding myself before every meeting: Listen! It's a hard lesson to learn, especially for someone like me. If you're either quick-witted or very opinionated, you really want to jump in. But, very often I've found that the solution to the problem (and that's what this business is all about, solving problems for clients) is given in the meeting if you listen.

Peggy Masterson
Senior Vice-President
Creative Group Head
Benton & Bowles

(Advertising Age, June 29, 1981. Copyright © 1981 by Crain Communications, Inc.)

Of all the skills we are taught in high school and college, few receive less emphasis than listening skills.[1] Instead, we concentrate most of our related time on speaking and becoming good senders of communication. But our success as senders is directly tied to our ability to understand the total communication process, and that involves listening. Listening involves much more than just "hearing" what someone is saying. In fact, being a good listener often requires greater skill than being a good speaker. When we are speaking, we can adapt and alter our messages at will. If we are able to tell that we are not being understood, we can change our messages. As listeners, we also become "senders" of communication in that we send back to the speaker information about the success of his or her message. And without being able to listen and respond to other people, we are unable to effectively use this communication which we receive.

When more and more professional women began actively seeking and succeeding in sales positions in many industries, management began to realize they possessed a quality many times overlooked by sales trainers—the ability to listen. Sales trainers had spent so much time telling trainees how to answer objections that they had overlooked the importance of understanding the objection in the first place. Not only was it necessary to listen to the words a customer was saying, but it was also necessary to look beyond the words to the feelings and motivations that prompted those words. With an emphasis stressed since birth to listen attentively and with the societal freedom to react to emotions and to be understanding, women turned out to be superb salespersons because they had acquired the ability to listen. If a customer was using bypass language, women knew how to look for the true meaning and then *rearticulate* that true reaction either in their own minds or directly to the customer.

Some of the best executives (both men and women) are successful because they have the ability to listen. They were able to reach goals they set for themselves because dealing with people was just as important as dealing with goods and services. Many times these people act not as managers in the traditional sense, because a tremendous amount of the work of the company has been delegated, but instead as safety valves by being able to listen to the problems of employees. Such people, when truly able to understand and communicate with employees, can do a great deal to help alleviate pressures for those employees before the pressures start affecting their ability to perform their jobs. A corporation can seem almost overbearing to some employees, and despite the releasing of tensions and problems to peers or immediate supervisors, there is no substitute for gaining the ear of management. And more times than not, the reason employees feel they do not have the understanding of their immediate supervisor is because the supervisor has not learned how to listen.

When a university with which the author was associated faced hiring a new president, it hired an interim president to run the university while the search process evolved. The person hired in the interim did not bring to the job the traditional credentials of a Ph.D. and academic experience. The individual had spent his career in business, not education. But during the time he spent as interim president, *he listened.* He listened to every level of the university from janitor to dean. He listened to every constituent of the university from alumni to student. He listened to every friend of the university from business executive to local civic leader. A quiet person who dressed casually and undertalked every conversation, the interim president kept the university running smoothly even though he made relatively few decisions. During his tenure, the university experienced a tremendous "calming" effect which was talked about long after he left.

In this chapter on listening, we examine "listening styles," and how we can look beyond the words in order to receive those feelings and motivations people are sending to us in interpersonal com-munication.

Approaches to Understanding Listening

Sometimes it helps to begin a new concept by highlighting what we have already learned. This helps to create frames of reference, to build categories or "boxes" in which we can put different concepts. Let's review our discussion of the different "approaches" to interpersonal communication. We talked about viewing interpersonal communication as a series of rules for specific behaviors to follow in order to succeed. We also talked about approaching interpersonal communication as a series of situations, such as the business executive with the new office holding the discussion with the vice presidents. In addition, we examined interpersonal communication as a developmental process.

We can approach the concept of listening from the same perspectives. For example, think of the "rules" you might follow to be a good listener, such as not interrupting the other person. Ask yourself how this particular situation is affecting your listening. Is the other person monopolizing the conversation? But should you let that person continue because he or she needs your listening's "safety valve" in order to release emotions? Does the situation demand your listening to be responsive more to the emotions of the other person? Can your listening be responsive to both? How will the way you listen in this conversation affect future conversations? Rules, situations, and the developmental process of listening are just as important as the rules, situations, and developmental process of "sending" communication.

As we discuss listening, we interweave many of these approaches. It is through studying this coming together of different approaches that we can learn to become more effective listeners.

Steps to Good Listening

Strolling through the campus of almost any college or university, we can witness a variety of "listening situations." Students may be casually chatting along walkways, paying some attention to each other and some attention to the sights and sounds of the moment. Rather than paying avid attention to what each is saying, they are content to just enjoy being with each other. At another place on campus, we might encounter two people discussing a very personal relationship. Each can feel the emotions of the other person, and each is paying undivided attention to what the other is saying as they share their experiences. Professors chatting with students, a police officer arguing with a driver about an improperly parked car, research assistants discussing the results of a new experiment—all are climbing the different levels of the listening process.

Sensing Listening begins by *sensing*. To really appreciate the process of listening, to *enjoy it* and *look forward to it*, we must be able to use our senses to absorb everything we can about the person talking. Many times we bypass sensing and jump ahead to hearing, and then wonder why we may not have "heard" what the person was saying (Figure 3–1). Using our senses to listen takes practice. If you were to take a walk in a forest, your senses would pick up the sounds of birds chirping, pine trees whispering in the wind, and twigs cracking beneath your feet. You would feel the cool, crisp air and see the wildflowers swaying in the sunshine. As we do in the forest, when we encounter other people, we need to listen to them with all of our senses. *Listen* to their eyes. Do they sparkle, or squint? Are they saying "I am sincere"? Are they saying "I want to talk more"? *Listen* to their handshakes. Are they saying "I am positive about meeting you"?

We can "listen" with much more than our ears. Every perfume and cologne manufacturer knows that and tries to convince us that the messages sent by someone wearing Enjoli, for example, will be received by people in a way different from messages sent by someone wearing Babe. A

recent television commercial promoted a subtle cologne by using the example of the man whose presence arrived at the office before he did. On the faces of the other employees was subtle rejection. They had received a message even before they could hear or see the person.

Even our ears hear more than mere words. They also hear the tone of a person's voice. Although most people are aware of voice tones, they often do not actually "hear" those tones because they are listening to the words of the other person. Stop and listen attentively the next time you converse with someone. Monitor all of the different changes in that person's voice and the relationship these changes have with the conversation. Do this for a series of conversations with various people. You'll find that each person's vocal qualities are unique. Scientists who specialize in reading voice prints know that with the right equipment, a person's voice is as identifiable as a fingerprint. By concentrating on a person's vocal qualities, you will begin to find that you can recognize that person's voice just as you recognize his or her face. By using your senses, you can mold your art of listening.

Attention Now that we are awakened to our sensory skills, we need to move to the next step in the listening process, *attention*. Simply sensing communication does not mean we pay attention to it.[2] We need to concentrate on the messages we receive.

How many times have we been in a conversation with our parents, our friends, or people with whom we work and the person to whom we are listening says, "I'm boring you, aren't I?" Or perhaps the more direct statement, "You're not even listening to me!" jolts us to a new level of alertness. We probably then realize we had sent feedback to the person which made it obvious we were not paying attention. Perhaps we were staring off into space. Perhaps we were shifting our feet while looking at the floor. Perhaps we asked a question that had absolutely nothing to do with what the person was saying or perhaps we asked about what that person just finished explaining. Perhaps we were just silent. The result was that the other person lost the commitment to continue because we had lost the commitment to listen. Not paying attention is the most basic violation of good listening behavior. Moreover, it is the most noticeable violation.

It is sometimes difficult to tell if people are understanding what we are saying to them. If we knew they didn't understand our message, we could adjust that message accordingly. But they give us no verbal or nonverbal clues. We may continue to converse uninterrupted. Only later do we discover that a serious communication breakdown took place. An order will not be filled, an examination will be failed, a group will not reach its goal, and we know someone may have been paying attention but was not understanding.

As students, we have all sat in a classroom listening to a lecture and little by little, let our concentration slip. We may not even have noticed our concentration slipping. We have been listening and paying attention to every word the teacher was saying. Then suddenly the lecture stops, and the teacher calls on us to answer a question that had been discussed not less than five minutes before. We are shocked, embarrassed, and frustrated. We do not even know where the question came from let alone what the answer is. The teacher says, "You weren't paying attention." But the teacher is partially wrong. We were paying attention. What we were not doing was understanding, and that caused our concentration to drift. Had the teacher known we weren't understanding, he or she could have repeated the material.

Some universities have what are known as instructional-response systems (Figure 3–2). At each seat is a series of buttons. The buttons are connected to a small central computer which is connected to a display monitor at the lectern. In large classes, the teacher can ask a question and give a series of possible answers, much like a multiple-choice test.

Listening in class, regardless of the year in school, may present special challenges. College students studying to be elementary or secondary school teachers find skill in interpersonal communication especially important. Knowing more about how and why children listen contributes to a teacher's ability to impart knowledge.
(Ken Karp)

FIGURE 3-2
Some classrooms are equipped with instructional response systems which monitor how well students listen and comprehend information. At any given point in a lecture, students can respond to an instructor's question by pushing a set of buttons attached to their desks. Back at the podium, the instructor instantly can see how many students answered the question correctly. *(Instructional Industries, Inc.; JW/University of Texas News Service/Frank Armstrong)*

Students then push the button corresponding to what they feel is the correct answer. The teacher is instantly able to see how many students understand the material. This electronic feedback system works particularly well in such subjects as mathematics in which sequential learning is necessary and in which problems can develop quickly if the student doesn't understand the material.

The problem is that we have no human electronic response system telling us if the person listening to us is truly understanding what we are saying. Moreover, we can look quite attentive while still not understanding what is being said. As a result, we must develop our own skills of listening so that we work at not only paying attention but also at providing feedback to the other person when we don't understand something.

> One ear heard it, and at the other out it went.
>
> *Chaucer*

Empathizing

To *empathize* means to enter mentally and with emotion into the feelings of another person. To a certain degree, empathy relates to the overlapping fields of experience or homophily we talked about in Chapter 1. Empathizing is one of the least understood yet vitally important steps in the listening process. We cannot casually empathize. Rather, we literally transpose ourselves into the other person's positions as a communicator and then develop an awareness of what that person is feeling. The saying "Do not judge me until you have walked a mile in my moccasins." in many ways expresses the role empathy plays in the

OOPS

An
irate banker
demanded that
Alexander Graham Bell
remove
"that toy"
from his office.
That toy was
the telephone.
A Hollywood producer
scrawled a curt
rejection note
on a manuscript
that became
"Gone with the Wind."
Henry Ford's
largest
original investor
sold all
his stock
in 1906.
Roebuck sold out
to Sears
for $25,000
in 1895.
Today, Sears
may sell
$25,000 worth of goods
in 16 seconds.
The next time
somebody
offers you
an idea
that leaves
you cold,
put it on
the back burner.
It might
warm up.

listening process. The therapist or psychiatrist should be able to understand and empathize with a patient in order to treat an illness. A mother and father empathize with their child. But in some situations, empathy gets pushed back in favor of more immediate steps in listening. In a corporate setting, the goals of the discussion and the desire of people to participate in specific kinds of behavior take precedent and often leave empathy far behind. Yet adding empathy to our listening can improve any interpersonal encounter. With empathy, we have the ability to gain a deeper insight into the person with whom we are talking. We cannot only monitor more types of messages the person may be sending but also become much more sensitive to those messages. If a person has been passed over for promotion and is participating aggressively in a business meeting, we may be less likely to react negatively if we can empathize and understand the reasons behind the behavior.

Remembering   Still another step in the listening process is *remembering*. Memory is a skill and, as a support to good listening skills, can be learned and improved. We accumulate information in any conversation. Yet sometimes remembering the information we accumulate is difficult. Consider the politician who was asked a question that took three minutes for the reporter to phrase. By the time the reporter completed the question, the politician had forgotten the first half of it and couldn't give a complete answer. The reporter wrote the next morning that the politician had avoided the question. But the truth was that the reporter had compiled so much information into the question, that it was virtually impossible to remember, let alone answer. We cannot effectively understand what is being said unless we remember what is being said. Thus, remembering, be it for a few seconds or a few minutes, is necessary in order to effectively respond to the sender.

Managing
Listening Steps
with Skill   Being aware of the various steps of good listening has little value unless we can manage the steps with skill and consistency. Simply remembering to use all our senses is not enough any more than simply being attentive is enough. What we need is a combination of *goal* and *emotional* listening. By goal listening, we mean beginning to establish for ourselves listening goals that we can follow. The first and most basic is to make a commitment to ourselves to become good listeners. Simply keeping the goal in mind is the first step towards effective listening. Every time we meet someone and exchange information, even a smile, we make a commitment to listen. We don't dismiss the presence of other people simply because they are not important to our daily lives. We may not be promoted for listening attentively to the office receptionist, but if we break this listening habit, we run the risk of someday not listening to someone who can promote us. Remember, in order to be effective, listening must become a habit.

After we have made a commitment to become good listeners, we can then begin to manage the individual listening steps, again with work and practice. Think of these steps as building blocks, like the building blocks of self-concept we discussed in Chapter 2. Yet building the good listening habit, as with any other building process, must overcome obstacles now and then. Let's examine some of these obstacles and ways in which you can overcome them.

Obstacles to Good Listening

Clearly, one of the most obvious obstacles to good listening is not applying the steps we have just discussed. But we want to look even deeper into what interferes with good listening and the inability to accurately receive communication. In the selections that follow, we talk about broad-based obstacles to listening, including selective exposure, selective perception, and selective retention, and we examine how these obstacles can affect interpersonal communication.

Selective Perception   Imagine that you go with a friend to hear a speech by a leading political candidate. Both you and your friend hold very strong but different views on a key issue that the candidate touches upon in her speech. When the speech is over, you discover that you and your friend have entirely different interpretations of what was said. Yet you both heard the same speech. How could the two of you differ so greatly on what you heard? Blame it on *selective*

FIGURE 3-3

Selective perception is an obstacle to good listening. We often make judgments about people by their appearance or what we perceive them to believe or represent. Examine the three faces. We may not care to listen attentively to the two grouches on either end or to the shouting sailor in the center. But if the two people on either end were smiling, and the sailor was a police officer, our listening behavior might change. *Now, turn the book upside down.* Remember this exercise the next time you find yourself guilty of selective perception which interferes with your ability to listen. *(Examples from old advertising cards from the early 1900s. Courtesy U&Ic)*

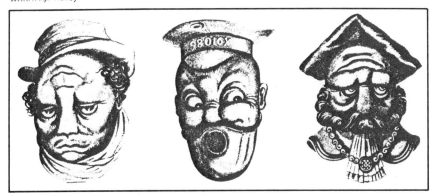

perception (Figure 3–3). This phenomenon explains that what we hear and, consequently, what we perceive is determined many times by our preconceived notions about someone or something. Although the same message might be sent to two different people, each selectively interprets or perceives the communication differently. If you perceive yourself as being liberal, then you might react more favorably to something a liberal candidate says than to something a conservative candidate says, even though they say the same thing! We often hear what we want to hear; we are all guilty of selective perception.

The first step in overcoming the selective perception hurdle is to recognize it. Then we can try our best to compensate for it. When we interact with someone we perceive has different opinions from ours, we should keep open minds. Look for opinion shifts. Look for common ground. Try to perceive how they feel about an issue while also asking why we perceive things the way we do.

Selective Exposure

Selective exposure is more closely related to whom we listen than to how we perceive communication.

We tend to think of listening as a skill employed when interacting with others. But we may be more selective than we realize in our interactions. We need to remember that whom we choose to interact with is another way of determining to whom we want to listen. We can inadvertently narrow our own perspectives by limiting our communication to only certain people with whom we agree.

Selective exposure means that we choose to come in contact with communication from others who we perceive possess certain beliefs. The word *perceive* forges the interrelationship between selective perception and selective exposure. Selective exposure can actually limit the number of people to whom we listen, and can therefore reinforce and solidify our opinions and beliefs. Once these opinions are solid, they further interfere with listening by strengthening our selective-perception processes. To be able to have an intelligent, open mind on matters of substance and to be able to interact and work cooperatively towards common goals, we must understand and tolerate different ideas and opinions. One way to achieve this is to avoid selectively exposing ourselves to communication—by not limiting the people to whom we talk, courses we take, books we read, television programs we watch, or anything else we perceive as mirroring our own beliefs.

Selective Retention

Earlier in this chapter we discussed that remembering is a key step in the listening process. Now we apply that step and skill to the concept of *selective retention*. Selective retention is the same as selective remembering. Just as we selectively expose ourselves to communication we perceive as having certain qualities, we selectively retain or remember communication which we perceive as having certain qualities.

For example, we may hear a politician's speech and remember only those things with which we are in agreement. At work, we may be having a disagreement with our boss over the best method to fill orders. When the boss tells us to do something, we may only remember the directions that agree with our own perceptions of the way things should be done. At home, parents ask their sons or daughters to do chores around the house. And sons and daughters have an uncanny ability to remember only the chores which are the easiest or the ones they want to do. In essence, we selectively remember communication.

When I was learning how to ski, my wife was gallantly trying to teach me the fine points of stopping and turning. On the advice of my enthusiastic instructor, we both headed up the chair lift to the top. Unfortunately, as I started down the run, the only thing I could remember was how to keep from falling off the side of the mountain and taking a short cut straight to the bottom. With constant instruction at various intervals on the way down, I arrived at the bottom, remembering absolutely nothing about how to stop and turn. Later, on a more moderate run, I gradually began to develop my skill and became an avid fan of the sport.

This experience on the ski slope can be applied to listening. When we enter into a conversation, we may carry with us a certain priority of information and opinions. Regardless of what communication is sent to us, we only remember what we feel is important and that with which we agree. Just as staying on the mountain was the first priority in my mind, we all have priorities in our minds in any situation. Even though I listened and paid attention to what my wife was saying about turning and stopping, it was not a priority, and I did not remember it.

Stereotyping   *Stereotyping* as used in this text means prejudging a person (Figure 3–4). We frequently prejudge people before we have an opportunity to interact with them. Closely related to selective perception, stereotyping sets up artificial barriers through which we selectively listen because we believe a person has certain qualities, stands for something, or represents something. We can be guilty of stereotyping in any number of interpersonal encounters. In many cases, we tend to stereotype people with others of the same group. Perhaps we have known someone in our past who had certain qualities, and now we perceive everyone like that person to have the same qualities.[3] I asked students what they felt were some of the most common stereotypes that they encounter in school that consequently interfere with good listening. They gave the following answers:

One student pointed out that she used to think other students who dressed in sloppy jeans and sweatshirts were not very intelligent. She had been raised to consider neatly dressed people as intelligent, as good to associate with, and as those who obtained leadership positions on campus. Not long after she had arrived on campus she met a student with long hair, patched jeans, and a patched shirt. The two found

"Personally I think anyone that doesn't agree with me would have to be an ignorant, feebleminded, incompetent . . . but I want to hear your honest opinions."

FIGURE 3-4

Sexual stereotyping is a common form of prejudice that sets up barriers to interpersonal communication. Many jobs which were once primarily held by men are now held by women, and vice versa. *(Photograph courtesy of Exxon Company, U.S.A.)*

themselves sitting next to each other at a college luncheon for student volunteers. During lunch, the two started to talk. In the process of the conversation, she learned that the student in patched jeans and the patched shirt was a straight-A student and had already been accepted to one of the best law schools in the country. It was clear that he was highly intelligent and had a high grade-point average and law-school admission scores to prove it. From that point on, she paid little attention to how people dressed, at least in judging their intelligence.

Another student pointed out that it is quite easy for a student to be stereotyped as either an athletic "jock" or a good scholar, but that stereotypes, again, preconceive that the two don't merge. After having heard that a star football player was very arrogant and difficult to talk to, she found herself at a party standing next to the athlete. She paid little attention to him and replied to most of his comments with light-hearted innuendoes. Two days later, her roommate had a date with the athlete and returned to the dormitory exclaiming what an unusual evening it had been and how she liked talking to him. She said he had invited her to a lecture by a foreign-policy expert. After the lecture, they spent the evening at a coffee shop discussing foreign policies of the superpowers. The first student was surprised and chagrined. She had paid little attention to the athlete and consequently to what he said since she had already stereotyped him.

An unprejudiced mind is probably the rarest thing in the world; to nonprejudice I attach the greatest value.

André Gide

Another student living in New England, who considered herself a liberal, had a roommate from Iowa. At first, the New Englander listened only halfheartedly to her roommate's discussions of politics, because she equated being from Iowa with being ultraconservative. One day, the New Englander discovered the Iowan had been elected president of a campus organization supporting a very liberal candidate for the U.S. Senate. This changed her perceptions of her roommate and, for that matter, her stereotypes about people from Iowa. The two found that they enjoyed much in common, and the New Englander spent much more time actually "listening" to her roommate.

One of the most interesting stereotypes I uncovered was that of a student who had stereotyped a friend with a high S.A.T. (Scholastic Aptitude Test) score. Such tests are required for admission to American colleges, and it is not uncommon for people to divulge their scores to other students, especially when the scores are high. One student became friendly with another whose S.A.T. scores were almost 300 points higher than his. When he discovered his friend's high scores, he started to withdraw from the relationship. He found himself "tuning out" of conversations because he felt he couldn't contribute anything worthwhile to someone with such high S.A.T. scores. This stereotyping was also lowering his self-concept. One semester later, when both students ended up with about equal grade points, the student with the low scores began to rekindle the friendship.

From I.Q. tests to S.A.T. scores to Graduate Record Examinations, schools are breeding grounds for stereotypes on intelligence. And although a great deal of emphasis is placed on such scores, they do not necessarily measure our abilty to communicate with each other or, for that matter, to succeed in life. We are reminded of the saying heard around law schools: The A students become law professors, the B students become judges, and the C students become millionaires. Grade-point averages, prep schools, and a host of other academic "regalia" can create barriers to good communication. Use your listening skills to overlook these barriers and improve, not hinder, the communication process. Look for things you have in common, such as places you have visited, restaurants you have enjoyed, people you know. You may find your perceptions about intelligence changing as you develop the ability to interact with anyone, regardless of how intelligent you perceive the person to be. Finally, stop and ask what intelligence is, anyway. Is it a good G.P.A? Is it a high S.A.T. score? Is it exemplified by a lawyer? Is it exemplified by a writer? Is it exemplified by a millionaire? We might discover that what we perceive as intelligence is really a form of stereotype we place on people, and it therefore hinders our ability to communicate. Only with an open mind can we effectively communicate with and especially listen to all people.

How many times have we heard about stereotyping of the handicapped? Perhaps this unjust and "unskilled" approach to listening is felt deepest when a handicapped person applies for a job. The interviewer, seeing or hearing evidence of the handicap, often concentrates on

ANYTHING YOU CAN DO THEY CAN DO, TOO

While you flex your muscles in front of your morning mirror and congratulate yourself on your nimble brain, consider this: The light over your mirror was perfected by a deaf man. While your morning radio plays, remember the hunchback who helped invent it. If you listen to contemporary music, you may hear an artist who is blind. If you prefer classical, you may enjoy a symphony written by a composer who couldn't hear. The President who set an unbeatable American political record could hardly walk. A woman born unable to see, speak or hear stands as a great achiever in American history. The handicapped can enrich our lives. Let's enrich theirs.

(© United Technologies Corporation, 1981)

that handicap and does not listen to what the person is saying. This may result in the interviewer stereotyping the person as being unable to do the job before ever considering what the person has to say on his or her behalf. In essence, stereotyping the handicapped and letting that block our ability to listen clearly to what a handicapped person is saying places a handicap on ourselves.

Source Credibility

Source credibility is how much we respect, believe in, and accept the sender of communication (Figure 3–5).

How intelligent we perceive the person to be about a given subject, even how dynamic the person is, are additional dimensions to the concept. People who possess these qualities influence us and form our opinions.[4]

Source credibility becomes an obstacle to good listening when we perceive someone as having little or limited credibility and therefore put little faith in what he or she says. We may politely pay attention to something the person is saying but do not really care to understand or remember what that person says.

Source credibility varies among people and even within a single conversation. If we are at a party and engage in conversation with someone, we may discuss a range of topics over the course of an evening. Suppose we are talking with an attorney. If the discussion deals with a point of law, we would probably perceive the attorney as being a credible source on that subject. On the other hand, if we learn the attorney had never attended an opera, we might place much less credibility on his or her opinions about opera.

FIGURE 3–5
Source credibility is the amount of believability, trust, and other qualities we place in a sender of communication. If we perceive someone as having little credibility, we may pay little attention to what he or she has to say. In others, we may place a great deal of attention, listen carefully, and understand and remember what they say. *(Mr. Rogers of the television program, "Mr. Rogers' Neighborhood." Copyright © Family Communications, Inc.)*

As with stereotypes and selective perception, we need to keep open minds and not prejudge individuals by giving them more or less credibility than they deserve. One way to overcome this obstacle to good listening is to learn more about the people with whom we interact.

Cultural Obstacles   In Chapter 2, we talked about the effect being in a foreign country could have on one's self-concept. We discussed how we try to familiarize ourselves with surroundings that are much like our own even if it means eating for a month at McDonald's. But just as our self-concepts may need readjusting, we may need readjusting to the difference in verbal and nonverbal communication cues of foreign cultures. A person from a foreign country may think of the things we consider good qualities of communication as strange. For example, some cultures do not encourage direct eye contact to the degree that other cultures do. Trying to read the nonverbal cues of another culture may result in our listening to conflicting information, misjudging behavior, or misunderstandings. When we have the opportunity to become more immersed in a culture, we can listen with a great deal more accuracy.

To better understand how cultural differences (Figure 3–6) can affect communication, consider the example of the American Indian, specifically the Navajo. A research study by George M.

FIGURE 3–6

Sometimes we feel that because a person is from another culture, he or she cannot contribute in a meaningful way to interpersonal interaction. Cultural obstacles have long been the cause of misunderstandings which have affected everything from friendships to international politics. (*A student from West Java with a puppet used in mock fights demonstrating Penchak Silat, a Javanese martial art. Courtesy, IT&T, "Big Blue Marble"*)

Guilmet, a sociologist at the University of Puget Sound in Washington, discovered that there was a considerable difference between the communication habits of Navajo Indian children and Caucasian children as perceived by their mothers. A videotape of four Navajo Indian and four Caucasian children playing in a Los Angeles day-care center was shown to Navajo and Caucasian mothers.

One child displayed by far the most intense verbal and physical activity of the eight children. The tape shows him running to the teacher and stating loudly that he wants help in using a cartridge tape device that shows cartoons. He also tells the child already using the machine: "My turn."

Eighty-five percent of the Caucasian mothers "stressed the positive . . . They described him as aggressive, excited, and interested. Only 35 percent of the Navajo mothers approved. . . . The other 65 percent thought he was mischievous. Not enough discipline."

Guilmet concludes that:

> Navajo and Caucasian mothers attribute distinctly different meanings to active speech and physical behavior. The Navajo mothers tend to perceive extremely active speech and behavior to be discourteous, restless, self-centered, and undisciplined. The Caucasian mothers tend to see the same as self-disciplined, exciting to observe, and advantageous for the child.[5]

We can see that if receiving communication from another person results in our judging the person as "discourteous, restless, self-centered, and undisciplined," then there is a good probability that the communication will fail. When communicating with someone from a different culture, take the time to learn the meaning of various verbal and nonverbal symbols which you do not understand. Instead of prematurely shutting out people, you may be able to adapt your own behavior to be more tolerant of their communicative styles.

Physical and Semantic Noise

Both physical and semantic noise can block the listening process. When we discuss the communication model in Chapter 1, we learned that noise can enter the communication process in a variety of places, all hindering the smooth flow and accurate interpretation of messages. We know, for example, that a baseball's breaking the living-room window will interrupt a conversation. We know that a stereo's blaring in the background can make it difficult to hear and thus understand what another person is saying. These are examples of physical noise.

Semantic noise can also interfere with our ability to listen. As we learned in Chapter 1, semantic noise deals with the meanings of words and phrases. Bypass words are some of the best examples of semantic noise; they make it difficult to understand the true meaning of the sender's message. With semantic noise, we must look beyond the meaning of the words. Unfortunately, we run the risk of being inaccurate in our interpreta-

COMMUNICATIONS PROBLEMS LINKED
TO 'FAULTY' INPUT

No one would argue that children who constantly cut up in school, fall behind in their work and pick fights with their classmates have a behavior problem.

But to brand them as simply anti-social or emotionally disturbed may be cruelly unfair.

In some cases, a pattern of unruly behavior and slow development may be the result of a child's frustration over feeling out of sync with the rest of the world. Faulty information processing in the brain may keep the child from seeing and hearing things the way they really are, so he has trouble relating to his environment—and the people in it—in a normal way.

Nancy Saleeby, a speech pathologist at N.C. Memorial Hospital, says a child's difficulty with speaking, writing and behavior in general—what she calls "the output of communication"—may stem from serious problems with hearing and reading—"the input of communication."

She explains that in the case of sound and language processing, for example, "the problem may have nothing to do with impaired hearing, but with what happens to the information once it gets past the ears and into the brain."

Saleeby works primarily with youngsters with serious behavior problems, many of whom are referred to NCMH for psychiatric evaluation.

"They are here because parents and people in the schools around the state have run out of ideas about what to do with them," she explains.

Working with audiologists and child psychologists, Saleeby administers an exhaustive battery of tests designed primarily to detect auditory (sound) processing disorders.

Tests are given to evaluate perceptual skills involved in speaking, reading and writing. Precise measurements are made of electrical activity along the auditory pathway in the brain to pinpoint the location of any physical breakdown that may cause incoming signals to become scrambled.

"We have found that about 80 percent of the children we see actually have an auditorily based learning disability or language disorder that contributes to their inability to communicate effectively with other people," Saleeby says.

After analyzing all the test results, Saleeby helps design behavior management programs for parents to carry out and makes recommendations to teachers and school health personnel on how to handle the child and help him fit in.

Occasionally, Saleeby says, solutions are relatively simple, especially in the case of mild perceptual difficulties.

For instance, if a child's main problem is an inability to selectively listen to different sounds, he may need only a pair of earplugs to help him tune out background noise in the classroom so he can concentrate on his work.

Therapy, such as memory training or exercises to develop association skills, can help alleviate other types of information processing disorders.

In most cases, however, therapy cannot correct a problem, only lessen its harmful effects.

"Sometimes we have to recognize that a weakness is going to be there forever," Saleeby says. "It's not going to change; the child is not going to outgrow it; and you're not going to accomplish anything by dwelling on it.

"Instead, you have to look for ways to help the child compensate for the deficit and learn to live with it."

(Courtesy, The Chapel Hill Newspaper, Chapel Hill, N.C.)

tions. But as receivers of communication, we must sometimes take on the responsibility of accurate interpretation in order to make up for what may be a shirking of responsibility on the part of the communicator to send accurate messages.

Switching Listening Styles

A train coming to a crossing at which it changes tracks must slow down to pass over the switch. If it doesn't, it risks jumping off the track and missing its destination. The same thing can happen when we listen. The message must travel between the sender and the receiver, and how we receive the message and what we do with it is much like the train's switching routes to follow different destinations. We must throw our own mental switches. Throwing those switches takes time, literally measured as a fraction of a second, and unfortunately, if the message does not slow down, it jumps the track. We either miss part of what is said or we may misunderstand what is said. These changes in the way we process messages can be called switching listening styles.

We throw four basic cognitive or mental switches to receive and process communication: (1) agree; (2) disagree; (3) think; or (4) question.[6] And any time we switch our "processing of the sender's message, we run the risk of jumping the listening track. Because we need to process information quickly, an information overload or a switching overload can cause us to miss or misjudge information we receive. For example, some kinds of information remain in our memory for a few seconds, then are lost. Moreover, some kinds of information and information processing take more "storage space" in our brain than others. To understand these concepts, try listening to the radio while you're reading a book. The task is not too difficult and is even easier if the station is broadcasting background music rather than a talk show. Now try watching television while reading a book. This becomes more difficult, and to some it's impossible. When watching television, we use more of the "storage and processing" systems in our brain than we do when listening to the radio. Consequently, we can't do as many other things or comprehend as much other information at the same time. The

Laughing Stock ————————————————— *by Charles Fincher*

same principle applies to cognitive switching. It takes more storage space to think and question than it does to agree with someone. Moreover, when the message switches from something we agree with to something we disagree with, it takes time to switch from one processing mode to another. In listening, it takes more space and more time to empathize and understand what a person is saying than to just sense and pay attention to what a person is saying.

In relation to our own listening skills, we can improve our ability to process information by first sensing and paying attention to what is being said. Then with these building blocks, we can begin to understand, empathize, and remember. When the message changes, we may need to start building these blocks all over again. Although these functions may only take a split second, the risk remains that our listening may jump the track. When it does, we may stop the person with whom we're talking and say, "Excuse me, would you repeat that?" Or if we are questioning something the sender said, we might stop and say, "Do you really feel that is the case?" By injecting these responses, we may inadvertently put the breaks on the conversation, which gives us time to "throw the switch" and begin to actively listen again.

Misreading Communicator Styles

The noted Swiss psychiatrist Carl Jung set forth the theory that humans comprise various psychological types. Guidance counselors have long used this notion in prognosis tests to try to predict our competence and happiness in future working situations. More recently, Jung's theories have been applied to human communication. Paul Mok, a consulting psychologist, uses the basic personality types to develop four predominant communicative styles:[7] (1) the *thinker*, the person who is deliberate in thought and action, is businesslike, and lives a highly structured life; (2) the *feeler*, an emotional, sensitive person who likes emotional involvement with people and may lead a more carefree life than the thinker; (3) the *intuitor*, a more imaginative individual but who can also be impatient with people who do not immediately see the value or lack of it in something or someone; and (4) the *sensor*, who likes to absorb the things around him or her using all of the senses—for example, a skier absorbing the sights, sounds, and smells of a snow-covered mountain.

What Mok and others suggest is that we can achieve much better communication by correctly reading the person with whom we are communicating (Figure 3–7). People in sales positions who must deal with many different personality types can immediately benefit from this notion. If they misread the correct communicative styles of clients, they may lose the sales. This is because if we misread the correct communicative style of an individual, we actually listen to the wrong signals. Much like utilizing the overlapping fields of experience we discussed in Chapter 1, we can adapt our listening behavior and responses in order to overlap our communicative styles with the people with whom we are talking.

It is a secret known to but few, yet of no small use in the conduct of life, that when you fall into a man's conversation, the first thing you should consider is, whether he has a greater inclination to hear you, or that you should hear him.

Steele

FIGURE 3-7

The next time you attend a gathering and interact with different people, ask yourself what listening styles are operating. Different situations can create different listening styles. Do you find listening is less attentive at social gatherings than in other settings? Should it be? *(Irene Springer)*

Left versus Right Brain Hemispheres Related to communicative style is the way people use the right and left hemispheres of their brains. Science has taught us that the left hemisphere controls our logical, structured thinking whereas the right hemisphere controls our more emotional responses. The sensor and the feeler would most likely process information primarily through the right hemisphere, whereas the thinker and the intuitor would process it through the left hemisphere. These are not hard and fast rules, however, as we indicated at the beginning of this text. People cannot be neatly fitted into inflexible categories. But it is important to realize that these hemispheres and the way we approach interpersonal communication can be related.

Sending Feedback

In Chapter 1, we learned that communication is a circular process: The sender communicates a message to a receiver, and the receiver, in turn, sends feedback to the sender. We continually alternate between being the sender and being the receiver of communication as we talk with another person. Feedback is extremely important for both roles. Through feedback, we are able to influence and even adjust the message being sent to us.[8] Without feedback, we have no way to alter the message, and the sender has no way to determine if what is meant to be communicated is being received with the desired effect. In some ways, the very discussion of feedback is a bit artificial because it tends to suggest that sending feedback from a receiver back to a sender is different from sending a message from the sender to the receiver. It isn't. Much of our discussion applies to any portion of the circular process of interpersonal communication. We separate the two processes in order to understand them better. We further divide feedback into positive and negative examples.

Positive feedback can take a number of forms. One of these is *clarification*. By asking for clarification (Figure 3–7), we are providing feedback that says, "What you are saying is important to me, and I want to be able to understand it." We can request clarification through a host of verbal and nonverbal cues. A frown accompanied by a smile may indicate we want to receive more information but of a different type than we have been receiving. We want something clarified. Or we can verbally request clarification by asking, "Would you please clarify that for me?"

Still another form of positive feedback is *evaluation*. Evaluation is feedback which is separated from the person with whom we are talking. It is normally objective and free from personal emotion or biased opinion. Evaluation is not to be confused with criticism, which in itself may be positive or negative. Suppose a wife asks her husband, "What do you think of this dress?" When her husband replies, "I like it very much," this exchange is an evaluative statement about the dress. If her husband had said, "I like it very much; you have good taste", the evaluation would have been accompanied by a compliment. But if he had said, "I can't stand it; how could you possibly see yourself in something like that?", the evaluation would have turned into negative criticism. The woman was not asking her husband to judge her ability to pick out clothes, just if he liked the dress. She wanted evaluative feedback. Considering our discussion on assertive behavior, the woman could have answered her husband's statement with, "I am interested in your opinion of the dress, not a personality assessment."

Empathy is another form of positive feedback. When we say, "I know how you feel" or "I understand what you are going through", we are empathizing with the other person. When sincerely expressed, empathy can enhance the self-concept of the sender and increase his or her desire for continued communication. In our discussion of the steps of good listening, empathizing was the last step, and in some cases the most difficult to achieve. As positive feedback, it is the kind of communication that can elicit some of the most positive responses and solidify a relationship between two people.

FIGURE 3–8

Imagine the importance of "clarification" and "evaluation" listening to an orchestra leader. Few people need keener listening skills. The most minute variation in tone must be identifiable immediately. *(Sir Georg Solti, Music Director of the Chicago Symphony Orchestra. Photograph by Robert Lightfoot III. Reprinted by permission)*

Start monitoring your own communication with other people. What types of positive feedback do you receive? How can you offer more positive feedback to others? To help your monitoring process, we now look at feedback you'll want to avoid—negative feedback.

**Providing
Negative
Feedback**

"Don't Rain on My Parade" is a song which describes that people don't appreciate negative reactions to their positive communications. The world is full of pessimists. They can ruin companies, lose friends, break up marriages, and perform a host of other ills. Do not become a person who rains on other people's parades. In the end, you'll only destroy your own parade. If a friend drops by to tell you about her new job, don't start listing all the reasons why she could get fired.

Another negative form of feedback is to respond *partially* to what people are saying. This habit can signify to the sender that you only value part of what he or she is saying. It also signals an inability to listen effectively because you have only heard part of the conversation.

Defensive communication and *denying* communication are other forms of negative feedback. Accepting criticism gracefully is an art. No one likes to be criticized, and it is only natural that we react to it with some form of internal hostility, sometimes expressed verbally. It takes a strong self-concept to accept legitimate and valid criticism. In most cases we react defensively. A teacher says, "I feel you could do better on this paper." Outside you agree. Inside you are saying, "I disagree. I know the paper is good; it is your perception of it that is wrong." Unfortunately, your disgust may manifest itself in defensive, nonverbal feedback. Noticing that you are upset, the teacher may withdraw further criticism, just when it may constructively improve your future class performance. Denying something, at least when the denial is unjustified, is much the same as defensive communication. Inside we know we are guilty, but outwardly we deny it. We may have allocated only thirty minutes a night to study our communication assignments. When a roommate suggests that we do not study long enough, we deny it, knowing inside we are wrong. Our roommate knows we are wrong, but because of our denial decides not to offer any further criticism.

Remember that listening skills are learned. We have the ability to understand and practice good listening skills, to improve our ability to react accurately to communication, and to become responsible receivers as well as senders of interpersonal communication.[9]

SUMMARY

Our success as senders of communication is directly tied to our ability to understand and practice good listening skills. Listening takes practice and an acute awareness of the many subtle forms of communication that occur in any conversation.

A number of important steps are necessary to assure good listening in any conversation. The first step is sensing—using our senses to absorb all of the different forms of communication sent to us. A second step involves paying attention to what is being said. Three additional steps are understanding, empathizing, and remembering. By employing all five steps we can improve our listening skills and avoid breakdowns in communication which result in misunderstanding and even conflict.

Equally important to understanding the steps to good listening is knowing what obstacles stand in the way of good listening. We may be guilty of selective perception, perceiving messages in ways which agree with our own predetermined attitudes. Selective exposure means we are guilty of exposing ourselves only to messages which we believe will be the same as our predetermined attitudes. Selective retention means we only remember those things which agree with our predetermined attitudes. Any one of these obstacles can hinder communication. In many of us, all three operate at the same time, resulting in what may become a total breakdown of the communication process. Other obstacles include how much we believe other people, called source credibility, and cultural obstacles explained through the example of how Indian and Caucasian mothers differed in their interpretations of children's behavior. The effects of physical and semantic noise, switching listening styles, and misreading communicator styles concluded our discussion of obstacles to good listening.

Directly associated with all of these listening styles is our ability to accurately send feedback. Sending feedback is often overlooked, especially if we fail to realize that even as receivers of communication we send messages back to the senders. Positive feedback can encourage and enhance the communication process. Negative feedback, especially when inaccurate, can severely hinder the communication process.

OPPORTUNITIES FOR FURTHER LEARNING

BANVILLE, T. G., *How to Listen—How to be Heard.* Chicago: Nelson-Hall, 1978.

BARKER, L., *Listening Behavior.* Englewood Cliffs, NJ: Prentice-Hall, 1971.

COLBURN, C. W. and S. B. WEINBERG, *An Orientation to Listening and Audience Analysis.* Chicago: Science Research Associates, 1976.

ERWAY, E. A., *Listening: A Programmed Approach.* New York: McGraw-Hill, 1969.

HAYAKAWA, S. I., *Through the Communication Barrier.* New York: Harper & Row Pub., 1979.

HIRSCH, R. O., *Listening: A Way to Process Information Aurally.* Dubuque: Corsuch Scarisbrich, 1979.

HOLTZMAN, P. D., *The Psychology of Speakers' Audiences.* Glenview, IL: Scott, Foresman, 1970.

MORAY, N., *Attention and Listening.* Baltimore: Penguin, 1969.

REIK, T., *Listening with the Third Ear.* New York: Arena Books, 1972.

RICH, A. L., *Interracial Communication.* New York: Harper & Row, Pub., 1974.

WAKEFIELD, B., *Perception and Communication.* Arlington, VA: Speech Communication Association (ERIC), 1976.

WEAVER, C. H., *Human Listening, Processes and Behavior.* Indianapolis: Bobbs-Merrill, 1972.

WOLVIN, C., *Listening.* Dubuque, IA: Wm. C. Brown Company, Publishers, 1981.

chapter four

Language and Meaning

PREVIEW *After completing this chapter, we should be able to:*

Understand the roots of language.

Explain how we acquire a language.

List the functions of language.

Discuss how we use language to communicate, to control, and to secure commitments.

Define semantics.

Describe how language symbols and referents are translated into meaning.

Discuss how grammar is the "glue" of meaning.

Distinguish between denotation and connotation.

Understand language variables.

Describe language style.

List different modes of speech.

These words uttered by the Latin poet Horace more than 2000 years ago still apply. Dictating the way we interact with each other, the rules and laws of interpersonal communication are chiseled by the hand of the sculptor who understands the use of language.[1]

Roots of Language Use

One-half century ago, the words used to revise a large dictionary came from usage shaped and molded not only by scholars but also by the local newspaper. The way in which words appeared in the press was an important consideration in determining their common usage and sentence structure. The only people writing prose to be read aloud were the playrights and the poets. Today, the "press" has a new meaning, and many journalists put pen to paper or finger to key to write the entire text of the evening news to be read aloud. With instant communication available from virtually any culture or from any region of the world, we may be finding ourselves living in a period of accelerated language change, one much more intense and compressed than in past generations—an interesting speculation to begin our discussion of language in interpersonal communication. It's also a speculation which highlights the fact that regardless of how fast "words may fade now blooming and alive," we are faced with a multitude of interpersonal encounters every day, each one demanding a different use of language. As a result, our emphasis in this chapter is not on precisely what words to use in a given situation but rather on the many facets of language and how we use and adapt these facets to fit our individual needs.

Understanding the characteristics of language and language use is important for two reasons. First, by being able to adapt our own use of language as well as understand how others use it, we can decrease the chances for noise to enter the communication process. At the same time, we increase the chances for a clear understanding of the true feelings and emotions behind the words. Second, because we first compose our thoughts in an unspoken "silent" language of *intra*personal communication, an understanding of language use will give us a larger storehouse from which to intrapersonally choose our words and sentences. Such a storehouse can add to our vocabulary the variations in meanings of a single word and the multitude of ways words can be arranged in sentences, phrases, or even primal utterances. When we're aware of the fine distinctions that are possible, we can consciously or subconsciously use them to express our thoughts. Even more important, the various *ways* these distinctions are made determine our ability to use new words with even greater clarity.

Acquiring Language

As normal children, we were about eight months old when we uttered our first words and those familiar sounds of "dada" or "mama." Later we acquired more familiar words such as "hi" or "bye-bye." But the snowballing effect of our ability to use language occurred around the age of eighteen months. At that age, we combined words, and this ability mushroomed our vocabulary.[2] Indeed, within two weeks after we first joined together words with meaning, we uttered as many as seventy different combinations. Even more astounding is that the next week, we were providing anyone who would listen with as many as 700 different word combinations. By the time we reached the age of six, we had increased our vocabulary to as many as 8000 words.

Acquiring Our First Words The road from babbling to 8000 words was not necessarily free from bumps. Along the way we encountered stern reprimands when words and actions together headed us for a hot stove or across a busy street. And when we tried to communicate with our parents in a language that they simply couldn't understand, we became frustrated. But we persevered.

And we persevered not only with our embryonic verbal language, but also through many forms of nonverbal behavior. During the time we were learning language, we were also learning to react and interact through eye contact and varying tonal qualities of our voices. Many of the games we played with adults were eye-contact games, such as peek-a-boo. Try playing peek-a-boo with a child and pay attention to how your own eyes change with expression and then to how a child's eyes change. The child is learning to react to visual as well as to audible stimuli. When you say "peek-a-boo," notice how the tone of your voice changes to meet the changes in tonal qualities of the child's voice. Psychologists have debated whether such "parent and child" language could be replaced by more "adult" talk and thus speed a child's learning of the language. More recently, however, research tends to suggest that "baby talk" is very appropriate, because the child is equipped to interact at the baby-talk level and not at the adult level.

Verbal and nonverbal cues from parents make important contributions to a child's ability to build a vocabulary and a working association with language. *(United Nations/W.A. Graham)*

The use of simple words referring to easily identifiable objects, and even substitute words and sounds such as "wa wa" for water, are normal for children because they are capable of handling the language at that level, and they can thus interact this way with others in their environment.

Building Sentences These same nonverbal cues provide additional help for the child when it comes time to develop words into more meaningful sentences. Learning sentences is partly internal and partly external for children because they learn to use certain words in ways that adults do not. As the child gradually begins to communicate with adults, he or she begins to assimilate certain rules of word arrangement, or sentences. If a mother or father looks at a child and says, "Please bring me the book," the child may go over to the other side of the room and pick up the book. With this accomplishment, the parents may feel the child completely understood their word arrangement and responded accordingly. Yet under closer observation, the child may merely have understood the word "book," could see where the book was, and watched his or her parents point to the book. It may have taken this entire combination of cues to help the child respond correctly.

As children begin to use words, regardless of what meaning they may have for them, they begin to pick up the sentence structure used by adults around them.[3] Here the use of more advanced vocabulary can help form correct and more complex sentences as the children progress from "baby talk" to "adult talk." Gradually they began to use the "rules" of grammar common to adult language and they acquire the ability to generate the responses they desire from those around them.[4]

Teaching aids, including audio-visual simulations and computer-based systems, are becoming more common in elementary school classrooms. Yet the importance of human interaction cannot be over emphasized. *(Kenneth P. Davis)*

The Importance of Interaction

Of all our experiences which helped us to develop language skills, few were more important then our interaction with adults. Sitting in front of a television set apparently does little to develop a child's ability to use language or increase vocabulary to any great degree. What does is interaction with adults who are willing to take the time to talk to a child. Talking is different from speaking or even reading to a child. Talking, both verbally and nonverbally, means interacting with children and responding to their communications. From this interaction, children can grasp the rudiments of the sender-receiver interface in human communication. A parent's hugging a child when he or she cries is a form of communication that produces appropriate feedback. Children thus learn how to develop different kinds of cries, each expressing a different emotion or need. These first human contacts are the forms of dialogue which will later result in the "coupling" necessary to learn language.

The problem with some forms of communication children receive is that no opportunity exists for feedback between them and adults. A television set used as a baby sitter is a form of limited one-way communication. A parent who simply reads a book without taking into account the way the child reacts to the book is practicing one-way, not two-way, communication. Even the ability of the child to utter one-word descriptions of feelings or things warrants feedback from an adult. Although the language may seem simple and perhaps unimportant, the child may be expressing the exact same feeling as an adult would, only using less complex language. A child's saying "toe hurt" does not mean his or her experience is any different from an adult's, even if the adult says, "This ingrown toenail is sending shooting pain up the arch of my foot."

We should remember that when we sent and received communication in acquiring language, we learned not only the ability to use words correctly but how to interact with others. We acquired certain "switching" skills which permitted us to judge when to speak and when to listen. Our own language development and even our personalities were influenced by these early interactions. As we grew older and matured, we acquired complex language "storehouses" from which we arranged words in a myriad of ways. Let's now examine some of these ways in which our language functions.

Functions of Language

Just as children use language to adapt to various environments, adults use language to encounter both themselves and others in their daily life styles.

Communicating through Intrapersonal Communication
Perhaps the most basic function of language is to communicate through intrapersonal communication. When studying interpersonal communication, we often overlook the role intrapersonal communication plays in helping us arrange our lives and even interact with each other. We know that children only use very simple words to express ideas, so we can assume that before language can be verbalized, there is no way to internally communicate with words as we know them. But as yet, we do not know exactly how we do communicate within ourselves and especially, what role language plays in that communication. To some degree, however, language does help us to organize our thoughts and actually arranges our self-concept.

To better understand both of these concepts, stop and consider the next time you interact with someone in a sensitive situation. At the very basic level, you predetermine the words you want to use by asking yourself, "What do I want to say?" Not only may you choose the exact words you want to say, but you may also weigh the amount of inflection you want to use with those words. Perhaps you are calling someone you have met just briefly to ask him or her to go to a dance and out to dinner with you. You might ponder exactly what words you are going to use before you pick up the telephone.

And what about your self-concept? Equally important to what words you choose is what your ego state is going to be after you make that telephone call. Part of the reason you are choosing your words very carefully is to help maintain your self-concept, which will either be elevated or lowered after you speak with your prospective date. If you receive an enthusiastic "yes," then your self-concept will be positive. You know this before you make the call, and thus take some care in thinking out what you are going to say. If you receive a "no" answer, then you are going

Words are the voice of the heart.

Confucius

to be slightly disappointed, at least for a few moments after the call. This is another reason to choose your words carefully. In the first instance, you would be using language "internally" to structure your sentences. In the second case, you would be using language to maintain or improve your self-concept. Each is an example of language's being used for intrapersonal communication.

Obeying Society's Rules

Once again we encounter the "rules" we first discussed when examining different approaches to interpersonal communication.[5] Society, like communication, consists of various norms to which we all try to adhere most of the time. Language is one instrument which assists us in obeying these norms. Specifically, it helps us to effectively communicate with others in a way that is acceptable and adhered to by society.

Using language to obey society's rules can best be exemplified by the various parlimentary bodies throughout the world. When world leaders meet to discuss important international issues, they carefully choose their words to convey specific meanings to a specific audience. Many such meetings have a variety of "political norms" which are inappropriate to violate. Even during heated disagreement, some bodies require certain "niceties" of its members. One leader disagreeing with another, for example, should first refer to the opponent as a "distinguished colleague."

Extremely rigid norms also exist in military organizations in which the required language for certain situations is "Yes, Sir" or "No, Sir." In some fraternal or lodge organizations, members are expected to address officers by their titles rather than by their names. Even in academic circles, formality sometimes beckons us to call a person not by his or her first name, but by the title of "professor" or "Dr." Even in a family structure, one member may refer to another using a third-person context—for example, "Your father feels you should" or "Your mother wants you to." And how many times have we been startled out of our daydreams with a stern, "Ms. Jones!" or "Mr. Smith!"?

Adapting to Situations

Directly integrated with rules or norms of behavior are situations. Different situations demand different kinds of language behavior. How you greet someone in a formal parliamentary setting differs from how you greet a cohort at a sales meeting.

For example, suppose you have a cup of coffee with a friend in a coffeehouse. Your conversation is casual, the sentences are structured in a certain way, and the words exchanged are lighthearted and straightforward. Now consider what happens when you sit as a member of a company's board of directors and address that same friend who happens to be the company's president. Your interpersonal interaction, the words that are exchanged between you, and the way you address each other and others in the room produce an entirely different language than what occurred over the cup of coffee.

The following conversations illustrate the point:

At the coffeehouse:

PRESIDENT: *What a day. The jerks in the trucking division can't get their schedules sorted out. The incompetents in shipping can't get the packaging straight. And that manager in division three! If he says one more word about his office being decorated, I'll personally strangle him.*

VICE PRESIDENT: *I know what you mean. We need to kick some people in the pants and tell them to get their acts together. I'd like to take that manager and throw him out of the building.*

In the boardroom:

PRESIDENT: *Bob, you're working in the trucking division. Is there any way I can help with the schedules? I very much want to assist you in any way I can.*

BOB: *Not really, I think everything is going fine.*

PRESIDENT: *Well, keep me posted. I'll be checking back with you. Sally, you have some fine people in shipping, but I noticed we are getting a bit behind. I've asked Mary to stop by and help.*

SALLY: *We appreciate her help. We're swamped with work.*

PRESIDENT: *Harry, I know you want the office redecorated, and I've asked the carpentry crew and the supervisor to check with you.*

Clearly, the situation in the boardroom with the managers necessitated a different kind of language than in the coffeehouse. The situations were entirely different. If the president of the company had opened up the meeting by addressing Bob with, "You jerk, why can't you get your schedules sorted out?" the atmosphere of the meeting and Bob's willingness to respond may have been entirely different. Similarly, if the president had looked at Sally and said, "You incompetent, why can't you get packaging straight?" Sally might have said some choice words of her own.

Although we might not think too highly of the president who talked one way to the employees' faces and another way behind their backs, such a dichotomy does serve to illustrate how people adapt language to fit different situations. Moreover, if the trucking division does not sort out its schedules, if the shipping department doesn't get its packaging straightened out, and if Harry complains one more time about his office, the company president may use even different language.

Control   In our discussion of interpersonal needs, we learned that one of our primary needs is that of control. In some cases we like to be controlled; in others, our needs center on our ability to control. A major source of that control is language.[6] Few methods short of physical contact offer such important contributions to fulfilling this

An example of using language to control others is found in the work of the auctioneer. The skillful use of words, sometimes at a pace almost too fast to comprehend, entices, cajoles, and can even embarrass a person to bid. *(Jim Kallett/Photo Researchers)*

interpersonal need as language. Yet control does not necessarily mean total dominance. Cashing a check, buying food at the grocery store, and having our cars repaired all necessitate some form of control over the people with whom we deal.

Frustration develops in any of us when we lack the control necessary to function successfully in society. This does not mean that we need to become domineering or abrasive. It does mean that we need to acquire the skills necessary to control when we want or need to be controlling.

Some of the most elementary uses of controlling language occur in everyday interaction with other people. "Please pass the milk," "Fill it up," and "I need it by Friday" are simple statements of control. We think little of being direct and stating precisely what we want when we interact with people who provide us services, especially services for which we pay.

On the other hand, we tend to alter our controlling language in certain situations. In some cases this altering is acceptable and perfectly understandable. If we are stopped for speeding, we would probably not go up to the police officer and say, "I'm in a hurry, and I want this ticket made out and you back in your car in exactly five minutes." Instead, we alter our controlling language. We might agree with the officer that we were speeding. On the other hand, we might suggest that the traffic flow caused our speeding, if in fact it did. By doing this, we would be injecting some form of controlling language, yet realizing that the situation did not lend itself to the amount of control we might be able to offer in another situation.

Consider your participation in a group discussion. You are a new employee with a large manufacturing firm. During your second month on the job, you are called to an important meeting with the division managers. Although you are new, you oversee one of the key manufacturing steps which will be critical in manufacturing parts for a new product line.

The day of the meeting arrives, and you have diligently studied every facet of the manufacturing process. You are prepared for the meeting and for every question that might develop. Midway through the meeting, you realize that the plans for the new product's development do not give your area of the plant sufficient time to produce parts on schedule. You sense that if you don't tell the division managers about this situation, your inability to provide parts on time may be blamed for a serious backlog of orders.

You realize that you are new with the company, and you don't want to sound out of place. But you also realize that if you don't assert yourself, more problems will exist later. You must gain control of the meeting and make the division managers listen to you. Yet you know you cannot alienate them because you're going to need to work with them in the future. Finally, you have the opportunity to speak:

> *"This new product seems exciting, but it will fail miserably and seriously damage our reputation with our existing customers."*

The room is hushed. You have captured control of the meeting. The division managers sit puzzled. You continue:

> *"I do not want to sound pessimistic, but by next March when parts from our area are not available, production will stop and orders will not be filled. As a result, bad customer relations will develop which could threaten business for our other products."*

One of the division managers speaks up, saying:

> *"But why won't there be parts?"*

To which you reply:

> *"Because we only have three machines, and even if they operate twenty-four hours a day, their capacity will still be below your demands for parts for the new product."*

The president of the company then asks you how many machines will be necessary to meet the new product's demands. Your research lets you supply the answer.

This example shows how language permitted you to gain control of the meeting and, in effect, the behavior of the division managers. But what would have happened if you had *not* been able to use language effectively? What would have happened if you had not clearly explained the consequences of the lack of parts and succinctly stated that the product would "fail miserably"? Less direct language might have also "failed miserably" for you, denying you the chance to clearly communicate your concern. At the same time, had you voiced your concern with "You jerks are going to make a real mess out of this." You might either have lowered your credibility to the point that it made you ineffective with the group, or you might be looking for another job.

Many times, more assertive language can help us add control to a situation. Stop and consider all of the different frustrating experiences which result from our lack of control. Then consider how language could prevent us from being controlled when we actually want to be in control. Perhaps a particular person continually insults us, not directly but rather through innuendo. Whenever we are in a group discussion, that person responds to our comments by saying, "That's not a very good idea." The person then proceeds to offer another opinion. The next time it happens, we might reply more assertively with, "Excuse me, but my ideas may have just as much validity as yours. I'm interested in hearing your ideas, but I do not appreciate your need to judge mine before we hear yours."

Securing a Commitment

The author knows a jeweler who has a reputation for never finishing his work on time. Although I appreciate his skill, depending on his completion schedule is impossible. I finally solved the problem by trying a different method: Whenever I took something to his shop for repair, I asked him specifically how long he felt it would take. After his answer, which was usually in the neighborhood of a "few weeks," I would state a specific date I wanted to return for the merchandise. I then made sure he gave me a commitment that the merchandise would be available on that date. By simply saying, "Great. You're saying I can pick up the watch on . . . ," I achieved a personal commitment from him, and the watch was usually ready. In those instances when it was not ready, I normally only had to wait an extra day or two, and then it was easy to recognize that the jeweler was embarrassed that he could not live up to his promise. In this case, language was employed to gain a commitment that put a person's reputation on the line. Such phrases as "Will you do it for me?" and "On what day can I expect it finished?" require a personal commitment from the person with whom we are dealing and lessen our frustrations caused by unmet expectations.

Perhaps no person is more skilled at using language to gain a commitment than someone working in sales, especially direct-contact sales. These people know how to use language to elicit a commitment to buy their company's product. Because of this ability, they're some of the highest paid people in business and industry. To watch a talented salesperson work with language is to watch someone use language as a tool, just as a carpenter uses a saw and hammer or a sculptor uses a chisel. At the heart of the sales presentation is what is called the "commitment," or what some salespersons call "asking for the order." Asking for the order takes on many different forms. Sometimes it's direct, such as "Can I sell you some today?" Although widely used, this request for commitment is risky, because it can generate the dreaded one-word reply of "No." Often, the request for commitment involves a more subtle use of the language. Consider the person selling a car. Many a customer leaves the showroom with a new car without ever having uttered the words, "I'll buy it" or "I'll take it." Instead the salesperson has sold the car by effectively using language to ask a series of

Salesmanship consists of transfering a conviction by a seller to a buyer.

Paul G. Hoffman

questions. Let's examine the following commitment-gaining language, which might take hours, days, or even weeks to fully develop:

"Do you like this year's new models?"
"Do you enjoy driving?"
"What kind of a car do you drive?"
"Have you seen some of this year's new features (explains them)."
"Please sit inside (the customer does)."

At this point, the salesperson has engaged the potential customer in conversation, and the customer has made a partial commitment to the car just by sitting in it. The customer may not buy the car, but the commitment of interest is much greater than when he or she first walked into the showroom. Moreover, the salesperson and the potential customer can now talk about something they have in common (the car and its features). The fields of experience between the two now overlap. Homophily, that important part of communication we talked about earlier in the book, exists.

"Here are the keys. Enjoy it for a few hours."

After the customer returns from driving the car, the salesperson again engages him or her in conversation. Most importantly, the salesperson determines what the customer's likes and dislikes about the car are and can then seek out and handle any previously unstated or hidden objections.

Sales Clerk: "May I help you?"

Me: "Yes, I'd like some picture hooks."

Sales Clerk: "What kind of picture hooks?"

Me: "Just picture hooks. I want to hang some pictures in my office."

Sales Clerk: "We have more than a dozen different kinds of things to hang pictures. They're all over there on that rack."

Me: "I want the best one."

Sales Clerk: "Which is best depends on a lot of things, sir."

Me: "Like *what* things?"

Sales Clerk: "Like what kind of walls you have—wood, plaster, marble, wallboard, cement, brick and . . . ."

Me: "And, what?"

Sales Clerk: "And what kind of pictures you want to hang—little, big, framed, unframed—plus . . . ."

Me: "Plus?"

Sales Clerk: "Plus, whether you'd like glue hangers, double-faced tape hangers, nail hangers, magnetic hangers . . . ."

Me: "I simply planned to buy some ordinary hooks—the kind that the little nail goes through that bent piece of metal that serves as a hook and holds that hook flat against the wall. Won't *that* do my job?"

Sales Clerk: "I really don't know, sir. If I don't completely understand your *problem*, it would be foolish for me to recommend a solution. And even *more* foolish for *you*, under the circumstances, to accept *my* solution."

(D.J. Maloney, "What's Your Problem?" Harris Profitable Finishing Innovations, 3 *Spring*, 1979)

Language and Meaning

Finally, the salesperson begins to ask for the order:

"You would probably want a radio and automatic transmission, wouldn't you?" (The question is almost always safe, especially on medium-sized cars in which a manual transmission is commonplace. The purpose of the question is to get an affirmative answer. Additional questions eliciting affirmative answers might follow.)

"Does your current car have air conditioning?" (Depending on the answer, the salesperson either affirms that air conditioning can be included with the new car or simply avoids the issue.)

"Would you like a bright or softer color?"

"When would you like delivery?"

By now, the car has been "psychologically" purchased, and all that remains is completing the paperwork. Notice that at no time did the salesperson ask "Can I sell you one?" Similarly, at no time did the customer say, "I'll buy it." The salesperson's skillful use of the language helped to produce the sale. The final question "When would you like delivery?" took the place of "Will you buy the car?" If the customer tells the salesperson a delivery date, it is the same as saying "I'll buy it." Skillful timing is necessary along with the right words. But without the words, without the use of language, the car would have never changed hands.

Interaction among Individuals

The correct use of language is necessary in order for people to successfully interact with each other. It's a basic fact of life.

First, we use language to draw together our fields of experience. We noted an example of this when the salesperson and the customer could talk about specific features they had discussed together. By using language familiar to each of them, their interaction could improve and continue. Language became the thread which stitched together their conversation. As more and more threads were added to their conversation, the fields of experience of the two individuals overlapped and created homophily.

Second, language becomes an exploratory device that enables us to look more deeply into each other's field of experience. The deeper we explore the other person's field of experience, the more opportunities we have to communicate with that person. In essence, the more we have in common, the more things we can discuss. We can explore someone else's field of experience in many different ways. Asking questions is one of those. "Where were you born?" "Where did you go to school?" and "What brought you to this area?" are good exploratory questions. "When did the two of you meet each other?" is a favorite question when engaging another couple in conversation, because a story lies behind every meeting, and the subject is one which is highly personal and about which both can talk. The answer to such a question can also offer hints about interests the couple enjoys. You might discover that they met at a tennis tournament. With that in-

HOT TUB CULTURE SPAWNS A DIALECT

SAN FRANCISCO (UPI) — North of the Golden Gate, the trendy residents of marvellous Marin are getting "upfront" about their curious speech.

They are willing to "interface" with us about "where they're coming from" and the "space" they're "into."

The "bag" into which they are is a new dialect called "psychobabble," or "Marin English," or the "language of the hot tub."

Robin Lakoff, a linguistics professor at the University of California, said in an interview that the new way of talking by some Californians, especially the upper middle class in Marin County, is a valid dialect and is not going to disappear.

Unlike a New York accent or Black English, which are marked by special inflections and grammatical constructions, Marin English is characterized by the way it pours new psychological meanings into ordinary words.

The words are usually simple ones that have concrete, physical meanings, often dealing with place, such as "center" and "behind." The verbs describe movement—"getting my head together." Prepositions are popular in the dialect—"into," "at" and "around."

Never before have such small words wrought such large meaning.

Thus, the "space" someone is in is not a space at all but the mental outlook he or she has.

"You appear to be open and direct. But you deflect any real communication. The closeness is only apparent. The other person feels he is the victim of a hoax that he can only vaguely penetrate. He doesn't know how to behave. He doesn't know what the rules are."

She said the use of concrete words for abstract ideas creates a kind of paradox. "It seems like direct and confronting language. But from another point of view it is very elusive. It slips from your fingers. It's hard to tell exactly what the meaning is."

This kind of vagueness often drives speakers of ordinary English up the wall.

Some people who consider themselves the guardians of pure English are determined to stamp out the language of the hot tub, said Lakoff. "But you can never stamp out linguistic change. It arises because people need it."

A MARIN–ENGLISH GLOSSARY

SAN FRANCISCO (UPI) — A brief glossary of some Marin English words and phrases:

"Into"—Interested in, absorbed by ("into meditation," "into ceramics").
"I know where you're coming from"—I understand what you mean.
"Where I'm at"—A position that has been reached in a process of change.
"Trip"—Experience.
"High energy trip"—Intense experience.
"Heavy"—Serious. Grave. Important. Powerful.
"Upfront"—Honest.
"Space"—Where a person's at.
"Off the wall"—Spontaneous.
"Blow Away"—Astonish. Dumbfound. ("The picture blew me away").
"Lay"—Inflict. ("Don't lay that trip on me").
"Come down"—Happen.

formation, you can begin to ask questions about their enjoyment of tennis, sports in general, TV coverage of sports, and so on.

Two key factors enhance our ability to explore another person's field of experience: (1) vocabulary and (2) the willingness of each person to participate in self-disclosure. The more extensive our vocabulary is, the more exact and refined our questions and disclosures can be. When we learn the fine distinctions between different words and can use those words with precision, we have truly expanded our vocabulary. At the same time, learning new words and the distinctions between them enables us to communicate with greater clarity. Although we do not want to sound like intellectual elitists in conversation, neither do we want to sound ignorant.

Without the willingness of both people to enter into a limited degree of self-disclosure, conversation will have a difficult time developing. Again, the key is using language effectively. Perhaps prefacing a question with a compliment will make the person feel more at ease. Or perhaps first disclosing something about ourselves will help. But to be effective, our self-disclosures need to conform to society's norms and rules of behavior. We would not think of going up to someone at a party and saying, "I like tennis, swimming, football, hiking, cycling, baseball, chess, and camping. Please tell me which of those sports you like so we can begin conversing." Rather, we gradually enter into a conversation and slowly pick up cues, moving the interaction to more common ground. "Wasn't it a beautiful day? We went cycling, then did some hiking in the woods behind town." This statement allows the other person to volunteer information about his or her own experiences, ask a question, or even let us know that he or she does not share our enthusiasm for cycling or hiking. If that person does answer in one of these ways, we can offer another comment or ask about the sports he or she does enjoy.

Vocabulary and self-disclosure accompanied by the skillful use of language makes human interaction not only possible, but rewarding and meaningful.

Interaction among Groups

Closely related to interaction among individuals is language's ability to provide interaction among groups who use language in a different way. Canada and Mexico, each with its own culture and languages, are immediate examples. If Canadians and Mexicans expect to communicate with each other, they need to learn each other's language.

Yet variations occur even within a given language. In some cases, these variations are in the words themselves. For example, we find various Latin terms immersed in the language of our judicial system. In other cases, the way in which words are used signifies their special place among groups. While in the hallways, two members of a state legislature might refer to each other by their first names. But when they're within the legislative chamber, references to "my distinguished colleague" would be more appropriate.

Certain subcultures possess their own language variations which contribute to their identity. Try walking into a game room or pool hall in the inner city and start to talk the same way you would if you were attending a high-fashion ball. To say you would stand out from the crowd would be an understatement. Similarly, try using the language of the inner-city pool hall while attending a high-fashion ball. The butler may usher you to the nearest door. Each social group has its own language which is determined by the various situations it encounters. We recognize that even different regions of a country have different dialects (Figures 4–1, 4–2, 4–3). The normal vocabulary, grammar, and pronunciation of one region may be completely foreign to another region, even though both regions are in the same country and use the same language. Understanding and accepting

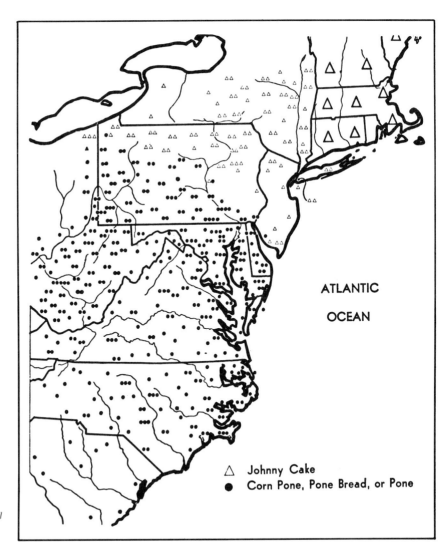

ATLANTIC

OCEAN

△ Johnny Cake
● Corn Pone, Pone Bread, or Pone

FIGURE 4–1
A form of corn bread commonly made without milk or eggs is pronounced differently in different regions of the eastern United States. *(R.W. Shuy, Discovering American Dialects. Champaign, IL: National Council of Teachers of English, 1967, p. 43)*

Language and Meaning

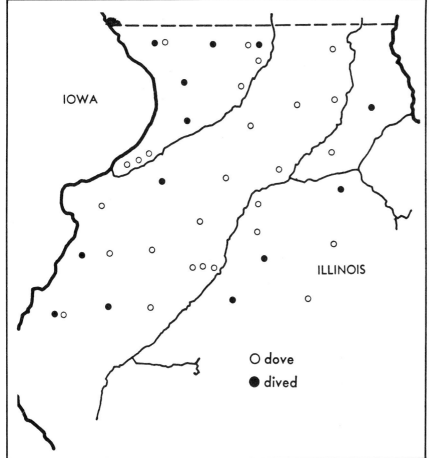

FIGURE 4-2
The different pronunciation of the word "dived," such as having dived into a pool, is found in different regions of Iowa and Illinois. (R.W. Shuy, Discovering American Dialects. Champaign, IL: National Council of Teachers of English, 1967, p. 44)

these dialects can be the first step in encouraging interaction among people of the various regions. Along that same line, the ability to adapt our language to the group we're with is often necessary in order for us to gain credibility with the group. Without this credibility, without feeling we "belong," we deprive ourselves of one of the important interpersonal needs we discussed earlier—inclusion. We don't need to cast aside our cultural identities, but being flexible in our use of language can help us communicate with certain groups. After all, learning the different meanings of words in different cultural settings enhances our vocabulary, and enables us to communicate with greater precision and understanding.

Keep in mind that we encounter many different groups in any single day and, whether we realize it or not, we alter our language to interact with these groups. People from different socio-economic backgrounds, different cultures, different countries, even in such different situations as the locker room or the board room require different language structures for successful interaction. What are the different

FIGURE 4-3

Changes in dialects occur through the movement of different populations. For example, the arrows show changes in residency shifts in the Detroit, Michigan area for people of Jewish (J), German (G), Italian (I), and Hungarian (H) descent. *(R.W. Shuy,* Discovering American Dialects. *Champaign, IL: National Council of Teachers of English, 1967, p. 40)*

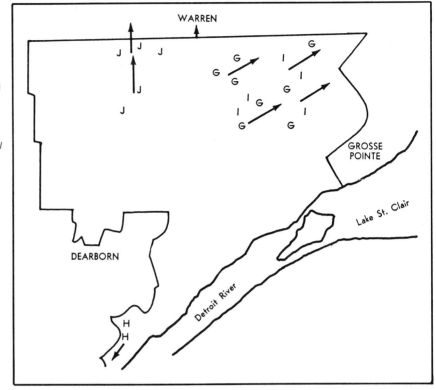

groups you encounter in any given day? How do you change the structure of your language to communicate with those different groups? Answering these questions is the first step in developing the language skills necessary to effectively communicate with greater understanding.

Understanding Meaning

An example of a personal encounter with misunderstanding the meaning of language involves the phrase "come apart at the seams." In the western part of the United States, some people use the phrase to mean to totally relax. In the eastern part of the United States, some people use the phrase to mean to be mentally unstable or become uncontrollable. For two people who have different meanings for the phrase, it's easy to see how misjudgments about the other's personality could develop if one says to the other, "Let's go home, I've had a rough day and really want to come apart at the seams."

Differences in meaning, both of words and sentences, alter the way we use language and the way other people interpret what we say. This, again, is why having an adequate vocabulary is necessary to assure better understanding. At the same time, as in the preceding example, it remains important to understand *where* differences in meaning can occur. Being alert to the "stress points" of language where "breaks" in the communication process can happen is an important step towards improving the way we use language in interpersonal communication.

Semantics: The Science of Meaning The study of meaning, or more appropriately the science of meanings, is called *semantics*. Originating from the Greek words for *significant* and *sign*, semantics has evolved into a broad-based area of scholarly inquiry. The results of research in the field are providing valuable insights into the way we use language and apply meaning to language's various signs and symbols.

(Cartoon by Sidney Harris, reprinted with permission)

Symbol versus Referent Written language, as we learned earlier in this text, evolved from simple drawings or pictographs on the inside of caves to more complex symbols, such as words. Yet words are actually nothing more than modern-day pictographs (Figure 4–4). In comparison, the pictographs were more complex than words, at least small numbers of words, because they meant a great many detailed things to the people who read them. A stick figure of an Indian standing with a shield, for example, was symbolic of all the ramifications of war.

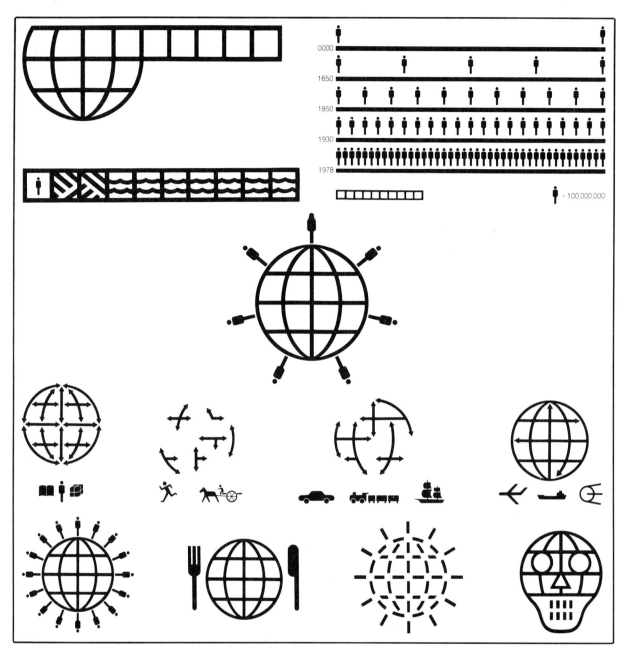

FIGURE 4-4

Examples of symbols designed to cut across language barriers are seen in these drawings designed to explain world population problems. The East-West Center in Hawaii invited visual communicators from the United States, Japan, India, and Iran to visually explore the question: "Is there a better way to convey essential information to people worldwide?" Reading across each row of symbols, the text reads: "As we unfold the earth—we find that it has limited usable land and resources, that populated areas comprise only one-tenth of the globe's surface—The world's population has doubled four times in the past 2000 years. Each time, the doubling has occurred at an ever-increasing rate. The earth, a home for more than four billion people, is a place of greatly increasing diversity and complexity—Ideas, people, and goods are moving faster and faster and intermingling. There are rising challenges in the changing world, caused by global situations of population, food, energy, and environmental pollution. (© East-West Center)

ali'i nui	Chief, chiefess, king, queen, noble, royal; big chief.
calabash	Bowl or circular vessel usually made of wood or gourd. In Hawaiian, 'umeke.
hao	Iron.
kākou	We, ourselves.
kama'āina	Native-born; literally, land child. Has come to mean a person who has lived in Hawaii a long time and is accustomed to Island ways.
kanaka	Human being, man, mankind, person.
kāne	Male, husband, masculine.
kano	Large hard stem, as on a banana bunch, sweet potato, or pandanas fruit; tool handle; hard; stiff.
kapa	Tapa, as made from wauke or mamahi bark; formerly, clothes of any kind.

Hawaiian was originally an oral language. It was translated by missionaries who arrived in Hawaii in the 1820s and felt the Hawaiians needed a printed Bible in their own language. Vowels in Hawaiian have the same sound as Classical Latin.
(Courtesy: Aloha: The Magazine of Hawaii, 3 *July/August 1980, p. 69)*

Today, we use words as the symbols which guide our thoughts and call forth images and meanings we have learned since birth. But keep in mind that words are symbols composed of symbols. Consider the word *flower.* If we went out and wrote these six letters, or symbols, on the side of a cave, the result would be similar to the pictograph of our early ancestors.

Now let's examine the different images that the word (symbol) flower creates in our minds. Somewhere in our experiences, flowers have played a part. Perhaps our vivid recollections date back to the time we suddenly came upon rows and rows of yellow tulips. Or perhaps we remember the delicate African violets our families raised. Perhaps we remember particularly beautiful roses growing by our homes or a dozen red roses someone gave us or we presented to someone else. All of these images of flowers are *referents* to the symbol *flower.* And while we were thinking of the different flowers we may have seen, others reading this passage had different thoughts of flowers they have seen.

Our discussion of the difference between the symbol flower and the referent for the symbol leads us into examining how misunderstandings can develop when different people place different referents on the same symbol. Assume, for example, that you and your friend decide to send a gift to a third friend.

> *"Let's send flowers."*
> *"Great idea," your friend replies.*
> *"I'll order them today. Will a $20.00 bouquet be OK?"*
> *"Bouquet? I thought live flowers, perhaps a mum plant, would be better."*
> *"Live flowers? Live flowers aren't romantic enough. I think cut flowers in a nice bouquet are more appropriate."*
> *"OK, cut flowers in a bouquet. But they're going to wilt."*
> *"They won't wilt that fast. Daisies last a long time."*
> *"Daisies?! Who said anything about daisies? We should send orchids."*

寿
福
禧
財
禄

Chinese symbols express the five happinesses: (top to bottom) long life, good fortune, happiness, wealth, and prosperity. The symbols represent an art form and a reflection of Chinese philosophy. Traditionally, they are hung vertically on the walls of Chinese homes. *(Courtesy: Supervisory Management, March, 1980, p. 37)*

The alphabet of the Cherokee Indians. Notice how much more complex it is compared to the twenty-six letters of the standard English alphabet. *(Courtesy, William M. Hardy and "Unto These Hills")*

Cherokee Alphabet.

D $_a$	R $_e$	T $_i$	δ_o	O $_u$	i $_v$
S $_{ga}$ O $_{ka}$	F $_{ge}$	Y $_{gi}$	A $_{go}$	J $_{gu}$	E $_{gv}$
$_{ha}$	P $_{he}$	$_{hi}$	F $_{ho}$	Γ_{hu}	$_{hv}$
W $_{la}$	$_{le}$	P $_{li}$	G $_{lo}$	M $_{lu}$	$_{lv}$
$_{ma}$	O $_{me}$	H $_{mi}$	$_{mo}$	Y $_{mu}$	
Θ_{na} $_{hna}$ G $_{nah}$	Λ_{ne}	h $_{ni}$	Z $_{no}$	$_{nu}$	C $_{nv}$
T $_{qua}$	$_{que}$	P $_{qui}$	V $_{quo}$	$_{quu}$	E $_{quv}$
U $_{sa}$ $_{s}$	4 $_{se}$	b $_{si}$	$_{so}$	$_{su}$	R $_{sv}$
L $_{da}$ W $_{ta}$	S $_{de}$ T $_{te}$	J $_{di}$ J $_{ti}$	Λ_{do}	S $_{du}$	$_{dv}$
$_{dla}$ L $_{tla}$	L $_{tle}$	C $_{tli}$	$_{tlo}$	$_{tlu}$	P $_{tlv}$
G $_{tsa}$	V $_{tse}$	h $_{tsi}$	K $_{tso}$	J $_{tsu}$	C $_{tsv}$
G $_{wa}$	$_{we}$	O $_{wi}$	$_{wo}$	$_{wu}$	6 $_{wv}$
$_{ya}$	B $_{ye}$	$_{yi}$	$_{yo}$	G $_{yu}$	B $_{yv}$

> "OK, orchids. But white flowers remind me of artificial snow."
> "White flowers?! I meant purple orchids. Those are the best to send."
> "Hold it right there. I suggest we send flowers; you agree. I imagine us sending a bouquet of cut daisies and you're talking about live purple orchids. Let's solve the dilemma and send candy."
> "Great idea! With or without nuts?"

Little needs to be said about the different referents these two people who encountered the word flower managed to picture in their own minds.

Symbols into Sentences

If a single word can create all the different imaginable conflicts in meaning we just discussed, imagine the misunderstandings which can occur when different words are combined into sentences. The potential variations of word arrangement in any language are enormous. Twenty-five words alone can provide the basis for millions, even billions, of possible sentences.

When my family was recently planning to visit relatives over a holiday, our original intention was to drive to our relatives' home. As a gift, we also decided to buy and give our relatives a frozen turkey to help supply part of the food for the holiday dinner. Because of a change in plans, only one member of the family could go, and instead of driving, he had to ride the bus. In a telephone conversation explaining the change in plans, the statement was made, "Since the turkey would melt with John on the bus, we'll send a smoked ham." Not until after the words were out did we realize all of the possible mental images that statement could create. What we wanted to explain was that since the bus ride would take over six hours, a frozen turkey might melt and spoil during that time. Instead, the statement, "Since the turkey would melt with John on the bus, we'll send a smoked ham," could have been interpreted to mean:

> Both John and the turkey will melt before the bus arrives.
>
> The turkey would melt before the bus arrives.
>
> The turkey will be on the seat with John.
>
> The turkey will be in the luggage bin.
>
> Regardless of where the turkey is, both the turkey and John are going to melt.
>
> John will be perched on top of the bus; therefore the turkey will melt.
>
> Neither John nor the turkey will make the trip; a smoked ham will go instead.
>
> The smoked ham will arrive by mail, not by bus.
>
> The turkey will remain behind and melt because John took the bus.

Thousands of other combinations of meaning could exist beyond those mentioned. Our language is enormously complex and contains many stress points, which can cause breakdowns in interpersonal communication. If we add such variables as facial expressions, tone of voice, and a host of other "cues," we can even increase the chances for these breakdowns.

Grammar: The "Glue" of Meanings

Before you throw up your hands in frustration and say that it is easier to go through life not talking, remember that the purpose of language is to enable us to communicate and to prevent communication breakdowns. Language strives for this with its *rules of grammar*, which encourage certain arrangements of words in order to achieve a universal understanding. When the arrangement of words adheres to these accepted rules, we refer to the arrangement as good grammar. Yet even though the rules of grammar may be standardized and somewhat inflexible, many different words and organizations of words can be used to obey such rules. Thus, we might say that the statements "Please go to the barn and bring back some milk" and "Please bring back some milk from the barn" are both grammatically correct, and either arrangement of words will produce the same results.

Denotation and Connotation

Another stress point in language occurs when we misunderstand the difference between *denotation* and *connotation*. From elementary school on, we have heard that the denotative meaning of a word refers to its dictionary meaning. Although truth exists in that statement, taking it literally has caused more than one communication breakdown. Dictionaries tend to look at multiple meanings of words. By using other words to form those meanings, they immediately risk creating the same misunderstanding that happened in the example of the two friends' ordering flowers. Perhaps a dictionary filled with nothing but pictures would solve the problem, but providing a picture of "insurance" or "love," for example, might be a bit impossible. The point is that a much better way to refer to *denotation* is to say it is a *precise or explicit meaning of a word*. Whether or not that word appears in a dictionary is not of consequence.

Connotation, on the other hand, refers to *something less precise and explicit* than denotation. Connotation derives from the word *connote*, which means to *suggest* or *imply*. With connotation, we lack the accuracy we have with denotation. And when we use words to communicate with each other, we often forget that although a denotative meaning may exist, the speaker in interpersonal communication may be using either his or her own denotative *or* connotative meaning of a particular word. Similarly, because of his or her own interpretation, the listener may receive a completely different meaning from what the speaker intended.

In using language for effective communication, we must keep in mind that different people, because of their backgrounds and life experiences, place different meanings on different words. In casual, everyday conversation between friends, we may take the meanings of words for granted, knowing no serious consequences will occur if we make mistakes. But this attitude can cause us trouble when we engage in more important conversations or are in situations where the emotional content of our messages becomes more intense.

To better understand how breakdowns in communication can occur between the denotative and connotative meanings of words, imagine that you are working for a company that produces spare parts for airplanes. You have been hired to write a manual which tells mechanics how to install certain parts. You work long hours on the project and finally present the manual to your boss. Two days later, your boss sees you in the hallway and says, "The manual looks good." You stop and say to yourself, "The manual looks *good?* He must think it's only mediocre. Why, I thought it was excellent, superb, even a fantastic job! All I get is the comment that the manual looks good?"

To you, the word "good" is the same as average, so-so, even failure. You remember in school that the teacher referred to your papers as excellent, creative, superb. You remember that a "good" paper meant a C grade in school because it was average and was what was expected. But to you, that manual is not average. What you fail to realize is that to your boss, there are only two kinds of reports—bad reports and good reports. The word "good" is explicit and precise to your boss, the exact opposite of bad, no more, no less. The connotation of the word "good" is thus causing an interpersonal communication breakdown.

When taking part in interpersonal communication, think about both the explicit meanings of words as well as how those words may fit into the other person's field of experience, and affect his or her interpretation of the words you use. You may find yourself appraising someone's performance on anything from his or her gourmet cooking skills to his or her on-the-job accomplishments. But each interpersonal encounter is different. Discussing a trip to the student store to buy textbooks is a much simpler process than explaining why you have fallen in love.

Language Variables

In a sense, we have already been talking about different variables in our use of language. Some consider meaning itself a language variable.

Our language does contain other variables, though, and we should be aware of them so that we may have as many "tools" as possible to build good skills of interpersonal communication.[7] Let's now examine such language variables as structure, concrete versus abstract language, language intensity, verbal immediacy, and vocabulary.

Words Joined Together: Structure

If we could go through life uttering one-word expressions and if everyone had the identical meaning for those expressions, interpersonal communication would be a simple process. Too simple. We would not have the ability to even begin to explain complex concepts, such as love and brotherhood. But with the added complexity of language comes new potential for misunderstandings. Not only are words themselves important and full of different meanings, but the way we join words together varies their meanings. The more complex a concept, the more words are necessary to explain it. And while we're concentrating on what words to use, we're also concentrating on how we arrange those words. Also, it stands to reason that the more complex our conversation is with someone, the more complex our words and the arrangement of those words need to be. Without such arrangements, our ability to communicate would be severely hampered.

Are such arrangements more complex today than in years past? This is an interesting speculation, because if it is true and if the rate with which that change is taking place is increasing, it poses important considerations for the study of interpersonal communication. Someone interested in new technology might suggest that we have so many new words entering our vocabulary every day, and the mass media bring them to us with ever-increasing speed, that our language is changing at a much faster rate than it did in the past. New levels of complexity in society and new words and arrangements of words to meet that complexity place new importance on our ability to communicate with each other.

Concrete versus Abstract Language

Regardless of how fast language may actually be changing or the complexity of the concepts we encounter may be increasing, we must remain alert to the need for clear and concise language to express our thoughts and ideas. Let's examine this need further.

Language—both words and the arrangement of words—can range between concrete and abstract.[8] *Concrete* words and sentences are *simple and direct.* "The dog went to the store" infers that the dog left one location and ended up at the store. On the other hand, if we want to describe the dog and what occurred on the dog's route in more detail, we might say, "The old dalmation padded down the winding, aspen-lined lane to the country store, sniffing the cows, barking at a rabbit, and stopping to lap up water from a stream along the way." We learned much more about the dog and the trip to the store in the second statement than in the first. The first statement employed concrete words and word arrangements. The second statement included more complex words and word arrangements. It was more abstract.

Which statement was more appropriate? That depends on what was needed to communicate effectively and to meet a specific communication objective. If we only needed to know where the dog had gone, then the concrete language of the first statement was perfectly acceptable and appropriate. But if we needed to display our ability to develop descriptive prose to our creative-writing teacher, the latter statement was more appropriate. Remember, although abstract language can help us to communicate complex thoughts, it is also suspectible to misunderstanding. Use abstract language only to the degree that the communication situation requires it.

Language Intensity

Imagine that you're conversing with a friend about someone you have both dated. Your feelings about the person in reference are rather neutral. You remember the evening the two of you went to dinner, then to a play, and then said good night. The words you use to describe the person are "nice," "compatible," "acceptable"; nothing too exciting, but nothing negative, either. As you talk about the person, you have very little intensity in your voice. Your friend, on the other hand, has a different impression of the person. With gusto, your friend describes the person as being "warm," having a "fantastic sense of humor," and being "great with people."[9] You are somewhat mystified about your friend's positive reaction. Perhaps there were qualities you missed. Just then, a third friend enters the room who has also dated the same person. The third opinion? With words such as "pervert," "klutz," and "inept," the person gets a totally negative third evaluation.

This example points to the way language of different intensity is used to describe a position someone holds about a person, an object, or an issue. In this case, the intensity of the language described the person from three different perspectives: neutral, positive, and negative. Although this example used language which clearly reflected negative or

118   Language and Meaning

positive opinions, much of what we say is more subtle. Descriptions are often not as clear-cut as "pervert" or "fantastic." And, as with anything else, we can sometimes misunderstand the intensity of language just as we misunderstand the meanings of words.

Research also suggests that the intensity of language plays a part in affirming or changing our opinions. Although the results do differ, some generalizations are possible. For example, one suggestion is that we tend to use less intense language when we face a stressful situation. In other words, we apparently try to lessen the stress through our use of language. One research study discovered that *actual* suicide notes exhibited lower language intensity than notes written by people who were role playing suicides.[10]

Other research indicates that language that is too intense can lower our opinion of the speaker when the speaker delivers a discrepant (at odds with our own ideas) message.[11] To better understand the concept, suppose we're thinking about buying a particular car, but decide to walk into another showroom just to see the competing models. The salesperson in the showroom begins to use intense language, speaking negatively about the car we are considering buying. Because we are already positively disposed to the car, the salesperson's remarks are not only an attack on the car, but on our personal judgment as well. As a result, our opinion of the salesperson is lowered. Countless orders are lost at all different levels in the selling process, from check-out counters to corporate boardrooms, because people do not realize this simple concept. The act of bad-mouthing the competition with high-intensity, negative language has lost billions of dollars in business. A much better approach would have been for the salesperson to remain neutral about the competing car and then praise the qualities of the models he or she was selling. Interestingly enough, had the salesperson shifted to the other extreme and been too *positive* about the competing car, our opinion of him or her might have also been lowered because we would have not expected excessive praise for a competing product.

Research has uncovered many other effects of language intensity.[12] Remember, intense language can creep into our conversations without our realization. Emotional involvement with an issue and strong opinions can cause us to become "internally" more intense and "outwardly" express this intensity. Learn and practice monitoring both your emotions and your language, because intense language can interfere with your reaching a goal, be it selling a product or yourself.

Verbal Immediacy

Just as our feelings about something or someone can influence the intensity of our language, the degree to which we associate ourselves with a concept can also influence our use of language. We call this *verbal immediacy*. Verbal immediacy refers to the degree with which we associate ourselves with a message. Stated another way, verbal immediacy refers to *the amount we approach or avoid a topic*.[13]

"The golden sun burst through the dawn mist, casting a luminous glow over the tranquil scene, as a hush was broken only by the distant melody of church chimes, the murmuring of leaves and the lullaby of a mother sparrow trilling to her young." So wrote David Goldman. And why did he write it, you ask? To try to put into one sentence what Wilfred J. Funk designated as the 10 most beautiful words in the English language: chimes, dawn, golden, hush, lullaby, luminous, melody, mist, murmuring, tranquil.

(Courtesy: The Idaho Statesman)

To better understand the concept, let's examine the following statements. The first one is considered to be an example of strong verbal immediacy. The others descend in comparison to the last statement, which reflects weak verbal immediacy:

> We will gain a rich appreciation of interpersonal communication while taking this course.
>
> You and I will gain a rich appreciation of interpersonal communication while taking this course.
>
> Perhaps you and I will learn about language while taking this course.
>
> Perhaps you will learn about verbal immediacy while taking this course.

The first statement was assuring and all inclusive. But in the last statement, the speaker was removed not only from the feelings and expectations of the other person, but also from the degree of involvement, as indicated by the reference not to the entire course but to just a small segment of it. In each statement, more and more disassociation took place.

Differences in verbal immediacy, much more than we are able to illustrate or discuss here, "result from variations in adjectives (the vs. that), verb tense (present vs. past), order of occurrence or references in a sequence (earlier vs. later), implied volunteerism (want vs. must), mutuality (Dave and I do X vs. I do X with Dave) and probability (Bob and I will vs. Bob and I may)."[14]

In what situations and in what ways are immediacy and language related? Research results suggest that we use *less* immediate language when we are in a stressful situation, and we disassociate ourselves from the source of the stress. A group of journalism students under the impression that their program was being cut by the university administration used fewer first-person pronouns when writing about that topic than they did in a less stressful situation.[15] Another researcher found that people's scores on anxiety tests increased when their language immediacy levels decreased.[16] Still another study found that former President Richard M. Nixon "used language that was lower in immediacy when he was communicating in relatively uncomfortable (for him) situations."[17] As with language intensity, examples of verbal immediacy number many more than I can share with you here.[18] When you are in a conversation with another person, start to monitor immediacy as well as intensity. How do both variables play a part in the communication you send and receive?

Vocabulary   We talked earlier about the importance of a vocabulary in making precise use of the language, achieving the ability to discuss and explain complex issues, and communicating with greater understanding. Vocabulary, as a language variable, works toward finding those key points in one person's field of experience which can interact with the key points of another's field of experience. The better we use our vocabulary, the more adept we are at cementing thoughts and ideas with each other through interpersonal communication.

Like language intensity and verbal immediacy, how we use the range of words in our vocabularies may be determined by a given interpersonal situation and what we encounter in that situation. Research results suggest that when we communicate in a highly stressful situation, we may use a much smaller variety of words than we would under non-stressful situations.[19] Other results suggest that people who use a wide vocabulary, and who are not doing so to show off, are perceived as being more competent, of a higher social and income status, and in control of themselves.

Language Style

If we combine all of the language variables we have just discussed and examine language styles—how the variables are used in interpersonal communication—the combinations are infinite. But why do people who possess the same vocabularies and understand the same rules of grammar still communicate in different ways? Part of the answer lies in each person's language style or, expressed in relation to spoken communication, interpersonal style. Different interpersonal situations necessitate the use of different words and different arrangements of words. Think of all the people with whom you talk and how your own style changes from one situation to another. We will examine *some* of the more easily recognizable language styles next.

Humor as Style   Although some may call humorous people the life of the party, others may look upon their constant humor and laughing mannerisms as boring or juvenile. Nevertheless, a humorist possesses a certain style in the way he or she uses language.[20] We all, at times, play the role of the humorist. We may offer a humorous anecdote, tell a joke, or relate a funny story as an interpersonal "strategy" to make another person laugh.

> *Good humor is the health of the soul; sadness its poison.*
>
> *Stanislaus*

Professor Kenneth Andersen offers a succinct description of humor as a language style when he states that humor is a response "arising from the perception of incongruity or from wit and word play."[21] In other words, the use of language to describe something or someone in a humorous manner describes the relationship between language and one type of style. Andersen suggests, "jokes of all sorts depend upon language for a portion of their effect. Dialect jokes, jokes based on group stereotypes, . . . and shifts in meaning are all basic to humor. Puns and many forms of verbal word play are recognized and often highly valued forms of humor."[22]

Appropriateness   We have all been in social situations in which the language being used is inappropriate. Using the language to offer inappropriate prose at inappropriate moments causes an unnatural strain on any interpersonal encounter. Yet cussing and swearing are not necessarily or automatically inappropriate. Under certain circumstances,[23] even cussing, swearing, or obscenity perhaps has its place.[24] Remember our discussion of that important interpersonal need, inclusion? The desire to be included, the desire to draw together other persons' fields of experience with our own can cause us to engage in inappropriate conversation. One person in a crowd tells a joke, another tries to better it, and suddenly the conversation has shifted to a style of language inappropriate to the situation.

Monitor your own conversation in a number of different interpersonal situations—for example, social gatherings or business meetings. Determine what style of language is appropriate for the occasion and then practice it. You may even discover that remaining silent can be a very appropriate style in certain circumstances.

Modes of Speech

Another way to approach language style is to examine different *modes of speech*. Modes of speech deal with *the way words are joined together in a particular pattern* to accomplish different communication goals. Consider the following modes of speech and notice how we use different language patterns in different situations:[25]

Impulsive. An impulsive pattern is characterized by *short utterances without the need for complex language structure.* You are riding a horse and get hit by a tree limb. "Ouch!" is your reaction. Your friend suggests that you go to a fine restaurant with delicious desserts. You immediately squeal, "Ooooooo." In most cases, we would characterize an impulsive pattern as "a speaker's vocal reaction to a situation."

Contactive. Slightly more complex than impulsive patterns are contactive patterns. Contactive patterns are most frequently *used when we are attempting to initiate "contact" or gain the attention of another person.* "Hello there." "How are you?" "How have you been?" are examples of contactive patterns. These patterns can be single-word statements, such as "Hello," but they're more often composed of word phrases. It's the *intention* in making the statement, not the number of words, that distinguishes an impulsive pattern from a contactive one.

Conversative. Although a very limited vocabulary may be employed, conversative patterns go beyond the impulsive reaction and the contactive phrase and approach "conversation." In a conversative pattern, *our language style approaches human interaction.* Messages are sent and received, and feedback takes place or at least is expected. Examples are cocktail party chatter and elaborated greetings, and farewells. A conversative pattern may take the following form: "Wendy, it's been so good to see you. I hope you'll get back to see us soon, and please say 'hello' to Larry. By the way, will he be coming with you next time?"

'WATCH YOUR LANGUAGE' IN COURT, SAYS LINGUIST

Judges and juries are influenced not only by what lawyers say in the court-room, but also by the way they say it, according to Sharon Veach, a Stanford University doctoral candidate in linguistics.

Veach says "courtroom language is public speaking" or formal language. Men, Veach says, usually fare better at public speaking than women because "they've been encouraged to project their voices, their personalities." As a result, Veach concludes, women can be at a disadvantage when they enter a courtroom.

"Women attorneys face the problem of making juries see them as lawyers and not as gendered beings," she says. Pauses and hesitations, emotional statements, the use of fillers such as "er" and "um," hedgers such as "I guess"— all of these ways of speaking cause jurors to perceive the lawyer as feminine and to filter all information through that perception, according to Veach. "If you can't make a juror forget about your sex, then you really have to watch yourself," she said.

"Have control over the formal language," she advises. "Sometimes you use [the word] 'approximately.' Sometimes you don't."

Veach gives other language tips:

—Men have more monotonic voices so they should try for greater variety in their voices. Women, because they have a wider range of intonation, should use more monotonic speech.

—Pitch of voice establishes authoritativeness. "Most women could lower their pitch and be taken more seriously."

—Use metaphors only "as a last resort." War and sports metaphors especially should be avoided. "They generally aren't clarifying and cloud the issues," says Veach.

—Don't interrupt.

—For practice, talk into a tape recorder.

Most important, says Veach, lawyers should realize that "every moment they're on a public stage."

Martha Middleton

(American Bar Association Journal, 67 February, 1981, p. 151)

Descriptive or Directive. In a descriptive or directive pattern, words are not only joined together in phrases but usually appear in a *definite sequence which tells a story or directs someone to do something.* Stop and consider how you would tell a friend the route you took to get to class or to travel home. Everything from street signs to landmarks would be included, and your words would be arranged in a way that would help your friend mentally travel the same route.

Elaborative. More complex than the patterns we have already discussed is the elaborative pattern. Here, language tackles the tasks of *moving from one concept to another, much the way paragraphs are used in a book.* One example of this pattern would be an insurance salesperson's description of a policy to a prospective customer.

Each day we encounter numerous modes of speech. When we get up in the morning, the language patterns we employ may be very minimal. "Oh what a night!" may be the prelude to further grunts and groans as we manage to get from bed to breakfast. Later we will add a "Good morning." Still later we might find ourselves giving directions or explaining a complex idea to a coworker or student. Our ability to adapt and function successfully using different modes of speech is important to our ability to function in society. Although debated and in some ways controversial, the British sociologist Basil Bernstein suggested that different social classes in Great Britain possessed different patterns of speech, ranging from the more restrictive patterns for lower classes to the more complex and elaborative patterns for upper classes. Bernstein's research has been interpreted to suggest that these different levels of language complexity cause lower-class children in Britain to fall behind their middle-class counterparts when they reach elementary school where the more elaborative patterns of language are employed.[26] Professor Frederick Williams suggests possible broader applications of Bernstein's concepts across countries and cultures; he states, "it can be argued that a child is socialized into the behavior patterns and capabilities of individuals in a particular social stratum because of the language capabilities which (the child) acquires."[27]

SUMMARY

This chapter on language has brought us from the poetry of Horace to the way in which we use different styles of language to communicate with each other and function within our society.

We first acquire the use of symbols and begin uttering sounds in infancy. Gradually we acquire our first words, and from approximately two to six years of age, we increase our vocabularies from a few words to about 8000. As we continue to increase our vocabularies and build sentences, we gain the ability to handle complex language tasks. Our opportunity and ability to interact with other people are very important to this stage of language growth. As we improve our skills of interpersonal communication, the very opportunity to interact interpersonally helps to build these skills. One is the offshoot of the other.

Language serves various functions in our lives, one of the most basic being the ability to communicate within ourselves through intrapersonal communication. As our use of language improves, we acquire the skills to internally verbalize more complex thoughts and processes and to solve more complex interpersonal problems that might confront us. Still another function of language is to assist us in meeting the expectations of certain societal norms through appropriate conversation. Language helps us to adapt to different situations. Whether we're bargaining for a pay raise or negotiating a family squabble, language is the key which can unlock understanding.

Two additional functions of language include control and gaining commitments. Control as a basic interpersonal need can many times be achieved by understanding the difference between assertive and nonassertive language. Directly related to control is our ability to gain commitments from people. Interaction among individuals and interaction among groups were other functions of language we explored.

In discussing the important role of meaning in language, we encountered the term *semantics,* used to describe the science of meanings. Important to understanding meaning is to be able to distinguish between the symbol (a word) and the referent (what the word means). Grammar is the glue that holds meaning together, while denotation and connotation refer to the difference between the explicit, sometimes called "dictionary," meaning of a word and how the word functions in a certain context. Language variables include studying the structure of language, or how words are joined together; concrete versus abstract language; the intensity of language; verbal immediacy; and vocabulary.

Concluding our chapter was a discussion of language style, which included humor, the appropriate use of words, and modes of speech, of which there were patterns of increasing complexity from impulsive to elaborative.

OPPORTUNITIES FOR FURTHER LEARNING

BECK, M. S., *Baby Talk.* New York: Times Mirror, 1979.

CARROLL, J. B., *Language and Thought.* Englewood Cliffs, NJ: Prentice-Hall, 1964.

CHOMSKY, N., *Reflections on Language.* New York: Pantheon, 1975.

CONDON, J. C., Jr., *Semantics and Communication* (2nd ed.). New York: Macmillan, 1975.

CROSS, D. W., Word Abuse: *How the Words We Use Use Us.* New York: Coward, McCann & Geoghegan, 1979.

DeVILLIERS, J. G., *Language Acquisition.* Cambridge: Harvard University Press, 1978.

ELGIN, S. H., *Gentle Art of Verbal Self Defense.* Englewood Cliffs, NJ: Prentice-Hall—Spectrum Books, 1980.

FARB, P., *Word Play: What Happens When People Talk.* Knopf, 1974.

GOODMAN, P., *Speaking and Language.* New York: Random House, 1971.

HAYAKAWA, S. I., *Language in Thought & Action* (4th ed.). New York: Harcourt Brace Jovanovich, Inc., 1978.

HOWARD, P., *New Words for Old.* New York: Oxford University Press, 1977.

McDONALD, D., *The Language of Argument* (3rd ed). New York: Harper & Row Pub., 1980.

MICHAELS, L. and C. RICKS, *The State of the Language.* Berkeley: University of California Press, 1980.

MITCHELL, R., *Less Than Words Can Say.* Boston: Little, Brown, 1979.

NEWMAN, E., *Strictly Speaking.* Indianapolis: Bobbs-Merrill, 1974.

PEI, M., *Weasel Words: The Art of Saying What You Don't Mean.* New York: Harper & Row Pub., 1978.

PEI, M., *The Story of Language.* Philadelphia: Lippincott, 1965.

POSTMAN, N., *Crazy Talk, Stupid Talk.* New York: Delacorte Press, 1976.

SHENKER, I., *Words and Their Masters.* New York: Doubleday, 1974.

WOOD, J. T., *Human Communication: A Symbolic Interactionist Perspective.* New York: Holt, Rinehart & Winston, 1982.

chapter five

Nonverbal Communication

PREVIEW   *After completing this chapter, we should be able to:*

Describe the basic functions of nonverbal communication.
Explain territorial and personal space.
Tell how body types, shapes, and sizes can influence interpersonal communication.
Discuss how body smell, color, and hair impact on how we interact with others.
Realize the importance of body movement in interpersonal communication.
Compare and contrast emblems, illustrators, and adaptors.
Give examples of messages communicated by posture.
Explain how facial expressions communicate information.
Define paralanguage.
Apply good voice qualities to interpersonal communication.
Explain the role of touching.
Discuss how our dress projects an image.
Understand the influence of color and time on interpersonal communication.

Without saying a word, she placed her warm hand on his chest, and he winced at the pain. Slowly his eyes began to close as her other hand stroked his blood-streaked hair. She could smell the powder burns from the spent cartridges and she could hear the wind from the coming storm racing through the willows below. She could tell from his tattered uniform he had been fighting since the War's beginning, and the scenes of Gettysburg, Vicksburg, and Winchester were etched in his brow.

No words were spoken, but the man and the woman still communicated everything they wanted to say in the preceding passage. How? They used nonverbal communication. Nonverbal communication uses images to communicate. Sometimes they're simple images, such as a lapel pin; other times they're more complex, such as portraits of private jets and yachts decorating the walls of a stockbroker's plush office. In this chapter, we will learn how these and other nonverbal messages affect interpersonal communication.

Functions of Nonverbal Communication

First, we will examine the functions of nonverbal communication.[1] Although various descriptive terms are used, nonverbal's basic functions are: repeating, substituting, complementing, regulating, and accenting verbal communication.

Repeating   A brief introduction to the nonverbal factors of emblems and illustrators helps us explain these basic functions. We examine these factors in greater detail later in this chapter. *Illustrators are movements which complement what we say*—for example, a hand gesture that emphasizes a description of a close football game. In many ways these movements *repeat* what is said. We say to our friend, "I caught a fish eighteen inches long," and hold our hands eighteen inches apart. The hand movements are nonverbal-communication messages repeating what we verbally say.

Substituting   *An emblem*, on the other hand, *can be a substitute for words* (Figure 5-1). An outstretched thumb pointed sideways communicates, "give me a ride" without our having to say the words. In this case, nonverbal communication is a substitute for verbal communication.

Time out; Referee's Discretionary or Injury Time Out followed with tapping hands on chest.

Ineligible Receiver Down Field on Pass

FIGURE 5-1

Football signals are forms of nonverbal communication which substitute for words.

Nonverbal Communication

FIGURE 5-2
Nonverbal communication, such as the conductor's outstretched arm, complements words.
(Prentice-Hall Photo Archive)

Ball Illegally Touched,
Kicked, or Batted

Complementing Complementing messages (Figure 5-2) are closely related to messages which repeat and substitute. If we hold our hands around an imaginary basketball while we tell our friend about an exciting basketball game, our hands would be complementing, through nonverbal messages, what we were saying using verbal messages.

First Down

Regulating We can actually control the flow of communication by using nonverbal communication. If we raise our hands when someone else is talking, it's a signal that we want to say something or that we want the other person to stop talking. A pause can have the same effect. Shaking our heads in a sideways motion can also prompt the other person to stop talking and ask us why we disagree.

Forward Pass or
Kick Catching
Interference

Accenting Nonverbal messages accent interpersonal communication by *highlighting certain words or phrases we verbally express.* Imagine that you are an architect designing a new building. At the top of the building you've planned a dome-shaped restaurant. As you describe the building, you talk about the proposed landscaping and the construction of the many floors and balconies. When you excitedly tell about the domed restaurant, your hands gesture in front of you in a dome-shaped pattern. Your hands' forming the shape of the dome is an example of the accenting function of nonverbal communication.

We see these functions in action as we discuss nonverbal communication in more detail. Let's begin our discussion by learning about both territorial and personal space.

Safety

FIGURE 5-1 (cont.)

U nderstanding Territorial Space

(© Elizabeth City News Company, Elizabeth City, N.C.)

Territorial space, although closely related to personal space, is generally defined by physical boundaries, such as the perimeter of a beach blanket or the goal line on a football field. Also referred to as territory or territoriality, our territorial space affects the way we communicate with others. In a study done at the Pennsylvania Correctional Facility, researcher Sheila J. Ramsey identified the different territorial spaces that existed among prisoners. She found:

> When in the yard or other open space, someone crossing the eight-to-ten foot barrier is perceived as trespassing. In closed quarters, depending on the need for privacy, the distance is reduced to two or three feet. The outer limits become important when being approached from the rear or when an approach is combined with direct constant eye contact. Conversational distance between two inmates is approximately two feet; between an inmate and a guard it increases to three feet.[2]

Not only humans can have territorial space. A dog, for example, may have an entire fenced-in yard in which to roam about. While the dog has the freedom to run and walk over a wide area, an intruder, person or dog, will find leaping over the fence a risky endeavor. Such an encounter would be violating the dog's territorial space.

Defending territorial space is a natural instinct for many wild animals.

Intruding and Defending Territorial Space

Defending territorial space is a definite activity, especially for animals. Wild animals, for example, may lay claim to a water hole or hunting ground. When other animals venture too close to the claim, the animal who owns the territory may or may not permit them to drink or hunt, depending on the "owner's" thirst or hunger at the time. Such patterns of behavior are particularly noticeable when natural resources are scarce, such as at a water hole in the desert.

Even more protective territorial space exists around a mother and her young. Intrusion into this space may result in much more serious conflict. Whereas an animal might growl and prance around a watering hole while other animals manage to drink, attack, physical harm, and even death can result if another animal, including a human, violates the territorial space of an animal with offspring. Consider the mother who may wince when a neighbor or relative barges into her baby's room, picks the child up, and begins coo-cooing at it. Not only is the mother protective of her child, but she also shares the territorial space of her baby's room; tension is the natural result when someone violates that space, especially without permission.

The Home Environment

Examples of territorial space abound in the home. Each member of the family usually has a certain area to which he or she lays claim, be it a work area or a favorite chair. Yet no one is particularly worried about encountering violence upon violating another family member's special space. On the other

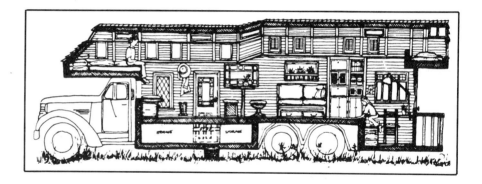

hand, some areas are more protected than others, such as a person's dressing or sleeping area. Chances are if a teenager announces that he or she is moving into the living room, the announcement would create more than just idle discussion at the dinner table.

Having our own space is very meaningful, especially during adolescence. As we became more concerned about ourselves, especially about the way we dressed and the way we looked, we began to work towards developing strong self-concepts, acceptance among our peers, and success in our social interactions. Such efforts demanded experimentation, and trial and error took place in varying degrees of privacy. We appreciated the ability to shave or fix our hair in private. The ability to change clothes and experiment with new apparel without fear of disapproval became important to us. Being able to develop an acceptance with the way our bodies were changing became important to us. Even the ability to participate in conversation with others required a degree of privacy, sometimes even our own extension telephone. We still appreciate this privacy as adults.

Social Relationships in the Home

Territorial space can be an especially sensitive area in homes in which children live with one natural parent and another parent through marriage. Because of the ties that were developed in the child's formative years with the natural mother or father, the child may feel less threatened when the natural parent enters his or her territorial space. On the other hand, when the parent through marriage enters the territorial space, the child may be more protective, less open, and even tense. Similarly, the parent through marriage may feel the same way when the child enters the parent's territorial space. Even though the spouse may be able to walk freely in and out of the bedroom, the child from a previous marriage may not. When understanding exists between parents and children about what causes these anxieties to surface, then the ability to respect another's territorial space is much easier, and the relationship between the child and the parent through marriage is less strained.

Nonverbal Communication

FIGURE 5-3
Increased heating and construction costs are forcing
many businesses to decrease the size of their office
space. *(Steelcase)*

Changing Uses of Territorial Space

Changes in the family structure, inflation, even the weather and energy costs may be changing the way we obtain, use, and adapt to our territorial space (Figure 5–3). Fifty years ago, it was not uncommon for large, extended families to live together in large homes. Parents, grandparents, and children may have lived together in·a house big enough for everyone to have territorial space. Then as our population became more mobile, families moved away from each other. People who grew up in one part of the country lived in another part of the country, and retired in still another. Today, as inflation makes it necessary for many families to live together again, and as soaring energy costs make it necessary for houses to be smaller, we find ourselves adapting to sharing smaller living quarters with more people. Similarly, businesses are finding large, spacious offices too expensive to heat. Yet reduced work areas can produce restrictive environments, and new frontiers in interior design will need to create the illusion rather than work with the reality of territorial space.

Public and Commercial Places

Many public and commercial places are also undergoing the same spatial changes in architectural design (Figure 5–4). While walking through the Atlanta International Airport recently, I noticed that where the underground passageways connected with the concourses, the ceilings were a grid of mirrors. Actually, the ceilings at that point were quite low, and the mirrors helped alleviate a feeling of confinement. It also helped keep

FIGURE 5-4

Where space does exist, spatial changes in modern architectural design create the feeling of openness in many public and private buildings.
(Citibank, N.A.)

the flow of people moving efficiently. The desire to avoid walking under a low ceiling could create a traffic jam of people during rush periods. Restaurants that use strategically placed mirrors to create the illusion of large areas are also following this architectural concept.

Territorial Space at School   Still another area of territorial space is at school. The typical classroom has well-defined territorial space (Figure 5–5). At the front of the room is the teacher's desk. Although a student may be able to approach the desk and talk to the teacher, the student cannot take the liberty of occupying the

FIGURE 5-5

School classrooms are examples of highly structured territorial space in which each student's desk defines that space. *(United Nations)*

chair behind the desk. Similarly, the student's territorial space is defined by the size of the classroom seat. And although it may not be large, it is something the student returns to day after day. Even when assigned seating is absent, a class gradually adopts a fairly constant seating arrangement.

In a living unit or a sorority or fraternity house where two or more people are assigned to a small room, each individual still develops his or her own territorial space. If one person enters and sits at another person's desk, it may seem awkward or unnatural to the person whose space has been violated. Somewhat jokingly, although with more seriousness than is realized, students may take colored tape and stick it down the center of their room, creating an imaginary wall over which room-mates are not supposed to cross.

Personal Space

Personal space is concerned with psychological traits rather than the physical structures of territorial space. One way to understand personal space is to imagine that a bubble exists around each of us. If we are shy and introverted, our bubbles may be very large. Large bubbles prevent people from "physically" coming too close to us. But our bubbles are very flexible. they change from one moment to the next, depending on a host of factors, all of which influence the way we communicate with others.

One student related how quickly our perceptions of personal space change by telling about her morning's experiences. She told that the day had started out really great with breakfast with her best friend. An hour later she arrived at school, and ended up in the elevator with an ex-boyfriend she couldn't stand. From the very small bubble that surrounded her at breakfast, she had acquired a large bubble by the time she met her ex-boyfriend. Conversation had flowed freely and intimately at breakfast but in the elevator, she did not want to even see, let alone talk to, her exboyfriend.

The Relationship of Territory to Personal Space

Even though personal space is different from territorial space, the two are interrelated. In many cases, the amount of available territorial space determines the amount of personal space we need (Figure 5–6). If we step onto a crowded elevator, we do not normally feel awkward if some-one's shoulder touches ours. But if we are in an empty elevator, and some-one steps on and stands with his or her shoulder touching ours, we feel very uncomfortable and probably get off at the next floor, or at least are relieved when a third person steps on. In these situations, available territory deter-mines how much personal space is adequate for us to feel comfortable. Park benches, movie theatres, library tables, and grocery lines are all places where our personal space is very flexible, determined by the available ter-ritory we share with other people.

COURTROOM POSITIONING

Courtrooms today come in many different shapes and sizes. Some give you elbow room; some make you feel like you are sitting in the stenographer's lap. It is up to you to size up the advan-tages of the courtroom in which you will be arguing —even if it means checking out the premises a day before.

If a courtroom is properly designed and sound-insu-lated, your voice should carry. If not, make sure the jury is between the witness and yourself. After all, it is not only your client you are trying to impress. Make sure the jury hears and sees what is going on.

Never, never give your back to a judge or jury while arguing. If there is a one in a million chance that he'll miss your point, he will.

Always look alert and poised. Slouching indicates disinterest and if you do not care, the jury won't either. If a witness has made some in-audible remark, repeat it to make sure that the jury caught it.

When you're in summa-tion, look each juror in the eye. Pause. Appeal to their sensitivities and don't try to be "cute." Remember—you are trying to make a positive impression on them and that impression is one of profes-sionalism. Make one mis-take and the straw pyramid tumbles.

(Source: Trial, May, 1979)

FIGURE 5-6

Personal space may vary, depending on the amount of territorial space available. *(Ken Karp)*

In interpersonal communication, both the sender and the receiver must feel comfortable with their personal space in order to communicate effectively. Violating another's personal space, such as standing in an empty elevator with shoulders touching, infringes upon personal space, and the ability to strike up a conversation with the other person is severely inhibited. We will now examine what research has taught us about personal space.[3]

Factors Influencing Personal Space

In addition to available territory, other factors play a part in how we define personal space.

Friendship One of the more basic and easily understood factors which influence personal space is friendship. Every day we encounter situations in which we locate ourselves closer to friends than we do to strangers. For example, assume that at the end of a class you decide to stop by the coffee shop for a sandwich. Upon entering you notice a close friend seated in a booth with someone you do not know. You decide to join them. You are much more apt to position yourself closer to your friend than to the stranger.[4] Assume now that you are working in a corporation, and a meeting is called to discuss a new product. As you enter the room, you know some of the managers. You are much more likely to choose a seat next to them than a seat next to one of the managers you do not know. We also use personal space as a means of communicating friendship. We may sit closer to someone as a nonverbal way of saying, "I want to be your friend"[5] or "I want to get to know you better." A risk is involved in such behavior, though, because violating another's personal space can hinder rather than further friendship.

Nonverbal Communication

Age and Status Strangers who are similar in age will approach each other physically closer than strangers whose ages are far apart.[6] Related to this concept is status. People of similar status will approach each other more closely than people whose statuses differ.[7] In many cases, status and age go hand-in-hand: Older people, especially in some organizations, have more status.

Stop and consider the people with whom you interact. If you go into your boss's office, do you stand as close to your boss as you would to one of your coworkers? Probably not. If you walk into the lunchroom and your boss is there, you would be more likely to sit across from your boss rather than next to him or her.[8]

Praise and Criticism It's a human characteristic to praise and avoid criticism, and this characteristic reflects upon our personal space. In situations in which we are receiving praise, there will be less distance between us and the person praising us than in situations in which we are receiving criticism, especially negative criticism.[9] If your boss called you into his or her office to praise you, you would probably not feel uncomfortable about sitting in the chair next to the boss's chair. But if you were called in for a serious reprimand, you might feel much more comfortable sitting on the other side of the room. The boss might even feel more comfortable having you there because the increased distance would prevent either of you from violating the other's personal space.

Sex Research has also suggested that males and females have different personal-space expectations when talking with people of the same sex. When men are talking to other men, they tend to stand farther apart than when women are talking to other women.[10] Some research studies have shown there to be as much as a one-foot difference in personal-space expectations.

Culture We often are insensitive to the personal-space expectations of different cultures.[11] Because we are more apt to encounter people of our own cultures, we form the habit of assuming that everyone behaves with the same cultural and social norms that we do. Cultures, however, differ in the way personal space is employed in interpersonal communication. In some cultures, it is appropriate for men to kiss each other on the cheek as a greeting. In other cultures, such behavior would be considered a violation of personal space. Certain cultures deem it inappropriate to look a person in the eye while being reprimanded, others consider this action a sign of disrespect. Obviously we cannot learn every cultural difference that exists, but we can be aware that differences do exist. Allowing people from different cultures more time to know each other and learning as many of the basic cultural differences as possible are just two ways to avoid obstacles to interpersonal communication.

Situation Situation is still another variable through which we can examine personal space. Because every interpersonal encounter is different, we must keep the situation in mind as a means of evaluating another person's personal space. If we attend a cocktail party or a social gathering and we know the people and the setting, we find the people there are usually congenial and relaxed. Violating another person's personal space in that situation by standing close or even putting your hand on that person's shoulder is unlikely. On the other hand, imagine that you are attending a high-level diplomatic function. Here the atmosphere is much more formal. Even though this gathering may also be congenial, the personal-space expectations are much different. People are not apt to stand as close to each other, and it would be highly inappropriate for ambassadors or heads of state to start slapping each other on the backs. The situation demands a greater distance between communicators. Edward T. Hall, a recognized expert on nonverbal communication, distinguished among different distances based on the amount of intimacy or formality of an interaction. The different distances were:

> (1) intimate distance, for private interactions or physical contact, which is 0 to 18 inches; (2) personal distance, for situations involving less sensory involvement, which is 18 inches to 4 feet; (3) social distance, for informal interactions with business associates and friends, which is 4 feet to 12 feet; and (4) formal distance, for public speeches and distances from public officials, which is 12 feet and beyond.[12]

Although we should *not* view these distances as any kind of absolute formula, in very general terms they do show the variations which can exist in different situations.

Topic Closely related to situation is the topic of discussion. If we are discussing a very intimate topic with a close friend, we would not hesitate to stand close to that person (Figure 5–7). If the topic is less personal, such as

FIGURE 5–7

The topic of conversation can affect how closely we stand when we talk to another person. Such close personal topics as secrets can encourage closer interpersonal contact than less personal topics.

politics, the distance may increase. Observe the way two people communicate when one tells the other person a secret. Even if one person does not whisper in the other person's ear, he or she will lean over and lessen the distance between them. In this instance, the topic is more intimate, just between two people, and has an atmosphere of perceived confidentiality.

Psychological Makeup Our discussion of personal-space expectations and violations would not be complete without touching on the effect of individual psychological makeup. Each of us is different, and although we can talk in general terms about such factors as friendship, culture, age, sex, status, situation, and topic, we cannot ignore the fact that our own psychological makeup will influence any interpersonal encounter we may have. Consider self-concept. When we feel good about ourselves and have high degrees of self-concept, it may be much more difficult for another person to violate our personal space. We seek out, desire to be with, and communicate with other people. Because we have self-confidence in our ability to relate to others, and therefore perceive others as liking us, we are not offended by people's being close to us, especially when we feel positive about the other person. This does not mean we go through the day hugging people, but a positive self-concept produces positive relationships with others, and when positive relationships exist, it is more difficult to violate the personal space.[13]

In working towards improving our interpersonal-communication skills we need to guard against violating others' personal spaces. Equally important is the ability to recover from a violation of our own personal space. Many times people misread our nonverbal messages and unconsciously violate our personal space. In these situations, we need to adjust to the violation as much as possible to keep communication flowing.

Body Types, Shapes, and Sizes

When we discussed communication models, we learned that the receiver of a message reacts to it by sending feedback back to the sender of the message. Although most of our examples included messages of words, we learned that words are but verbal symbols. We also communicate with nonverbal symbols. The amount of distance we place between ourselves and the person with whom we are talking is a nonverbal symbol. If we love the person, we may stand closer; if we do not like that person, we stand farther away. But of all the nonverbal symbols we communicate, some of the most meaningful are communicated with our bodies—how we move, our facial expressions, our gestures, and our postures. Because communication with our bodies is more subtle and less intentional, it may be more credible. In other words, we continually think about what we say, but we may pay less attention to our eye movements, how much we blink, whether or not we rub our hands, and a host of other nonverbal messages. Skillful receivers of nonverbal communication are also skillful senders of communication because they read all of the messages others send, not just a portion of them. Although estimates of the different nonverbal symbols we send at any given moment run into the thousands, we will concentrate our discussion here on the obvious movements.

Forming Impressions by Body Type As a child, I spent part of each summer camping in the Greenbrier River area of West Virginia. Just outside of Hinton, West Virginia, perched on a horse-shoe mountain top at a bend in the Greenbrier, was Camp Thomas E. Lightfoot. There I spent two weeks in close fellowship with peers and counselors from West Virginia and parts of Pennsylvania.

One of the most interesting examples of how people make impressions of others was the conversation between campers about the counselors. Many of those impressions were made on the basis of physical shapes. This was especially true when older campers were describing counselors to youngsters who had not been to camp before. The conversations would go something like this:

> "You'll know Junior. He's big, really big. He can pick you up with one hand. I hope I get in his cabin."
> "I wonder if Mousy grew any this year. You wouldn't believe how tiny she is. Why, I'm bigger than she is!"
> "Wow, I hope I get in Dave's cabin. He's real nice. You'll like him. He's short, kinda fat, and loads of fun. He's my favorite."

By the time the bus had rambled through the West Virginia mountains into the southern part of the state, every new camper had a visual image and a personality image of the counselors with whom they would spend their next two weeks. In every case, the counselors who stood out from the crowd were the big and the small and the skinny and the husky. How the campers would relate to the counselors, and their first impressions of them, were formed by judgments based on the sizes and shapes of the counselors' bodies.

Understanding Body Types There are three major classifications of body types: the endomorph, the mesomorph, and the ectomorph. Many of us are combinations of all three. Think of the endomorph as short and fat. The ectomorph (Figure 5-8), on the other hand, is best described as tall and skinny. In between is the mesomorph, best described as muscular and athletic. In some societies, although not all, the mesomorph is the ideal, the physically fit person who is admired, and the one we associate with good physical health. Less desirable is the endomorph, because being fat is often associated with being slower and less active, and with looking less attractive in clothes, among other stereotypes. The ectomorph, something a diet commercial would want us to emulate,

FIGURE 5-8

Ectomorphs are tall, skinny body types.

may also be perceived as fragile. Such a person may be excluded from sports, prone to illness, and may possess other, less desirable traits.

Body Types as Stereotypes How does this relate to nonverbal communication and interpersonal interaction? A problem exists when we let these stereotypes interfere with the communication process. Suppose that you are waiting to tryout for the basketball team. Into the gym comes a very tall, thin candidate. Immediately everyone looks up and greets the person with either a smile or a "hi." The person sits down at the end of the bleachers, and the next three people who arrive sit down close to the tall, thin person. Soon they are talking with each other and laughing and joking. It is clear the tall, thin person is perceived as being a good basketball player, someone with whom others want to associate and communicate. No one actually knows the tall, thin person; it is just assumed that because the person's body type is that of an ectomorph, he or she must be good at basketball. But when practice starts, the tall, thin person cannot dribble the ball, cannot pass the ball, and cannot shoot the ball. The stereotype was wrong. Being tall does not mean a person will be a good basketball player any more than being short means a person will be a bad basketball player (Figure 5–9).

FIGURE 5-9
While we tend to think of tall people as better basketball players, the game involves a great many assets beyond height. Positions such as that of point guard demand speed, agility, and the ability to play a strong offensive and defensive game.

Overcoming Stereotypes Our perceptions about body size can cause us to make inaccurate judgments about people. The key is to look beyond the stereotype. Avoid making snap judgments about people, and then adopting a certain communicative strategy for them based on the stereotype. For example, don't automatically assume that a person who is overweight is a social outcast. Perhaps to compensate for being overweight, the person has developed a tremendously outgoing personality and is most enjoyable to be with. Don't, on the other hand, assume that everyone who is overweight is walking around with a positive outlook on life; some may personally feel rejected and find interacting with others difficult. The point is *do not assume anything!* Interact with people before judging them. Talk and listen. Then adapt your own communicative skills to ensure that positive interaction takes place.

Our Bodies' "Natural" Clothes

Although we know that the clothes we wear each day affect in some ways how others perceive us and how we perceive ourselves, sometimes we fail to consider the effects our "natural" clothes have on others. Our body smells, colors, and hair can have just as much impact on how we interact with others as how we dress.

Body Smell We only need to look through the pages of a magazine or turn on the television set to witness the importance that is placed on how we smell. Advertisements for perfume, cologne, baby powder, aftershave, mouthwash, deodorant, soap, and other products make sure we do not forget that smelling right can mean everything from finding a date to making it to the top of the corporate ladder.

Each of us has certain emotions and reactions we associate with different smells. Many of these emotions are the result of prior experiences. When we communicate with other people, the smells each emits can play dominant or subtle roles in the interpersonal interaction. For example, perhaps at some point in our lives we had an intense love affair with someone who happened to wear a certain aftershave or perfume. The scent became the trademark of the individual just as much as the clothes he or she wore. Because we were close to the person, the scent also became etched in our minds. When we encounter these smells that have a given meaning for us and bring forth memories of past interactions, we need to be alert to the role that smell plays in the way we communicate. Stereotypes about people who wear a certain aftershave may be as accurate or erroneous as stereotypes about dress or body types. The key is to sort out the smell from the total communicative experience and determine what role it plays in the way we send and receive messages.

Body Hair Some years ago I moved from Purdue University in Indiana to a faculty position at the University of Oregon. Located in Eugene, the University is situated in the Wilamette Valley between the Coast Range and the Cascade Range of mountains. What I immediately noticed when I arrived on campus was the large number of male students wearing beards. Beards had been present at Purdue but not to the extent they were present at Oregon. When I commented on the apparent phenomenon, one of my colleagues pointed out that so much hiking, camping, and skiing was done in the area that the students found beards easier to care for than trying to shave in the wilds or having the icy wind hit

"I'll tell you why nobody likes you . . . it's because you have bad breath . . . BAD BREATH!"

The allure of perfume

Does perfume make a woman as sexy as the ads promise? Robert A. Baron, a Purdue University psychologist, looked for the answer and came up with some unusual results—at least among college students.

Males, it seems, are attracted to perfumed females *only* if the women are wearing jeans, sweatshirts, or the like.

For the well-dressed female, perfume seems to have the opposite effect: It turns men off.

In the experiment, Mr. Baron paired up males and females and then asked the males to rate how attractive they found the women. Half of the women in the experiment wore two drops of a perfume called Jungle Gardenia, the other half did not. Some women in each of the groups were neatly dressed (blouses, skirts, stockings), the others wore the most casual campus garb.

The women in casual clothes who wore perfume were seen as warmer and sexier than those who did not wear perfume. In nice clothes, the scented women were seen as colder and less romantic than the women who did not wear Jungle Gardenia.

Among the possible conclusions that can be drawn from his study, Mr. Baron says, is that perfume and dressy clothes "may be too much of a good thing."

Whatever the conclusion, Mr. Baron warns: "Unquestioning faith in the benefits of perfume, cologne, and similar products does not seem justified."

(The Chronicle of Higher Education, October 10, 1980, p. 14. Reprinted with permission)

their faces on a ski slope. Somewhat jokingly, he also noted that some of the students with beards liked to "leave the impression" that they hiked, camped, and skied.

The observation was particularly meaningful because I had just completed a course on communication theory and had read about some of the impressions people had of individuals who wore beards. Certain corporate atmospheres found beards particularly inappropriate. Those wearing beards in such settings were thought to be somewhat anti-establishment and did not fit well into corporate decision making. Later, after talking to some business leaders, I found that beards were more accepted in the northwest for the very same reason my colleague had suggested, the outdoor life style.

We find that body hair communicates a symbol like any other type of message. Stereotypes abound. "Long-haired people are liberal." "Short-haired people are conservative." "People with beards are antiestablishment." "Clean-shaven people support the establishment." "Blondes have more fun." Although we may agree or disagree with each of these assertions, we nevertheless make judgments about ourselves and about others based on body hair. How hair is worn, colored, and styled all play a role in interpersonal communication.

Skin Color Prejudice of any kind interferes with interpersonal communication. Unfortunately, society has created many barriers to communication through its creation of racial barriers. Whether we're willing to admit it or not, skin color does effect the way people communicate. For example, we may feel that someone with the same skin color as ours may have a cultural heritage similar to our own and is therefore easier to communicate with and to get to know. The language that is used, the references, and the past experiences may be similar. Stop and consider the people with whom you interact. What role does skin color play in the way you communicate with other people? Should it play that role? If communication is less than satisfactory, what can you do to improve your communication?

Body Movement: Basic Patterns of Communication

The importance of body movement in interpersonal communication is readily seen in an examination of the performing arts. Take dance, for instance. Unlike other forms of expression, such as the theatre where the voice plays a dominant role, dance relies almost totally on body movement to communicate (Figure 5–10). Carefully choreographed movements expressing love or hate can be exhibited by the same two dancers on stage: They can perform a caressing embrace or they can turn their backs to each other and fold their arms. No words are necessary to communicate the feelings. The positions and movements of the dancers' bodies communicate them all.

FIGURE 5-10
Dance is an example of an art form which uses nonverbal communication expressed in body movements. *(American Dance Ensemble, Douglas Bentz and Robert Parola)*

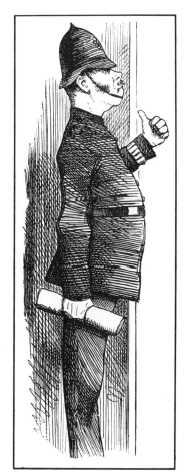

In studying interpersonal communication, we want to become more sensitive to the ways in which our bodies communicate information. We will start by understanding what are referred to as emblems and illustrators in nonverbal communication.

Gestures: Emblems and Illustrators

Gestures are primarily thought of as hand movements. They are also some of the most obvious forms of nonverbal communication. To help us understand them, we will break gestures down into two types of movements: *emblems* and *illustrators*. We should be aware that although our arms and hands are the most frequent expressors of emblems and illustrators, they are *not* the only parts of our bodies that gesture.

Emblems   To distinguish between emblems and illustrators, remember that illustrators are movements which accompany speech. Emblems, on the other hand, do not need speech to communicate meaning. An example of an emblem is putting the tip of our index fingers on the tip of our thumbs with our other fingers extended. This sign

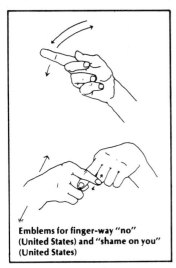

**Emblems for finger-way "no"
(United States) and "shame on you"
(United States)**

FIGURE 5-11

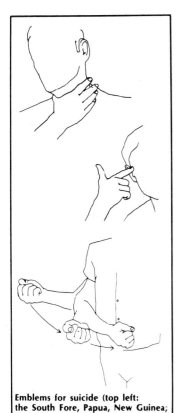

**Emblems for suicide (top left:
the South Fore, Papua, New Guinea;
top right: United States; bottom:
Japan)**

FIGURE 5-12

(Both figures are from P. Ekman,
"Movements with Precise Meanings," Journal of Communication, Summer, 1976,
p. 14-26. © 1976 by Journal of Communication)

for "OK" or "success" is immediately recognizable without the need for ac-
companying words to identify it. Let's now examine specific characteristics
of emblems:[14]

> *Emblems Have Direct Translations.* We immediately know what an em-
> blem means, as in the preceding example. The index finger placed
> over slightly puckered lips means "Be quiet." Placing a cupped hand
> behind our ear means "We can't hear" or "Speak louder." Facing the
> palm of our hands out at the end of our outstretched arms means
> "Stop!" or "Halt!" or "Do not come closer!"

> *Emblems Have Precise Meaning.* Confusion is at a minimum when
> emblems are used. The receiver of a true emblem has no difficulty
> understanding what is meant. When a motorist passes someone
> alongside the road with an outstretched arm and a thumb pointing
> in a certain direction, the motorist knows precisely that the hitch-
> hiker is saying "I want a ride."

> *Emblems Are Directed towards a Specific Receiver.* Receivers of em-
> blems know that the emblems are directed specifically towards
> them. Motorists passing the hitchhiker know that the "thumbs-up"
> emblem is directed right at them at that particular time.

> *Emblems Are Consciously Sent.* When we send emblems, we con-
> sciously know we have communicated information. We may not
> always know when we communicate with illustrators. In an intense
> conversation, we send thousands of nonverbal cues, many of which
> we do not even realize we send. We may compliment the leader of a
> discussion group while our faces say we have contempt for the per-
> son. But we may not realize our faces show contempt. On the other
> hand, if we were to snub our noses at the person, we would be con-
> sciously aware of our "emblems."

> *We Take Responsibility for Emblems.* Because emblems are con-
> sciously sent, we are able to take responsibility for them. We may
> not, however, always want to; for example, children who look inno-
> cent after being caught making faces at the teacher may not want to
> take responsibility for their actions.

Again, remember that emblems can be communicated with body movements other than those using our hands and arms. Emblems can also occur
during conversation (Figure 5-11), although our examples have stressed
nonconversive examples to help distinguish between emblems and illustrators. If, in the middle of a conversation, one person touches the end of
an index finger with his or her tongue and then draws an imaginary number
one in the air, the action serves as an emblem meaning "That's one for me"
or "You got me on that point." Such an emblem would have a precise meaning based on the context of the overall conversation but would still be conscious, precise, and translatable.

Emblems also differ across cultures (Figure 5–12). In the United States, pointing your index finger at your temple with the thumb upright translates as "shooting yourself in the head." In Japan, an emblem depicting suicide is pushing a closed fist near your stomach to depict the plunge of a knife in your vital organs. In still other cultures, grasping one hand about the throat is an emblem for suicide.[15]

Illustrators We now turn our attention to illustrators. Found more frequently than emblems in interpersonal communication, illustrators complement our words rather than replace them (Figure 5–13). The typical expressive gestures used in talking are examples of illustrators. As with emblems, illustrators can still be identified, but they are less precise and pronounced. We have all been in situations in which we cannot think of the words we want to say. We stop, hesitate, motion our hands outwards in a circular motion, and say, "Oh, you know what I mean." Hopefully the other person will know what we mean, although there remains ample room for confusion and misunderstanding. Let's examine some specific characteristics of illustrators:[16]

Illustrators Are Not Precise. Using illustrators when we don't know what words we want to say is one example of how illustrators are

FIGURE 5–13
Found more frequently than emblems, illustrators complement words rather than replace them.

less precise than emblems. In conversation, we must keep in mind that even though nonverbal movements are important and natural to our ways of speaking, they may also cause misunderstanding, especially when illustrators are used as substitutes for words.

Illustrators Increase When We Are Involved in What We Are Saying. The next time you talk to your friends about a movie they have seen, one they liked and were excited about, notice how expressive they are with their hands. Their range of emotion is great, and the expression of that emotion through nonverbal communication is equally great. Telling of a harrowing experience, something unusual, or something that left an impact on us are all incidents in which the use of illustrators will increase.

I enjoy riding amusement-park roller coasters, and remember my mother telling me about my reaction to my first ride on a roller coaster at a park near Ligonier, Pennsylvania. I apparently came off the roller coaster with my mouth hanging open. When asked about the ride, I could only sway frontwards and backwards while saying, "It was terrible!" Some years later, I tackled the "Screaming Eagle" at the Six Flags amusement park outside of St. Louis, Missouri. When my son was asked how he liked the ride, he said, "You wouldn't believe it," and could only hold his hand on his head and close his eyes. When the Kings Island Amusement Park near Cincinnati, Ohio unveiled "The Beast," heralded in advertisements as the "biggest, baddest, meanest roller coaster of them all," temptation was too great. After that ride, however, shortly after a large picnic lunch, the illustrator consisted of holding our stomachs, uttering the words "I want to sit down," and looking for the nearest bench.

Illustrators Can Complement Words. Imagine that you live in an apartment building with a spiral staircase. Try describing the staircase to a friend, explaining in detail how the staircase is built from top to bottom. See how quickly you point your index finger up or down and begin turning it in a spiraling motion. Even if you deliberately try not to use your hand to help you describe the staircase, you soon find your hand wanting to move. When words just do not do the job, illustrators are called in to help. When used properly, illustrators can significantly increase your ability to communicate. You may find yourself working for a company to whom it is necessary for you to deliver a report. Consider not only the words you are going to use but the gestures which will highlight those words. Consider what gestures or other illustrators will help you clarify a point, distinguish between two issues, or drive home a conclusion.

Even though our discussion of illustrators must be general, research has identified subcategories of illustrators. Consider some of these in light of how you might use them while carrying on a conversation. Ask yourself under what topics or in what situations would each category find a use? The subcategories are:

> *batons:* movements which account or emphasize a particular word or phrase.
>
> *ideographs:* movements which sketch the path or direction of thought.
>
> *deictic movements:* pointing to an object, place, or event.
>
> *spatial movements:* movements which depict a spatial relationship.
>
> *rhythmic movements:* movements which depict the rhythm or pacing of an event.
>
> *kinetographs:* movements which depict a bodily action or some non-human physical action.
>
> *pictographs:* movements which draw a picture in the air of the shape of the referent.[17]

Adaptors   Earlier in this text, we discussed the role that intrapersonal communication plays in interpersonal communication. Especially when we are alone, body movements which we classify as adaptors help us to orient ourselves or to adapt to our environment. We tend to decrease our use of adaptors when we are around others, because they can become distractive and interfere with interpersonal communication. One example of an adaptor movement would be scratching. Perhaps we are studying and are having trouble thinking of the answer to a question or the solution to a problem. We breathe deeply, rub our chins, and scratch our heads. If we face the same problem in a meeting of corporate executives, we would be less visual in attempting to find solutions. We might only lightly bite our lower lips or wrinkle our foreheads, for instance.[18]

Posture

Most of us have grown up with someone in our family who monitored our posture. "Stand up straight," "Don't slouch," or "Straighten your shoulders" used to echo in our ears because someone cared about how we presented ourselves to others. Many times the comments came when we were slouched down in our chairs, at a table, or in a sofa. They may also have come when we were being fitted with our first suits or formal gowns. As we grew older and left home, the comments stopped. Unfortunately, bad posture didn't always stop. And whether we want to admit it or not, posture communicates information just as much as hand and arm movements.

Messages Communicated by Posture   Look at the people around you and notice how their postures communicate information. What messages are being sent?

Some of the most common positions of the body, slouching or sitting with our arms folded, communicate such messages as disinterest or defensiveness. A person who is tense and uncomfortable may stand artificially erect. On the other hand, when participating in a group discussion, a person's slight slouching posture may indicate an air of confidence, relaxation, and being in charge of the situation. But do not plan on slouching at the next round-table discussion just to project an image of being in control. You may discover that others do not perceive you that way, and instead you might be labeled as someone who does not pay attention. A good posture for most interpersonal interaction is to sit or stand upright enough to project an image of being alert and interested in the conversation.

Observing Posture in Others

One way to become sensitive to your own posture and how it affects communication is to observe others. We can ask ourselves a series of questions which form a good foundation for observing the positioning and posture of people engaged in interpersonal communication. The next time you observe two people talking, ask yourself the following questions:

Do both people have the same posture? Why?

If one is sitting and the other standing, how does this relate to the perceived status one has in comparison to the other?

Are the people relaxed or tense?

Does posture change during the conversation? Why?

Are the people leaning towards or away from each other? Why?

Do their posture and the positions of their bodies tend to restrict others from entering the conversation?

How far apart are they?

Do the positions of their arms or legs suggest personal warmth or coldness towards each other?

When one person changes posture, does the other? What could this suggest?

How long is a given posture maintained?[19]

By observing others and monitoring our own postures, we can begin to use our postures to aid, not hinder, our interpersonal communication.

Facial Expressions

Of the various types of nonverbal communication, facial expressions are some of the oldest, identifiable means by which we have reflected emotions and personality states. If we had had the opportunity to attend the ancient Greek theatre, we would have seen actors wearing facial masks to portray different moods. Other cultures have also adopted masks to display feelings—for example, tribal masks worn in ceremonies and masks held on poles to illustrate pain and pleasure. Perhaps no other part of the body has been given such attention in nonverbal communication as the face.

> Never bend your head. Always hold it high. Look the world straight in the face.
>
> *Helen Keller*

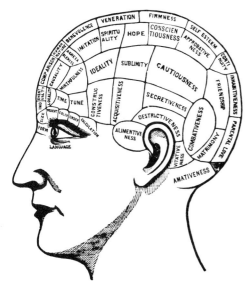

FIGURE 5-14

The unscientific study of the face and head for centuries has centered on a so-called "science" of physiognomy.

A Note on Physiognomy The rather unscientific study of the face over the centuries has centered around an area of inquiry called physiognomy.[20] Not an exact science as far as being able to prove its ideas, physiognomy has nonetheless managed to fascinate us since the time of Aristotle. Basically, it represents the study of the face and skull as indicators of various personality types (Figure 5–14). Some confusion has resulted in trying to use the term to apply to both the features of the face at rest, such as a high forehead or a snub nose, and the way our faces move as a medium of expression, such as puckering our mouths or wrinkling our foreheads. The latter belongs more to the contemporary study of nonverbal communication, whereas the former links to the speculations of soothsayers. Nevertheless some distinguished people and corporations through history, including Socrates and A. T. & T., have studied physiognomy to better understand human interaction.

Although we do not have scientific evidence to suggest that a person with a long forehead is more intelligent than someone with a short forehead, or that someone with deeply recessed eyes has a better memory than someone whose eyes are less recessed, we do have a form of image conditioning developed from childhood that stereotypes certain faces. Take nursery rhymes, for example. The chumpy face of the innocent little pigs facing the protruding features of the big, bad wolf is a stereotype that forms in our minds. Mass media and the theatre continue our conditioning through everything from advertising to pantomime. What facial stereotypes come to mind for a small-town sheriff, a librarian, a chef, or a gangster? Because of all of this conditioning, we may react subconsciously to certain facial types. The teacher who looks like a Boston bulldog may leave an initial impression on a young child of being less than a sweet, understanding person when the opposite may be true.

Nonverbal Communication

Functions of Facial Expressions

Facial expressions serve many of the same functions as other types of nonverbal communication. One way to view these functions is to use the categories established by Professor Mark Knapp. Examining facial expression as "interaction management," Knapp sees the face able to "(1) open and close channels of communication, (2) compliment or qualify verbal and/or nonverbal responses, and (3) replace speech."[21] Knapp points out that these different functions can occur simultaneously.

Try applying these functions to your own experiences. Imagine that you are taking part in a class discussion. If the class is large, you might raise your hand in an effort to secure your turn to speak. But if you are talking with just one other person, raising your hand would be inappropriate. In this instance, you might partially open your mouth to signal that you have something to say. Perhaps you wrinkle your forehead while tilting your head slightly downward and then look up at the person. In each case, you send the message, "I have something to say." To complement what you are saying, you may show a sly smile to signify that you offer a heretofore-untold piece of information. Watch the facial expressions of people gossiping. Notice how they use their faces to add life and importance to what they say. To replace words, facial expressions must be forms of "emblems" we discussed earlier. Depending on the subject being discussed, a yawn might mean "Let's go home," or "I'm bored," or "I'm tired."

Facial expressions are nonverbal labels a person wears. An expressive, smiling face communicates an image about the person that affects the way we react to that individual and the way we communicate with him or her. (Barbara Hendricks of the Chicago Symphony Orchestra. Courtesy: Columbia Artists Management, Inc.)

Facial Expressions as Labels Some people use their faces as constant reminders of their feelings, almost as identities like special perfumes or certain types of clothes. Let's examine people whose faces identify them as "withholders," "revealers," "substitute expressors," and "ever-ready expressors."[22]

Each type of person employs his or her face as an identity. "Withholders" keep feelings from appearing on their faces. More expressionless than others', withholders' faces are difficult to read to determine their feelings. To some degree, withholders hinder the flow of communication because nonverbal communication is received but seldom sent. "Revealers" are just the opposite. A secretary said of her boss, "I know the minute she arrives at the office what kind of a mood she's in." Another phrased it this way: "She wears her feelings on her face." In each case the people in the office learned their boss's face was one of that person's most accurate means of communication. "Substitute expressors" show different facial expressions than what they are feeling. Unless you like thinking in reverse, it can be difficult to communicate with such people. "Ever-ready expressors" are like hunters with loaded guns waiting to shoot. At the slightest reaction to emotion or any other stimulus, these people's faces say it first. Many times such individuals are simply labeled, "very expressive."

Components of Facial Expressions Even though the face works as a whole to communicate emotion, research has anlayzed different components or portions of the face as having more importance than others in expressing certain emotions.[23] The next time you talk with someone, watch how the different portions of that person's face express different emotions. For example, research

FIGURE 5-15
The most accurate indicators of fear are found in our eyes and eyelids.

tends to support the notion that our eyes and eyelids are the most accurate indicators of fear (Figure 5–15). When we are afraid, our eyes are wide open and we may look straightforward with a "blank stare" until the threat passes or we learn to control our emotions. Happiness, on the other hand, is expressed primarily through our mouths and cheeks, but our eyes and eyelids also play important roles.

Many experiences and displays of emotion are expressed through different portions of our faces simultaneously or in rapid succession. Although we cannot go through life looking at only one portion of an individual's face to see if it registers a particular emotion, we should become sensitive to the way people use facial expressions to communicate. Many times, by concentrating on a given portion of the face while attempting to understand the emotion being expressed, we can gain a more accurate reading of what a person feels and may be consciously or unconsciously trying to express.

Applying Facial Expressions

Although we would find it awkward to adjust our facial expressions to serve as "emblems," we can learn how these expressions can play more important roles in interpersonal communication. Thousands of variations in facial expressions exist, and many of them are beyond our control. But others are within our control.

The simple advice "Try meeting people with a smile." is not trite when we consider that it begins communication with a feeling of positiveness for both the sender and receiver. A sales manager complimenting a salesperson can be more effective by adding a smile instead of maintaining the facial expressions of a stern drill sargeant. Facial expressions can act as both reinforcement and nonreinforcement. Decide what you want to say, then coordinate your facial expressions to convey your intended message. Many teachers, for example, fail to realize that their facial expressions are nonverbalizing the exact opposite of what they are verbalizing. Suppose a student is called upon to answer a question. The teacher, wanting to reinforce the student's correct response, says, "That's a good answer and certainly well thought out." But the teacher's face shows a wrinkled forehead, eyebrows together, and rigid lips. Although the teacher thinks he or she has positively reinforced the student, his or her face has, instead, said the exact opposite.[24]

Communicating with Our Eyes

Just think how impossible it would be for writers to tell love stories, for movie producers to bring romantic interludes to the screen, and for television drama to grasp our attention if it were not for our ability to communicate with our eyes. No one would be able to cast an alluring glance

across the room, be wide-eyed with terror, stare down an opponent, or send daggered looks towards an enemy. The twitch of an eyelid can bring a totally different meaning to what someone says. Our eyes tell people when we want to communicate and when we do not want to be bothered. They express love, hate, and every emotion in between.

Understanding "Mutual Gaze" To understand the role our eyes play in interpersonal communication, we first need to know the meaning of the terms *eye contact* and *mutual gaze.*[25] If you have ever taken a course in public speaking, you have probably heard the term *eye contact* used. It refers to looking at the eyes of the people in the audience. But if you're looking at the audience, you're usually looking at more than one person, and you're usually a distance away from those people. When two people are in an intense conversation, sitting only a few feet apart, and are looking at one another, the term *mutual gaze* refers to the action of their eyes. Thus, mutual gaze has a more direct application to our discussion of interpersonal communication.

Applying Eye Behavior to Communication How do we use our eyes to communicate with different people in different situations? Some of the ways include:

Receiving Messages. Using our ability to glance away from another person in order to process the messages being sent to us, we can create mental regroupings of our thoughts. This permits us to

It was definitely a love match, we could see it in their eyes.

David Frost commenting on the marriage of Prince Charles and Princess Diana

retune to the conversation and better understand the messages we are receiving. This is especially important when we are receiving information which is difficult to comprehend. Glancing away from another person can also result from embarrassment, anxiety, or another emotional state.

Sending Messages. Glancing away from another person may help us understand what that person is saying, and we can use the same approach to send information. We can state something complex more easily if we momentarily break the mutual gaze to determine what we are going to say next. Think of the times we try to explain something complex to other people. Notice how we break away from gazing at another person long enough to collect our thoughts or to think about what we are saying. Research has suggested, however, that we still look away more often when listening than when talking. When we are talking, we are in control of the communication channel and want to keep control of the channel as long as we have something to say. Thus, we are more apt to gaze at the other person to avoid being interrupted.

Controlling Information Overload. Along with breaking our gaze at another person when we simply have too much information to comprehend, regardless of its difficulty, we break away from mutual gaze to try to sort out and arrange the priorities of the information we are receiving.

Judging Senders and Receivers. Watch two people talking to each other. Are they friends or strangers? You can answer this by observing how much time they spend in mutual gaze. Researcher David R. Rutter found that, on the average, strangers spend more time looking at each other than do friends. He concluded that such behavior meant that friends know each other and therefore need less visual monitoring of the other person.[26] Strangers, on the other hand, know little about each other and spend a great deal of time "monitoring" the other person.

Controlling the Communication Channel. We can also use our eyes to help control the communication channel. When we want to communicate with other people, we look at them. If we do not want to talk to other people or if we want the conversation to end, we may look away.

Expressing What We Feel. Our eyes help us to "express" what we feel. If we are emotionally involved with what we are saying, we may open our eyes wider than if we are noninvolved or bored with the topic. These findings should be viewed with a moderate degree of skepticism because research has also suggested that people who approve of each other (which could mean that they are friends) spend more time in mutual gaze than do people in disapproving situations.

156   Nonverbal Communication

Other factors affect how we use our eyes to communicate. For example, shyness, the situation, the competitive atmosphere, and the sex of the senders and receivers all influence what role and to what degree our eyes play a part in nonverbal communication.

Qualities of the Voice

If tomorrow morning we were asked to stand before Congress or Parliament and deliver a major address, we would think very carefully not only about what we would say but about how we would say it. We would consider how our voices would project to the gallery, what role the public-address system would play, the difficult words we would need to pronounce, the tone of our voices, whether our voices would be authoritative or soft-spoken, and how we would articulate each word and syllable. For such formal speaking occasions, we tend to pay attention to how our voices complement our words. However, when we speak to someone on a one-to-one basis, we forget many of the ways in which our voices send messages, regardless of what words we speak. We let our defenses down. Let us now look at the ways we can use our voices to make the most of every interpersonal encounter.

Paralanguage The word *para* means alongside. Paralanguage, therefore, is language alongside language. Specifically, *paralanguage is the way we use the sounds of our voices to utter words*. The play and the movie "My Fair Lady" were based on paralanguage. Stop and listen to a person who speaks with an accent. The way that person uses his or her voice may be different from the way you use your voice. You both could use the same words, but each of you would use different paralanguage. If we want to get scientific, we could analyze each person's voice using a voiceprint. A voiceprint provides a detailed "drawing" of a person's voice. In fact, some scientists claim that a voiceprint is much like a fingerprint in that no two voiceprints are exactly alike.

Paralanguage can be broken down into different categories. For example, the *quality* of your voice is a form of paralanguage. In "My Fair Lady," Professor Henry Higgins found Eliza Doolittle selling flowers in the streets of London. By improving the quality of her voice, Eliza later passed for royalty at a formal ball.

Is your voice breathy? Does it become breathy in certain situations? The *resonance* of your voice is a form of paralanguage. Radio announcers are commonly known for their deep resonance. *Tempo* means the way in which you vary the rate of speech and your use of pauses. Learning to read paralanguage permits us to add another dimension to effective interpersonal communication.

Applying Good Voice Qualities to Interpersonal Communication

When interviewed by an employer, a prospective secretary was told, "You, more than anyone else in this company, will determine its success or failure." The secretary looked a bit startled and asked why. The employer replied, "Because every bit of new business we receive comes from people who call us on the telephone. But more importantly, the first call doesn't necessarily bring new business. It's usually the second or third call that makes the difference. One hundred percent of their impression of this company depends on the quality of your voice. You have the job of every employee on your shoulder." The secretary suddenly realized the importance of being able to identify and use good vocal qualities. Sloppy English, a down-home lazy sound, or a drill-sergeant tone of voice left an instant impression on everyone who called the company.

In dealing with other people, especially when we use the telephone, we sometimes forget how important it is to project a positive image, not with what we say but with how we say it. From answering the phone, to asking for a date, to handling calls from the company president, voice quality takes constant practice and constant monitoring. It is sad that so many adults have never learned the importance of good voice quality, especially those who wonder why they have never improved their jobs or positions in life. Many times it is because the impressions they continually left behind did not take into consideration the corporate image—which happened to be themselves.

Touching

A popular bumper sticker reads, "Have you Hugged Your Kid Today?" From the very moment children enter the world, touch becomes an important and, at times, the only means of communication with other people. Gradually as their eyes open and they take in the wonders of the environment, they begin to expand their communicative behaviors. Still later, social norms begin to influence touching behavior. From a kiss to a handshake, touch communicates the full range of emotions with nonverbal flair.

The Importance of Touch in Early Life

Psychologists tell us that the amount of touching an infant receives can directly affect how well adjusted the child is later in life.[27] Yet historically, Americans have actually discouraged touching their children under the belief that touching transmitted infection and disease. What we may not have realized was that children who are not touched may be more susceptible to disease than children who are touched.

As children enter elementary school, touch is a major form of reinforcement.[28] Because sexual connotations are not associated with touching at the preschool and early elementary levels, teachers are freer to appropriately touch children to alleviate their fears of alienation, rejection, or other feelings they may have.

As children develop a sexual awareness, touching behavior becomes limited between teachers and students and, in many cases, between parents and children. The latter can cause difficulties, because the transition into puberty can be an emotional trauma. The time when an individual's identity is being challenged may be the very time that touch and affectionate support from a parent is needed. Psychologists refer to this need for touching behavior later in life as *anchoring*. Anchoring, when used to complement verbal, positive stroking, can play an important role in developing a positive self-concept and instilling confidence. Suppose a youth makes a major personal decision, such as to enroll in a special honors course in school. When the youth tells a parent about the decision, the parent compliments the youth and, at the same time, hugs the youth. Later when the youth is facing another difficult decision, the parent, by giving the youth a hug, can call forth that same confidence.

Who Touches Whom Where Although children may have great latitude in their touching behavior, social norms gradually define the appropriateness of that behavior. Once again, the situation plays a large part in when, and what kind of, touching is appropriate. Consider touching by people of opposite sexes. In one study, researchers examined the relationship between unmarried, opposite-sex friends on the basis of four types of touching behavior—pat, stroke, squeeze, and brush. Monitoring the touching of more than eleven different parts of the body, the researchers found that strokes generally communicated sexual desire and warmth, whereas pats communicated playfulness and friendship. They were not able to say conclusively what messages squeezes and brushes conveyed.[29]

How we interpret messages relayed by touch also depends on what parts of the body are touched. For example, touching of the hands is almost universally interpreted as pleasant and as communicating warmth. On the other hand, touching of the pelvic area is interpreted as sexual. But here, again, the situation plays a part. A football coach slapping a player on the buttocks as the player heads into the game to make the big play is much different than similar touching while walking along the beach. Touching of upper portions of the body occurs more frequently among friends than does touching of lower portions of the body (Figures 5–16, 5–17). Of all the parts of the body, however, the head is the most frequent area of touching contact. It also receives considerable variations of that contact depending on the relationships involved: parent and child, same-sex friends, and opposite-sex friends, for example.

Changing social norms can also affect what kind of touching takes place and under what circumstances. For example, a research study compared touching that was acceptable in the mid 1960s

FIGURE 5-16

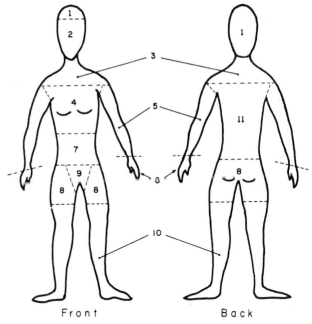

Front   Back

The human body diagrammed into 11 areas.

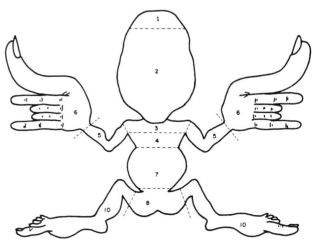

FIGURE 5-17

Relative size of body parts based on the extent of their cortical representation. (Numbers on the diagram refer to corresponding areas in Figure 1.)

with touching that was acceptable in the mid 1970s.[30] The research found: "Female friends of males touch the chest and stomach and hip region with greater frequency, and male friends of females touch the entire torso, from the chest down to the knees, with greater frequency."[31] The subjects used in the research were college students. We should not generalize across other age groups.

Cultural Differences in Touching Touching behavior differs among different people, and it also differs among cultures. For instance, one research study found that American couples in coffee shops touch each other an average of only two times per hour.[32] In France, that figure jumps to 110 times per hour. But if you think this captures the "touching" prize, you haven't been to the Caribbean. The same researcher found that couples in Puerto Rico touch each other an average of 180 times per hour. Of course, other variables can enter into such research, including lighting, proximity to other tables, sounds, and other nonverbal factors. Is there any place in American society outside of the home where a greater degree of touching appears to be socially acceptable? Yes, in airports. There, one researcher observed that 85 percent of the people touch each other during the period surrounding arrivals and departures.[33]

Dress

(Photo courtesy of The National Broadcasting Company, Inc.)

When we mention projecting an image, dress immediately comes to mind. It is impossible to escape the bombardment of fashion advertisements and fashion magazines promising us a new love or the right job if we purchase the correct wardrobe. When we stop to think, however, that people do form impressions about the way we dress, especially critical first impressions, perhaps those ads are not that farfetched.

> *Be neither too early in the fashion, nor too long out of it; nor at any time in the extremities of it.*
>
> *Lavater*

Learning about Proper Dress

Many people fail to dress right because they simply haven't been taught how. We can spend hundreds of dollars to attend charm schools or executive-image courses, or we can take the time to read some fashion magazines or books about proper dress and learn much of the same information. A series of executive-look books for both men and women are available in most stores, and although they are written for the mass popular audience, they do contain common-sense advice on such topics as coordinating a wardrobe and what fashion colors can mix or match.

Dressing for Occasions

When we use the word *occasion*, we do not mean a school dance or a job interview, although these are important. By occasion, we mean learning to judge what is appropriate in different situations. We all know how embarrassing it would be to show up at an informal picnic wearing evening clothes or at a formal dance wearing blue jeans. Yet we may unknowingly violate other occasions by equally improper, although more subtle, means. For years one large corporation has had a rule that executives should always wear navy blue suits, white, long-sleeved shirts, and black shoes. Although such attire has been overdone by some conservative corporate atmospheres, learning not to offend others is one of the best rules for dress. This does not mean that if you show up in a khaki-colored suit that you will be asked to leave. But the adage of dressing not for the job you have but for the job you want is good advice in any situation. By doing so, you signal to your superiors that you will dress to fit your new position when it is awarded. And a superior prefers to avoid the risk of poor dress habits' creating embarrassing business situations when someone else can be promoted whose choice of clothes presents much less risk.

Dress and Self-Concept

While teaching at Purdue University, a public-speaking professor named Bruce Kendall had a rule that students delivering speeches were to dress up in appropriate attire. For men, this included a coat and tie; for women it meant a nice dress or suit. Although he did not grade speeches on the way the students dressed, Kendall knew that looking good had a great deal to do with positive self-concept and, therefore, gave the students more self-confidence in giving their speeches. Feeling good about the way we look means that we will relate positively to others, and therein lies one of the key steps towards good interpersonal communication.

olor

Before concluding our discussion of nonverbal communication, we need to briefly alert ourselves to the influence of color on interpersonal interaction.

Major magazines know by looking at sales figures that certain color combinations on the front covers sell better on the newsstands than other color combinations. In some cases, this research has even suggested that certain audiences prefer certain colors. In our dress, colors not only say something about ourselves but also provide that all important self-concept. Consider how much you are aware of the colors you wear. When you buy a pair of jeans, other than fashion jeans, do you wash them to fade them before you'll wear them? Do you sometimes want to wear something bright to make you stand out in the crowd? Do you sometimes want to wear something dark or neutral to blend in with what others are wearing and to belong, as it were? If you answered yes, then you are sensitive to colors.

In some situations, dressing in darker greys, blues, and blacks can increase the wearer's credibility better than lighter colors. Notice how attorneys dress when they are in court. Light, flashy colors can be distracting, although your being too polished can lead some people to believe you are trying to hide something. Different seasons, different parts of the country, and a host of other factors determine what colors affect us and when.

When you are concerned about what color of clothes to wear, analyze the situation. What will other people be wearing? What colors will project the image you want to project in relation to the other people who may be present? To what degree do you want to stand out from or blend in with the crowd? You may need to weigh your own self-concept against the norm. Wearing what you feel comfortable in may be more important than what others expect you to wear.

Colors of the surrounding area may also affect interpersonal communication. Observe those colors when you enter a room. How does the color reflect on your mood and the mood of others? Warm, muted shades, for example, are more relaxing than hot, intense shades.

Time

In American culture, time communicates messages. In fact, the importance of this elusive element has even found its way into our figures of speech: "Time is Money" "Time is of the Essence" "Time Waits for No Man—Or Woman."

Consider the different ways that time helps or hinders our communication. If you begin your day without enough time to do everything necessary before leaving for school or work, the people around you may see an impersonal, hassled individual who continually spouts harsh words. "Hurry up and get out of the bathroom." "Isn't breakfast ready yet?" "Don't bother me now!" are phrases which communicate little care about the feelings of others. At work or at school, the pace may continue with even greater consequences to fellow students or workers.

DOONESBURY
by Garry Trudeau

Being late is another message communicated with time. You have made an appointment to arrive for a job interview at 9:00 A.M. Instead you arrive at 9:05. How will five minutes affect the interview? First, it may affect your own self-concept. You may perceive yourself as a person who has just indicated to a prospective employer, "I am not interested in this job." During the interview, you may feel awkward and anxious and may talk too fast, thinking that you have already wasted five precious minutes. And the prospective employer may have received the very impression you fear—that you are not interested in the job and that if you are hired, you will be late for work just as you were late for the interview.

When speaking, the timing of silence or pauses can have a profound effect on meaning. Consider what happens when a person finishes a sentence and then simply stops talking.[34] How long will you wait until you feel obligated to say something, regardless of whether or not you had planned to speak or had anything important to say? When a person who is criticizing another finishes with the criticism, what will the silence communicate? Such phrases as "Well, what do you have to say for yourself?" "What do you think your punishment should be?" and "You're fired!" are communicated without a single word simply by the silence. Consider what happens in a classroom when the teacher asks a question. If no one knows the answer and the teacher just stands there mute, you can literally feel the tension consuming the room. After such an experience takes place, the rest of the class period may also be filled with tension. Actually, the length of the silence was in itself a form of verbal punishment.

SUMMARY

Nonverbal communication creates images without words. These messages repeat, substitute, complement, regulate, and accent our language.

Two major factors affecting nonverbal communication are territorial space and personal space. Territorial space can be defined by physical boundaries. Whether we're at home, school, or work, territorial space influences our social relationships. Personal space, on the other hand, is best described as psychological space. Friendship, age and status, praise and negative criticism, sex, culture, situation, topic, and psychological makeup are some of the means by which we determine our personal spaces.

Many of the impressions other people have of us are formed by what our bodies look like and what we do with our bodies. For example, the basic shapes of our bodies can be classified as endomorphic, mesomorphic, and ectomorphic. The first refers to a short and fat body, the second to a muscular body, and the third to a tall and skinny body. Although it is important to understand body types, it is equally important not to draw stereotypes from them. Smell, hair, and skin color also send nonverbal messages.

Our body movements can be grouped into emblems, illustrators, and adaptors. Emblems replace words and have very specific meanings. Illustrators complement words and have less specific meanings. Adaptors help us adjust to our environment. Our postures also send nonverbal messages as do our facial expressions.

Other components of nonverbal communication include our eyes, vocal paralanguage, touching behavior, dress, and color. Through mutual gaze, we can control the channels of communication and adapt our eye behaviors to help us send and receive messages. Paralanguage is language which travels alongside our words. The tempo, pitch, and resonance of our voices are examples of paralanguage. Touch plays a part in early life and gradually adapts to social norms in less intimate relationships. Our dress plays a big part in our self-concept, and color can influence emotion and establish credibility.

In some societies, time is an important factor in interpersonal relationships. Being kept waiting and being late for appointments can project impressions of disrespect as well as affect our self-concepts.

OPPORTUNITIES FOR FURTHER LEARNING

ACKERMAN, P. and M. KAPPELMAN, *Signals: What Your Child is Really Telling You.* New York: Dial Press, 1977.

BAUM, A. and Y. M. EPSTEIN, eds., *Human Response to Crowding.* New York: John Wiley, 1978.

BIRREN, F., *Color and Human Response.* New York: Van Nostrand Reinhold, 1978.

BOSMAJIAN, H., *The Rhetoric of Nonverbal Communication: Readings.* Glenview: Scott, Foresman, 1971.

BURGOON, J. K. and T. J. SAINE, *The Unspoken Dialogue: An Introduction to Nonverbal Communication.* Boston: Houghton Mifflin Company, 1978.

GOFFMAN, E., *Relations in Public.* New York: Basic Books, 1971.

HALL, E. T., *The Silent Language.* New York: Doubleday Anchor Books, 1973.

HOPSON, J. L., *Scent Signals.* New York: Morrow, 1979.

KNAPP, M. L., *Essentials of Non-Verbal Communication, Brief Edition.* New York: Holt, Rinehart & Winston, 1980.

MAYER, L. V., *Fundamentals of Voice and Diction* (6th ed). Dubuque, IA: Wm. C. Brown Co. Publishers, 1982.

MEHRABIAN, A., *Public Places and Private Spaces.* New York: Basic Books, 1976.

MORRIS, D., *Gestures.* Briarcliff Manor, NY: Stein and Day, 1979.

MORRIS, D., P. COLETT, P. MARSH, and M. O'SHAUGHNESSY, *Gestures: Their Origins and Distribution.* London: Jonathan Cape, Ltd., 1979.

NIERENBERG, G. I. and H. H. CALERO, *How to Read a Person Like a Book.* New York: Hawthorn, 1971.

ZAKAS, S., *Lifespace: A New Approach to Home Design.* New York: MacMillan, 1977.

chapter six

Relationships

PREVIEW   *After completing this chapter, we should be able to:*

Discuss the role of communication in a relationship.
Describe "circles of experience" and how we merge them to form relationships.
Compare and contrast the depth and breadth of a relationship.
Explain how communication can break down in a relationship.
List and define Knapp's stages in the coming-together and coming-apart process.
Understand variations in relationships.
Distinguish between an orthodox relationship, sharing, and a cohabitant relationship.
Realize that the changing values in our society can affect our interpersonal relationships.
Describe communication variables in relationships.
Understand the issues in researching relationships.

When actor, writer, and director Alan Alda of M*A*S*H fame was interviewed about his movie "The Four Seasons," he explained that he had wanted to write about friendship because it is such a powerful force in our lives. People, he noted, work very hard at being friends, and it is a very difficult and sometimes painful process. One of the reasons it is painful is that when people become closer to each other, they see deeper into each other's lives. That makes them vulnerable because their deficiencies may be noticed.

The Role of Communication in a Relationship

Relationships, of which friendships are a part, are powerful forces in our lives. And all of them can sometimes be very painful. Interpersonal communication can be considered the glue which holds any relationship together. It can also be said that the lack of this glue or glue that is improperly mixed, just like two chemicals that violently react to each other, can tear a relationship apart.

This chapter does not tell you how to glue together every relationship. Although interpersonal communication can sometimes determine whether relationships will progress beyond mere acquaintance to intimacy, it can also determine when such relationships should stay at the level of an acquaintance. At the very beginning of this book, we talked about a student who expressed her satisfaction with a dating relationship because of the "good talks" the couple had. In this chapter, we talk more about those "good talks" and how the different factors of interpersonal communication affect our ability to develop relationships and dissolve them.

What we talk about is not necessarily new. We have already touched upon the basics of interpersonal needs and the different approaches to interpersonal communication in Chapter 1. In addition, we have examined self-concept, how to improve listening skills, the role of language and nonverbal communication, and interpersonal communication in small groups. We now want to examine how these concepts apply when we're developing relationships, from acquaintances to intimate encounters.

The Depth of a Relationship

We can examine relationships in many ways.[1] We can break them up into beginnings and endings and not worry too much about what happens in between. Our concentration in these instances would be on the interpersonal communication at the "hello" and "goodbye" stages. Or we can examine relationships by relying on the developmental approach to interpersonal communication.[2] This approach follows the relationship from its beginning through its development to greater levels of intimacy. In some relationships, this development stops at friendship, an elusive quality in itself. In others, it gets much more intimate, as in relationships that husbands and wives share. We can, then, view relationships in terms of the different levels of involvement with each individual's circles of experience.

Circles of Experience

Imagine that the set of circles within circles in Figure 6-1 represents one individual, and that each ring represents different levels of information about the individual.[3] At the center circle is our core of experience, our most private thoughts and feelings. Existing here are things we do not divulge to any other individuals regardless of how intimate our relationships with them become. Perhaps an inner circle of experience represents a favorite place where we can go to be alone and ponder the world. Although there would be nothing earth shattering about telling our best friend or even our wife, husband, or lover about such a place, we cherish it as part of our individuality and simply have no desire to divulge it to anyone. Other inner circles may be even more intimate, such as sexual fantasies.

In many ways, these inner circles are not harmful to a relationship. When they become so or when they interfere with our own self-concept or ability to function with others, then it may be time to consult professional help. As we learned earlier in this text, inclusion can be a powerful interpersonal need, and sometimes penetrating our center core serves a purpose, if only to release pent-up emotions and share them with other people. The question invariably becomes: To whom do we divulge our private thoughts, and what will be the consequences?

Nearer the outside of the circle are pieces of information we don't mind revealing: our favorite colors, our favorite foods, or our feelings about the weather, for example. In between the outer and inner cores is a host of other information which may not be terribly confidential but which may be something we don't want to broadcast to the world; our grades in school can be in this category. Divulging such information is called *selective disclosure*.

FIGURE 6-1

We all have different circles of experience, the most "public" information about ourselves represented by the outer circles and our innermost "private" thoughts represented by the inner circles.

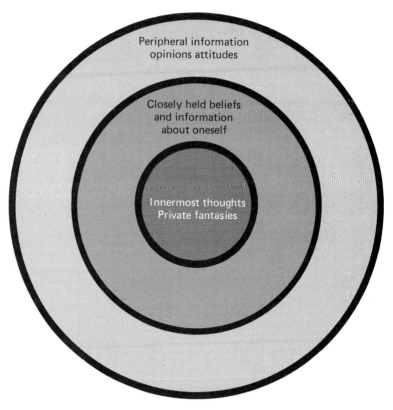

Peripheral information opinions attitudes

Closely held beliefs and information about oneself

Innermost thoughts Private fantasies

Real friendship is a slow grower and never thrives unless engrafted upon a stock of known and reciprocal merit.

Lord Chesterfield

Merging Circles of Experience How do our circles of experience affect our interpersonal relationships? Suppose we've just met another person. This person also has a series of life experiences which can be represented by circles (Figure 6–2). Our first greeting with the person enables both of us to penetrate a very small part of each other's circles.[4] Our exchange might be, "How's it going?" "Great! How's everything for you?" "Just fine, thanks." We've exchanged information on a very superficial level.

Earlier in this text, we examined a communication model and discussed how communication between two people is based on *homophily*—the shared characteristics between individuals. Now examine our two circles and let them represent two people engaged in a relationship. In this relationship, we assume that homophily is represented by the amount of overlap between the two circles. In a beginning relationship, such as the first greeting just described, or a casual acquaintance, the two circles overlap only slightly (Figure 6–2). The things that are shared between the two individuals may be very limited. In very close relationships between two people, a great deal more overlap of the circles of experience exists (Figure 6–3). The two people have found common ground, discovered in large part through interpersonal communication, and are building upon shared experiences.

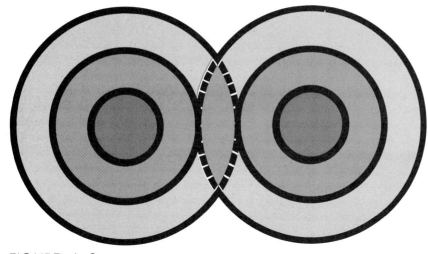

FIGURE 6-2

In casual friendships and acquaintances, we share less intimate information about ourselves with each other.

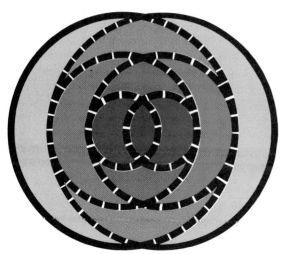

FIGURE 6-3

In close and intimate relationships, we share our innermost thoughts. Yet some information still may remain "private."

The Breadth of a Relationship

We have been discussing relationships in terms of how much one person penetrates the inner core of another person. We should also remember that relationships have breadth as well as depth. The two terms tend to be confusing, because they hinge on how people define breadth and depth. For our purposes, the word *depth refers to the degree of intimacy in any given topic area. Breadth refers to the number of different subjects covered in a given topic area.*

Research has labled three
dimensions of interpersonal attraction: social attraction,
physical attraction, and task attraction. Read the statements
associated with each dimension and evaluate your relationship with another person based
on these statements.

To best understand breadth and depth, let's consider
the example of money. Suppose we reveal to a friend how much money we
make a year. Because this disclosure is more important than our feelings
about the weather but not as important as our most private thoughts, on our
concentric circles this information might appear halfway between the outer
perimeter and the inner core. Sharing knowledge of our salary has a certain
depth. Yet if, in addition to our salary, we also disclose how much income tax
we pay, how much interest we earn on a savings account, what stocks we
hold, and other similar information, then our revelation takes on considerable more breadth.

The Flexibility of Breadth and Depth

To conclude our discussion of breadth and depth, we should understand
that the two dimensions: (1) can differ from one individual to another; and
(2) are flexible. We used the example of salary information's being midway
between the outer perimeter and the inner core of our circles. That may be
fine for one person but not for another. Another person may consider this
same information very important and would not dream of revealing it except to someone very close, and perhaps not even then. Similarly, within the
same topic, some information may be more critical than other information.
How much you have in your checking account may be less important to you
than your salary. Whereas you may not hesitate to tell a friend how much
money is in your checking account, you might only tell someone very close
to you the amount of your salary.

Communication Breakdowns in Relationships

Reflecting upon all that we have discussed in this chapter, we can see the
tremendous potential for communication breakdowns in a developing relationship. The most obvious problem comes from misreading just how far
into another person's circles of experience a given topic lies. Consider two
people who go out on a date. Both are highly attracted to each other, but one
person misjudges the level of the relationship in terms of what is the appropriate type of interpersonal interaction. This indiviual asks: How do you
feel about having babies? How the other person feels is not the point. What
is the point is that the other person does not consider that this is an appropriate question to ask at this stage of the relationship. As a result, that
person builds up a psychological defense, and the conversation regresses to
superficial topics.

Consider a business-related example. An employee
discusses a problem with a supervisor. Listening to the employee, the super-

visor senses that the real problem has nothing to do with the company but rather with the employee's personal relationship with her husband. The supervisor is faced with making a decision. If he or she asks the employee about personal matters, it may help solve the problem, but he or she also runs the risk of penetrating the employee's inner circle of experiences and of creating a defensive, nonproductive reaction. On the other hand, the supervisor realizes that until the employee feels comfortable about discussing her personal problem, she will be less than productive at work.

Every day in every type of relationship, opportunities exist for communication breakdowns. The problem is especially acute in developing relationships because neither person is quite sure of the breadth or depth of topics which are appropriate at these early stages of the relationship. To better understand these concerns, let's examine a hypothetical relationship.

Earlier we talked about examining relationships during their beginning and ending stages. We also discovered that we would miss a great deal about what happens in between if we just studied the point at which people say "hello" and "goodbye."[5] As a result, we divide a relationship into more component parts for the following case study. Various scholars have used different terms and different divisions to explain developing and deteriorating relationships. In his book *Social Intercourse*, Mark Knapp chose to divide the "coming together" of stages of interaction into: initiating, experimenting, intensifying, integrating, and bonding. Because all relationships do not stay together, we also examine what Knapp calls the "coming-apart" process. Here the interaction stages are labeled: differentiating, circumscribing, stagnating, avoiding, and terminating.

Friendships are fragile things, and require as much care in handling as any other fragile and precious thing.

Randolph S. Bourne

Case Study of a Relationship

We follow the development of these communication patterns as two students named Jim and Janet meet in a college chemistry class. One day Jim arrives late for class and the only seat vacant is next to Janet. Jim moves across the row of seats, excusing himself as he maneuvers his way to the empty place. Sitting down, he looks at Janet and whispers,

> "Hi. Kind of a tight squeeze, isn't it?"
> "I guess so," Janet replies.
> "Has the prof said anything important?"
> "Not yet, she's just going over last week's notes."
> "Great. Guess I didn't miss too much."

By now the professor is concentrating on new material, and the conversation between Jim and Janet stops as each begins to take notes.

Finally class ends, and the two walk out of the room together. When they reach the hallway, Janet looks at Jim and says,

> "Do you understand this material?"
> "Some of it. I felt like cutting class last week to go to the mountains but was afraid I would be lost forever."
> "I know what you mean. I really don't think I was cut out to be a chemistry major."
> "The exam next week has me petrified. I need a C to make sure I get through the course."

Jim and Janet walk more slowly as they continue to talk, then introduce themselves to each other. Gradually the other students pass them. Jim, after a brief moment of silence, looks at Janet and remarks:

> "I noticed your Long Beach sweatshirt. Is that your home?"
> "No, I visited some friends there last month and picked it up then. Actually, I'm from Santa Barbara, but we haven't lived there since I was young. My father is in the Navy, and he's stationed at San Diego. Where are you from?"
> "L.A. I'm not sure how I ended up going to school in Oregon."

Both begin to sense the other's need to get to the next class. After walking part way across campus, they come to a point at which each goes in a different direction.

> "It's been nice talking to you," Jim says a bit haltingly. "May I call you?"
> "OK," Janet replies with a bit of hesitancy.

Over the next weekend, they date twice. At the end of the second evening together, Jim asks,

> "If you aren't busy this weekend, would you like to get together and study for the exam? We could go to the beach?"
> "I'd love to."

The weekend at the beach turns out to be fun for both Jim and Janet, although not much studying is done. They spend a lot of time talking about each other's interests, families, friends, hobbies, feelings, and opinions about sex and personal commitments.

For the next few weeks, they are with each other almost constantly. When one is seen alone on campus, it isn't unusual for one of their close friends to ask where the other one is. Jim liked the Long Beach sweatshirt so much that Janet has arranged for a friend to get one for him. Each seems to care for the other's needs. They review their chemistry notes together to make sure the other has not missed anything. Each is frequently the guest for meals at the other's apartment.

Spring comes, and both Jim and Janet manage to land jobs near Seattle. By the end of the summer after their senior year, they are engaged.

At first everything is fine, but then problems creep in. Each has spent enough time with the other to begin to know feelings even when they aren't talking to one another. Gradually, when they do talk, their conversations deal more with things they do not share than with things they do. Finally, it becomes obvious that the relationship which had developed in the atmosphere of a college campus is not working in the real world. Each becomes involved in his or her own world and finds the other less and less interesting.

By Thanksgiving, the relationship has deteriorated to the point that both Janet and Jim realize it is better not to say anything to each other rather than bring up old memories which only cause hurt feelings. Any topic of discussion is on dangerous ground. Although they still see each other and remain engaged, their time together is spent avoiding conversation. Comments such as, "I'd rather not talk about that"; "Do we have to dwell on that again?"; and "Let's just skip the whole thing" become more and more frequent.

Between Thanksgiving and early December, the relationship seems to be in limbo. One topic of conversation which is definitely off limits is the relationship itself. They deliberately go out with other couples to avoid having to talk about each other. When the evenings with the other couples end, Jim and Janet begin to feel awkward and engage more in unrelated small talk than in things of substance. Although each feels uncomfortable in the other's presence, neither wants to take the responsibility for dealing openly with the fact that nothing between them seems positive or even remotely related to what their lives had been like when they dated on campus.

Then one afternoon in mid-December, Janet tells Jim she wants to be with her parents over the holidays, and she feels he should also spend the holidays someplace else without her. At first Jim is defensive, then agrees to the temporary separation. He wants them to be together up until the time Janet leaves for home, but she disagrees and tells him her work is too demanding. She simply cannot spend much time with him.

It isn't long after New Year's that Janet's phone rings. Jim wants to see her and talk. She agrees, and they make arrangements to meet for lunch at a local restaurant that had been their favorite place when they first arrived in Seattle. When Janet arrives, Jim immediately notices she is not wearing the engagement ring.

"I really do not care to order," Janet exclaims as she sits down, making no effort to unbutton her coat.

She then glances away from Jim saying, "It's over. You know it's over. I know it's over. There is no use torturing each other any longer with false hopes and illusions."

For the next few minutes, both utter a few putdowns, then realize they are being childish. It is over. Both understand that a relationship which had been created in the world of the college campus amid weekend parties, peer approvals, few obstacles, few worries, and few distractions has now taken on a different perspective.

K napp's Stages of Interaction

Who knows, maybe Janet and Jim will get back together again. No way? Possibly, but in the meantime we want to analyze their relationship in terms of Knapp's stages of interaction.[6] As we have already learned, these can be broken down into the stages which exist in the coming-together and the coming-apart processes.

Stages in the Coming-Together Process *Initiating* Initiating is the beginning stage of any relationship, whether it lasts a lifetime or a few minutes. Initiating represents the first contact with another. For Janet and Jim, that occurred as Jim sat down next to Janet in chemistry class and said, "Hi. Kind of a tight squeeze isn't it?" We could conclude that the initiating stage ended when the professor began to lecture. During the initiating stage, interaction is on a superficial level, with little breadth or depth.

Not all relationships begin quite as naturally as Jim and Janet's. Baseball player Tom Seaver reportedly met his wife when he was a student at Fresno State. Friends dared him to tackle a particular coed. He did. Such tactics apparently had some effect on advancing the relationship because Seaver and the coed were married to each other two years later.

The late movie producer Nicholas Schenck reportedly tried a similar tactic. While aboard a friend's yacht, he noticed a "pert young woman" on the wharf. Unable to control an urge to push her in the water, and not even knowing if she could swim, he gave her a shove anyway. When she reacted by blinking the water out of her eyes and giving him a big smile, they hit it off, and were eventually married. A friendly warning: Do not assume that these dramatic examples are supported by research which might suggest similar results on all occasions (or even a few).[7]

Experimenting By the time Jim and Janet reached the hallway, their relationship had progressed to the experimenting stage. Here, the interaction took on more breadth. Their personal "circles" began to merge as they exchanged the basic information about how well they were mastering the chemistry course. Although each may have been in some way attracted to the other, it wasn't the time for one of them to suggest spending the weekend at the beach. A required period of small talk takes place. The talk is

"safe" with little risk to the other person. Mild disagreement has little consequences. Having a person tell you he or she doesn't understand chemistry is
less of a blow than being turned down on an invitation to spend a weekend
at the beach. Still, the small talk did perform a basic function. It lessened the
risk for deeper interaction. ("We've agreed on some things; maybe Janet will
agree to go to the beach.") When the potential of a much more intimate encounter is on the mind of either person, the experimenting stage can be
looked at as a security blanket, something to cushion the fall if the conversation, upon approaching more personal depth, results in one person's saying
"no."

Intensifying For Janet and Jim the intensifying stage occurred at the
beach. Although we were not privy to the conversations which took place at
the beach, we can assume that very personal information was exchanged.
We read that they talked about each other's interests: "families, friends, hobbies, feelings, and opinions about sex and personal commitments." Their
beach talk was far more personal and informal than that which occurred in
the hallway outside the chemistry class. Nonverbal communication played a
bigger role. For example, at times, touching may increase while verbal interaction decreases. Even though it may be perfectly natural to walk silently
on the beach holding hands, such behavior would have been awkward and
unacceptable the day they first met and were walking across campus from
chemistry class.

Integrating The integrating stage appeared when Janet and Jim began to
view themselves, and to be viewed by others, more as partners than as individuals. Their own commitment to interaction was seen in Janet's giving
Jim a sweatshirt, in helping each other with chemistry, and in fixing meals
for each other. Friends confirmed the integrating stage by asking where the
other person was when seeing one of them alone. Jim and Janet's interaction with each other and with other people took on a dual quality. The word
"I" was often replaced with "we."

I am reminded that it is also possible to "rhetorically
lapse" back to previous stages of a relationship even after bonding takes
place. When my wife, Denise, and I decided to build a new home, we agreed
to do much of the work ourselves. Because of her schedule, she was unable
to begin the painting and staining until I had completed a floor-to-ceiling
stone hearth in the recreation room. After days of lugging stone, sand, and
cement by myself, I began to catch myself using the word "my" instead of
"our" when talking to her about the house. She pointed this out to me, and I
realized that it was not until a few weeks later when we both began to work
on the house together that I stopped having to catch myself saying "I" and
the word "our" seemed perfectly natural. When I was writing this book,
Denise suggested that I ask my readers what would have happened if she
had not worked on the house. Any ideas?

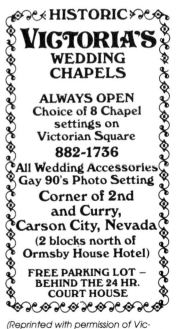

*(Reprinted with permission of Vic-
torian Square, Carson City, Nevada)*

Bonding The bonding stage of Jim and Janet's relationship occurred when they became engaged. In *Social Intercourse*, Mark Knapp succinctly refers to the bonding stage as "a public ritual that announces to the world that commitments have been formally contracted."[8]

Stages in the Coming-Apart Process

Differentiating As Janet and Jim's relationship began to come apart, they talked more about what they did *not* share than what they did. At this point, it was becoming obvious that something was going wrong with the relationship. Although they may not have openly engaged in heated arguments, they were in disagreement and did not see each other in the "we" stages that had preceded this stage of the relationship.

Circumscribing The circumscribing stage was recognized by Jim and Janet's carefully avoiding interaction that referred to their relationship. When one said, "I'd rather not talk about that" or some other similar phrase, the circumscribing stage had arrived.

Stagnating Gradually they began to feel uncomfortable with each other, and the relationship lapsed into stagnation. The period between Thanksgiving and mid-December was undoubtedly painful for both Jim and Janet. Conversations were most likely unpleasant.

Avoiding Avoiding the unpleasantness and pain became the avoiding stage. The decision to spend the holidays apart typified this. If the convenience of the holidays had not occurred, we might assume that the two would have gradually just stopped seeing each other.

Terminating The engagement ring no longer worn and the verbal confirmation of the ended relationship were all rituals of the terminating stage of the relationship.

Variations in Relationships

Not all relationships follow the exact sequential pattern we described in our example of Jim and Janet.

Micro and Macro Relationships

Smaller or *micro* relationships can take place within longer *macro* relationships. During the time that Jim's and Janet's relationship was coming apart, there may have been short periods when things were going smoothly, when the relationship reverted back to the kinds of interpersonal interaction that occurred when they first met.

| Omitting Stages of Interaction | In some relationships, interaction stages may actually be omitted. Bonding may never take place or termination may not exist until the death of one of the partners. Some relationships stay together and do not venture, in a macro sense, through the coming-apart stages. |

| "Parking" Stages | These "ideal" stages occur as the relationship parks or stops at a given stage at which the partners, for "better or worse," try to meet each other's needs. Couples reach a point at which they accept each other's differences and do not feel they are sacrificing their own identities in accepting those differences as part of the relationship. |

Types of Relationships

(Robert Wagner and Stephanie Powers of the television series, HART TO HART. Courtesy: Spelling-Goldberg Productions)

In addition to considering the interaction stages and the variations in those stages, still another way of examining interpersonal interaction is to analyze different types of relationships. We look at three types of relationships based on previous research centering around such things as the amount and type of interaction, values and beliefs, nonverbal "space," and sensitivity to interpersonal interaction.[9]

Orthodox Relationships

Both partners in an orthodox relationship have traditional beliefs. Each partner functions in the "we" state with little individuality in the relationship. If we were monitoring the interaction among partners in an orthodox relationship, we might find their identities to be tightly linked to the relationship itself, as opposed to being linked to their own uniqueness as individuals. We might also assume that as an orthodox relationship developed, interpersonal communication was quite successful at the integrating stage when the two people merged into one. To others, such a couple might be known as "the Smiths" rather than as John Smith and Mary Smith. Least satisfactory to this type of relationship would be the avoiding stage, because in the face of conflict, orthodox couples would rather meet together and talk things out instead of avoid each other.

Each individual is dependent on the other individual, and each does not hesitate to express feelings and wishes to the other person. Self-disclosure is the norm in an orthodox relationship. Few things are kept hidden from the other partner, and each individual builds upon the strength of the other. Each person in an orthodox relationship does not hesitate to express affection for the other person, and orthodox couples are more likely to express satisfaction with the relationship itself. Because of this high degree of emotional and psychological linkage, both partners find it easy to agree on issues which directly affect their relationship. More traditional sex roles are common in such a relationship, such as the woman's taking care of the children while the husband works.

Sharing

A variation on the orthodox relationship is one which we can label sharing. Sharing takes place between the individuals, but each individual retains a great deal of autonomy in his or her own life. The autonomy itself can be one of the things the couple has "in common." Couples whose partners pursue their own careers fall into this category. Other qualities of the sharing relationship include a couple's outspokenness, which is directly related to the individuals' autonomy. In many ways, this outspokenness will carry over into social situations as well, and the partners may openly disagree with each other. Orthodox couples, on the other hand, may be more reserved in social situations, reflecting their "public" commitment to their relationship and support for each other. Affection is more difficult to express among sharing couples. Also, because they do not hesitate to disagree on matters in which each is ego-involved, each tends to be less satisfied with the other person's ability to communicate interpersonally.

At first, it may seem that in traditional bonding terms, such as engagements or marriage, sharing relationships are off to a rough start. This may not be the case. Because of each partner's strong self-concept —strong enough to permit autonomy to exist in the relationship—enough

180   Relationships

TO WIDOWERS AND SINGLE GENTLEMEN
WANTED

By a lady, a situation to superintend the household and preside at the table. She is: agreeable, becoming, careful, desirable, English, facetious, generous, honest, industrious, judicious, keen, lively, merry, natty, obedient, philosophic, quiet, regular, sociable, tasteful, useful, vivacious, womanish, xantippish, youthful, zealous. Address all inquiries to: XYZ, Simmons Library, Edgeware Road, London.

individual self-worth is present to sustain each other's independence. Such individuals are also tolerant of varied sex roles for each partner. They might share equal chores in housework. Each might contribute substantially to the family income. They can be tolerant of role reversal in which the man stays at home to take care of the house while the wife works.

Cohabitants Consider a couple who exists in what we commonly call "separate worlds." Both in verbal and nonverbal communication, interaction plays a small role in their relationship. Although they may sleep in the same room, much of their time is spent in different parts of the living quarters, outside of each other's presence. Although they may have little in common, they avoid conflict by staying out of each other's way. Although they stay together, there is little commitment from both partners to the relationship itself. Because of the separateness, they are mostly inexpressive to the other partner. Affection, empathy, and understanding may be perceived as not existing in the relationship.

We have examined three types of relationships. Now let's ask ourselves what can happen and what kinds of communication patterns can result when an individual with the basic characteristics of a sharing person is involved in a relationshp with someone who is a cohabitant or an orthodox? How can a knowledge of interpersonal communication help each individual adapt to the other person?

Changing Values and Relationships

"Society is changing." "It's a new era." "We are a liberated society." Those comments reflect the changing values in our society which can have profound effects on both the kinds of relationships in which people engage and on the various stages of interaction that take place.

NO-FAULT RELATIONSHIP

No Fault is clean, pristine.
We join in love, serene,
and know that each may choose
to separate, cut the tape.
But I still hesitate.

Inside I feel you may not try
when things get tough. "Enough!"
The struggling flame you'd snuff.

And we would not reach
comfort and security
that only comes from surety.

by Denise

Making and Dissolving Bonds

We have centered on three examples of relationship types. But we do not need to look far to see that our changing society makes it difficult to classify any relationship as exclusively adhering to any one given type. Take, for example, the cohabitants. Looking back into history, we might find that a similar relationship would have advanced through the bonding stage, and then because of the stigma of divorce, the bond would never have been dissolved.[10] What effect do such things as no-fault divorce, living together out of wedlock, "palimony," and less traditional relationships have on life styles and the different stages of interaction in relationships?

Free Choice and Economics

If we viewed a cohabiting relationship in the 1980s, some might feel it would be foolish to keep the marriage together. Others, who deeply believe in traditional values built upon family or religious experiences, may feel differently. The point is that in some segments of our society, both choices are being made more freely than in the past. Economic conditions may cause a cohabiting relationship to exist and even be practical. The bonding stage never occurs, but two people, for economic necessity, decide to become roommates and share the cost of rent and food.

Levels and Variety of Involvement

The same couple may be considered as cohabitants on one issue and orthodox on another. For example, both are autonomous in their relationships, pursue different careers, and need little support from the other person. On the other hand, they may be intimately involved sexually, not share that intimacy with anyone else, and, in their verbal and physical interaction with each other, be very supportive and able to participate in a great deal of shared affection.

Communication Variables in Relationships

At any given stage of a relationship, different factors can influence the way people communicate. Nonverbal communication is one example. You would not go up to someone you just met and place your hand on his or her genitals. Yet such behavior occurring in private by two people who have been sexually intimate for years may be acceptable. Intercultural factors can also play a part.

Nonverbal Communication The part played by nonverbal communication in relationships in western culture can be plotted as a sequence of steps starting with eye-to-body contact. Despite what may lie in our hearts, we look at bodies first. Depending on the situation, we may then greet the person in some type of eye-to-eye and voice-to-voice contact. The twelve-step process towards reaching sexual intimacy would, including the steps we have just discussed, be: (1) eye to body; (2) eye to eye; (3) voice to voice; (4) hand to hand; (5) arm to shoulder; (6) arm to waist; (7) mouth to mouth; (8) hand to head; (9) hand to body; (10) mouth to breast; (11) hand to genitals; (12) genitals to genitals and/or mouth to genitals.[11] Variations do exist. A dating relationship may start with voice-to-voice contact, such as calling up someone for a date based upon seeing his or her picture in a student yearbook. That same date may end with a good-night kiss without one person's having ever put an arm around the other person's waist.

Stop and consider the relationships in which you may have been involved. Regardless of whether or not such relationships reached sexual intimacy, think about the sequence of noverbal contact you had with the other person. Now consider what could have happened or actually did happen, if, based on societal or cultural norms, some of the sequences were violated. What effect did (or could) it have had on your relationship with the other person? If such violations did occur, did they set back the relationship? In what ways did the relationship regain lost ground (or did it ever)?

Language If you have gained some sensitivity to the way nonverbal communication plays a part in the development of a relationship, then you should readily realize that language plays an equally big part. An intimate discussion on the first date may not be comfortable for you to listen to or take part in. For others, such a discussion might be perfectly natural and lead to an increased level of self-disclosure.[12]

(Pam Dawber and Robin Williams from the television series, "MORK & MINDY." © Paramount Pictures Corp. All Rights Reserved. All uses restricted without written permission from Paramount Pictures Corp.)

COURTSHIP: Student Love Ritual Easy To Spot

Seattle, Wash. (UPI)—St. Valentine or Don Juan probably could have learned a thing or two from David Givens.

Givens spent a good part of the last three years scrutinizing the getting-to-know-you rituals of males and females in student dining rooms at the University of Washington.

Givens isn't a spy or a voyeur. He's not even a romantic. He's an anthropologist, and he kept a close watch on coquetry in the interest of science—and a doctor's degree.

What he learned about love among the coffee cups and salt shakers is as old as Adam and Eve. And it isn't likely to change despite women's lib or any macho renaissance.

Givens, who chronicled his findings in an article published in the Psychiatric Journal, said flirtation, seduction and courtship fall into patterns regardless of how magical it may seem to the participants. In fact, he said, the processes are so invariable they can be categorized.

A cafeteria conquest usually starts with a girl sitting alone. The male enters and sits at the farthest corner of the same table, and the attention phase commences.

The male turns so the front of his body faces the woman, but he keeps his head turned. He looks at the table, then off to the side. Before long, his gaze begins to sweep across her gaze.

If the glance is returned, both begin tossing their heads and smiling as they adjust the muscle tone of their bodies. Stomach is sucked in, posture improves and the chest is expanded. Both begin stretching, and they casually groom themselves, hands touching clothing, face and hair.

If all is going smoothly, the recognition phase begins. The two look at each other and then down, in unison. They smile at the same time. They toss their heads and tension builds.

This once was called "love at first sight," Givens said. Then both move into submissive postures. Shoulders come up and forward, heads tilt to the side, feet go into a pigeon-toed stance and they clasp themselves.

According to Givens, this body language was designed by nature to show that a person is harmless, regardless of intentions.

If at this point neither has cut off the process by going blank or refusing to return glances, the two now enter into the introduction phase. They talk to each other. What they talk about doesn't matter, Givens said, because the non-verbal language continues. Voices become higher pitched than normal and softer.

The two still glance up and down at each other in unison, and hand motions are rotations of the palms, not the more aggressive pointing motions. As they talk, tension continues to build. They stretch. They yawn. They laugh loudly. But each time they laugh, they look away. Their body motions are in "close harmony, like they are dancing the same rhythm," Givens said.

From then on, nature, whatever it has in mind, takes its course.

There's only one problem with this courtship ritual, Givens said. As soon as it works, it is discarded and that, he said, often is what's wrong with marriages.

"Romance goes out the window. You can tell established couples because there is none of that interaction going on. It is very boring to watch."

As for himself, Givens said he is so self-conscious about his signals, he sometimes is immobilized in dealing with women.

By the way, Givens is 34 and single.

Topics of Conversation A study conducted by researchers Fern Johnson and Elizabeth Aries asked parents of students at The University of Massachusetts about their interactions with their friends.[13] Results of the research suggested that close adult female friends conversed "more often than do close male friends about personal topics or personal problems." Doubts and fears, family problems, and intimate relationships were some of the topics discussed. Moreover, women reported more in-depth conversations about such topics than did men. Male friends exceeded female friends in the frequency of interaction and in the depth of the interaction, but only for the topic of sports.

We could speculate on precisely what causes the differences; the researchers suggested that females may find themselves talking alone with friends whereas males spend more time in groups in which more personal topics of conversation may be less appropriate.

Ask yourself: When I converse with my friends, what do we talk about? Do you find similar patterns to those we've just discussed? Does the topic vary depending on how long you've known the other person? Compare your observations with someone of the opposite sex. See what he or she talks to same-sex friends about and if the topic varies depending on how long or how well they know each other. Do you feel there may be regional differences that could account for the topics of conversations among same-sex friends? Compare people you know from different parts of the country. Are there differences between New Englanders and Southerners? Midwesterners? Westerners?

Trust Few factors can have more influence on a relationship than trust.[14] Trust is critical for two reasons. First, trust is a necessary ingredient for self-disclosure. If two people are going to create homophily and sharing, the type of deep sharing necessary for intimate communication, self-disclosure must take place. For self-disclosure to take place, positive reinforcement is necessary. If, in telling someone about yourself, you disclose personal qualities which you hold important to your self-concept, you do not expect those disclosures to be met with negative criticism and condemnation. You trust the other person not to criticize or condemn.

Second, trust is important to keep the relationship intact and, in developing stages, to keep it progressing. A violation of trust, such as responding negatively to self-disclosure, relating intimate information about another to a third person, or violating a "contract" of the relationship, may cause the relationship to falter. We will now discuss self-disclosure and contract in more detail.

Self-Disclosure Self-disclosure is, as we learned earlier in this text, necessary to develop commonality and for effective communication to take place.[15] The particular type of self-disclosure plays a part in advancing or hindering a relationship. For example, research results

CHANGES—THE DAYS OF CANDLELIGHT
AND PORK CHOPS

Nine years ago today, a wide-eyed boy and a romantic girl were married at a church on a hill in Washington state. The sun was shining—an event itself in that part of Washington—and the happy couple observed that this was a sign of things to come.

They were married two days after graduating from separate universities. It was a large wedding, due largely to refusal by the mother of the bride to accept anything less. At a prearranged lull in the ceremonies, the bride and groom lighted two long, wax-covered wicks, joined the wicks to light a white candle, and extinguished all the flames but the last. The candle burned steadily for the duration of the ceremony, a symbol of their lives becoming one. It was the bride's idea.

The newlyweds returned from their honeymoon to an immediate separation. She spent two months in her native Washington, completing requirements for a teaching certificate, while he found work and a place to live in another state. He bought a bed for $25 at a garage sale and spent several weeks of spare time refinishing a headboard and set of captain's chairs.

Their first "home" was a second-story apartment with no drapes and a 2-inch gap between the carpet and the bottom of the front door. She arrived there from Washington on a Sunday evening; he began a new job the following day. That night they celebrated their first dinner at home—candlelight, new china and pork chops.

The first trouble in Camelot was a miscarriage that was two anxious, painful months in the making. She cried and bled a lot; he called emergency numbers and stayed up worrying. The doctor said it would have been a girl.

No one was hiring speech therapists then, so she had to settle for a dollar-an-hour job serving Kentucky Fried Chicken. No one really expected it to work out. One day a man ordered two dozen wings. She hollered at the kid in the back room to "slaughter a few more," then went in the back room herself and got everybody to make slaughtered-chicken noises. The speech-therapy people called the following week.

Her therapy job put them in the black. They saved and bought a genuine, simulated-wood-grain coffee table, and a new couch to replace the trunk in the living room. The couch cost $125; the coffee table was a steal at $7. They saved some more money and bought a portable, black-and-white television. No subsequent purchase, not even their first home, was half as exciting.

Time brought more money, better opportunities. They moved to a new town, rented a nicer apartment, collected things. After four years alone they had a daughter, who was followed closely by a second. Only death would have affected the proud parents more profoundly. Parenthood brought new dimensions to every emotion.

The days and their events, so sharp and well-defined in those early times, became blurred, less meaningful, in the ever-faster progression of years. Suddenly they weren't newlyweds anymore. Suddenly the babies were toddlers, then people. Suddenly the youthful parents could see the approaching specter of middle age.

One night they took their wedding book from its drawer in the nightstand and looked at its pictures together.

"My God," they said in a single voice, "look how young we were."

They bought a house, sold it and bought another. Of nine years of marriage, seven were sácrificed to the god of remodeling. Life became a collage of bent nails, broken boards, splinter-filled fingers, leaky plumbing, falling plaster, missing tools, short circuits, spilled paint, smelly solvents, endless messes and bitter, angry words.

There were other setbacks, the usual ones—automobile accidents, illnesses, surgery, job problems, money problems, and so on. Somehow they did what they swore they'd never do. They let themselves slip into a routine that had little time for anything but itself: 1) Get up, 2) feed the kids, 3) go to work, 4) come home, 5) work on the house, 6) collapse. On weekends delete 3 and 4.

A rare weekend of introspection brought them to their senses in the nick of time, and they came to date their years together in terms of it. The time after that passed in relative tranquility, but the old pressures were never far away.

Routine gets the upper hand because its demands are immediate and continuous. Work must be done, children must be cared for, homes must be maintained. It isn't easy to be romantic when rain is pouring through the ceiling and the kids are tracking mud across the carpet and the weeds are running amok in the garden. It isn't easy, but what is marriage without it? Somehow there has to be time.

Nine years isn't such a long time, but to that bride and groom it sometimes seems a lifetime since that sunny day on a hill in Washington. They are different. His eyes have narrowed; she keeps finding gray in her hair.

Tonight they'll go to dinner at the nicest restaurant they can afford. They'll have a tipple or two; she might get sentimental. If the time is right, they might say they love each other.

Things change. It won't be candlelight and pork chops, but it will be enough.

Tim Woodward

(Courtesy: Tim Woodward. © The Idaho Statesman. Reprinted by permission)

suggest that intimate information disclosed too early in a relationship will be perceived as inappropriate and will thus hinder the relationship. Deviant disclosure will be even less liked than normal but intimate information. Research suggests that as one person discloses more intimate information at the appropriate stage of a relationship, the other person will follow. Even the way we self-disclose information is important. You can whisper something about yourself and get an entirely different reaction than if you shout it. Although a few people feel that buying space on billboards and hiring skywriters is a great way to say "I love you," the best route may be to mention it quietly in intimate conversation.

Violating Contracts of a Relationship We tend to think of such things as engagement, marriage, and similar ritualistic bonds as forms of contracts, but unwritten contracts also exist between people. Interpersonal communication plays a part in such contracts, because when they are violated, serious breakdowns in communication occur.[16] Let's return to our example of Jim and Janet. Although they dissolved their engagement, each agreed not to discuss their relationship with friends or, perhaps more importantly, with other lovers or mates. This contract is not in writing and may not even be expressed verbally. It is an unwritten contract both will abide by so that despite their broken engagement, they remain friends.

Suppose that at a cocktail party one of the two learns from a complete stranger the story of the broken engagement and ruined love affair. The contract has been violated and broken. The result is that whereas Jim and Janet had managed to piece back their relationship to the point that they were no longer avoiding each other, they now cease to even remain friends.

Cultural Differences
Our examples of the nonverbal steps towards sexual intimacy discussed earlier apply to western cultures. Other cultures have variations on what is appropriate. For example, greeting a same-sex friend by kissing the person on one cheek and then on the other is appropriate in some cultures but not in others.

If you remember back to Chapter 5, we talked about touching behavior in different cultures. We learned of one research study which found that American couples observed in coffee shops touched each other an average of only two times per hour. The same researcher found that in Puerto Rico, the average was 180 times per hour.

Ask yourself what difficulties a relationship might encounter if two people from different cultures were attracted to each other, one from a high-touch culture and the other from a low-touch culture. Would the relationship progress faster or more slowly? By whose standards?

A study conducted by researcher Robert Shuter examined the communication patterns among both white and black populations.[17] Using people recruited from business and social agencies, Shuter found, among other things, that blacks are sensitive to changing their initial greetings based on another person's race and sex. He also found that in initial greetings, black males and black females ask significantly more questions of each other than they do of blacks of the same sex or of whites of either sex. He concluded that for blacks of the opposite sex, a greater frequency of questions is associated with different levels of intimacy. His research also pointed out that previous research that does not distinguish between races may be flawed.

Issues in Researching Communication in Relationships

The study just referred to directs our attention to some of the difficulties in gaining accurate information about what precisely does happen to interpersonal communication at various stages of a relationship. We need to keep in mind that relationships vary among individuals, and no set formulas exist to predict precisely what type of interaction will take place in them or even if they represent a particular stage of involvement. For example, much of the research which examines developing relationships deals with data obtained from questionnaires. Many times the subjects are college students. Many times the information is gathered "after the fact."

Moreover, we learn from information which can be verbalized easily. Ask yourself how you would tell someone doing research on relationships precisely the time you fell in love and precisely the time you fell out of love. It would be difficult *to define* love, let alone determine the time it starts and ends.

Anyone who has been romantically and intimately involved with another person realizes just how close to one's inner core the relationship penetrates. Yet the very fact that the relationship does penetrate close to the inner core may make it difficult to relate the "total" experience to someone else, such as a researcher. We have already seen how easily communication breakdowns can occur when two people misjudge the level of a relationship. Equally perplexing are the kinds of research difficulties that exist in gathering and interpreting information about people's relationships.

Adapting what we know about communication patterns between individuals is a difficult, somewhat illusive process. But it is not insurmountable, and you can take part in the experience. By taking a serious approach to learning about the good qualities of interpersonal communication and by adapting those qualities to your own relationships, you will be in a much better position to have meaningful, satisfying experiences, whether they be intimate or casual. You may not avoid the experience of breaking up or feeling the pain of a deteriorating relationship, but you will be able to understand it. And understanding in itself is a very valuable commodity.

SUMMARY

Our discussion began by centering on the difference between breadth and depth in a relationship. Each is defined in terms of information about ourselves. This information is represented by different circles of experience which, during a relationship, come together. Depth refers to the penetration into our personal lives that we disclose and share with others. How wide the range of topics is that we disclose or share refers to the breadth of our relationship. Knowing how wide a variety of topics can be and knowing the depth of our conversations and interactions with others permits us to be sensitive to the many communication breakdowns that can occur the deeper and more involved a relationship becomes.

We examined interaction in a hypothetical relationship between Jim and Janet and then applied that to Mark Knapp's stages of interaction: initiating, experimenting, intensifying, integrating, bonding, differentiating, circumscribing, stagnating, avoiding, and terminating. We examined also different types of relationships.

As examples, we learned about orthodox relationships in which both people are closely tied to the relationship itself; sharing relationships in which both individuals have an autonomy and are less attached to the relationship than in orthodox couples; and cohabitant relationships in which people exist together but have little in common, have little interaction, and express little affection for one another. Because of changes in our society, it is more difficult to categorize any given relationship. The relative ease with which some people make and dissolve bonds, economic necessity, and the different levels and varieties of involvement all contribute to this difficulty.

In conclusion, we examined communication variables in relationships and some issues surrounding research on relationships. Our discussion included the role of nonverbal communication, language, topics of conversation, trust, self-disclosure, and violating the contracts of a relationship. Some of the issues surrounding research include the ability to gather accurate information from a variety of subjects and settings as well as learning about the inner-core thoughts of an individual, which are not easily disclosed.

OPPORTUNITIES FOR FURTHER LEARNING

ALTMAN, I. and D. TAYLOR, *Social Penetration: The Development of Interpersonal Relationships.* New York: Holt, Rinehart & Winston, 1973.

BERNE, E., *Games People Play.* New York: Grove Press, Inc., 1964.

BULEY, J. *Relationships and Communication: A Book for Friends, Co-Workers and Lovers.* Iowa: Kendall/Hunt, 1977.

DAVIS, M. S., *Intimate Relations.* New York: Free Press, 1973.

DUNN, N., *Different Drummers.* New York: Harcourt Brace Jovanovich, Inc., 1977.

EDWARDS, M. and E. HOOVER, *The Challenge of Being Single.* Los Angeles: J. P. Tarcher, Inc., 1974.

EPSTEIN, J. *Divorced in America.* New York: Dutton, 1974.

HESS, H. J. and C. O. TUCKER, *Talking About Relationships* (2nd ed). Prospect Heights, IL: Waveland Press, Inc., 1980.

HYATT, I. R., *Before You Marry Again.* New York: Random House, 1977.

LIDZ, T., *The Person* (rev ed.). New York: Basic Books, 1976.

MAY, R., *Sex and Fantasy: Patterns of Male and Female Development.* New York: W. W. Norton & Co., Inc., 1980.

MORRIS, D., *Manwatching.* New York: Harry N. Abrams, Inc., 1977.

MOULTON, J. S. and R. R. BLAKE, *The Marriage Grid.* New York: McGraw-Hill, 1971.

O'BRIEN, P., *Staying Together.* New York: Random House, 1977.

PATTON, B. and B. RITTER, *Living Together: Female/Male Communication.* Columbus, OH: Charles Merrill Pub. Co., 1976.

REIK, T., *Of Love and Lust.* New York: Jason Aronson, 1974.

ROGERS, C. R., *Becoming Partners: Marriage and Its Alternatives.* New York: Delacorte Press, 1972.

SCHOENFELD, E., *Jealousy: Taming the Green Eyed Monster.* New York: Holt Rinehart and Winston, 1979.

SHERESKY, N. and M. MANNES, *Uncoupling: The Art of Coming Apart.* New York: Viking, 1972.

VILLARD, K. L. and L. J. WHIPPLE, *Beginnings in Relational Communication.* New York: Wiley, 1976.

ZUNIN, L. and N. ZUNIN, *Contact: The First Four Minutes.* Los Angeles: Nash Publishing, 1972.

chapter seven

Interacting in Small Groups

PREVIEW   *After completing this chapter, we should be able to:*

Describe the characteristics of small groups.
Give examples of the functions of small groups.
Compare and contrast types of small groups.
Understand the content of small-group interaction.
Explain the process of interpersonal interaction in small groups.
Discuss power and status among group members.
Distinguish between roles and role conflict in small-group interaction.
Understand the value of trust.
Describe how group size affects group interaction.
Explain how leadership affects personal communication in small groups.
List the qualities of leadership behavior.
Discuss the relationships of leaders to groups.

Venture through the rolling hills of New England, and when you travel down the winding road to the small village or the seaport town, look for the store that still sells candy in the jar and pickles from the barrel. Look for the potbellied stove in the corner, and then let your imagination flow. Let it flow to cold winter days when people used to come and sit by the stove and talk about politics, the weather, the wood supply, the price of fish, or the cost of yarn. If we could have taken part in those stove-side discussions, we would have learned a great deal about small-group interaction. We would have learned why the mayor sat in a particular place and why the store owner sat in a particular place. We would have learned to listen and to not interrupt. We would have seen how a leader emerged for every discussion. And we would have heard about the new ideas, the advice, or the talk around the stove later at our evening dinner tables.

Interacting in Small Groups

Today, some of the country stores, the potbellied stoves, and the discussions still exist. Discussions also take place in the halls of Congress, on college campuses, and in major corporations. Many times group discussion becomes the showcase where leaders and administrators are put "on stage," and where others evaluate their overall effectiveness. If a corporate executive cannot lead and participate in a group discussion or display appropriate and effective communication behavior, then he or she may be thought of as being incompetent during times when not on display.

In this chapter, we will examine how interpersonal communication functions in small groups. Whether we sit in a dormitory room with friends or in a plush office with a board of directors, the knowledge of interpersonal interaction in small groups will help us become responsibly involved in group decision making, personal or professional.

Characteristics of Small Groups

To understand how interpersonal communication affects our abilities to interact in small groups, we will begin by examining the different kinds of small groups. In some ways, these distinctions are academic. All groups are social, although we explain the particular social characteristics of a small social group. Similarly, problem-solving groups can be also task-oriented groups, although we examine what commonly distinguishes one from the other.

Group Size   Whereas one-to-one communication involves two people, group communication requires at least three people. And additional people mean more relationships and "channels" for interpersonal communication.[1] A group with ten people, for example, has forty-five possible relationships; a group of twenty people has 190. When the numbers increase, the changes in factors affecting interpersonal communication also increase. If we break down the relationships still further into nonverbal and verbal communication, the number of possible relationships between members of the group can reach into the thousands. Most of the groups in which we participate have three to five members, and it is in this range that we reference our discussion.

Cohesive Bonding   Something acts as a cohesive force to bond a group together.[2] This may be the task assigned to the group; one example would be a special committee of students appointed by the president of the university to study recreation activities on campus. Another example would be the monthly conducting of business by officers of a sorority or fraternity. In each case, something shared by all members of the group became the bonding force to bring and hold the group together. The members of the special committee shared the fact that they had been appointed by the president. The sorority or fraternity officers shared the fact that they had been elected to their respective offices. These bonds which create and hold groups together are also aids to interpersonal communication. Earlier we learned about homophily—shared experiences between two people which aid communication. In groups brought together for a specific purpose, some homophily automatically exists between group members because they collectively share the experience that brought them together. The key is to retain the cohesive bonding while accomplishing a goal.

Degree of Interaction   For our discussion of small groups, we assume that they participate in frequent face-to-face interaction. Based upon that assumption, we distinguish them by the frequency of their meetings. Small groups in formal settings usually meet on a frequent and regular basis. Such is the case for various clubs, organizations, academic and government committees, or groups charged to meet until a job is accomplished or a goal is met. These frequent interactions permit us to view interpersonal communication in small groups as a developmental process, not as a single situation. As the members become better acquainted, as they realize what to expect from the group, as they learn to whom to address their remarks and what the reactions to those remarks will be, the group begins to change to meet the demands of these more developed relationships. Understanding small-group communication as a process of successive interaction is important to being a responsible participant in small groups.[3]

Interacting in Small Groups

Member Roles Every person participating in small-group communication has a particular function. A leader, for example, is responsible for guiding the group's progress and assuring that every participant's view is heard. The members of the group are responsible for providing information to the group. A group of nurses might be called together by the hospital administrator to discuss the hospital's food service. One nurse may work in intensive care, another may work in obstetrics, and still another may work in orthopedics. During the small-group discussions, each nurse provides information about the food in her particular area.

In less-formalized small groups, members may play different roles. While playing bridge or at a social gathering, the role of the individual may be to interact with other people rather than to solve a particular problem. Yet regardless of what type of small group is gathered together, each individual in it has a role which complements that of the other group members.

Member Rewards Each member of the small group receives some form of reward for participating. An easy way to remember this reward structure is to divide it into two categories: direct and indirect.

Direct Rewards Direct rewards evolve from outcomes of group decision making, tasks accomplished, or problems solved. Assume that you live in a dormitory which has unlimited visitation hours. Although you appreciate the freedom to have people in your room at any hour, you also realize that such a policy results in interrupted study time, infringement on other people's privacy, and a security problem. As a result, the directors of the living unit decide to bring together a committee to discuss the problem and determine if changes in the visitation policy would improve the unit's living arrangements. Each floor of the unit is asked to elect a representative to serve on the committee, and you are elected to represent your floor. Your committee meets regularly until it finally devises a new visitation policy. Specifically, the policy specifies study hours during which visitation is not permitted, requires visitors to go directly to the room of the person they are visiting and not to wander in the halls, and establishes a sign-in desk at which every visitor must be identified by his or her host or hostess.

The direct rewards obtained from participation in the small-group discussion were the goals the group accomplished. For example, the visitation policy permitted time to study, it helped eliminate the problem of guests wandering in the halls and infringing on other people's privacy, and it aided security by having people sign in and be identified by their host or hostess.

Indirect Rewards You also reaped indirect rewards from participating in the small-group discussions. You may have found new friends in the group,

---

WHY DOES EVERYONE HATE MEETINGS?

Three kinds of people attend meetings. Those who want progress, those who don't, and those who want to impress the chairman. 98% of the talk goes to 2% of the problem. Remember the story of the board of trustees who agreed unanimously to spend millions for an atomic reactor, then fell in wild dissension over the request by the freshman basketball coach for a new blackboard. Maybe the air is too soporific. Maybe the carafes of ice water tend to lubricate the long-winded. Maybe the chairs are too comfortable. (A fast food chain designed its chairs to be purposely uncomfortable so people wouldn't linger over their coffee.) At your next meeting, remove the chairs, empty the carafes, turn the thermostat down to 55. A stand-up meeting could be a stand-out.

(© *United Technologies Corporation, 1981*)

and you definitely made some personal contacts which later may prove to be beneficial. Especially meaningful was your election by your peers to serve on the committee. It reaffirmed your self-concept and instilled self-confidence. During the meetings of the committee you also had the opportunity to see how a discussion group works and how responsible interaction can achieve goals. In addition, you experienced well-being by fulfilling that important "inclusion" need of interpersonal communication as you regularly met with people who considered your suggestions.

The next time you are asked to serve with a group, consider both the direct and indirect rewards you will achieve, for yourself and others.

Meeting over Time   Especially in more formal situations, small groups meet over a specified time period. This factor of time determines not only the kind of interpersonal interaction that takes place in groups but also how we approach that interaction. Forgetting that groups meet over time can cause serious problems in group decision making. Let's examine this phenomenon further.

In Chapter 1, we discussed that we could approach the study of interpersonal communication as a developmental process and used a group discussion as an example of this process. In group discussions, interactions with others become building blocks upon which future meetings and future interactions are built. In essence, we interact with someone in a group discussion, and what we say will affect our relationship with that person the next time the discussion group meets.[4] Will what we say improve or hinder interpersonal communication? Will what we say improve or hinder the decision-making ability of the group?

Later in this chapter, we learn how what we say affects the very next comment of others in the group. We also discover that being *too* concerned about our interaction with others can create much goodwill but little results in both group decision making and progress towards goals.

Now that we have considered some of the characteristics of small groups, we will examine the reasons why they function.

Examples of Group Functioning

Looking at different situations can help us pinpoint the reasons why small groups function.[5]

Implementing Policy   The previously described student committee meeting to devise new visitation policies for the living unit was actually implementing policy. Implementing policy is a frequent function of small groups and is most common in government agencies whose committees meet to devise rules and regulations affecting, for instance, business and services. Such organizations as the Small Business Administration, the Federal Trade Commission, and the Federal Communications Commission regularly meet as policy-implementing bodies.[6]

Policy-implementing bodies can also operate in business and educational settings. Boards of directors meet to review the profit and loss of a company and implement policy to change corporate direction. School administrators and teachers meet to establish policies for student athletic-eligibility requirements or academic probation, among others.

Recommending Policy
Groups also function in the capacity of an advisor. The committees of legislative bodies, as opposed to legislative agencies, meet to discuss and recommend policy to larger groups. A comittee of Congress will discuss a legislative proposal and may recommend passage of the proposal to the full House of Representatives. A corporation's personnel committee may meet to discuss who should be promoted and then recommend the names of those people to the persons responsible for their promotions. A committee of teachers might meet to discuss salary requirements and recommend that those requirements be implemented by a local school board.

As we can see from our examples, the output of a policy-implementing group may be considerably different from that of a policy-recommending group. Whereas the group implementing a policy takes responsibility for its actions, the advisory group places the responsibility for its recommendations back on the individual or group to which the recommendation is made.

The other three functions of small groups can best be explained by examining the different types of small groups.

Types of Small Groups

Small groups can be categorized into task-oriented groups, problem-solving groups, social groups, brainstorming groups, T-groups, and therapy groups. To some degree, they overlap each other. As we discuss each type, think of what you have already learned about interpersonal interaction and consider what communicative freedoms or restrictions would be inherent in each group's interaction.

Task-Oriented Groups
A *task-oriented group* sets out to accomplish a specific goal.[7] In many ways the task-oriented group is related to the problem-solving group because both have a task to accomplish. Yet the task group can exist without being a problem-solving group (Figure 7–1). An example of a task-oriented group might be a city council which meets to accept bids on new playground construction. We could assume that the decision to construct the playground in the first place, or solving the problem of inadequate recreational facilities, oc-

Task-oriented groups function to accomplish a specific
goal. *(Irene Springer)*

curred in a meeting of the city council's parks and recreation committee. Another example might be a group of students meeting to set the theme and plan the entertainment for a school dance. No specific problem needs to be solved, but the group does have a goal to accomplish by the end of the meeting.

Groups, including task-oriented groups, have agendas which they follow to guide them from their initial interaction to their final goal. In some groups these agendas are complex and defined; in others they're simple and flexible. Interpersonal interaction in the group is a direct result of the agenda, whether spelled out by the discussion leader or caused by the simple emergence of issues within the discussion.[8]

In task-oriented groups, interpersonal interaction has the opportunity to take place with a moderate amount of restrictions. The group realizes at the beginning of the discussion that it has a goal to accomplish, and it proceeds towards accomplishing that goal. This does not mean that the discussion is void of disagreement, but the amount of disagreement is less than that which sometimes can occur in problem-solving groups.

Problem-Solving Groups   *Problem-solving groups* seek solutions to problems (Figure 7–2). They may either implement those solutions or recommend that other bodies implement them. Problem-solving groups follow slightly different agendas than task-oriented groups, and they often exist in somewhat more restrictive atmospheres. Part of this results because something may be wrong or need changing when the group meets. Unlike a task-oriented group which knows beforehand what direction it will take, problem-solving groups often do not. The purpose of the group is to find a solution, and the collective efforts of the group are designed around that goal. All of these characteristics determine the group's interpersonal interaction.

FIGURE 7-2

Problem-solving groups function to seek solutions to problems. The group may either implement the solutions or recommend that others be responsible for implementation. *(Western Electric)*

Brainstorming Groups

Brainstorming is a particular type of interpersonal interaction, and when it dominates the interaction of a particular group, the group is referred to as a *brainstorming group*. Brainstorming permits one of the freest atmospheres of discussion to take place. The primary objective is to generate as many ideas into the discussion as possible so that the "right" idea or the "best" solution will not inadvertently be missed because of interactive restrictions.

As a process, brainstorming can be employed at many different points along the small-group decision-making route. In a problem-solving discussion, a certain amount of time can be set aside to give everyone a chance to offer solutions. With the emphasis on quantity rather than quality, the discussion leader can encourage even the more hesitant members of the group to offer solutions. Brainstorming can also be effective in a task-oriented agenda when the discussion centers around different ways of achieving a goal.

The key to effective brainstorming is for every member of the group to understand that criticism of any other person's ideas or comments is inappropriate during a brainstorming period. Such criticism runs the risk of stifling discussion. Remember, the goal of a brainstorming session is to stimulate, not inhibit, interaction. Regardless of how unusual or out of place suggestions may be, they are perfectly legitimate in an open, unrestrictive, brainstorming atmosphere. Because ideas may be presented in rapid succession, it is sometimes best to have someone write down each person's comments.[9]

Therapeutic Groups

Although much of our discussion has been of small groups in corporate and other organizational settings, small groups naturally function in other situations for a variety of purposes. In counseling and psychiatric sessions, *therapeutic groups* bring people together to enhance their abilities to deal with others and with life in general. The people who participate in such groups range from highly psychotic individuals who take part in therapy groups to those persons who simply want to enhance their awareness of others by participating in "encounter groups." Such encounter groups have also been called T-groups or training groups,[10] confrontation groups, and sensitivity groups. Differences and similarities exist between traditional therapy groups and the T-groups. To better understand how interpersonal interaction works in each setting, we will briefly explore these differences and similarities.

Similarities of T-Groups and Therapy Groups   T-groups and therapy groups are primarily intensive communicative experiences. In other words, the participant's own role and experiences become the product of the group's goals:

> The intensive group acts only upon itself, emphasizing intrapersonal aspects in that intermember communication is designed primarily to serve the individual self. In an effort to exert self existence, establish a self image, or dissolve tension within the self, group members turn toward themselves rather than toward others as the object of influence.[11]

Both groups also concentrate on emotional arousal. Researchers B. Aubrey Fisher and Wayne S. Werbel point out: "Members are encouraged and expected to drop their facades and inhibitions and reveal as honestly as possible their feelings about one another. Such openness typically leads to emotionally arousing confrontation and even interpersonal conflict."[12]

Still another similarity involves what can be called the "here-and-now" orientation of such groups. Each participant's taking responsibility for what is being said and what is happening at that moment can become the main task of the T-group.[13] Feedback is in reference to what is being said at the moment, without any need for an external referent, such as a particular problem to be solved by the group as a whole. The agenda, to a certain extent, is set as the group moves through its discussion.

Differences between T-Groups and Therapy Groups   One of the basic differences between T-groups and therapy groups lies in the characteristics of the people who participate in each group. T-group members generally consist of well-functioning individuals who are seeking greater competence in their abilities to experience life. Therapy groups, on the other hand, are often made up of individuals who want relief from problems with which they cannot cope. Even everyday stress may be too much to handle, and they seek relief through group counseling.[14]

Another difference lies in the task each group faces. Whereas T-groups try to resolve conflict within the individual, therapy groups permit that conflict to become a tool by which the individual can search out and resolve interpersonal dilemmas and stress. Acceptable discussion content for therapy groups includes personal thoughts of which members may be deeply ashamed, such as hostility towards loved ones, lust, and a lack of self-confidence.

Another distinguishing factor between these two types of groups is learning goals. Fisher and Werbel point out:

> Individuals in training groups are trying to learn new skills, but clients in therapy groups are trying to unlearn old modes of behavior. The latter group typically takes longer to achieve their goals. Training groups are born out of the knowledge they will soon die. Therapy groups require much more individual change among their members before they cease to exist.[15]

Fisher and Werbel also explain that it is often sufficient in a T-group for the members to recognize their problems in order to surmount them. "Not so in a therapy group in which problem areas must be continually explored for each member until his or her goal is reached."[16]

Social Groups   Still other groups which operate outside the traditional organizational or formal setting are social groups (Figure 7–3). Many groups meet by chance—for example, students dropping by a dormitory room after dinner, a group of fishing enthusiasts meeting on the pier during the height of the season, or bridge players spontaneously arranging a game of bridge. Cocktail parties, receptions, luncheons, and similar settings are where social groups congregate. Al-

FIGURE 7–3

Social groups primarily provide friendship, and may meet outside of a formal organization. Cocktail parties, luncheons, and spontaneous gatherings are some of the many examples of social groups. *(Irene Springer)*

though such groups do not have fixed agendas, and the makeup of the groups may change from one minute to the next, we should not be any less concerned about the qualities of good interpersonal communication necessary to interact within these groups. Good interpersonal communication transcends group settings. We should not cast our interpersonal skills gleaned from long sessions in corporate boardrooms aside when we sit around a table chatting with friends.

Interpersonal Interaction in Small Groups: The Process

We have been discussing the characteristics and types of small groups in order to distinguish small-group communication from interpersonal communication on a one-to-one basis. Now we shift our attention towards the process of interpersonal interaction in small groups.

Content of Small-Group Interaction To better understand small-group interaction, we first examine the content of that interaction. If we were to observe or record a small-group discussion and then classify into categories what people said, our categories and their descriptions might look like this:

Supportive Analyses— messages which, through argument, insight, or presentation of information, confirm a solution.

Argumentative Analyses— messages which, through argument, insight, or presentation of information, dispute a solution.

Procedural Communications— messages dealing with problem-solving methods, criteria for making decisions, clarity of wording, or comments on the experimental situation.

Expressions of Unity— messages showing agreement or acceptance.

Expressions of Disunity— messages showing disagreement or rejection.

Solutions— messages which recommend a course of action or state a policy for guiding action.

Expressions of Personal Involvement— messages relating personal experience, affection, commitment, or personal dilemma.

Phatic Communications— messages showing superficial interest; often joking or accommodating.[17]

By looking at each category, we can see that certain messages expressed at the wrong time will have a profound effect on the outcome of the discussion. At one time or another, we have all said something or have reacted to what someone else has said without realizing its consequences. The problem is especially troublesome in small-group interaction, because the possible combinations of how people will react to what we say and how we say it are compounded.

Responsibility for Group Cohesiveness One of the most important things we must keep in mind is that every member of the discussion group has some responsibility for group cohesiveness. Stop and examine the categories we have just listed, and reflect how certain ones would be inappropriate at a given point of group interaction. For example, after someone has offered a solution to a problem, what would it do to the group if we were to engage in intense and loud expressions of disunity? If such comments were made during a brainstorming session, they would be completely out of place. If we used highly charged and personal language, we might trigger an argument and create barriers between ourselves and the person to whom we were talking. Moreover, those in the group who like the person we attacked would build their own barriers against us. The same reaction might be obtained if we engaged in superficial or joking communication after a person expressed what he or she thought was a brilliant idea. Thus, our being sensitive to the content of group interaction and our own responsibility for group cohesiveness is important for effective interpersonal communication in a group setting.

Understanding the "Chains" of Interaction We have artificially categorized the content of communication, but we also need to understand that what we say also affects what other people say. Research has shown that certain comments elicit other comments, and these comments are linked together in a chain of decision making.

For example, by using our categories of content in small-group interaction, we can predict that in certain kinds of groups, certain sequences of interaction will take place. Assume that we have a group which meets to solve a parking problem on campus. During the initial stage of the interaction, the comments are mostly congenial and "expressions of unity." We could predict that if one person utters an expression of unity, it will be followed by another expression of unity. Later in the discussion, the sequence of comments—also called the structure of the discussion—may change. During that period when problem solving begins, we are analyzing the interaction between two people whose ideas do not mesh, and we might predict that a "solution" statement from person A will be followed by a "argumentative analysis" from person B. We might also predict that such an exchange will only go on so long until other members of the group will draw the discussion back on course through a sequence of "procedural communications" or "expressions of unity."

Our examples have been hypothetical, and certainly analyzing interpersonal interaction is much more complex and involved

FIGURE 7-4

To remain cohesive, groups must have members who are sensitive to listening and turn taking. Both are missing in this discussion group. *(Prentice-Hall Photo Archives)*

than our treatment permitted here. Keep in mind, however, that group interaction is a developmental process. Various sequences of interpersonal interactions are linked together to form the basic for group decision making.[18]

Listening and Turn Taking Before examining some of the specific factors which affect interpersonal interaction in small groups, a few comments on the roles of listening and turn taking are appropriate (Figure 7-4). By now, we should realize that for any discussion to move toward its goal, two elements must be present and practiced by every member of a group: listening and turn taking. Again, the multitude of relationships that can exist in even the smallest groups and the need for the group to remain cohesive necessitate the practice of good listening skills. At the same time, insensitivity to the appropriate time to talk and the appropriate time to listen can stifle a good idea, reduce our interpersonal effectiveness, and build up resentment from other group members.

Factors Affecting Interpersonal Interaction in Small Groups

Take as many half minutes as you can get, but never talk more than a half minute without pausing and giving others an opportunity to strike in.

Jonathan Swift

We now want to fine tune our awareness of what takes place in a small group when different variables enter into the interaction among group members. Naturally, many more variables exist than space permits us to touch upon here, so we will concentrate on the most basic ones. After we examine these variables, our attention shifts to the role of leadership in small groups and how interpersonal communication among group members can be affected by different leadership styles.

Interacting in Small Groups

**Power and
Status among
Group Members**
When researchers Fredric Jablin and Lyle Sussman
were investigating brainstorming groups, they discovered some interesting things about people who
contribute a great number of ideas to a brainstorm-
ing session.[19] Specifically, they learned that people who generate numerous
ideas in a brainstorming group perceive other people as being more equal in
status. They also perceive themselves as high-status group members.
Perhaps it would be ideal if all groups could function productively in a
leaderless atmosphere in which the quantity of information, not the quality,
determines the success of the group. In most groups, however, power and
status directly affect the interpersonal interaction of the group.

Relationship of Power to Status Before going further, we need to define *power* and *status*. Many times we link the two concepts together, but
they are actually distinct from each other. In group interaction, the discussion leader may have the power, through rules of order, to control interaction. But this does not necessarily mean that the leader has status. Researcher Patricia Bradley points out that: "Power is the ability to control
one's own need satisfaction and often the need satisfaction of others.
Whereas high power persons are able to facilitate or prevent the need
satisfaction of those low in power, low power persons are dependent upon
highs for their need satisfaction."[20] Yet Bradley also notes that high-status individuals do not necessarily have such control: "Although status is related to
the amount of desirability, satisfaction, or prestige inherent in a given position, differences in status do not, in principle at least, necessarily provide the
opportunity for high figures to control the need satisfaction of lower ranking individuals."[21]

Some Effects of Power and Status in Groups With the distinction between power and status in mind, we can examine the role each plays in
group interaction by coming to grips with the term *ego-defense mechanism*.
Having an ego-defense mechanism means protecting our egos. Stated
another way, it means keeping our self-concept and guarding our self-
confidence. It also can mean exercising that interpersonal need we learned
about earlier in the text—control. In group interaction, power and status
center around protecting our egos and retaining some degree of control
over our selves and our relationships with others.

To better understand these concepts, let's create an
example of a discussion among business executives. Sam is of low power
whereas his boss is of high power. Thus, his boss has control over Sam and
can determine whether the relationship will be good or bad, productive or
unproductive. Let's also assume that his boss determines whether Sam ad-
vances in the company. What has research suggested about the interpersonal relationship between Sam and his boss?

First of all, among members of the group, Sam's boss
will have more communication directed at him than Sam will. Not only will

Sam's boss receive more messages but the messages will be longer.[22] If Sam perceives that his boss has the ability to influence Sam's upward mobility in the company, then when Sam communicates with his boss, Sam's comments will be friendly, supportive, and agree with what his boss says.[23] In other words, Sam wants to make a favorable impression on his boss. Because of the tendency to agree with his boss and to filter out negative comments, the accuracy of the communication to his boss may suffer. Sam may have access to facts which do not support his boss but will withhold those facts if Sam perceives that a chance for promotion will be jeopardized. As part of a "psychological link" between Sam and his boss, Sam will also *express* more liking for people who are like his boss than like other low-power people who may be participating in a discussion.[24]

We can see from the preceding examples and research trends that unless a leader is skillful, unless a leader has the power to permit open and free discussion and uninhibited responses, the discussion can get bogged down in "niceties" and false flattery at the expense of accurate information and group productivity.

Roles and Role Conflict

In discussion groups in which the roles of group members are easily identified and adhered to, everyone has a fairly good understanding of what each person's relationship is to other members of the group. In some situations, this will determine how interaction will take place. Consider a teacher leading a class discussion. The teacher is the person in authority. Although the teacher may try to make sure that everyone's ideas are expressed, the teacher still holds final control over the group. If the teacher interrupts, then whoever is talking stops. If the teacher changes the subject, the group shifts gears. The roles of the teacher and student are easily defined. Authority figures—whether they be teachers, gang leaders, high-ranking individuals on a board of directors, or police officers in traffic congestion—play a big part in determining group interaction. Depending on how much authority people have and how they use it, regardless of whether or not they are "officially" designated group leaders, they will influence group interaction.[25]

Role conflict also plays an important part in group interaction. It can be experienced at any time by any member of the group (Figure 7–5). When it does occur, it can affect the behavior of a single individual as well as the interaction of the group. Stop and consider some of the different situations in which role conflict can take place. Assume that you are a member of a committee deciding personnel cuts for a large company. You have two close friends working in one of the company's divisions that is steadily losing money. And you know of no other place in the company where these people can be transferred. The company president asks your opinion of the losing division. Speaking in front of the other corporate officers, you find yourself hesitating; your verbal statements are contradicted by your nonverbal cues. You know you will sound ridiculous if you

FIGURE 7-5
To better understand the feelings of others and to deal with role conflict, members of this discussion group role-play the identities of different characters. *(Irene Springer)*

suggest anything other than eliminating the division. Yet you are sensitive to the people who work there, especially your two friends. Other members of the group who have no personal relationships in the division are puzzled by your hesitation. You begin to feel self-conscious and wonder if you will be perceived as being weak and ineffective as a future administrator. The process is painful. You have experienced role conflict, and not only has it affected your own behavior but it has affected that of the group as a whole.[26]

The key to good interaction is to keep roles and role conflict from interfering with the communication process. Sometimes this is difficult, especially when members of high authority are mixed together with perceived low-status people. Brainstorming, a process and type of group we discussed earlier in this chapter, is specifically designed to overcome these obstacles, but it is not practical in every group situation. Being able to recognize that roles play a part in interaction and that role conflict can occur at anytime is a first step in becoming a sensitive member of a group and a responsible and effective participant.

The Value of Trust Think of how difficult it would have been for us to develop our abilities to communicate with others if we had not been able to trust other individuals (Figure 7-6). We traditionally think of trust as something we want from others, sometimes more in their absence than in their presence: "I am dating a very wonderful person, and we have a meaningful relationship based on trust. Therefore, if I am away or must spend the weekend studying, the other person will not go out with someone else behind my back." "My

FIGURE 7-6

An important part of our development and our ability to interact with others grew out of our willingness as children to trust one another. That same trait plays an important role in shaping our ability as adults to interact in small groups. *(Copyright, Family Communications, Inc.)*

coworker and I are a team; my coworker would not cut me down behind my back." These statements imply the trust we place in someone else; we have certain expectations about what the other person will do, especially in relation to our own feelings and behavior. Similarly, it is our responsibility to earn the trust others may place in us.

Trust is implied in interpersonal interaction from the time we begin to talk. A child trusts that a parent will react positively to his or her beginning words. Think of how difficult it would be for a child to learn to talk if every time the child uttered a new word, an adult or parent said, "Be quiet!" The child would gradually become reserved, withdrawn, lack self-confidence, and be hindered in his or her ability to interact with others. Now consider how important trust is when we meet another person for the first time and begin to engage in self-disclosure. In our earlier discussions in this book, we talked about the quality of homophily or "overlapping" feelings, emotions, and things we share with other people. Homophily is the common ground upon which interpersonal communication is based. Self-disclosure plays an important part in building this common ground. But how much self-disclosure would take place if trust were not present? Self-disclosure would cease and so would the creation of common ground between two individuals. On a date, one person may say, "I enjoy hiking and camping." The other person replies, "I do not see how anyone can sensibly go out for days at a time and live on hard ground, eat burned food, and fight off bugs and snakes." In essence, the second person has just said, "Anyone who likes to camp and hike is stupid; therefore you are stupid." A much more tactful way to have expressed those feelings would have been to say, "I'm glad you enjoy camping and hiking. I enjoy golf and tennis."

Not only does trust help us to develop our communication skills and build relationships with other people, it also assures good group interaction.[27] Lack of trust can destroy group interaction. If certain members of a group feel that when they present an idea, they will be humiliated or chastized, they will not participate in the discussion. The result may be the loss of the very idea that solves the problem. At the same time, the morale of the entire group may be affected. Research has taught us that trust-destroying communication between two people can hinder the interaction among all members of the group. Even though the trust-destroying exchange may only be between persons A and B, persons C, D, E, F, and however many other people may be in the group can become defensive, protecting their own ideas against attack. They may feel stifled in their own comments or begin verbally attacking other members of the group before those members can verbally attack them.

Even though we may not personally like another member of a group, may not like or respect his or her ideas, and may intensely disagree with that person, we must not destroy that person's trust that we will react responsibly to what he or she says.

Personality Being able to "read" the personalities of different group members is important for the group leader. It is equally important for other members of the group who may be affected by particular personality types. Especially recognizable is the dominant personality who may try to control a discussion or interrupt other group members. Some people have more dominant personalities than others, and sometimes individuals who are part of a group cannot recognize when their dominance is hindering group interaction. Left unchecked, a dominant personality can monopolize conversation, stifle the comments of other group members, and cause the group to flounder out of control of the leader. If you see yourself as having a particularly dominant personality, guard against interrupting others and spending more than your share of time talking.[28]

Group Size The difference between your discussing an issue with a friend and discussing the issue in a city-council meeting is clear. The friend permits much more opportunity for you to be heard than does the city-council meeting. The friend may be more responsive to your feelings or more courteous and less impersonal than the city-council meeting. Part of the difference in your interaction between you and your friend and you and the council meeting is the number of people involved in the conversation. With your friend, two people are involved. In a city-council meeting of a large city, hundreds of people may be involved, especially if you are part of the audience. Size makes a difference in group interaction. Formulas, however, do not exist to tell us at what point certain kinds of interaction take place. We cannot say, for instance, that with three members, all members will be heard, but if the group is increased to ten, each member's opportunity to speak will be reduced by two-thirds. We cannot say this because other variables come into play. Still, group size does affect group interaction, as the following factors indicate.

Time for Interaction   With larger groups, each member has less time for interaction (Figure 7–7). Sheer numbers dictate this constraint, especially when the group has a limited time to interact. An hour set aside for a meeting of three people will produce a completely different atmosphere than an hour set aside for a meeting of twelve people. Your chances of being heard will be fewer, and the time you have to interact may be much more limited.

Providing Input   The more people present for a group discussion, the more chance for input. Two, three, four, or however many heads are better than one. If you have a particular problem to solve and are responsible for bringing together a group of people to solve the problem, think of the advantages of inviting every person who might be able to contribute information and possible solutions. You will sacrifice the chance for everyone to interact as much as you and they might like, but you will have access to information which might not otherwise have been available.

FIGURE 7–7

The amount of time each member of a group has for interaction is, to some degree, determined by the size of the group. *(Joseph R. Barber, A.T.&T.)*

Reaching a Consensus   Even though involving more people may improve input into the discussion, such involvement can hinder the discussion when it comes time for the group to reach an agreement. The more people, the more chance for disagreement. Group members or leaders accustomed to reaching a "consensus" rather than taking a vote for majority rule sometimes find larger groups difficult to deal with. The simple law of averages means that everyone may not agree, and the time necessary for a person to persuade others to a certain way of thinking, or even for every member to be heard, may prohibit true consensus decision making in larger groups. At some point, the leader may simply need to say, "It is time to vote on the issue."

Adhering to the Agenda   Just as large groups may find it difficult to reach a consensus, so may they find it difficult to stay with a given set of priorities, or stay with an agenda. Group leaders, in wanting to be democratic, try to permit as many views to be heard as possible. At the same time, however, they run the risk of permitting someone to discuss new topics which are not part of the original agenda or set of priorities.

Sequential Structure   Sequential structure of a group refers to the in-dependence of messages in sequence to one another. For example, consider the following dialogue from a problem-solving group:

PARTICIPANT A: *"I feel we should route all of our trucks through Kansas City. Then we would have full loads before reaching our service depots in Wichita and Topeka. After we fill up in Wichita, we can make additional stops in Hutchinson, Salina, Hays, and points west."*

PARTICIPANT B: *"That's a good idea, but why couldn't we go through Kansas City and then route south through Olathe and Emporia, and let the next truck service Topeka?"*

The interaction of participant A and participant B was in sequence, and both statements were interrelated. Good group discussion follows such a sequen-tial structure, with one comment related to and following another.

Larger groups, however, risk a lack of sequential structure. Let's look at another interaction, this time between participants C and D:

PARTICIPANT C: *"Let me make another suggestion. Bring one of the trucks out of Chicago and let it service such places as Peoria, Normal, Springfield, and Urbana. Have a dif-ferent truck leave St. Louis and work west towards Kansas City."*

In the future, group discussion may require new interpersonal skills when we interact via a video medium such as through teleconferencing. *(Courtesy of Bell Laboratories, A.T.&T.)*

The conference is a monster. It gobbles up, on the average, 45 per cent of the time of executives.

But a teleconference, by reducing travel, saves you time. This leaves you free to handle urgent problems, clear up detail work, and concentrate on your strategic planning. You become more productive.

A teleconference, operating through the Bell network, can connect several cities at once. To include more people, you can use a device as simple as a Speakerphone. Or go full scale with a conference room that lets you receive hard copy or demonstrate something on a Gemini® 100 electronic blackboard.

With a teleconference you can reach the offices of your company, customers, or vendors. You bring in people who could not otherwise attend. You review policy, resolve problems, introduce products, train personnel.

You can do all this because of the amazing range of capabilities of the Bell network, the world's largest and most advanced information management system.

You are already part of the network. Use it. See how easy it is to put our knowledge to work for you.

The knowledge business

PARTICIPANT D: *"Have we had our trucks inspected this year? I was noticing the other day that the police are cracking down on inspection violations."*

Participant D's comment is not related to participant C's. "As the size of a group increases, it becomes easier for members to ignore messages and pursue other topics of conversation, since the intended receiver of any message may not be clearly understood, and the responsibility for providing a suitable response falls on no one participant."[29]

Accentuating Personality Types Earlier, we discussed that a dominant personality can affect group interaction. The larger the group, the greater the chance that only the dominant personalities will be heard. Those of less-dominant or even submissive personalities may consequently feel isolated, and eventually may withdraw from the group altogether. Not only are there fewer opportunities to be heard in a large group, but also when one does speak, many more people are watching and listening.

Cohesiveness Some larger groups may be less cohesive than smaller groups. Part of the problem is that because there are many members, each member tends to perceive himself or herself as having less at stake in the outcome of the group. Yet subgroups within the larger group can be cohesive. These may be informal subgroups, such as students getting together to study for exams, or formally appointed subcommittees created to discuss one part of an issue.

Whether you're a participant or leader of a group, stop and ask yourself, how big is this group in comparison to other groups in which I have participated? Will the size make a difference? To what things related to interpersonal communication should I be alert? How can I responsibly control these factors to aid group interaction and help the group reach its goals?

Rewards What we personally obtain from a given small-group interaction can influence our own interactions. Stated simply, if it pays us to interact and take part in the decision making, we will do so. If we have no vested interest in the outcome or find that what we do or say is met by negative reinforcement or trust-destroying behavior, we'll cease participating. Assume that we sit on a committee which determines raises in pay. Our own raise will be affected by the committee's decision. Because we definitely have a vested interest in the outcome of the group, we may be quick to take part in the decision making.

Time Serious time constraints on a group can influence interaction almost as much as the size of the group. Both are directly related to each other. In the most basic sense, the larger the group, the more time necessary to arrive at a decision, and the more time necessary for everyone to have an opportunity to participate.

A sequence of group meetings can also influence group interaction. Groups which must meet once and arrive at a decision at that meeting may have completely different interaction patterns than ones which know they will be meeting again to continue working towards a decision or completing a task. Keep in mind, however, that many different variables can influence interaction in a group, and the fact a group meets once or many times is not an absolute predictor of what interaction can take place. Although research suggests that the personality of an individual and the amount of communication apprehension (fear of communicating) a person has will influence how he or she will interact in small groups, such other variables as attitude towards a topic, behaviors of other group members, and communication environment can all play a part.[30]

> *All problems cannot be solved, but some problems are diluted by time.*
>
> *Robert Half*

Leadership Behavior

Up to now, our discussion has centered on the interaction among participants in small groups. We now switch our discussion to the role of the leader in a small group and how leadership affects personal communcation. We examine the qualities of leadership and relationships of leaders to groups.

Qualities of Leadership

To understand the qualities that distinguish leaders from other group participants, let us begin with a definition of *leadership:* "Leadership is influential behavior, voluntarily accepted by group members, which moves a group toward its recognized goal and/or maintains the group."[31] From our definition, we can begin to extract and identify qualities of a leader.

Exerts Influence Our definition used the term *influential behavior.* To be effective, a leader must be able to exert influence over the group. This does not mean that an all-powerful or authoritarian individual makes a good leader, but it does mean that a leader lacking control or lacking influence

"All those in favor say 'Aye.'"
    "Aye."   "Aye."   "Aye."
        "Aye."   "Aye."

(Drawing by H. Martin: © 1979 The New Yorker Magazine, Inc.)

over a group will not produce results. Exerting influence and maintaining good interpersonal relations with other members of the group takes talent. Skill in interpersonal communication is an important quality in maintaining good interpersonal relations.

Possesses Credibility The credibility of a leader is another quality that can spell the difference between success and failure of a group. More importantly, the group must perceive the leader as being credible. A leader may have the title of "leader," but unless the group respects the leader and is willing to adhere to his or her influence, the group's progress towards its goal will be limited. Sometimes the inherent authority of a leader provides the needed credibility to function in a group. A sergeant meeting with a group of privates may lack certain qualities of leadership, but the rank itself can provide the credibility needed to reach the group's goal. This does not mean that the group will "like" the leader or even be satisfied with the group's achievements, but the power inherent in the rank will eventually get the job done. We can see immediately that nonvoluntary adherence to a leader's influence violates our original definition of a leader. Authority figures are not necessarily leaders, and in some situations, such as that just discussed, a fine line exists between when someone is "voluntarily" or "involuntarily" taking part in group interaction.

Is Committed to the Group's Goals Despite all of the personal qualities a leader may possess, the leader's success will be limited unless the group perceives him or her as being committed to the group's goals. Consider the student who is appointed the leader of a group to plan a class field trip. The student lets it be known that instead of going on the field trip, she would be much happier spending the day studying for exams. From the outset, the group proceeds but with little enthusiasm. When the leader attempts to influence the group's progress, she is perceived as suspect. Suggestions from the leader are met with suspicion. A good leader is perceived by the group as being committed to accomplishing a task. Without that commitment, credibility suffers, the ability to exert influence is lessened, and the productivity of the group and the satisfaction of the members with the group's progress is reduced.

Is Capable of Group Maintenance Simply being committed to a group's goals and following an agenda is not enough to be a sensitive and responsive leader. Maintaining the relationships that exist between group members is also important. At any moment, members of the group can become involved in dialogue which, unless skillfully handled, can endanger the cohesiveness of the group. Many times when ideas are being bantered about, when members of the group become highly involved with their own opinions to the point that they take personally comments which are in disagreement with those opinions, then interpersonal relationships can break down. Carried to the extreme, the interpersonal relationships between members of

> *The right of commanding is no longer an advantage transmitted by nature; like an inheritance, it is the fruit of labors, the price of courage.*
>
> **Voltaire**

the group can become so strained that the group ceases to function. Here is when good leadership qualities come into play. Being sensitive to these "breaking points" in interpersonal communication means a leader can help steer clear of crisis situations that may develop and can keep the group cohesive and progressing uninterrupted towards its goal.

Is Capable of Adaptive Behavior When crises do occur or when interpersonal relationships between group members become strained, then the leader may need to adapt to the situation and place his or her emphasis on group maintenance as opposed to reaching the group's goals.[32] From a strictly personality standpoint, this means that a leader may have to shift from being a director to being a negotiator.

To better understand the need for adaptive behavior, we can examine the relationships leaders have with different types of groups.

Relationships of Leaders to Groups Keep in mind that although leaders must possess all of the qualities we have just discussed, leaders interact with groups in different ways under different conditions.[33] Depending on these conditions, the success of a group can be measured in terms of (1) its productivity and (2) the amount of satisfaction the participants have in the group's final product (goal reached). The two are not always compatible, and one sometimes must suffer from an abundance or lack of the other. Imagine a series of combinations between a group and different types of leaders. For the purpose of example, we assume that two types of groups exist (although many more exist as combinations of the two): (1) interpersonal groups (IG), which put their highest premium on good interpersonal interaction and affection among members; and (2) task groups (TG), which put the highest premium on the task at hand or accomplishing a goal. Now imagine two types of leaders: an interpersonal leader (IL) and a task leader (TL). We can see that by placing the groups and leaders in a grid, four combinations exist:

	IG	TG
IL	IG IL	TG IL
TL	IG TL	TG TL

By examining the combinations, we can see that varying degrees of productivity and interpersonal relations will exist with the different combinations.

Interpersonal Leader: Interpersonal Group In this combination, the productivity of the group may be severely limited by an overemphasis on everyone's getting along with everyone else. Good relations among the group members takes precedent at the expense of meeting the group's goals.

Interpersonal Leader: Task Group Although this combination has some advantages—namely, the ability of the leader to keep the group cohesive —there is no indication that the leader will be able to successfully lead the task group towards its goal. The result may be the group's moving ahead on its own and leaving the leader behind. Nonappointed leaders may emerge to "bypass" the appointed leader and move the group forward.

Task Leader: Interpersonal Group In this combination, the leader may have a particularly difficult job moving the group forward because it continues to be stymied by members' desiring not to offend each other. As a result, the leader may be successful in moving the group forward but only after considerable resistance. Even if the goals of the group have been achieved—for example, by solving an assigned problem—the group may rate the leader's effectiveness as low and perceive the leader as authoritarian.

Task Leader: Task Group In a task leader: task group combination, the goals of the group may be reached, but the leader and the group may have little interest in the interpersonal relations among members. At first this may sound fine and productive, but consider what happens over time. If the group meets for a number of meetings and no attention is paid to the interpersonal needs of the group, the friction within the decision-making group may carry on even after the group completes its business. Although the group works well during the meetings, the overall morale of an organization may suffer. Tension may set in and disrupt the normal routine.

Keep in mind that our examples only show some of the extremes of combinations of leaders and groups. We started our discussion by noting the importance of leaders' possessing adaptive behavior— behavior which can adapt to the needs of the various combinations, even at different times in the same discussion. Adaptive behavior in which the leader and the group recognize the task, but in which both participants and leaders are skilled in good interpersonal communication, will produce both satisfaction on the part of the participants and productivity for the group as a whole.

> *Leadership is the ability to get men to do what they don't want to do and like it.*
>
> *Harry Truman*

SUMMARY

In learning about small-group communication we began by talking about the characteristics of a small group. Group size determines the number of possible interactions and can range into the thousands when relationships between group members and the intervening factors of verbal and nonverbal communication are considered. For our purposes, we characterized small groups in the general range of three to five members. In addition to group size, other characteristics of a small group include cohesive bonding, the degree of interaction among group members, member roles, member rewards including direct and indirect rewards, and the time over which the group meets.

We examined examples of group functioning, specifically groups implementing and recommending policy.

Of the various types of groups, we examined task-oriented groups, which strive for specific goals, and problem solving groups, which are designed to solve specific problems. A third type of group is a brainstorming group, which permits the freest interaction to take place. In brainstorming groups, members are encouraged to say whatever comes to mind under the assumption that the best comments will arise in an atmosphere in which the freest possible communication takes place. Therapeutic groups function in clincial settings. Social groups traditionally operate without fixed agendas, and the consistency of the groups frequently changes.

To better understand the content of small-group interaction we examined supportive analyses, argumentative analyses, procedural communications, expressions of unity, expressions of disunity, solutions, expressions of personal involvement, and phatic communications. Other factors include responsibility for group cohesiveness, the chains of interaction, and listening and turn taking.

When groups interact, power and status among group members contribute to the interaction. Roles and the conflict of member roles play a part. Trust, something basic to communication, especially when self-disclosure is invovled, functions in the small-group setting as well. Personality, group size, rewards, and the time a group meets affect the interaction.

At the core of a group is the leader, who is sometimes appointed, but who sometimes evolves from the group without being appointed. A good leader can exert influence in the group, possesses credibility, is committed to the group's goals, and is capable of adaptive behavior.

OPPORTUNITIES FOR FURTHER LEARNING

BAIRD, J. E., Jr., and S. B. WEINBERG, *Communication: The Essence of Group Synergy* (2nd ed). Dubuque, IA: Wm. C. Brown Company Publishers, 1980.

BEEBE, S. A. and J. T. MASTERSON, *Communication in Small Groups: Principles and Practices.* Glenview, IL: Scott, Foresman, 1982.

BRILHART, J. K., *Effective Group Discussion* (4th ed). Dubuque, IA: Wm. C. Brown Company Publishers, 1982.

BURGOON, M., J. K. HESTON, and J. McCROSKEY, *Small Group Communication: A Functional Approach.* New York: Holt, Rinehart & Winston, 1974.

BURNS, J. M., *Leadership*. New York: Harper & Row Pub., 1978.

CRAGAN, J. F. and D. W. WRIGHT, *Communication in Small Group Discussions: A Case Study Approach*. St. Paul: West Publishing Company, 1980.

FISHER, B. A., *Small Group Decision Making: Communication and the Group Process* (2nd ed). New York: McGraw-Hill, 1980.

GOLDBERG, A. A. and C. E. LARSON, *Group Communication: Discussion Processes and Applications*. Englewood Cliffs, NJ: Prentice-Hall, 1975.

GOURAN, D. S., *Consequential Decision Making: The Dynamics of Informed Choice*. Glenview, IL: Scott, Foresman, 1982.

ROSENFELD, L. B., *Human Interaction in the Small Group Setting*. Columbus, OH: Charles E. Merrill, 1973.

SCHEIDEL, T. M. and L. CROWELL, *Discussing and Deciding: A Desk Book for Group Leaders and Members*. New York: MacMillan, 1979.

STURGIS, A. F., *Standard Code of Parliamentary Procedure* (2nd ed). New York: McGraw-Hill, 1966.

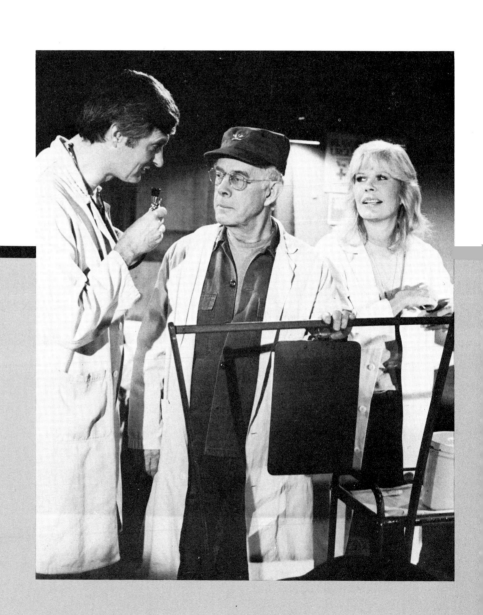

chapter eight

Interpersonal Communication in Organizations

PREVIEW   *After completing this chapter, we should be able to:*

Understand the importance of communication in organizations.

Be aware of the dynamic qualities of an organization.

Compare the classical, human-relations, human-resources, and systems approaches to management in organizations.

Give examples of the formal, informal, internal, and external communication networks.

List examples of upward and downward communication in organizations.

Describe the special problems created by rumors and grapevines.

Explain the different communicative roles individuals perform in an organization.

Discuss the power variable in organizations.

Give examples of applied interpersonal skills in organizations.

Understand the importance of planning and preparation for interviews.

Assess our own qualities to better prepare us for interviews.

Apply good interpersonal skills during an interview.

When I began writing this chapter, I was consulting for a corporation which had made a major commitment to developing the "human resources" of its employees. Numbering about 700 people, the company was large enough to attract and pay highly talented people. The company had introduced a corporate-wide appraisal program in which employees, in cooperation with their supervisors, established goals and worked towards fulfilling those goals.

This combination of corporate commitment to personal and professional development of its employees and the entire goal-setting and appraisal process signified that the corporation was sensitive to much more than profits. Management was sensitive to human resources, recognizing the importance of nurturing the relationships between each level of management. It also signified management's understanding that communication should not always flow in one direction—down from management. Through the appraisal program, employees could discuss their concerns with their supervisors. As an added benefit, realizing that the talents of one employee might be used in another division of the company opened up new lines of communication.

This same commitment to human resources was pointed out recently in a discussion of high-technology companies located in northern California's industrial area known as "Silicon Valley." One firm there had realized that incorporating technology in the production process and pressure for profits could improve productivity only so much. So it decided to break ground in a new frontier by recognizing the human needs of the employees and improving communication between employees and management. The company developed an innovative employee-benefits program which included flexible working hours, recreation facilities, and numerous opportunities to interact and socialize with management and each other. Productivity increased, morale was high, and the company gained a reputation for exhibiting high growth and having an awareness of modern management practices.

The Importance of Communication in Organizations

The preceding are examples of good communication in action within organizations. Communication has been called the glue which holds organizations together. Proving this analogy true is a world filled with organizations which have failed because of a lack of good communication. Consider the simple task of answering the telephone. In many small businesses, the entire image of a company rests with the person who answers the telephone. This individual must be able to listen carefully, take messages, and be courteous. If the person cannot listen and makes mistakes, customers will go elsewhere. What happens to businesses in which management closes its ears to employee complaints and refuses to take seriously any communication which travels up through the organization instead of down from the top? If the working conditions are poor, the morale is low, and the workers have developed their own underground management structure, top management can arrive one morning to find locked gates and picket signs.

Business Communication Situations Corporate communication skills can greatly affect an organization's ability to reach goals and motivate people. One study by researcher Michael Hanna identified eleven troublesome communication situations faced in business: (1) listening; (2) motivating people; (3) giving directions; (4) delegating authority; (5) group problem solving; (6) handling grievances; (7) private one-to-one conferences; (8) using the grapevine; (9) formal presentation; (10) conference leadership; (11) negotiation and bargaining.[1]

Stop and think of your own working situations, from part-time jobs to full-time positions. In what situations did communication affect the success or failure of an action? What communication skills could have helped the situation?

The ability to participate in group discussion is especially important because management decisions are often made through group processes. The manager or employee who cannot listen effectively will find little opportunity for real advancement, especially as he or she approaches responsibilities which include appraising others and handling grievances. In short, the ability to be successful and advance in any organization depends on the ability to communicate effectively. Even responsibilities for bottom-line profits fall back on someone's ability to convince others to purchase the goods or services of the company.

Being alert to communication situations and possessing the communication skills to interact with others is, however, only the first step. Also important, at any level of an organization, is the ability to *understand how communication flows* within the organization and the *forces* which act upon communication. In this chapter, we will examine these *dynamic* qualities of an organization.

The Dynamic Qualities of an Organization

Some of the oldest, most successful corporations have acquired an image of being static, unmovable, and crawling along with the sheer weight of their size and influence on the economy and society. Part of this image, although in many cases untrue, has evolved from an antiquated view of what corporations and organizations are all about. Too often these views have developed from an organizational-chart mentality in which communication channels and the relationships between individuals are as lines of command connecting the office of the president, the vice presidents, the supervisors, and so on.

Another way to view an organization is to realize that lines of communication may or may not follow the lines of command on an organization chart. Relationships among employees may mature, strengthen, and even go through bonding stages. They may also deteriorate. Supervisors, managers, even presidents change, and the content of communication and the communication channels change along with them. Thus, when we consider that any organization is a series of changing relationships between people, and communication is constantly flowing throughout these relationships, we can begin to visualize the *dynamic*, ever-changing nature of organizations.

Approaches to Understanding Management in Organizations

How have we viewed organizations over the years? That question needs to be answered to understand the way we approach organizational communication. In the following paragraphs, we will discuss four ways of examining organizations: the classical approach, the human-relations approach, the human-resources approach, and the systems approach.[2]

Management can be learned theoretically out of a book, but management, in my opinion, depends to a much greater degree on native talent and perhaps intuition and in some instances, I must say, a little luck.

Monford Orloff

Classical Approach One small company with which the author is familiar has a chief executive who tries very hard to leave the impression that he is a modern-thinking company president who knows a great deal about modern management techniques. His meetings are set up with clearly defined objectives. But he is the only one who sets the objectives because he resists advice from his subordinates. He is also the only one who knows what the objectives are because he never hands them out at the meetings. His meetings start at a certain time and always end at a specific time, regardless of whether or not the agenda is completed. He has a beeper phone and a small compact dictating machine attached to his belt. Although he constantly issues memos, he pays little atten-

226   Interpersonal Communication in Organizations

POST-MORTEM

Skyrocket McPhann
Was a city-desk man
With a voice like the Fourth of July
And a hide just as thick
As his temper was quick
When his schedules got knocked
    into pi.

When he got on the trail
Of a banner-head tale
And somebody bungled the story,—
The things that he'd call him
Would blister and maul him
And leave him all shaky and gory.

To hell with the reason!
To him it was treason
For any reporter to blunder,
And any excuses
Increased his abuses
And deepened the roar of his
    thunder.

They cautiously cussed him
And swore that they'd bust him,
Some day, in the midst of a panning.
They'd show the old bastard
They hadn't been mastered—
They would if it cost them a canning!

But on they kept slaving,
In step with his raving,
As month after month rambled by,
And none of them threw him
What all swore was due him—
A hellish good sock in the eye!

Then, at last, came a night,
As the fancy guys write,
When the flu knocked his nibs for the
    gong!—
And no man on the staff
Could remember to laugh
Or to whistle or break into song.

But each told the other
He'd viewed as a brother
And always regarded with pride
The best city ed
That had ever been bred—
And some of them damned nearly
    cried.

And now when they gather,
On pay days, to lather
Their tonsils with gin, every man
Insists on a toast
To the city-room ghost:
"Skyrocket (Here's to him!) McPhann!"

(J. E. Allen, Bulldogs and Morning Glories. Brooklyn: Linotype, 1945)

tion to the ones he receives. He also acts annoyed when employees seek to communicate with him and complains openly that such communication takes up too much of his time. In the rear of the building that houses the company is a separate section where materials are packaged and shipped. Here he has established complex quota systems recorded on large tally boards.

Aside from his being looked upon by many of the small-town employees as a complete nitwit, his modern ideas would be looked upon as antique by anyone knowledgeable in organizational behavior or organizational communication. He is a living example of the classical approach to organizational theory in which the organization chart is the only chart to live by, and the workers' output is divorced from their own feelings or relationships with others in the company.[3] He is threatened, insecure, and only manages to keep the employees in line by letting them know that if a union is ever voted in, the company will go under. Because the employees are paid little and jobs in the small community are scarce, his tactics keep the company in operation despite his tenuous relationships with the employees.

> The mind of man is fond of power; increase his prospects and you enlarge his desire.
>
> Gouverneur Morris

Human-Relations Approach

Another company in the same town has a manager with practically the opposite characteristics. A casual, likable person, he believes in a very democratic way of running the business. He frequently invites employees to his home for meals. He makes sure everyone is satisfied with the working conditions. The employees speak of him as a "nice," "pleasant" person for whom to work.

When the competition in town began to cut into his company's profits, the "nice, pleasant" manager set out to meet the competition with a series of staff meetings about pricing and other market factors. Gradually, however, the talented people in the firm became restless, and the leading salesperson left to join the competing company. Morale was affected, other employees became concerned and restless, and the company ran into serious financial trouble.

Even though morale may be improved, although sometimes temporarily, productivity can suffer under a "pure" human-relations approach to management.[4]

Human-Resources Approach

The company I spoke of at the beginning of this chapter looks at management from a human-resources approach.[5] It recognizes that individuals within the company have talents which can be nurtured to increase their productivity and improve the "bench strength" of management. As part of that commitment and recognition, it operates a company-wide training program to recognize these individual talents and to give employees the opportunity to develop their own skills without leaving the company. Moreover, the company recognizes that the responsibilities of an employee's job may not be as wide as the breadth of that employee's talents. Thus, while this breadth of talent is developed to make the worker as productive as possible in the job to which he or she is assigned, the company becomes alert to other jobs and responsibilities within the company to which the employee could be promoted.

Liaison with other divisions of the company was developed to improve and increase awareness of all opportunities within the company. Managers were made more aware of the opportunity pools that existed, and the person responsible for training kept track of the individual's professional and personal qualities that could be nurtured to make him or her even more effective in the new position.

Systems Approach

In the final chapter of this book we will talk about the interpersonal conflicts that can develop in a high-growth company. These conflicts are especially noticeable between different divisions of the company. For example, the pressure to produce means increased production for the manufacturer. The marketing people must plan campaigns, the salespersons must increase sales, which in turn puts more pressure on manufacturing, which in turn puts more pressure on marketing, and so on. The entire "system" operates at a higher and higher rate of productivity which is maintained by hiring more people. The emphasis is on horizontal communication between different "parts of the whole."

Along with the increased productivity and more personnel, transfers and promotions occur at a rapid pace. Although all three divisions—manufacturing, marketing, and sales—are dependent on each other, the relationships between division heads have little time to develop. Because the company is expanding so rapidly, division heads rarely remain at their jobs more than a few months before they are promoted, transferred, or replaced by more "aggressive" high-growth-oriented managers.

This interrelationship is indicative of the systems approach to studying interpersonal communication in organizations. Each division, and the corresponding persons who make up the divisions, are functionally dependent and interrelated to each other.

We can see from the four approaches to management that the four companies described operate in different ways. We might assume that one would be more successful than another and say to ourselves, "I would only want to work for the one with a commitment to human resources." Perhaps you would be correct. Consider, however, that all four approaches can be found within the same company, because a corporate commitment to a given management approach does not mean that that approach exclusively is practiced by everyone in the company. Rather, these approaches sometimes work best when they are viewed as "management philosophies," indicating that perfection is impossible.

Moreover, roles and approaches shift depending on the specific tasks to be accomplished and the personalities of the individuals involved. For example, in the company practicing human resources, there may be times when a manager must instruct a supervisor in very business-like language to further reprimand an employee for being late for work. This "classical" approach to a single situation may be necessary to solve a problem or clearly state objectives.

In each approach, communication varies. We can see this more clearly by examining communication networks in organizations.

Communication Networks

To understand how communication varies in organizations, we will examine communication networks: formal, informal, internal, and external. Although we have deliberately separated these networks to better understand them, they can be closely interrelated.

Formal Networks Formal networks are the easiest to identify. They are decreed everyday by such things as organization charts, appointed committees, and other identifiable characteristics which are known by management and employees. In getting the job done, meeting goals, accomplishing objectives, and performing other

---

WHAT ARE WE GOING TO DO ABOUT FRED?

"He smokes too much. Not only that, I saw him coming out of a bar at ten o'clock this morning. He's disruptive. He has the whole office staff laughing all the time. Let's get rid of him."

"Hold on, Fred did come up with the idea that's our big money maker."

"That's past history."

"It may be past history to you, but his idea is paying your salary."

"But wait, my attorney told me he took a second mortgage on his house."

"I remember the day I had to take a second mortgage. I also don't remember any earth-shaking ideas that came off our squash court. I'm promoting Fred. My bet is he'll come up with our next big money maker."

Is there a Fred in your organization? Do you know how lucky you are?

(© United Technologies Corporation, 1981)

"task functions," formal networks carry communication between people who are in positions to make decisions and carry on the work of an organization.

Examples of formal networks are found in many different settings: A college dean forms a committee of the heads of the living units to solve a housing crunch. A company supervisor brings together a group of employees to plan a change in office space. The company president issues a memo to the supervisors discussing the upcoming management meeting. The division managers meet to determine the future directions the company will take. All of these are examples of formal communication networks. Easily identifiable are the people who comprise the networks, their roles in the organizations, and the contents of the communications the networks carry.

Informal Networks

If formal communication networks were the only ones which existed in organizations, management would have little difficulty dealing with employees. Organizations, however, do not operate exclusively via organization charts and appointed committees. That three people might be brought together at a corporate board meeting does not mean that they will always interact with machine efficiency or that their meetings will produce predictable results. Human nature, with all of its variables, spawns relationships and communication which may have very little to do with formal communication networks.

One organization with which the author is familiar is headed by a manager who subscribed to the classical approach of directing the organization. He saw himself as head and made little effort to share his power with anyone else. His greatest weakness was his inability to listen. Upward communication, even simple questions from subordinates, was difficult to handle because he perceived communication as only being appropriate when it flowed downward. When a problem did arise, he rarely waited to hear more than one side of the story and immediately made a decision to solve the problem based on the chain of command. The manager's background, which included experience with small organizations and minimum-wage employees, did not give him the ability to deal with a more complex organization and the many different relationships that existed among skilled staff. He was most fearful when an employee communicated outside the division. Horizontal communication or communication to his superiors was life threatening and was met by serious reprimand.

Not long after his arrival, a series of informal networks began to develop. Because communication to the manager was, for all practical purposes, blocked for the employees, they began to communicate with another staff member who had equal professional seniority to the manager. This "phantom" manager, in an attempt to keep morale high and under pressure from other employees, began to make management decisions using the secretaries (who also found it difficult to talk to the manager) as a source of information and a channel of communication around the manager. Small subgroups began to form, and when committees were formed by the manager, the members of the committees made decisions based on the wishes of the informal subgroups to which they belonged. Finally, enough informal networks had been developed that the organization moved along in spite of the manager. When the periodic evaluation of the manager took place, the corporate officers replaced him with the "phantom" manager.

Internal Networks Our discussions of formal and informal networks dealt with communication that was internal—that is, inside the organization. For most of our examples in this chapter we deal with internal communication for three reasons. *First,* the great majority of communication directly concerns the people within the organizations. *Second,* many organizations are themselves "private" entities. Corporations, for example, do not typically make all of their records available to outsiders. Competitive business strategies, such as protecting patents, new models, and marketing plans, demand a certain amount of secrecy. *Third,* employees are "private" persons, unless they are politicians or public figures. Their private lives both at work and elsewhere are protected by law; thus, organizations are not at liberty to divulge this information to such outside publics as the press. The private nature of organizations was expressed by reporter John Lewis of the *Wichita Journal* in Wichita, Kansas, who noted in a symposium on corporate communications that "The corporation is, in fact, only a legal fiction that serves as a vehicle for a complex set of relationships between individuals."[6]

External Networks Although corporations and other organizations have traditionally been mostly concerned with internal communication networks, more and more attention is being paid to external networks. External networks carry information beyond the confines of the employees or people who make up the organization. Examples would be the general public or the news media, which help carry information to the public.

Even though business strife, such as worker unrest, has for centuries found its way into the press, the power of the electronic media and the speed with which it disseminates information has made business leaders keenly aware of the importance of these external networks of information. A television newscast can send the price of a stock up or down depending on how favorable the news is to the company.

External networks link the organization with people outside of the organization. For example, a public relations director is part of a network of people which not only includes corporate management but also members of the news media. Formal and informal networks operate in such a relationship. The public relations director may be asked by management to talk to a reporter—an example of a *formal* external network. At the same time, the reporter's secretary who happens to know when a good story is needed can be a valuable *informal* contact for a skilled public relations person.

Another notable external network is composed of the employees' families. Informal and even formal organizations of employees' families can exist, and the information flow within them can be faster than communication carried through more formal channels.

M essage Flow in Organizations

Our discussion of external networks was concerned with the channels used to carry communication. We can also become better organizational communicators by studying the *direction* in which messages flow.

Downward Communication   The manager who was replaced by the phantom manager was a person filled with the importance of downward communication. In that example, however, formal communication in any direction other than downward placed a serious handicap on the manager's effectiveness. Downward communication does serve important purposes in any organization. Traditionally, downward communication has been tied to a classical approach to management, but even in the most forward-thinking organizations, downward communication is still very necessary. The following are some of the functions of downward communication:[7]

Job Instruction. Job instruction includes directives from management on what is to be done, how it is to be done, and what results are to be expected.

General Information. General information to assist in getting the job done also finds its way into downward communication. For example, management will share with subordinates information about how another company is approaching a problem.

Rules and Regulations. Today, virtually every organization is faced with a host of government rules and regulations. In many companies management has the responsibility, sometimes legal, to disseminate information about these rules and regulations to employees. Job discrimination, equal pay, and working conditions are just some of the issues that flow from top to bottom. Other information may flow from the top to the first or second level under top management—for example, legal decisions affecting the company and competitive pricing policies.

Performance Appraisal. Companies which foster a human-resources approach to management are usually sensitive to carefully appraising the performance of employees. Telling employees how well they do their jobs, how they can improve, and how the company can help them improve are three types of appraisal information that can flow downward from management. At the same time, we should remember that truly effective performance appraisal necessitates two-way, and thus upward, communication as well.

Management Philosophy. Organizations, especially larger corporations, utilize such diverse methods as internal public relations and motivation seminars to develop employees' awareness of the philosophy and goals to which the company subscribes.

In conclusion, we need to know that although downward communication is important, it does have some pitfalls. Too much downward communication can overload the system to the point that much of the communication goes unheeded. A lack of sensitivity to timing can also destroy the effectiveness of the communication. Reprimanding an employee the morning after his house burned down may not be the wisest management decision. Inadequate communication can have the same effect—for example, firing a popular employee without fully explaining to key staff members why the decision was made.

Upward Communication Organizations which are sensitive to employee feelings and opinions permit every opportunity for upward communication.[8] Some of the common examples are:

Self-Appraisal. Self-appraisal is often required by organizations that have a well-developed performance appraisal program. Employees communicate to supervisors how they feel about success on the job, and then the supervisor responds to the employee's assessment.

Appraisal of Others. Sometimes requested, sometimes not, employees will communicate to supervisors about the performance of other employees. For supervisors, this form of upward communication is standard because they commonly report to the next higher-level person who has the responsibility for every employee. Yet in other situations, appraisal of others may take on the characteristics of "tattletale" communication.

Organizational Policy. Opinions of how things operate and of policies and procedures are forms of upward communication. This type of communication can be very valuable if received by management with an open mind.

When communicating upward in an organization, research suggests that to get the best results, communication should (1) be positive; (2) be timely; (3) support current policy; (4) go directly to the person who can act on it (although not necessarily an "end run"); and (5) conform to the perceptions of the receiver.[9]

TEAMWORK SAID KEY TO MANAGING

NEW YORK (UPI) — American management theories are based too much on a "John Wayne culture" of individualism and elitism, says a UCLA professor who has served as a consultant to many big companies and governments in 42 countries.

Dr. Ichak Adizes was born in Yugoslavia and educated in Israel and at Columbia University in New York. He presently teaches at both Columbia and the University of California at Los Angeles and operates his own consulting firm.

"The professors and textbooks in American business schools describe the perfect manager and give the impression such men and women really exist. They don't," Adizes said.

"American managers seem to assume that anybody with enough drive and

Horizontal Communication

Horizontal communication occurs between people at similar levels of responsibility within an organization.

Horizontal communication can be used to form some of the strongest relationships between people, because it often occurs in an atmosphere of mutual trust. Such communication can be voluntary and left out of an appraisal. Suppose a police officer on patrol has a question about procedures. Since the sergeant may evaluate the officer negatively because he or she does not know what procedure is appropriate, the officer is much more likely to turn to a fellow officer for advice.

Horizontal communication is sometimes difficult to monitor. It is one of the reasons management should be receptive to the upward flow of communication. A lid on upward communication can result in its being diffused horizontally within the organization. This can cause serious problems if the communication is negative and creates tension and a loss of morale within the organization.

External Communication The first three directions we have discussed dealt with communication within the organization—internal communication. External communication, as we learned, flows beyond the organization. Corporate public relations people talking to the news media exemplify external communication.

Controlled Communication Much external communication is under management's control. As we learned earlier, organizations are becoming more and more aware of the effects of external communication. In the Kansas symposium on corporate communications, James Boyd of the Vulcan Materials Company said: "Business must recognize the growing need of the community to be informed and to respond to that need when an interest is shown. Business, for its part, wants assurance that the information it imparts is treated in a manner which is fair."[10] Frank Hedrick of Beech Aircraft Corporation suggested that through external communication, a broader understanding and appreciation of the system of free enterprise is necessary to avoid government encroachment.[11]

In another forum, James D. Robinson III, Chairman of the American Express Company, suggested that the business community must have a change of attitude towards the function, power, and role of communications, and that business leaders must be committed to philosophically "speaking up" and "speaking out" on issues. He quoted *Wall Street Journal* columnist Vermont Royster as saying: "Only when the business community recognizes that its chief executives must be less narrow of thought, less inarticulate . . . and less fearful of the fray, will the voice of business be heard in the land."[12]

Uncontrolled Communication: Whistle Blowing Another type of external communication, one management does not control, is called whistle blowing. Another term, *leaking,* has been used to describe unauthorized communication in which an employee takes a grievance or complaint to the public or the press.[13] Little is known about whistle blowing because the person who blows the whistle often ends up being fired.

In a whistle-blowing incident, the employee becomes aware of something he or she feels is unethical, immoral, or illegal and which will endanger the public. When little or no action is taken after complaints have been made to immediate and higher-up supervisors, the employee takes the complaint outside the organization to the public, the press, or a government agency. Many times the employee subsequently is forced out or becomes isolated within the organization. In other cases, the employee may voluntarily resign on the issue from which the complaint generated.

education can become a perfect manager. This leads them to put all their emphasis on competition, instead of cooperation. It leads them to want to work alone instead of building competent management teams.

"People should learn to get along with others. That's ninety percent of good management," Adizes said.

He said the real secret of Japanese management success, which has been so noticeable in recent years, is that the Japanese culture eschews elitism and individualism and is based on cooperation and mutual respect, recognizing the need for complementary diversity in the management team.

Instead of having one top manager trying to solve ten problems and possibly failing at each as may happen in an American firm, Adizes said, in a Japanese company ten managers will work on one problem at a time, each from a somewhat different point of view but with mutual respect, until they solve it.

He said the tragic aspect of American elitism and individualism is that, as companies get bigger, it leads inevitably to just the opposite of what is intended—to stale conformity, rigid authoritarianism and inability to adjust to changed circumstances.

(Reprint courtesy UPI)

Special Problems: Rumors and Grapevines

If you have been part of any organization for any length of time, you are aware that information cannot always be trusted as being accurate and that informal networks often operate unpredictably. Both of these phenomena can involve rumor and the use of the grapevine.[14]

Rumors History has been filled with examples of information run amuck. Two major automobile companies, Volkswagen and Chrysler, fought unfounded rumors that the two were going to merge. A fast-food outlet fought rumors that it had worms in its hamburgers. Political conventions are notorious for rumors about candidates for office, running mates, and cloakroom deals. False shortages ranging from gas, to aluminum foil, to toilet paper have plagued merchants for years. Rumors are unavoidable. Simply defined, they consist of sometimes difficult-to-confirm information passed through informal channels of communication. Sometimes they prove uncannily accurate. Other times they have little basis.

Rumors are passed from one person to another for a number of reasons, such as the desire to verify information. One person says to another: "Have you heard anything about Joe's leaving?" "No, but I'll sure try to find out!" The desire to be included in a group which possesses the information is another motivation for rumor transfer. "Don't leave me out on a limb. Tell me what you know." Wanting to give something to someone else can aid rumor transmission. "You're my friend, so I'll tell you what I know."

Psychologists Gordon Allport and Leo Postman classified rumors into four types:[15]

Wedge Drivers. Some of the most serious rumors divide or simply relay untrue and damaging information. "I heard he is using his office to carry on a horse-betting scheme."

Pipe Dreams. Pipe dreams can best be described as wishful thinking. "I heard the old grouch is resigning." Unfortunately, he ends up staying.

Bogeys. Bogeys are untrue rumors which create fear or lower morale in an organization. "I heard we are close to bankruptcy."

Homestretchers. Homestretchers anticipate something. "It has all but been confirmed. The president is stepping down next week."

Many organizations, although realizing rumors are inevitable, do try to control them. Some organizations operate special phone numbers and rumor clearance centers that a staff member can call to try to verify information.

236   Interpersonal Communication in Organizations

When these centers are operated in an atmosphere of trust and commitment to the free flow of information, they can be helpful. Although they will not stop the spread of information through informal channels, they can help keep it accurate.

Grapevines Closely aligned to rumors are grapevines, which are informal communication networks which carry rumors. Research suggests that grapevines are not the same as the informal networks used on a regular basis for job-assistance information, such as asking a coworker how to complete a task. Grapevines are irregular, can change rapidly, and carry information which is about 75 to 95 percent accurate although not complete. Management, because information via the grapevine is not totally complete, simply considers it 0 percent accurate.[16] Research has also found that only about 10 percent of the people involved with a grapevine actually transmit information. The rest of the people aware of the event or issue receive the information from those 10 percent.

To use interpersonal communication responsibly in an organization, we should keep aware of the inadequacies of rumor and grapevine-centered communication. Such communication can be incomplete, and when we are spreading information, we may only have part of the facts. When all of the facts become known, we need to ask ourselves how the total story affected our credibility.

Communication Roles

Regardless of whether we participate in rumor transmission, ask for help with our jobs, or deal with top management through established channels, we serve given communication roles in an organization.

Identifying Role Behavior Depending on the situation, the topic under discussion, the task to be performed, or the goal to be reached, our roles may change. Figure 8–1, represented in an article by Donald MacDonald, shows the different role relationships that can exist in an organization:[17]

> *Group Members.* Each dot in Figure 8–1 represents a person, and the entire figure shows one set of interrelationships among individuals. It can be a company, a professional association, a hospital, or any other organization. Within an organization are groups with *group members.* You may be appointed to serve on a committee, become a member of the board, or work as part of a construction crew. In each case, you are a member of a group.
>
> *Bridging Groups.* At the same time, you belong to a group that may communicate with other groups. The persons responsible for

FIGURE 8-1

Networks and communication roles. *(D. MacDonald, "Communication Roles and Networks In a Formal Organization,"* Human Communication Research, 2 *(Summer, 1976), pp. 365–375. (Used with permission of publisher & author)*

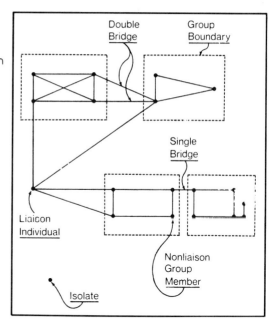

bridging the gap between the groups form *bridges*. Figure 8–1 represents both *double bridges*—connecting with two people—and *single bridges*—connecting with one person. Additional bridges may also exist. Examples of such bridges can be found in large committees which break up into smaller subcommittees in order to solve parts of a problem. In solving the total problem, it becomes necessary for one subcommittee to communicate with another subcommittee.

Liaisons. In any communication network, *liaisons* serve a paramount purpose in transmitting and receiving information. Usually such people have high status in the organization, at least among the staff if not on a formal organization chart. Liaisons are the "linkers" of information. The liaison person may be appointed—for example, a desk sergeant in a police station. Or the liaison person may evolve because of his or her personal characteristics; it may be someone to whom everyone turns to talk something out or ask questions. Liaisons can act as the links between multiple groups of people. They can also be members of a group.

Nonliaisons. Nonliaisons are group members who do not have contact with other groups.

Isolates. Isolates are the most removed from the decision process.

Fulfilling Communication Roles   From our knowledge of the various roles people play in an organization, we can see that to be an effective part of any organization, it is necessary to both have and to use properly many of the skills of interpersonal communication we have been talking about throughout this book. In decision making, the ability to work effectively within a group is critical to achieving even the simplest goals. Even more responsibility rests upon a group member acting as a bridge between groups. The ability to accurately communicate information, understand the give-and-take process of listening and reacting, and be sensitive to the interpersonal dynamics of organizations all determine the difference between success and failure. It also may determine how the individuals involved serve most of their roles from liaison to isolate.

Think of organizations in which you participate. Who are the group members who are the bridges and who are the liaisons? What interpersonal skills do they possess, and do they use them effectively?

The Power Variable in Organizations

A supervisor walks into a meeting of subordinates and says, "The president of the company says we have to increase production by 20 percent by the end of the month. If anyone does not raise his or her own productivity by 20 percent by the end of the month, I will fire you, and you will not receive a recommendation from the company." At the end of the month, overall production has increased by 31%.

Basis of Power Our example did not say anything about interpersonal communication, about self-concept, or about group processes or nonverbal communication. All of these helped the supervisor to communicate the message to the subordinates, but the very *power* of the supervisor to control the jobs of the subordinates may have been the only incentive for meeting the goals.

Power plays a major role in all organizations.[18] Sometimes it is subtle, such as a coworker's knowing more than a colleague about the operation of the grapevine. At other times it is overt, such as the company president's unquestioned authority to hire and fire.

In studying communication in organizations, we should remember that power can play an important part in interpersonal interaction. Because power usually evolves from above, we tend to pay more attention to messages reaching us through downward communication. If we are closely associated with power—for example, by being an executive assistant to a president—we will pay attention and react differently to communication from the president than, say, from a vice president. Because of the power relationship to communication, it is important to know the basis of power:[19]

The Power to Reward. People who can reward us have power over us. They can determine how much we are paid, what hours we work, whether we are promoted, and other "rewards," both tangible and intangible. The power may not always be evident or even stated, but whenever someone else has something of value to us, we

Isadora and Her Avocado Plant.

Isadora—do you have a plant at the office?

Well, yes, I do.

What kind is it?

It's a Schefflera.

Do you have a deep, abiding relationship with it...like ours?

Let's say we're just friends.

Just a silly office affair.

(© 1977 California Avocado Commission, Irvine, California)

Interpersonal Communication in Organizations

239

find ourselves operating in a power relationship. For some people, any kind of power imbalance is unsatisfactory. Many times such individuals find their greatest satisfaction in being the owners and operators of their own companies in which they sign paychecks, make the decisions, and reap the profits. They also take all the risks.

The Power to Coerce. Coercing power is often interrelated to the power to reward. If a person has the power to reward, he or she also has the power to punish. Perceived power to coerce can be just as powerful as actual power, and the person holding that power does not need to set examples by firing people to gain results.

The Power of Knowledge. Knowing how to do something can mean knowing how to succeed. Whether it is investing money or assembling an automobile, those who have knowledge are in a position of power to give or withhold that knowledge from someone else. Showing a new employee the ropes, training a salesperson, and helping a recruit learn the basics are examples of using knowledge as a basis for power.

Power through Identification. A manager the author knows left for a vacation. Not long after he had gone, the organization began to have problems. Even the substitute manager was unsuccessful in keeping things under control. The problem was that no one in the organization identified with the manager, no one wanted to be like him, and many people actually disliked him. Because no one *identified* with him, when he left, they stopped behaving like a group of coerced subordinates and more like individuals. The substitute manager did not have the time to develop his own management style before the organization began to flounder. People who exercise power through identification find they can manage an organization even when absent. Employees identify with the manager and carry out that manager's wishes whether or not the manager is present.

Power by Agreement. When someone enlists in the military, he or she agrees to the rules of power which are part of the military structure. Admirals have power over ensigns, majors have power over captains, sergeants have power over privates, and so on. In organizations, similar power by agreement is found at all levels, and one joins the organization with a general agreement to operate within these constraints. Companies' social clubs and professional societies all consist of people who are part of the organization because they recognize and agree to abide by the power structure which is part of the organization.

What kind of power we best respond to or what kind of power we can best administer depends on our individual psychological makeups. Remember that communication is an important part of an organization, and that power plays a major role in determining the results of that communication.

240 Interpersonal Communication in Organizations

Power Relationships We have talked a great deal in this book about communication as a process of sharing. Power can also be viewed as a sharing process. One cannot have power without having someone over whom to have power. The success of using power is determined only by how another individual responds to that power. If a police officer walks up to an individual and tells that person to be quiet, the police officer has used power. If, on the other hand, the person's response to the officer's request is to yell even louder, the police officer has had little original success in using power.

We hear the phrase *balance of power* used to describe the relationships between two countries. A balance of power can also exist between people, both in and out of organizations. The president of a company hires a talented executive assistant. Because the president needs more time to consider the growth and expansion of the company and wants relief from daily personnel problems, he entrusts more and more authority to the executive assistant. It is not long before the executive assistant is handling all personnel problems effectively.

One day when the president tours the assembly line, he asks a supervisor to have lunch with him. To his surprise, the supervisor tells him that she appreciates the offer but that the executive assistant wanted to have lunch sometime this week, and before the supervisor can have lunch with the president, she needs to check with the executive assistant. The president discovers that by placing responsibility with the executive assistant, he has also shared his power with the executive assistant.

This example shows that power relationships are an exchange, much like that of goods and services. Because the president wanted to spend more time helping the company expand, he had to give up much of his direct power to the executive assistant. Of course, the president still has at his disposal all sorts of other bases for power and can overrule, even fire, the executive assistant. But then the president would be back spending even more time on personnel problems. While understanding the basis for power, do not forget the costs implied in the use of power.

A pplied Communication in Organizations

We will now turn to some concrete applications of communication skills in organizations. First we will review some of the typical and frequent situations in which those skills are important and then we will concentrate on one application, the *interview*.

Collective Interaction Every organization operates through a pooling of talent. Some of the most effective uses of that pooled talent occur from solving problems through mutual interaction. The ability to adapt to the goals of an organization, to the priorities at hand, and to the personality and temperament differences of

Great copy Marty, we love it but we have to make one small change.

Couple more changes Marty.

Just some small corrections Marty.

Just one final change and Ar Arrf. Arrf. Arrf.

MARTIN FRIEDMAN

(Reprinted with permission from the October 22, 1979 issue of Advertising Age. Copyright 1979 by Crain Communications, Inc.)

members are skills necessary for your own acceptance and effectiveness in small-group communication.

Public Presentations A friend who finished taking a course in public speaking said she thought the course was useful but had no idea when she would ever use what she learned, because she was joining an accounting firm and did not expect to be giving many public speeches. A year later when she returned to campus, she found that making public presentations was a way of life at her company. Explaining to prospective clients the services of the firm and explaining investment practices to a group of trainees were just some of the assignments she shouldered during her first year with the company.

One-to-One Interaction Earlier in this chapter we talked about approaches to management, one of which was the human-resources approach. In such an approach, the appraisal interview plays a big part. Many companies use appraisal interviews on an annual basis to review an employee's performance and to set goals for the coming year. The appraisal interview is an example of one-to-one interaction.

Other interview situations are also common in corporations. Perhaps the most common is the job interview. Still another type is the exit interview, the meeting with a supervisor or other company official to discuss your leaving the company. In smaller companies, the exit interview may be a very informal conversation between you and the person to whom you submitted your resignation. In other settings, it is a formal corporate policy carried out under rather strict guidelines which cover such items as future recommendations, severance pay, and other personal and professional matters.

There are three things to aim at in public speaking: first to get into your subject, then to get your subject into yourself, and lastly, to get your subject into your hearers.

Gregg

Interpersonal Communication in Organizations

To conclude our discussion of interpersonal communication in organizations, we will now examine the job interview.

An Interview: Planning and Preparing

One of the tragedies of higher education is that many colleges and universities permit students to spend thousands of dollars in tuition and living expenses over a typical four-year period and *never* teach them a few critical skills about what they should do when they leave school and head into job interviews. Career placement and planning services exist, but unless students voluntarily seek out these services, they often go unnoticed. Few professors take the time to incorporate information about job searches and interviewing into courses, although communication and business programs are exceptions. Many students consequently make a complete mess out of finding jobs. This situation is equivalent to training for four years to run the mile event in the Olympics and then starting the race with your legs in chains.

Through consulting, working in industry, and advising students, I have encountered hundreds of people who are intelligent, have good grades, have good communication skills, but who make stupid and ignorant mistakes that cost them choice jobs after graduation. In some cases, their entire careers falter because the first job creates a mental set into which they place their battered self-concepts and unfulfilled dreams. The language used here may seem harsh, but so is a life of always coming in second because you weren't aware of some of the basic skills necessary to get off to the right start.

In the following pages we will only scratch the surface of what you should learn about handling a job interview. Thus, do not be foolish enough to stop here. Learn all you can from career-placement services. Take advantage of seminars. Read, practice, and learn everything about what may be the most important interview of your life, your job interview.

Understanding Yourself

No one knows you better than you, but sometimes before people enter a profession, they forget to ask the all-important question, Who am I? Think about that question. You'll probably ask it often in your lifetime, but preparing for a job interview is one of the most important times you will ask the question. A first career can have a direct effect on a life-long vocation. Getting into a profession in which you are unhappy and unsettled can burn up negative energies that could be directed much more productively to another kind of work.

Personal Qualities Let's examine some of the questions you might ask yourself:

Motivation. Try asking: What kind of a person am I? Am I self-motivated? What are my accomplishments? What have I done in life or in school that would lead me to believe I would be happy and successful in a certain profession? Have I voluntarily taken courses which would apply directly to my professional goals? Have I taken courses, even though they might have been tough, to improve my skills and provide me with a worthwhile learning experience that will pay off in big dividends in my chosen profession? If you answered yes to the last question, you might ask if the experience was enjoyable and satisfying. These are questions that can be beneficial in providing the real reasons why you might want to enter or avoid a given career.

Being in Charge. Do you like to be in charge or do you prefer to work under someone else's direction? The obvious answer may seem to be, "I like to be in charge." Ask yourself if that is really the case. Have you consistently volunteered for leadership positions in your school? When you have been assigned to group projects have you readily accepted the role of leader? Did you actively solicit or were you elected to officer positions in clubs or fraternal organizations? If you were, did you enjoy the experience and the responsibility? These are questions that you will need to ask many times in your professional career.

Self-Assessment. Do not ever stop asking yourself these questions. Self-assessment and self-analysis should not occur only at that point in your professional development when you are graduating from school or moving on to your next job. Asking important questions about your own abilities and goals is a necessary function at every point in your professional career.

The Resume Everyone has his or her own idea about what a resume should contain and what it should look like. Thus, keep an open mind, not only to the advice you read here but also to the advice you receive from counselors and placement directors.

Appearance Every resume is different. Resumes reflect a person's individuality. But how that individuality may be expressed varies greatly. Becoming too tied to a hard-and-fast rule can force you into artificiality. For example, I remember a placement director who consistently stressed that a resume should be limited to a single page. Because of a strong work-study program at the college, many students graduated with two or three different job experiences listed on their resumes. This, along with the stress on awards and activities in the school, resulted in resumes that easily filled two pages. References could neatly be placed at the bottom of the second page.

Yet instead of being flexible and realizing that their own abilities filled two pages much better than one, students tried to jam everything on one page, using the smallest type style they could find. Everything was single spaced, and margins were one-eighth inch on all sides. The end result was a messy jumble, which left the impression that the applicants were not only lacking in neatness but also in common sense.

Make sure you have adequate margins. One inch is usually appropriate, although larger margins can work effectively if you are centering a smaller amount of material on a page. Also, choose a good typewriter. Don't type your resume on an antique ribbon typewriter that looks like it's on its last legs. It communicates to an employer that you may not care enough to take the time to find a good typewriter. Consider having your resume set in type at a professional printing house. Many companies are using typewriters which automatically adjust margins. Thus, in the future a resume with uneven margins may look as though it has been typed on outdated equipment.

Show your resume to as many people as possible and *no less than four*. Have the people reading the resume check it for spelling and content. If they don't understand something, by all means change it. If your roommate or guidance counselor cannot understand something on your resume, there is a good chance management will not be able to, either. And you may never land an interview to explain it. Good examples are Greek organizations which exist on many college and university campuses. The Alpha Beta Alpha might be a highly trained group of award-winning broadcast journalists. On the other hand, it might be the dormitory dishwashers' club. If the content is confusing, consider how you could reword it to better explain what you are trying to say.

Functions The resume itself has many different functions. Most importantly, it serves as a general introduction. Everything about you must be communicated in a resume. The resume is a first impression, and remember, you only have *one* chance to make a first impression.

Second, your resume may become part of a permanent file. Your resume will not only be looked at on the day you are considered for hiring, it may also be looked at on the day you are considered for promotion. This time, your credentials may be competing in a completely different league.

Third, and most pertinent to our discussion, a resume can help you land an interview. Few people are hired because of their resumes alone. They need to meet their prospective employers in person and talk about their qualifications. Putting your best foot forward on a resume is the first step to putting your best foot forward in an interview. The resume must make the employer want to meet you in person. Think about that when you are writing your resume. While reading it, the employer should be able to say, "I think this person would be a positive asset to our organization, and I would like to talk with the person further." Those are the kinds of reactions that *must* pop from the pages before you will be invited to meet management on a personal basis.

Strategy First, plan a strategy for your resume. Do not start writing without thinking. Ask, "What are the important qualities I want to communicate? What kind of experiences have I had in school? Did I take advantage of certain work opportunities? What type of awards have I won?" In other words, what will communicate you as being a professional person to a prospective employer?

Don't forget to include your personal qualities. What are your hobbies; what are your interests? What are those things that will make the person stop and say, "I'd like to meet this individual in person."?

Consider whether you want to use a functional resume or a chronological resume. Both have advantages, although some people feel the chronological resume is better for recent graduates. Functional resumes are especially appropriate when you have had good experience, but the titles of your jobs have not accurately reflected your abilities. A chronological resume lists, usually in order of the most recent first, the various activities and professional experiences you have accumulated. A functional resume lists the talents or abilities you possess without any reference to job titles or chronology.

The Introductory Letter

Do not forget to include an introductory letter with your resume. Just like the resume, it also must be perfect, well phrased and neat. Never send an introductory letter or a resume to a "Dear Sir." Find out who is going to be making the hiring decision and type the letter to that person. Talk about some of your personal qualities. Explain why you're interested in the company. It's easy to spot a form letter, and you need to make your letter stand out from the crowd. Show some enthusiasm and interest in your letter. Do not make it sound like a dry business letter, but at the same time keep it professional. Remember, it's the first impression management will have of you. A resume is a source of information, but an introductory letter must converse on an interpersonal basis. Will management enjoy talking with you, or will you be just another person taking up valuable time? Without being overbearing, sell yourself and express your unique qualities to management.

Asking for the Interview

Do not forget to ask for a personal interview in the letter that accompanies your resume. Do not forget to close your letter with a statement that will elicit some kind of response. "I'll look forward to hearing from you" is all right, but even better is a statement that you will be in the area and will be in contact with the person to set up an interview, or to simply request an interview and indicate that you will call on a given date to set up a time.

Always follow through with a telephone call. Just because a person does not write back or telephone you confirming an opportunity to hold an interview does not mean the person is not interested in hiring you.

Appearing for an Interview

Remember, be persistent and try for the interview, because even though you may not be considered for an immediate opening, other jobs will open up later. If you are in the forefront of management's mind, you will be in line to be considered much quicker than if your resume and cover letter are merely placed in a file.

Now it is your responsibility to put your best foot forward, including being prompt and prepared. This also includes being well dressed. Remember, you are being viewed not only as the person who will do the job, but as a person who will represent the company. Pay close attention to the important details of nonverbal communication, especially your

appearance. Clean hair, shined shoes, clean fingernails, pressed clothes all make an important difference. If you are a man, many suggest that you wear a suit and tie rather than a sportscoat. Be careful, too, of the little subtleties of good grooming. Ties that don't coordinate well, suits that look cheap, colored shirts, neckties that tie too far above the waistline, socks that are too short, and casual shoes can all spell a quick end to any consideration. Take the time to learn how to dress well, not just to dress.

Take into consideration the style of your hair and if you have a beard. You may think you're cool, but management may not know you well enough and may feel that long hair will just get longer and sloppier and that your beard is attempting to hide something.

Nonverbal factors should be of prime importance to women as well as to men. A woman in a skirted suit can present an air of professionalism. A skirt is more professional than slacks, even though when you are on the job you might be able to wear slacks. Makeup should be appropriate and not overdone. Leave your purse behind. Nervous fidgeting and not knowing what to do with it can be disastrous. If you have one, take along a tasteful briefcase for the "management" look. It has been said that a person should not dress for the job he or she has, but for the job he or she wants.

All of these things may seem like common sense, but you only need to spend an afternoon walking the halls of a placement bureau or talking with a corporate recruiter to see how many people have never learned even the basic lessons of presenting themselves.

Interacting with the Interviewer

When you meet a recruiter, or whoever is conducting the interview, greet the person *by name* but make sure you *pronounce it correctly*. If there is any question, check with a receptionist or someone who is sure of the correct pronunciation. Avoid being chummy. Nicknames and first names are absolutely out unless someone requests to be called by his or her first name or nickname or you have known the person for a long time. If the interviewer moves to shake hands, return the action as if you mean it. A limp handshake is not appropriate. Shaking hands communicates a positive attitude for women as well as for men.

Applying Interpersonal Skills Practice your skills of interpersonal communication during the interview. When serving as Assistant Director of the Career Planning and Placement Center at Eastern Illinois University, Robert Jones summarized nine skills important to an employment interview:

1. Follow the cues given by the interviewer. Let the interviewer take the initiative. Usually you can tell what the interviewer expects very early

in the interview. You may need to be a talker, but you also may find you need to be a listener.

2. No two interviews will be exactly alike.

3. The interview is a two-way process; do your share of talking if allowed. Remember, you must sell yourself just as a business sells its product to the consumer.

4. Avoid too many "yes" or "no" answers.

5. Try to be friendly and relaxed.

6. Be frank and sincere.

7. Think about the interview from the interviewer's point of view.

8. Be concise and prompt with your answers and questions. Don't be a compulsive talker.

9. Terminating the interview may be as important as making a good first impression. Thank the interviewer for his or her time and consideration.[20]

Handling Questions Be prepared for all sorts of questions. Answer honestly, but be on your toes. Some of the questions may become personal. What are some of the typical questions asked during interviews? Frank S. Endicott, Director of Placement at Northwestern University, surveyed companies and asked them to list frequent questions asked by corporate recruiters. Here are more than ninety questions Endicott found in his research:[21]

1. What are your future vocational plans?

2. In what school activities have you participated? Why? Which did you enjoy the most?

3. How do you spend your spare time? What are your hobbies?

4. In what type of position are you most interested?

5. Why do you think you might like to work for our company?

6. What jobs have you held? How were they obtained and why did you leave?

7. What courses did you like best? Least? Why?

8. Why did you choose your particular field of work?

9. What percentage of your college expenses did you earn? How?

10. How did you spend your vacations while in school?

11. What do you know about our company?

12. Do you feel that you have received a good general training?

13. What qualifications do you have that make you feel that you will be successful in your field?

14. What extracurricular offices have you held?

15. What are your ideas on salary?

16. How do you feel about your family?

FIRST INTERVIEW A CRUCIAL START

CHICAGO—A crucial interview for many new managers is the first one—with the company's executive recruiter. The degree of sophistication with which a candidate interacts with a recruiter can literally make or break his career, says James J. Drury of Keating, Grimm & Leeper, a search firm.

Here are some of the more common "turnoffs" that Drury mentions:

• Unprofessional personal appearance: long sideburns, double-knit suits, tinted eyeglass lenses, unshined shoes, ankle-length socks and discount store ties.

• Poor eye contact and stone face during an interview.

• Jaded attitude toward recruiters.

• Answers that are too short or too long.

The Chicago Sun-Times

JAUNDICED EYE

A kid with good sales form

A new category appeared the other day in the classified section of my local newspaper right between Motorcycles and Recreational Vehicles. It caught my eye because there was only one ad in it:

SKATEBOARD FOR SALE

1978 Flyer, fiber wheels, all fiberglass body, oversized ball bearings permanently lubricated, only 18 miles logged, must sell, owner retired.

It also gave a phone number to call "after school," so I waited until 5:00 p.m. and dialled, hoping to learn about what obviously was a budding industry. A mature female voice answered, and when I asked about the ad she yelled for "Jackson," who came on the line as professionally as any car salesman I ever talked to. "This is Jackson; may I help you?" It was the voice of a 10 year old.

"Jackson," I said, "my name is Lavenson and I'm calling about your 1978 skateboard. It's the first time I've seen a used one advertised. What's wrong with it?" Since I had no idea what I'd do with a skateboard, I was hoping his answer would give me an excuse to turn it down after putting the junior salesman through his paces.

"Nothing is wrong with my skateboard. It's in mint condition."

"You say in your ad that it only has 18 miles on it. Are those *original* miles, or did you buy it used?"

"I bought it new, and it's still under warranty. It has permanently sealed bearings and never needs servicing. It's won me two trophies for pool forms."

"What are pool forms?" I asked, suddenly feeling older.

"Figure eights in a swimming pool, of course. Don't you know *anything*?"

"I guess not. How much you asking for your vehicle?"

"Will this be cash or do you want to finance?" Jackson asked. For a moment I thought my banker was talking.

"Cash!" I fairly spurted with indignation, wanting to tell this upstart he was talking to a mature rich kid.

"Thirty-nine dollars. The helmet is extra."

"Helmet? What's that for?" I wanted to know.

"My parents made me buy it before they decided to make me sell the skateboard."

"Just why are you selling it, Jackson? And what does it mean, you're 'retired'?"

"I broke my leg," Jackson replied matter-of-factly. "I was doing a figure eight in a pool when some guy started to fill it."

I suppressed a gasp, but my hesitation on the phone triggered a follow-up worthy of the best sales pro: "Take my word, the skateboard doesn't have a scratch on it."

"Jackson, I think I'll pass on the skateboard," I said, hating to hang up the phone, "but please call me when you put an ad in the Jobs Wanted section."

By Jim Lavenson

(Reprinted with permission from the March 1979 issue of Sales & Marketing Management, © 1979 by S&MM.)

17. How interested are you in sports?

18. If you were starting college all over again, what courses would you take?

19. Can you forget your education and start from scratch?

20. Do you prefer any specific geographic location? Why?

21. Do you have a (boyfriend/girlfriend)? Is it serious?

22. How much money do you hope to earn at age 30? 35?

23. Why did you decide to go to this particular school?

24. How did you rank in your graduating class in high school? Where will you probably rank in college?

25. Do you think that your extracurricular activities were worth the time you devoted to them? Why?

26. What do you think determines a person's progress in a good company?

27. What personal characteristics are necessary for success in your chosen field?

28. Why do you think you would like this particular type of job?

29. What is your father's occupation?

30. Tell me about your home life during the time you were growing up.

31. Are you looking for a permanent or temporary job?

32. Do you prefer working with others or by yourself?

33. Who are your best friends?

34. What kind of boss do you prefer?

35. Are you primarily interested in making money or do you feel that service to other people is a satisfactory accomplishment?

36. Can you take instructions without feeling upset?

37. Tell me a story!

38. Do you live with your parents? Which of your parents has had the most profound influence on you?

39. How did previous employers treat you?

40. What have you learned from some of the jobs you have held?

41. Can you get recommendations from previous employers?

42. What interests you about our product or service?

43. What was your record in military service?

44. Have you ever changed your major field of interest while in college? Why?

45. When did you choose your college major?

46. How do your college grades after military service compare with those previously earned?

47. Do you feel you have done the best scholastic work of which you are capable?

48. How did you happen to go to college?

49. What do you know about opportunities in the field in which you are trained?

50. How long do you expect to work?

51. Have you ever had any difficulty getting along with fellow students and faculty?

52. Which of your college years was the most difficult?

53. What is the source of your spending money?

54. Do you own any life insurance?

55. Have you saved any money?

56. Do you have any debts?

57. How old were you when you became self-supporting?

58. Do you attend church?

59. Did you enjoy your four years at this university?

60. Do you like routine work?

61. Do you like regular hours?

62. What size city do you prefer?

63. When did you first contribute to family income?

64. What is your major weakness?

65. Define cooperation!

66. Will you fight to get ahead?

67. Do you demand attention?

68. Do you have an analytical mind?

69. Are you eager to please?

70. What do you do to keep in good physical condition?

71. How do you usually spend Sunday?

72. Have you had any serious illness or injury?

73. Are you willing to go where the company sends you?

74. What job in our company would you choose if you were entirely free to do so?

75. Is it an effort for you to be tolerant of persons with a background and interests different from your own?

76. What type of books have you read?

77. Have you plans for graduate work?

78. What types of people seem to rub you the wrong way?

79. Do you enjoy sports as a participant? As an observer?

80. Have you ever tutored a younger student?

81. What jobs have you enjoyed the most? The least? Why?

82. What are your own special abilities?

83. What job in our company do you want to work towards?

84. Would you prefer a large or a small company? Why?

85. What is your idea of how industry operates today?

86. Do you like to travel?

87. How about overtime work?

88. What kind of work interests you?

89. What are the disadvantages of your chosen field?

90. Do you think that grades should be considered by employers? Why or why not?

91. Are you interested in research?

92. If married, how often do you entertain at home?

93. To what extent do you use liquor?

94. What have you done which shows initiative and willingness to work?

How would you answer some of these questions? Obviously, many have no right or wrong answer, but if you are asked the question, you must respond. It's a good idea to consider these questions and many more that you can think of and practice the answers. Sit down with a friend and role play. Even videotape your answers, then play them back and see how you would look to an employer.

And what about some of those answers? Frank Endicott also looked at some of the negative factors evaluated during an employment interview that lead to the rejection of an applicant.[22] Consider some of the following negative characteristics which might be communicated in an interview. Examine closely the ones which would be corrected by the use of good interpersonal-communication skills:

1. Poor personal appearance.

2. Overbearing — overaggressive — conceited — superiority complex—know-it-all.

3. Inability to express oneself clearly—poor voice, diction, grammar.

4. Lack of planning for career—no purpose and goals.

5. Lack of interest and enthusiasm—passive, indifferent.

6. Lack of confidence and poise—nervousness—ill-at-ease.

7. Failure to participate in activities.

8. Overemphasis on money—interest only in best dollar offer.

9. Poor scholastic record—just got by.

10. Unwilling to start at the bottom—expects too much too soon.

11. Makes excuses—evasiveness—hedges on unfavorable factors in record.

12. Lack of tact.

13. Lack of maturity.

14. Lack of courtesy—ill-mannered.

15. Condemnation of past employers.

16. Lack of social understanding.
17. Marked dislike for school work.
18. Lack of vitality.
19. Failure to look interviewer in the eye.
20. Limp, fishy handshake.
21. Indecision.
22. Loafs during vacations—lakeside pleasures.
23. Unhappy married life.
24. Friction with parents.
25. Sloppy application blank.
26. Merely shopping around.
27. Wants job only for short time.
28. Little sense of humor.
29. Lack of knowledge of field of specialization.
30. Parents make decisions for the individual
31. No interest in company or in industry.
32. Emphasis on who one knows.
33. Unwillingness to go where company sends him.
34. Cynical.
35. Low moral standards.
36. Lazy.
37. Intolerant—strong prejudices.
38. Narrow interests.
39. Spends much time in movies.
40. Poor handling of personal finances.
41. No interest in community activities.
42. Inability to take criticism.
43. Lack of appreciation of the value of experience.
44. Radical ideas.
45. Late to interview without good reason.
46. Never heard of company.
47. Failure to express appreciation for interviewer's time.
48. Asks no questions about the job.
49. High-pressure type.
50. Indefinite response to questions.

If, after a personal interview, you have not heard anything from the employer within a week (unless he or she has indicated it will be longer), follow up with a personal telephone call. Management may have been out of town, or something may have developed that postponed the hiring decision.

Be persistent. Do not give up. Yet do not be pushy. The difference between the two can be an *extremely* fine line, and if you cross over it, you'll be perceived as aggressive and abrasive. The best advice is to use common sense and judge each situation individually.

SUMMARY

Our discussion of interpersonal communication in organizations has centered on the role and flow of messages and applied interpersonal-communication skills as reflected in the interview situation. Good interpersonal communication is important for success in any organization. Many times referred to as the glue which holds organizations together, communication influences management styles and contributes to everything from productivity to morale. Eleven troublesome communication skills in organizations include: listening, motivating people, giving directions, delegating authority, group problem solving, handling grievances, utilizing private one-to-one conferences, using the grapevine, making formal presentations, exhibiting conference leadership, and negotiating and bargaining.

Although we tend to think of organizations in terms of organization charts, a much more dynamic way to approach them is to examine the communication relationships that exist. These become the bases for decision making, often bypassing more formal structures.

Four approaches to management were discussed in this chapter. The classical approach is most closely tied to the organization chart and "chain of command." The human-relationships approach places a priority on people's interacting with each other and high morale. A pitfall of this approach can be low productivity, whereas a pitfall of the classical approach can be low morale. The human-resources approach seeks to develop the individual's full potential within the organization as a means to achieving high productivity. The systems approach assumes all the different divisions of a company function as an interrelationship.

Within any organization are different communication networks, which we classified as formal, informal, internal, and external. Each can interrelate to the other. Formal networks closely follow assigned channels of communication, whereas informal networks develop among individuals. Networks operating within an organization are called internal, while those operating outside the organization are called external.

Communication also flows in different directions within organizations. Downward communication from supervisor to subordinate can include job instructions, general information, rules and regulations, performance appraisal, and management philosophy. Upward communication from subordinate to supervisor includes self-appraisal, appraisal of others, and organizational policy. Horizontal communication between employees of equal stature often involves task sharing. All involve internal communication. Yet external-communication flow is also present and leaves and enters the organization as an interchange with the public.

Rumors and grapevines are special problems in organizational communication. Rumors are identified as wedge drivers, pipe dreams, bogeys, and homestretchers. Most rumors flow through informal communication channels called grapevines.

Regardless of what positions we hold in an organization, we fulfill certain roles in our relationships with other people. These relationships are often based on a power structure which can affect interpersonal interaction. While learning the bases of power—reward, coercion, knowledge, identification, and agreement—we also learned that power is a shared process between individuals.

Examples of applied communication in organizations include collective interaction, public presentations, and one-to-one interaction of which the interview is a prime example. Good interviews, especially job interviews, include preparation and planning. A resume and the use of effective interpersonal-communication skills all contribute to a successful job interview.

OPPORTUNITIES FOR FURTHER LEARNING

ALLEN, R. K., *Organizational Management Through Communication.* New York: Harper & Row, Pub., 1977.

ALMANEY, A. J. and A. J. ALWAN, *Communicating with the Arabs: A Handbook for the Business Executive.* Prospect Heights, IL: Waveland Press, Inc., 1982.

ARNOLD, C. C., et al., *The Speaker's Resource Book, Rev.* Glenview, IL: Scott, Foresman, 1966.

BORMANN, E. G., R. G. NICHOLS, W. S. HOWELL, and G. L. SHAPIRO, *Interpersonal Communication in the Modern Organization* (2nd ed.). Englewood Cliffs, NJ: Prentice-Hall, 1982.

BOWER, S. A., *Painless Public Speaking: Develop and Deliver Your Train of Thought Anytime, Anywhere.* Englewood Cliffs, NJ: Prentice-Hall—Spectrum Books, 1981.

BUYS, W. E., T. SILL, and R. BECK, *Speaking by Doing.* Skokie, IL: Nat. Textbook Co., 1981.

CAPPS, R., C. H. DODD, and H. J. WINN, *Communication for the Business and Professional Speaker.* New York: MacMillan, 1981.

DELLINGER, S. and B. DEANE, *Communicating Effectively: A Complete Guide for Better Management.* Radnor, PA: Chilton, 1982.

DIEKMAN, J. R., *Get Your Message Across: How to Improve Communication.* Englewood Cliffs, NJ: Prentice-Hall—Spectrum Books, 1979.

DYER, W. G., *Team Building: Issues and Alternatives.* Reading, MA: Addison-Wesley, 1977.

FISHER, R. and W. URY, *Getting to Yes: Negotiating Agreement without Giving In.* Boston: Houghton-Mifflin Co., 1981.

FRANK, A. D., *Communicating on the Job.* Glenview, IL: Scott, Foresman, 1982.

GOLDHABER, G. M., *Organizational Communication* (2nd ed.). Dubuque, IA: Wm. C. Brown Company Publishers, 1979.

HAMILTON, C. R., C. PARKER, and D. D. SMITH, *Communicating for Results: A Guide for Business and the Professions.* Belmont, CA: Wadsworth, 1982.

HOWELL, W. S. and E. G. BORMANN, *Presentational Speaking for Business and the Professions.* New York: Harper & Row, Pub., 1971.

KATZ, D., and R. KAHN, *The Social Psychology of Organizations.* (2nd ed.) New York: John Wiley, 1978.

KOEHLER, J. W. and J. I. SISCO, *Public Communication in Business and the Professions.* St. Paul: West Publishing Company, 1981.

McCULLOUGH, W., *Hold Your Audience: The Way to Success in Public Speaking.* Englewood Cliffs, NJ: Prentice-Hall—Spectrum Books, 1978.

MILES, R., *Theories of Management: Implications for Organizational Behavior and Development.* New York: McGraw-Hill, 1975.

MYERS, G. E. and M. T. MYERS, *Managing by Communication: An Organizational Approach.* New York: McGraw-Hill, 1982.

OLSON, R. F., *Managing the Interview: A Self Teaching Guide.* New York: John Wiley, 1980.

OUCHI, W. G., *Theory Z.* New York: Avon, 1981.

PASCALE, R. T. and A. G. ATHOS, *The Art of Japanese Management.* New York: Warner Books, 1981.

PROCHNOW, H. V. and H. V. PROCHNOW, Jr., *The Toastmaster's Treasure Chest.* New York: Harper & Row, Pub., 1979.

SAMOVAR, L. A., S. W. KING, and M. W. LUSTIG, *Speech Communication in Business and the Professions.* Belmont, CA: Wadsworth, 1981.

STEWART, C. J., and W. B. CASH, Jr., *Interviewing: Principles and Practices* (3rd ed.). Dubuque, IA: Wm. C. Brown Company Publishers, 1981.

THOMPSON, J., *Organizations in Action.* New York: McGraw-Hill, 1967.

TOWNSEND, R., *Up the Organization.* New York: Fawcett Books Group—CBS Publications, 1970.

WEICK, K., *The Social Psychology of Organizing* (2nd ed.). Reading, MA: Addison-Wesley, 1979.

WHYTE, W. H., Jr., *The Organization Man.* New York: Simon & Schuster, 1956.

WYDRO, K., *Think on Your Feet: The Art of Thinking and Speaking Under Pressure.* Englewood Cliffs, NJ: Prentice-Hall—Spectrum Books, 1981.

chapter nine

Interpersonal Communication in the Family

PREVIEW   *After completing this chapter, we should be able to:*

Be aware of the dimensions of family interaction.
Explain the communication forces at work in the family unit.
Discuss the tension between individual autonomy and interdependence in families.
Distinguish between firm, open, and orderless patterns of family interaction.
Recognize the illusion of ideal patterns of family interaction.
Describe the role of power in family interaction.
View the family as a small group engaged in small-group interactions.
Discuss the family in terms of formal, informal, closely knit, and loosely knit communication networks.
Discuss obstacles to family communication.
Improve our communication with the elderly.
Understand communication patterns in the extended family.

The summer after we moved to Chapel Hill, our fifteen-year-old son, John, spent three weeks in Germany living with a German family. The day he returned, we asked one of our friends if he would like to accompany us to meet John at the airport. Our friend, Larry, had recently returned from a tour of military duty in Germany. After the plane landed and our son had picked up his baggage, we all went out to dinner.

The conversation at the dinner table turned out to be primarily interaction between John and Larry. Although feeling a bit left out and wondering how a father could get some attention from his returning son, I began to observe the changes in communication patterns which were occurring and how they were really an example of changes which would be much more long range than the hour we spent having dinner.

John displayed both a dependence and an independence during our talk. He was dependent on our immediate family as a source of warmth and love which made coming home a pleasant experience. At the same time, he had achieved a new independence through experiences ranging from passing through customs to enjoying a European culture. He wanted that independence to be recognized, but at the same time appreciated sharing his experiences with the rest of our family. A new communication network outside our family developed with Larry, who could relate to his experiences in Germany. Our interaction with John became more adult-adult oriented as opposed to parent-child oriented.

If we were to characterize families' communication patterns today, we could best describe them as ever changing. This phenomenon of change in all families has frustrated researchers' efforts to study and predict communication among family members.[1]

As we examine interpersonal communication in the family, we will deliberately talk more about general trends than specific instances. The variety and flexibility of communication patterns that exist within different families demand this approach. However, an exploration of these general trends should uncover some similarities of communication patterns that we find within our own families. And knowledge of these trends should give us the tools to make our interactions with our families more meaningful.

Perhaps host and guest is really the happiest relation for father and son.

Evelyn Waugh

Interpersonal Communication in the Family

Defining the Family

A family is many things to many people. A family can be defined as an organized system of interaction based on changing relationships between people who may live together.[2] Let's dissect this definition and apply it to some concrete examples.

Interactional Qualities How and when families talk with each other varies. In some families, the maximum amount of interchange takes place at the table at mealtime. Here all members sit down at a given time, talk about their experiences during the day as they eat, and leave the table after everyone finishes the meal. In other families, "mealtime" as such does not exist. In many single-parent households, dual-parent households in which both parents work, with flexible working hours, and with other changes in life style, sitting down together for an evening meal may be almost impossible for some families. To force a regimented system of behavior upon so many demanding schedules may prove fruitless and be more an attempt to keep order than assure emotional bonds.

But whether a family meets together at the evening meal, whether a single parent meets a son or daughter for lunch, or whether a husband and wife converse over a bedtime snack, established and recurring communication patterns based on developing relationships are nurtured. The patterns reoccur because each member of the family has been conditioned on what to expect from other members of the family. When Harry talks everyone listens. When Hilda talks everyone obeys. When Jerry talks no one else can get a word in. When Mary talks she always gets a different opinion from Jerry.

These interaction patterns may be different from our interaction patterns outside the family. Our "outside" patterns may be based on shallower relationships of shorter duration, and we may be less dependent on them than we are on our family-interaction patterns.

Developmental Qualities Our definition of a family specified people who may live together. Such a situation, especially over time, can contribute not only to recurring communication but also to developmental communication. The developmental quality of interpersonal interaction has been stressed throughout this book, from its function as a basis for understanding the communication process to its role in developing relationships. This characteristic of interpersonal communication is equally important among family members.

Some people who do not understand these developing qualities become disenchanted with their own family's communication patterns. Children in conflict with parents or parents in conflict with each other label as "less meaningful" and "deteriorating" those communication

Selfhood begins with family and society, becomes modified by ideas and emotions, but ultimately grows to maturity in the context of trial and error.

Bruce McClellan

patterns which are better understood as "changing" or "developing." Stop and consider the changes that take place between the time a son or daughter is twelve years old and, say, twenty years old. The way in which a twelve year old relates to a parent and the way a twenty year old relates to a parent are quite different. Yet in some families, both parents and children fail to understand these developmental changes so that communication breaks down, and emotional traumas create barriers, not bridges, to communication. Understanding the changing and developing nature of communication patterns among family members when one or more of those members moves through stages in his or her own biological and psychological development ensures that communication channels can remain open, and interaction can continue.

Situational Qualities Established, recurring, and developing communication patterns that exist between family members can all be altered by different situations. To understand this situational nature of family communication patterns, consider the example of one member's borrowing the family car. Suppose when you ask to use the car, the other member of the family you asked says "yes," and you enjoy a drive to the beach. However, the next time you ask for the car, you are told it has been promised to another member of the family. So you negotiate with the other member, trading your use of the car for the next week for his or her use of the car now. At still another time, you are refused the use of the car. You try to negotiate. No chance; you walk.

In each case, the situation was different and the communication patterns were different. You interacted one way when you were given the use of the car, another when you had to negotiate the use of the car, and still another way when you were refused the use of the car. Each situation was different, producing different responses.

Communication Forces in the Family Unit

Earlier in this text we talked about the need to have control over our own lives and how this need shows up in our interpersonal interactions. Just as it affects our social and working relationships, the need for control affects our interpersonal relationships with our family members.

The Family Members' Need for Autonomy: The Independent Identity Our personalities begin to develop while we're infants. Sometimes this development contrasts with our parents' wishes. For example, while we generate new ideas and explore new experiences, those caring for us balance our explorations with a need for order, even for our safety. If we want to play in traffic, we will be stopped. If we try to see what the red glow of a stove burner feels like, we will be stopped. But our desires to search out new experiences, to be independent, and to achieve identities continue into adulthood.[3]

Within the family, this desire for autonomy and identity influences our communication patterns. We seek to be recognized among other members of the family. Sometimes this desire for autonomy results in sibling rivalries, sometimes in strained relations between parents and offspring. We only need to think back over our childhoods and adolescences to remember those first assertions of our autonomies. The first time we made choices of what to wear, what clothes to buy, or what food to order in a restaurant were big occasions.

This need for identity remains throughout our lives. Even after two people have reached a "bonding" stage, the necessity to retain an identity continues to play a part in the relationship.

The Need for Interdependence

While each family member strives for autonomy, the family as a unit must hold together. The family by its very nature is *interdependent*. At times this means sharing the rent or sharing the bathroom. At other times it means emotional interdependence, the need to turn to someone else who immediately understands us and can empathize with our problems. Some people view the family as a source of strength. Achievements are accentuated and failures are minimized because of strong family ties and the family-support system.

Thus, in family interaction, the individual's need for autonomy is balanced against the family unit's interdependence on one another. Consider the following dialogue:

WOMAN: *If we are careful this month, we will have enough money left over to put some in savings.*

> Family life is too intimate to be preserved by the spirit of justice. It can only be sustained by a spirit of love which goes beyond justice. Justice requires that we carefully weigh rights and privileges and assure that each member of a community receives his due share. Love does not weigh rights and privileges too carefully because it prompts each to bear the burden of the other.
>
> Niebuhr

MAN: *That sounds good, but Jennifer needs braces. At some point, we need to think about when we are going to start her treatment and how we are going to pay for it.*

WOMAN: *I realize Jennifer needs braces, but we also need to consider a cushion in case of a family emergency.*

MAN: *We have some life insurance to fall back on, and don't forget the stocks we own.*

WOMAN: *I don't consider the few stocks we have much of a cushion.*

MAN: *I understand your feelings. We do need some savings, but what about Jennifer?*

WOMAN: *I feel strongly that Jennifer's braces can wait at least another few months. I want to put the money in savings.*

MAN: *All right. The money goes in savings.*

We can see from the interaction that both people considered the balance between individual family members and the family as a whole. The decision had to be made whether the extra money would go into savings and be a support for the entire family or whether the money would benefit a single member of the family. At the same time, the woman was exercising her own individuality as an autonomous family member responsible for making financial decisions. In this case the man agreed, although disagreement and the man's own assertion of autonomy might have been exercised in a different situation and in a different family. The interaction which did occur reflected both the individual's desires for autonomy and the recognition of the interdependence of each family member upon other family members.

Resolving Conflict over Autonomy and Interdependence Recognizing the forces which pull between autonomy and interdependence is a first step in avoiding and resolving conflicts that exist when these two forces are at odds with each other. The next time a family argument develops, pause long enough to consider how autonomy and interdependence are colliding. Ask yourself if your own desire for autonomy conflicts with your family's need to be interdependent. If it does, can you avoid the conflict by recognizing the force and dealing with it in a positive way? Consider the following dialogue:

SON: *Dad, I know there's room at the cottage for the three of us. Crystal would have her own bedroom, and she can even help us drive. I don't see what the problem is. She has spent the night with us before, and you never objected. Why all the fuss now?*

PARENT: *There's no fuss. I just don't feel that a week at the beach needs to include your girlfriend. Besides, we've planned the trip for more than a month, and there was no mention of her coming along.*

SON: *So I brought it up at the last minute. I've brought her home for dinner at the last minute, and you were glad to see her.*

PARENT: *Look, let me be open and up front with you. Since your mother and I divorced, you know the time you have had to spend with either of us is limited. She lives five hundred miles away, and I'm at work all day. That doesn't leave much time for the two of us to be together, and I feel guilty that you can't spend time with your mother when you're not with me. I guess there is another side of it I don't like to admit. Your dating and bringing Crystal along makes me feel a bit like I'm getting very old. After all, being at the beach has always been a family activity. I don't want to lose that. Your wanting to bring Crystal along makes me feel alone and left out as though you would rather be with her than me. Needless to say I can't blame you, but it still hurts a little just the same.*

SON: *I'm sorry. I didn't realize how you felt. I can see the problem much more clearly now.*

In this example, the autonomy-interdependence conflict was based upon an emotional relationship. The parent's desire to keep the family interdependent was in conflict with the son's desire to bring his girlfriend along to the beach. But this time, father and son were able to talk things out because the father disclosed some inner feelings. In many family situations, someone may not be as quick or as willing to tell how he or she feels. Pride alone can stand in the way of self-disclosure. Unless one person is sensitive enough or knowledgeable enough to understand the forces which act upon the family unit, a host of communication breakdowns occur.

When you find yourself in a family dialogue which borders on conflict, ask yourself if you can negotiate a compromise. See if you can recognize the forces at work and communicate clearly what you feel or if you can help someone else to see the problem in a broader perspective. Although you may not be totally successful, understanding what each family member has at stake is a start in the right direction.

Distinguishing Patterns of Family Interaction

We can become even more sensitive to family interaction by viewing it as different patterns of communication.[4] We must be careful, however, not to place a particular value on a given communication pattern. Research has not suggested that any one pattern is more successful or creates any greater happiness than any other. While viewing these patterns, keep in mind that individuals, families, and situations differ.

Firm Patterns   If we were forced to use such labels as "downward communication" or "tough-minded," we might apply them to a member of a family who had control over other family members, whether the control was earned or taken, and on whose shoulders much of the decision making fell. We're hesitant to make an analogy with organizational communication, because comparing the way families operate with the way organizations operate is risky if not irresponsible. The tough-minded classical manager who rules through strong downward communication and even fear is not the same as the tough-minded parent who rules with love. At the same time, however, the family authority figure who keeps order through one-way communication directives could be said to be perpetuating a firm communication pattern.

A firm pattern of communication is designed to keep order and stability within the family. It can exist between one member of a family, such as a parent, and others who may be less capable of making decisions for themselves, such as young, dependent children. In these instances, the safety of the offspring is considered along with keeping order. As the children grow older, the firm pattern of communication may be replaced by a more open pattern, but only in certain areas. Although the child may be able to openly negotiate permission to walk to the movie with a date, requesting the family car for the weekend is out. Psychologically, these firmer patterns may never completely disappear as far as children's relationships with parents are concerned.

Where problems exist is in the interpretation of varying *degrees* of firmness. Consider that we are given the freedom to make decisions on our own. We are permitted to leave home and go to college, make decisions about schedules, and handle relationships with peers. We also handle our own finances. Yet when vacation time arrives, we may return home to family-communication patterns more firm than we have been accustomed to. We're suddenly not in control anymore. Yet a host of brothers and sisters still at home may require our parents to maintain order through a firm pattern of communication.

Many times we rebel against firm patterns of family communication. But such patterns can be part of the natural evolutionary process of families and generations. When parents are much older and unable to care for themselves, the children may instill a firm pattern of communication with their parents.

A HAPPY HOME RECIPE

4 cups of love
2 cups of loyalty
3 cups of forgiveness
1 cup of friendship
5 spoons of hope
2 spoons of tenderness
4 quarts of faith
1 barrel of laughter
Take love and loyalty, mix it thoroughly with faith. Blend it with tenderness, kindness and understanding. Add friendship and hope, sprinkle abundantly with laughter. Bake it with sunshine. Serve daily with generous helpings.

Open Patterns   Like firm patterns, open patterns of communication are simply a matter of degree. They evolve because the family has found it can function effectively in an open atmosphere of discussion, with each member working toward their individual autonomy and needs while not sacrificing the interdependence or cohesiveness of the family unit.

The key to a truly open pattern of communication is the ability of the members of the family unit to understand and accept continual change. As members of the family grow older, as new people are brought into the family unit through birth or bonding, the patterns are necessarily altered. Involving all members of the family in *two-way* communication is a difficult process and requires flexibility and understanding. Such "ideals" are not easily achieved. But when members of a family understand good interpersonal-communication skills, open patterns have the best chance for success.

Open patterns should not be confused with a lack of caring about members of the family or with sloppy communication skills. Rather, they are characterized by two-way communication in which the family unit retains its stability but is receptive to individual messages.

Orderless Patterns The least stable communication pattern is an orderless pattern. Again, this does not mean that an orderless pattern is bad, just that it is unpredictable. Each individual member of the family is given as much freedom as possible to seek out his or her strengths and communicate feelings to other family members. Other members, in turn, accept this free exploration of thoughts and ideas and support such interaction. Orderless patterns are indicative of considerable self-disclosure in which each member of the family explains and tests feelings and opinions.

Orderless patterns are much like brainstorming where all ideas are considered and encouraged, sometimes regardless of the consequences. The price for this free expression is a lack of stability.

Subpatterns When we evaluate communication patterns in our own families, we need to be alert to communication subpatterns. If patterns are firm, they may be firm between some but not all family members. One parent's communication patterns with young children may be different from communication patterns between the parent and a grandparent or with another parent. Age, generation, issues, and degree of relationship can play a part in determining a communication pattern.

The Illusion of the Ideal Pattern After reading about these various patterns, it is easy to make value judgments about our own families' communication and whether we would like a more firm, open, or even orderless pattern. Sometimes we equate more happiness with a certain pattern. Perhaps we feel that other family members should be more open to our ideas. Or we might desire more firmness and one way communication in our quest for more direction in our lives. As the saying goes, the grass always looks greener on the other side of the fence. Because we are not part of another family, we naturally see the positive sides of other people's interactions. A guest for dinner or the weekend often sees families on good behavior, and fails to realize that in the day-to-day interaction, everything isn't always polite and ordered. Some scholars even suggest that families have much more disagreement than agreement.[5] The very fact that a family creates bonds unlike those elsewhere in society can make disagreement less threatening to family members than it would be to people involved in interactions outside the family.

Again, we should not assume that one communication pattern is better than another. Every family is different, and a family's cohesiveness may make it better able to accept a certain pattern.

Recurring Patterns

Even though communication within families is a developing process, communication patterns do become repetitious. They become repetitious because of the family's striving for a balance between individual autonomy and family interdependence. Once the family has a workable communication formula, it encourages the communication of that formula.

By their very nature, these recurring patterns are difficult to change; this can create problems, especially when some family members don't get along with each other. Suppose two children have a rivalry and disagree with each other whenever they interact. Each sees the other as a threat to personal credibility, as a competitor for the love of a parent, and as a generator of other conflicts that can occur in close family relationships. They fight over territorial space, clothes, or other possessions. Because the family has worked to develop recurring patterns of communication, changing the patern to resolve the sibling conflict or prevent it takes a strong commitment and a knowledge of interpersonal skills.

Power in Family Interaction

As with organizations, power in families can affect how members communicate and relate to each other. Traditionally, we have thought of power in a family as being invested in the head of the household, the person who holds the purse strings, the person who can say yes or no. In many situations, this individual does hold power in family interaction and family relationships. But to truly understand power, we must look beyond a single individual. Besides, the definition of the term *head of the household* is rapidly changing in our society. We must thus look to *every* member of the family, since each member takes part in that power-based family interaction.

The Balance of Power

Every member of the family utilizes some form of power to survive as an individual. This use, again, relates to that omnipotent need for self-identity and autonomy. To achieve and protect that identity, therefore, members of a family set up power structures around which they interact with others. Each interaction is different, and the degree of power varies with the topic or issue and the people who are interacting with each other.

Imagine that you want to borrow some money from a member of your family. The person who has the money has power over you, and your interaction will reflect this. You do not simply approach the person and say, "Give me your money!" Your communication is more like, "I need a loan and wondered if you could lend me ten dollars until I pick up my paycheck this afternoon." But the person lending you the money wants to negotiate a deal. Since the person is required to mow the lawn, he will give you the money if you agree to mow the lawn for him. Now you possess power over him. And you negotiate. If he wants the lawn mowed, he must give you the money first. The power relationship has now become *two way.* In this example, both people have power, although we could argue over who has the most power. Yet in another situation dealing with another issue, the power balance may be entirely different.

Applying the Basis of Power to Family Interaction To further understand power, we can apply to the family setting the factors we discussed in the chapter on interpersonal communication in organizations.[6]

The Power to Reward Members of a family have the power to reward in both tangible and intangible ways. If you need money, the people who have money have power over you, as our example just showed. In a family, however, the intangible rewards of attention and love are present. We may feel a need for the love and attention that another member of the family can offer. This can range from a young child's relationship to a parent to two people in romantic love with each other. Although these emotions cannot be bargained and traded like dollars, the overt expression of them can be, "Let's make love" or "I have a headache."

The Power to Coerce In many families, the power to coerce is more *implied* than *applied.* Young children realize that their parents have the power to punish them, although as they grow older, they also realize that the means of punishment are gradually reduced.

The Power of Knowledge Young children's social and physical development depends on the knowledge of their elders. Help with school work, learning how to drive, and acquiring manners require the transfer of knowledge from one person to another; the person possessing the knowledge has power over the person receiving it.

Power through Identification In families with strong emotional bonds, power through identification exists. During a child's development, the youngster goes through stages in which he or she emulates an older member of the household. During this time, the person being emulated may have a degree of power over the youngster and can set examples. In some cases, this emulation can continue into adulthood.

Power by Agreement We tend to think of power by agreement as contracts or written documents by which people abide. In a family, power by agreement is present, but not in such formalized form; children may agree to arrive at meals on time, go to bed at a certain time, be back from a date at a certain time, and perform household chores. Parents, in turn, may agree to feed, house, clothe, and take care of the children.

The Family as a Small Group

In essence, the family is a small group of individuals. Thus, the skills of small-group interaction play an important role in family communication. We can apply those small-group skills to the family setting mindful of some variations.

Applying Small-Group Skills
If we are asked to take part in a corporate board meeting, we would pay close attention to the way in which we interacted with other group members.

After all, we would be evaluated by peers, the profits of the company might be at stake, and our future relationships with our coworkers would depend on our use of good communication skills.

When we get back home and interact with our family, we often neglect those skills. For some reason, we may feel it's not as important to use them around our families. We may even feel that we can get away with not using those skills with our family. Arguments, conflict, and hurt feelings are just some of the consequences of such neglect. As discourteous as it is, we tend to live in our own worlds. Recognizing other people's perceptions of the world sometimes takes practice. Consider interacting in a family in which people have different perspectives from yours. To fail to recognize these perspectives means that homophily is absent, communication is one way, and people hear but do not listen.

Assume that you sit down with a parent, a younger sister, and an older brother. The conversation takes the following form:

YOURSELF: *I want to set aside fifty dollars from my job and buy some new clothes this month.*

PARENT: *There is a sale at Anthony's. All of their men's stock is at half price through the end of the month.*

SISTER: *Get some new slacks. And get rid of those ones that look like you stepped out of a carnival. I saw some on Bobby last week that were fantastic.*

BROTHER: *Buy jeans. My last pair lasted five years.*

YOURSELF: *All good ideas. I'll consider them.*

You could have reacted to each of the three opinions by disagreeing. Each person had a different perspective on buying clothes. Your parent, who is concerned about making ends meet, wants you to take advantage of the sale. Your brother has had years of use from a pair of blue jeans and considers quality first. Your sister could care less about either money or quality; she's concerned about looks. How did you handle the discussion? You recognized and appreciated each person's perspective and opinion.

You could have also interrupted, lacking sensitivity to the "taking-turns" approach, which may have caused a breakdown in communication. You might have failed to see the relationship between your sister and your parent. Contradicting one may have caused hard feelings with the other. You could have failed to consider that you might like to ask a member of the family for advice. Shutting off communication at this point in the conversation might have prevented that person from giving you that advice. Overall, you were sensitive to the developmental nature of interpersonal relationships and reacted by respecting the thoughts and opinions of others.

In the chapter on interpersonal communication in small groups, we examined the content of small-group interaction. We learned that every person in a group has a responsibility for group cohesiveness. Apply that same principle to family communication. Remember that the content of small-group interaction can include supportive statements, statements of unity, and solutions to problems as well as arguments against solutions, expressions of disunity, and messages which show superficial interest. Be alert to these different messages found in all small-group communication and be constantly aware which statements support group cohesiveness, promote positive relationships, and work towards solutions to problems that each member understands, appreciates, and accepts.

We often fail to see the distinction between family discussion groups and other discussion groups. At work or at school, the people we deal with may be our same general age. This commonality plus their position in life and the shared task to be accomplished may make their perspectives on issues similar to ours. Do not assume that every group interaction will share the same characteristics. That we sometimes rely on our families to be supportive causes us to forget that family members react to communication just as do other people. Abrupt criticism and insensitivity to other people's feelings and opinions can have the same negative consequences inside the family and out.

Leadership Behavior   Unlike board meetings, small-group communication in the family is usually spontaneous and without an appointed leader. This does not mean that leadership can be discounted. If a group discussion has a recurring theme, a leader may emerge. Many times the leader will be the person who initiated the communication. Yet if the topic changes, which it often does within a relatively short period of time, the leadership may also change.

Imagine that three members of a family are sitting around the table after dinner. Within a period of fifteen minutes, three topics are discussed. The mother initiates a discussion about the lawn. A brother named Bill initiates a discussion about a course in which he is enrolled. A sister named Mary initiates a discussion about planning for a highschool dance. We assume that Mary is younger than Bill. During the discussion about the yard, the mother, although not appointed a discussion leader, leads the discussion. Bill listens most of the time, and Mary offers some opinions. When Mary initiates the discussion about the school dance, Bill tends to monopolize the conversation. He tells Mary about his own experience and explains to her exactly how the dance should be planned. When Mary makes a suggestion, Bill disagrees, then asks their mother for her opinion. Bill assumes he has a right to lead the discussion since he is older and had already experienced planning a high-school dance. But Bill fails to see that not only has Mary initiated the discussion, but she is the one personally involved in the planning. Sometimes the difference in age, experience, and perceived status within the family causes people to assume leadership positions at a time when they actually might improve family relations by deferring to the person who initiated the discussion and has the most at stake in its outcome.

Small-Group Permanence Earlier, we said that the family represents variations from other small groups. One of the most distinct is its *permanence*. The board of directors at a company changes, sometimes quite rapidly. In a family, however, the group will last for the members' lifetimes. This permanence has both assets and liabilities. It does retain a relative stability over time. Members know how other members react and have adjusted their communication patterns accordingly. On the other hand, the security and permanence may mean that more members may be more prone to risking disagreement which can cause strained relationships.

Be alert to these characteristics in your own family interaction. Ask yourself how much the permanence and consistency of the family as a small group permits members to disagree and what are the consequences of this disagreement.

Families as Communication Networks

More complex than the small-group perspective of a family is to view it as part of larger communication networks.[7] By doing so, we take into consideration not only communication patterns within the family but communication patterns beyond the family. The "extrafamily" relationships become important when they influence patterns of communication among family members. A family is seen by others not only by how members relate to each other, but by how they relate to those outside the family.

To understand families as networks, we will break families down into (1) formal; (2) informal; (3) closely knit; and (4) loosely knit networks. These four divisions are *interrelated*, but to help us understand them, we will discuss them separately.

Formal Networks Formal networks are lines of communication which are understood and accepted by all members of the family. Many times these formal networks are keys to family decision making and problem solving. The family lawyer, doctor, and minister are members of a family's formal communication networks. These professionals and their decisions, the accuracy of their communications, their opinions, and their credibility all influence the family. Suppose family members sit down to discuss the legal ramifications of adding on to the family business. Even though the lawyer might not be present, the communication that has taken-place between the lawyer and the family becomes part of the discussion and the decision making. The perceptions other people have of the family may also be determined by the capability of the lawyer. "The Jones retain Jane Doe as their lawyer. Therefore, the Jones must be a fine family." The same can be said for the family's other formal networks.

Informal Networks   Informal networks also play a role in family interaction. Some of the Jones' valued customers can be part of their informal communication network. The customers do not have the same relationship to the family as does the lawyer, but their advice still may be sought about the decision to expand the business. The interaction with the customers may not be as formal as that with the lawyer—meetings may be by chance instead of by appointment—and the credibility may not be the same. Nevertheless, the customers, many of whom the Jones know on a personal basis, are important links in the network.

Neighbors, friends, club members, and other social acquaintances may all be part of a family's informal communication network. Johnny plays with Mary. Mary gets in a fight with Johnny. Mary's mother gets in an argument with Johnny's mother. Mary's mother tells her problems to Mary's father, who happens to be Johnny's father's best friend. We can easily see how these outside relationships can directly affect family interaction.

Closely Knit Networks   For our purposes, closely knit networks consist of people outside of the family unit with whom at least one member of the family is related. In many cases, relatives not living with the family—for example, aunts, uncles, and cousins—are part of closely knit networks. Frequent communication takes place within the network, and a close emotional bond may exist among the members. Closely knit networks are nutured through frequent visits, telephone calls, family reunions, and similar reaffirmations.

Loosely Knit Networks   Loosely knit networks are made up of a family's casual acquaintances, those people who have limited emotional involvement and contact with family members. Such individuals do not readily or profoundly affect the relationships or communication among members of the family unit. Unlike the members of closely knit networks, members of a family's loosely knit networks probably do not know one another.

FAMILIES APART—'NEXT TIME IS
ALWAYS SO FAR AWAY'

Amtrak's morning train from Seattle is on time to the minute. It stops at the station in East Olympia, where five people—two women, a man and two little girls—are exchanging goodbyes. The women hug each other. Another chance will not come again for months. It is no casual hug.

The station at East Olympia is a monument to the decline of rail travel. There was a depot once, but it died of neglect. In its place is a three-sided shelter in the pines, a sort of glorified lean-to. The town is several miles distant by way of a dirt road through the forest. There are no taxis, no ticket windows, not even a telephone. A stranger arriving in the middle of the night could be forgiven for thinking he had been left to die in the wilderness.

The stop is of the half-minute variety. The luggage isn't completely aboard when the porter says it's time to go and the wheels begin to move. The man, the girls and the younger woman lean from the doorway with last goodbyes. The other woman stands on the platform, waving. She smiles, but doesn't fool anyone. Her eyes betray her best attempt at bravery.

The train stops again in about 20 minutes. The man and woman are surprised by the number of passengers that file from the ornate brick station and aboard the train at Centralia. The children, for the most part, are quiet. The oldest, who is nearly 7, says she wishes she could stay at her grandmother's house for a million years.

The subject of her wistful thoughts is in downtown Olympia by now. It is her first day on a new job, after 16 years on the old one. It doesn't seem fair. Starting over is tough enough all by itself.

Centralia behind, the man and woman begin the inevitable conversation. Perhaps they could visit sooner next time. Perhaps in the spring. The woman says six months between visits is too long. Her husband agrees, but the old obstacles waste no time presenting themselves. Not enough time, too many miles. It helps to talk about next time, but not very much. Next time is always so far away.

They talk some more, and then no one feels like talking. The children begin to play with their dolls. Western Washington glides by, white in the windows of Amtrak's Superliner. It is snowing, not just in Western Washington but throughout the Northwest.

On the trip over, the train had to back up and make three runs at a snowdrift in the Blue Mountains. Then it pulled onto a siding and waited for a three-diesel snowplow. Nothing could have been more reassuring to the holiday-minded passengers than the sight of that churning snowplow. It was a happy trip. Now the thought of getting stuck doesn't seem so bad.

More towns. Kelso-Longview, Vancouver, Portland. The Columbia River Gorge is lovely, even under a foot of snow, but the scenery is lost on the parents of the little girls. Unlike their daughters, they have found no suitable distractions. Their thoughts remain with the woman they left on the platform at East Olympia.

The man is thinking about something that happened at her house that morning. He was in the living room, searching for things that might have been overlooked in packing. She was in the kitchen, preparing a hot breakfast to brace her granddaughters for the rigors of train travel. He overheard her

Interpersonal Communication in the Family

talking to them, and suddenly he realized she was crying. It wasn't surprising, really. He half expected it.

She is not the sort who would manufacture tears to make them stay longer—or move closer—and that made it worse. She didn't know anyone else could hear, and would have been upset if she had known. The conversation was meant to be private, between her and her only grandchildren. She was telling them how she felt about them. Her voice sounded terrible, all shaky and broken.

The man stayed in the living room longer than necessary, pretending to look for things he knew were already in the suitcases. Another man might have known what to do, but he was not another man, and he felt clumsy and helpless. And a little guilty.

It was he, after all, who had taken her daughter to live and raise children in another state. She was happy there, but sometimes she got a certain look in her eyes, and he knew she was thinking about her mother, and he would wonder for the hundredth time if he had done right by them. There had been chances to move. Perhaps he was wrong to love Idaho so much.

When it was quiet in the kitchen, he sneaked down the hallway, opened his suitcase, and made a show of being busy.

More stops. Hinkel, Pendleton, LaGrande. This time the train crosses the Blue Mountains without incident, putting yet another barrier between people who want to be together. How many other families are aboard, leaving behind the people and places they know best?

The train arrives in Boise early in the morning. The man and woman carry their sleeping daughters to the car, load the luggage and drive home. It is cold inside. The man stays up a long time, fussing with the wood stove and wishing it were a heat pump. When he does come to bed, he lies awake for a long time.

He wonders if she knows that her daughter isn't the only one who misses her, and if she has any idea how bad he feels about the separations. He wishes he had told her how much he wished that it didn't have to be the way it was. Most of all, he wishes he had gone into the kitchen that morning and given her a hug.

He hopes she'll read this someday, and that she'll understand.

(Courtesy: Tim Woodward. © The Idaho Statesman)   **Tim Woodward**

Communication Roles

Within family-communication networks, different family members have different roles. One member of the family may have the role of maintaining the networks. A parent who frequently exchanges letters with relatives may fill this role. Other family members may act as liaisons between two different networks. For example, suppose Sam is a member of the Jones family. He is thus part of the Jones' family-communication networks. When Sam marries into the Smith family, he also functions as part of the Smith's family networks. In addition, he serves a third role of being the *liaison* or the *link* between the two networks. The next time you attend a wedding reception at which two families meet for the first time, notice how the initial greetings center around the "links" in the network. "Oh, I see, you're Sam's uncle. Well, then who is Tillie? Ah, she's Sam's aunt. How nice."

Obstacles to Family Communication

In order for communication to flow freely within communication patterns and networks, it must overcome various obstacles. By analyzing your own family-interaction patterns, you will undoubtedly come up with many more obstacles than we can treat here. A few of the more common ones, however, include generation differences, stress, nonverbal obstacles, and stereotyping.

Generation Differences If the "generation gap" were responsible for everything it is blamed for, most of the communication problems people face could be solved by concentrating our research efforts on this single phenomenon.[8] Yet although the generation gap is often a scapegoat, in some cases it is a very definite block to interpersonal communication. It becomes particularly troublesome when emotional and social distances develop between different family members.

Let's look at a situation in which a family is dealing with financial matters. For parents who have lived through hard economic times, their primary goal in life may be to earn a good living. In fact, a lack of happiness for them is associated with the truama and stress of not being able to make ends meet. Sons and daughters, on the other hand, who may not have shouldered the responsibilities of a family or tough economic times, may be more concerned about the quality of life as opposed to income. This does not mean that they are not concerned about earning money, just that money is considered a secondary goal to quality of life.

The conflict between making a living and making a life can be illustrated by what happened at a chemical company. When reprimanding employees, the company forced them to take days off without pay. Management found that telling employees who were forty years old and older to take days off without pay was effective; it hurt their economic security. Yet when the company told its twenty-five–thirty-five–year-old employees to take days off without pay, the response was, "Hell, we'll take the whole week!" The younger workers took economic security for granted and did not see the threat. Thus, the company changed its policy and made younger employees who made mistakes work overtime.[9]

Families can face numerous other such issues. An acceptable dating partner, appropriate clothes to wear, and satisfactory living arrangements with peers can all be areas about which different and deep-seated generation-related opinions can create obstacles to communication.

Stress Traditionally, the family has been looked upon as a sanctity from the stress of a job and the outside world. Yet the family environment sometimes can be more stressful than the world from which we are supposed to escape. "I need to get back to work to rest from my vacation" is a joking phrase which may often not be so far from the truth.

People react to stress in different ways. Some people return home after a stressful day and want to be alone. They may want to collect their thoughts and ponder the day's activities. Not wanting to talk to other members of the family, doing exercise routines alone, and going upstairs to lay down for an hour may be some of their reactions. Other people may want to talk out their problems and frustrations. They desire to be with other people to whom they can relate and explain how rough the day was. When these two opposite types of people happen to meet at the end of the day, for instance, a husband and a wife, additional stress is almost unavoidable. The wife may feel that her husband doesn't care about her because he's avoiding her. The husband may perceive his wife's need for attention as a continuation of the stress he left behind. The resulting communication, if it takes place at all, may be explosive.

To be able to communicate under stress, it is important to understand these different reactions to stress. Try to determine how the person with whom you're communicating handles stress and then adapt to that style. If the person wants to unload his or her problems, try to be a good listener. If he or she wants to be alone, try to give the person that freedom.

Nonverbal Obstacles

In our discussion of personal and territorial space, we learned that different people require different amounts of both. The size and architecture of houses and the size of families can create some awkward situations and resulting barriers to communication. Rooms on different floors and seating arrangements which do not permit face-to-face communication can produce artificial barriers. Similarly, when adequate territorial space is unavailable for all family members, friction can result. The future may not hold a solution for such problems. Because of high energy costs, unpredictable interest rates, and inflation some experts predict that much smaller houses will be the norm for the future.

For children between the ages of six and twelve, conflicts between verbal and nonverbal cues can be troublesome. For children older than twelve, when the verbal and nonverbal cues are in conflict, the nonverbal cues will be read as correct. To better understand these nonverbal obstacles, consider the use of satire. Because adults are more adept at understanding figurative meanings of words, they will be able to understand the point of a satirical story much more than will young children, who take words at their literal meaning.[10]

Stereotyping

Stereotyping can promote as many obstacles to effective family communication as it can to other communication. One of the stereotypes we discussed when learning about listening skills was the assumption that people from a given class or background have certain traits. When the family network stretches to include such people, the same unjustified stereotypes can be imposed. What friends we should associate with and who is the right person to date can be some of the barrier-filled discussions that ensue. As family members associate with individuals outside the family and as networks expand to include new friends and associates, open communication without prejudice, although sometimes difficult, is a step towards understanding.

Communicating with the Elderly

In what has been called the "Aging of America," television documentaries have focused on older citizens, Congressional subcommittees have investigated their benefits and life styles, and older citizens themselves have become a powerful, organized force in society. Changing economic conditions spawn predictions that more senior citizens will be residing with their families in the future as generations share living space to cut costs. For the elderly, this social adjustment may be traumatic. As part of our continuing research efforts into communication skills, we are becoming more sensitive to the needs of the elderly and ways to bring them into meaningful interaction with each other and with younger generations (Figure 9–1).[11] Much of the adjustment to aging has a foundation in interpersonal communication, beginning with self-concept.

Challenges to Self-Concept

We have learned that one of the first prerequisites of positive and satisfying interpersonal communication with others is a positive self-concept. Self-concept has its roots in our value system, our past, our perceptions of the future, and the answer to the question "Who am I?"

The elderly face constant challenges to their self-concepts, which can make interpersonal communication difficult.[12] For many elderly persons, the work place was the source of self-esteem. Colleagues and coworkers were present to provide the positive reinforcement for jobs well done, to reaffirm competence, to praise, and to mold.[13] People's perceptions of themselves were closely tied to this network of positive reinforcers. Upon retirement, the source of this reinforcement disappeared. Not only were there no people to offer praise, but there was no setting in which praise could take place. Thus, one of the main sources of self-concept disappeared.

Perceived or actual mental and physical health and perceptions of the future can also influence self-concept.[14] If a person is less than active and healthy, the ability to interact positively with others deteriorates. Sometimes this becomes a self-fulfilling prophecy: The worse one feels, the worse one perceives himself or herself; and the worse one perceives himself or herself, the worse one feels. The future, the ambitions

A youth was questioning a lonely man. "What is life's heaviest burden?" he asked.

The old fellow answered sadly, "To have nothing to carry."

Interpersonal Communication in the Family

FIGURE 9-1
As part of a Chicago-based "Executive Volunteer Corps" program, retired volunteer executives offer experience and advice to aspiring entrepreneurs who are starting their own businesses. (Colonial Penn Group, Inc.)

and aspirations which were a vital and vibrant part of one's younger years, now become less helpful to self-esteem because of the limited opportunities to make a valuable contribution to society through employment. Forced public-assistance programs fanned by corporate retirement programs, some lucrative enough to *financially force* individuals into early retirement without consideration for their emotional health, compound the problem.

Even the mass media's treatment of the elderly may compound the problem. From books to television, the elderly are portrayed as less than competent, in ill-health, not self-sufficient, and even law breakers as typified by the movie "The Over the Hill Gang."

Improving Self-Concept and Communication In communicating with the elderly, positive steps can be taken to make interpersonal communication more fulfilling.

Avoid Stereotyping Our own conditioning to the elderly is influenced by what we hear and read. It must be balanced by what we actually experience. Do not fall into the trap of assuming that just because a person is elderly, he or she is less active, less alert or intelligent, less sensitive, or less able to relate to others or to younger generations. Case after case proves those assumptions wrong. When we set stereotypes aside, we can interact with another person through appreciation and mutual respect as opposed to pity.

Do Not Avoid Communication Avoiding communication with the elderly can be another self-fulfilling prophecy for both the sender and receiver of communication. When one has the opportunity to frequently interact with others, communication is more positive than interaction which occurs as a temporary respite to isolation. Just including an individual in discussions and activities can promote positive communication.[15]

Look for Homophily   Homophily means sharing. Look for common ground with the elderly. At first, the common ground may not seem important and even may seem superficial. Discussions about the weather, television programs, and news events are a start to any conversation, but they can lead to a deeper understanding of the background and experiences of the elderly. Even if you cannot share the same experiences, asking about and sharing new perspectives is meaningful and important.

Communicate as an Equal, not a Subordinate   We sometimes treat an elderly person more as a subordinate than as an equal, even when pity is not involved. Our communication habits, from nonverbal cues to language, fall into patterns somewhat similar to those we use when communicating with a child. Respect an elderly person as an equal and work to communicate on this basis.

Participate in Positive Stroking   You can replace the reinforcement no longer provided to the elderly by the work place by your own "positive stroking." Compliments freely yet honestly given about abilities and contributions can help supplement the lack of positive reinforcement from other sources.

Take the opportunity to improve your interpersonal skills with the elderly. Be responsible for initiating communication, and be alert to the pitfalls which prevent effective and meaningful communication. The role of the elderly in our society is changing. We're all recognizing that contributions to society, levels of mental and physical health, accomplishments, and potential are not always related to chronological age.

Divorce, Separation, and the Extended Family

The statistics on divorce and separation are such that many readers of this book are either the children of parents who are divorced, or are themselves divorced or remarried.

The breaking up of a relationship has occurred with much less stigma in recent years, a contrast from a few years ago when divorced persons were generally shunned by society. Today, although prejudices sometimes still exist, most people view divorce and separation as a much better alternative than the continuation of a destructive relationship. Many psychologists and marriage counselors report positive results from divorce, especially among individuals who are married but uncaring, unloving, and in some cases emotionally, if not physically, injurious to one another.

Since the high rate of divorce is a relatively new phenomenon, we cannot draw on long-term research as we can in other areas of psychology and communication. Thus, much of what we know about communication in situations of divorce and separation comes not from large-scale surveys, but from the clinical files of marriage counselors. Even then, a large body of unreported experiences exists where parties have not the background, finances, or wherewithall to seek counseling before a separation or divorce takes place. Add to this the fact that every divorce and separation is unique, and we can see why analyzing the phenomenon is still risky.

Challenging Self-Concept: Spouses To understand what happens to interpersonal communication during divorce or separation, we will begin by examining what happens to the self-concept of the parties involved—spouses as well as children.[16]

The breaking up of a relationship is a force which can significantly lower a person's self-concept. Remembering that self-concept is one of the key components of good interpersonal communication, we can see immediately that such communication is affected when a person experiences an "uncoupling," either legally or emotionally.

For example, a sense of failure can grip both individuals. The best intended plans have not succeeded, and both parties, whether admitting it or not, may feel responsible for the failure. If nothing else, each has incorrectly judged the other, or they would not have been joined together in the first place. The inability to successfully judge the qualities or characteristics of one's mate is a very personal kind of failure.

If the dissolving of the relationship is particularly unpleasant and drags out over a long period of time, the fatigue of these emotional battles can take its toll. Small victories and put-downs, either through interpersonal interaction or through legal sparring of attorneys, can be somewhat hollow vindications. Destroying one's mate may outwardly signal a form of satisfying revenge, but it takes little time to look in the mirror and ask, "What kind of a person have I become that I should need to enter into these battles?" It takes an incredible amount of maturity to keep self-concept intact in the face of threats to our judgments about love and relationships.

Second, communication between the two parties lessens or becomes "only for the sake of the children." Yet during the time of the relationship, the parties may have come to rely heavily on each other as a form of identity, albeit in an atmosphere of conflict. Suddenly each person's identity is in limbo.

In the chapter on relationships, we discussed how at a certain stage of a relationship, the "I" is replaced with "we." Now the "we," which makes up the whole person, is sliced off. Each individual temporarily becomes only half a person. Such occurrences may result in temporary, even intimate, reconciliations as each party seeks out the "lost" emotional partner. In other cases, another person or lover may enter the scene. When this occurs too soon after the divorce, the new relationship may be superficial or awkward, since the newly-divorced party may still be carrying the "we" part of the other party. It will take time before the new self-concept can function independently of the "we."

Acquiring a new self-concept may be further complicated by the couple's children, who have inner desires for parents to get back together again. Children may have a difficult time understanding why two people they love so much should not love each other. Even unintentional attempts at bringing the parents together, such as arranging lunches or times when the old family structure can be recreated, may inadvertently retain the "we" when the "I" is striving to rebuild itself.

Still another attack on self-concept comes from diminished friendships. Friends who want to remain neutral during marital discord avoid both parties, not wanting to play favorites or offend either party. Thus, the friendships and interaction which used to reinforce each person's self-concept are absent and loneliness sets in. Withdrawal then occurs, which can create more loneliness.

Changes in residence can be another threat. The familiar surroundings which once were the "security of home" abruptly change. Since one party must usually move out, the need to adapt to a new residence, even a new town or a new part of the city, presents a new challenge. Many times we overlook the fact that divorce and separation are synonymous with a physical move, with all of the challenges to the self-concept a move can bring, except that those challenges are operating when the emotional well-being of the parties is simultaneously under fire.

Personal possessions usually enhance a person's self esteem and become part of his or her identity. To some, success may be defined by owning a nice home or driving a nice car. Yet divorce usually involves a splitting up of property, and one party may lose some of these possessions. The party also loses part of his or her self-esteem in the process. Instead of returning to the well-furnished house in the suburbs, the party may drive a "clunker" to an empty apartment. All the party has worked for, perhaps measured by what he or she was able to purchase by working hard and moving up the ladder, is gone. The person is abruptly back to square one, feeling forced to start all over again. The blow to self-concept is very real.

Challenging Self-Concept: The Children of Divorce

Children of divorced parents, no matter what their age, also experience the same attacks on their self-concepts. Since a child's identity is made up of himself or herself and two parents, the child, depending on how custody is awarded, now finds himself or herself developing an identity with only one person. The structure in which he or she is viewed by friends is also shattered. If the child has friends who are also the children of divorced parents, the sharing of feelings and experiences may help to more rapidly rebuild self-esteem. Until that time, however, interactions with others may be awkward. This is particularly true if friends of the children were friends of both parents. They may be haunted by such question as, How can I explain my parents' divorce? What will my friends think of me now that I come from a single-parent family?

Guilt can be a particular problem if a child has been forced to take the side of one parent. The inhumanity of some of our courts of law and the antiquated ideas and incompetence of some judges still leave their marks on children. When a child sits in a courtroom and hears his or her parents attacking each other, when the child is forced to testify against a parent, or when the child is caught as a pawn between two parents because a judge or the attorneys find the child the only ammunition to win the case or settle the dispute, that child may be consumed with guilt. It takes a very mature child to realize that the sometimes artificially induced conflict of a legal confrontation should not be the image of a parent that the child carries from that day forward. When these legal skirmishes can be set aside and the relationship between parents and children move forward, then the rebuilding of self-esteem of all parties can begin.

While we could continue to discuss other factors which affect self-esteem, the examples presented thus far should make us more sensitive and aware of the difficulties faced by those who experience the termination of a relationship. If you are a child of divorced parents, ask yourself, now that you have thought more about what your parents have experienced, can your relationship with them improve? Can your communication with them be more productive? Can you, through interpersonal communication, help improve the self-concept of a person who has or is now experiencing a divorce or separation?

Changing Networks of Communication

Examine for a moment how divorce and separation alter the networks and channels of interpersonal communication. Most immediate is the disruption of the channels of communication among family members, especially between the separated or divorced parties. Direct communication may be replaced by indirect communication through intermediaries. One party communicates with an attorney, who in turn communicates with another attorney, who in turn communicates with the second party. Distortion of messages naturally increases via this new, more complex network. When A talks directly to B, the message may be slightly different than the message which passes from A through A's attorney to B's attorney to B. Party B, who now may receive conflicting information, may not know who to believe. Tensions increase, the parties become suspicious of each other, and breakdowns in communication occur.

Outside of the immediate family, a disruption in communication also happens. Whenever two people join together in a relationship, they also join together their respective families. Over a span of time, the networks between these two families may become very active and intertwined. The breaking up of the relationship disrupts these communication networks. Such breakups can be especially difficult for children and their grandparents. When the child becomes the custody of one parent, maintaining communication with the other parent's side of the family can be difficult. New networks may develop when one of the parties finds another mate, and children find themselves building relationships with the new family.

The interpersonal networks between the children and the divorced or separated parents may even change. One parent may become possessive of the child as a means of hurting the other parent. As a result, breaking the ties between the child and the other parent or reducing the communication which takes place between them is not uncommon. Even though a custody agreement may stipulate that a child is to spend six weeks each summer with the noncustodial parent, the custodial parent may sabotage that arrangement. Vacations, little league baseball, riding lessons, and summer camp may be scheduled in conflict with the six-week visitation period. The child is faced with choosing between these fun activities and seeing the other parent. The other parent, in the meantime, is faced with the guilt of denying the child the pleasure of these fun activities or the agony of not seeing the child during the legitimate visitation.

Under such circumstances, many children, especially young ones, do not perceive what is happening. They want to enjoy the activities, not realizing the hurt being inflicted on the other parent. The custodial parent rationalizes the activities as something good for the child and something he or she is providing which the noncustodial parent is not. But the end result is a lessening of the interpersonal ties between the noncustodial parent and the child.

When a child is older and understands the responsibility to keep the channels of communication open, extra efforts can be made to lessen the severity of the absence. If the child must participate in activities which interfere with visitation, perhaps he or she can visit the noncustodial parent at another time, making several shorter visits. More frequent phone calls and letters are also vital communication links. Ideally, each parent is mature enough to assume the responsibility for arranging for the child to spend time with the other parent. Unfortunately, the ideal does not always exist.

Merging Families Few communication situations can be more challenging than when two families merge. Here, understanding, as well as skill in interpersonal communication, is necessary to negotiate the relationships which will develop when one parent becomes "bonded" to another parent.

Most basic when two families merge is the fact that the number of people with which communication takes place increases. From our chapter on small groups, we saw how rapidly the number of possible relationships increases when just one additional person is added to a group. When families merge, those possibilities jump dramatically.

.Second, some relationships are more developed than others. Rarely does everyone start out on an equal par. The children from one family have had a longer relationship in that family than they have had with members of the newly-merged family. Thus, time is necessary to let relationships develop at their own pace. Unfortunately, the mere logistics of living together prevent this. Two families find themselves eating together, brushing their teeth together, even sharing each other's clothes. These "forced" relationships necessitate skill and understanding. While two brothers may verbally spar with each other, neither taking the other too seriously, the same sparring with a new member of the family may seem rude and insensitive.

Available territorial space is subdivided and this adds to the tension. A child who once enjoyed a bedroom all to himself or herself now finds the space shared with new "brothers" and "sisters." Adjusting to reduced territorial space can be frustrating and conflict-producing. Added to this is the fact that one of the merged families is adjusting to a new environment, having moved in with the other family. Familiar surroundings and neighborhoods are gone, and self-concept is a little shaky.

Children who do not have the maturity to cope with the "merged" situation force parents to negotiate crisis after crisis. Not only does the negotiation put a tension-filled, time-consuming drain on the parents, but in the eyes of the conflicting children, no negotiated settlement is satisfactory unless their side wins. This may place an additional burden on the parents' ability to effectively develop their own new relationship. They may not have time to communicate with each other because they are too busy communicating with the fighting children.

Applying Interpersonal Skills to the Extended Family   How do we cope with the new demands of the extended family? First we can understand that divorce and separation challenge the self-concept of all parties involved. In understanding these challenges, we can be more sensitive to the feelings and actions of others. Realize that low self-esteem can create unnatural communication. Thus, during these times, both parents and children can help to reassure each other that they are still respected, loved, and that they want to communicate and spend time with each other.

Second, the time when it may seem natural to withdraw from a parent or individual who is going through a divorce may be the very time that increased communication is necessary. The ability to empathize and listen will be especially appreciated.

Third, realize the changes that will alter traditional family communication networks. Stop long enough to evaluate these changes and determine if you can play a role in keeping the channels of communication open.

Fourth, when families do merge, understand the new parents' need to develop their own relationship. Also understand that any good relationship, be it step-family or friend, needs time to develop. Time and "breathing room" may mean less communication now, but more enjoyable and meaningful communication in the future.

SUMMARY

We began this chapter on interpersonal communication in the family by considering the qualities of interaction, developing relationships, and varied situations in which communication evolves. We learned that communication patterns are developed in an atmosphere which balances the individual's need for self-identity with the family's need for interdependence. We labeled these patterns as "firm," which reflects one-way communication from an authority figure; "open," in which each individual's self-identity is retained along with the interdependence of the family unit; and "orderless," in which individual autonomy is supported to the point that family stability is sacrificed. There is no ideal pattern, because families determine their own criteria for satisfying family structures. Patterns do, however, seem to be recurring and operate to retain the autonomous-interdependence balance.

Applying small-group communication to family communication, we found that such skills as group cohesion, turn taking, and leadership behavior can lead to more effective family communication. Families can also be viewed as communication networks. The formal network consists of individuals who provide services to the family. Informal networks also provide valuable information and relationships but are less structured than formal networks. Closely knit networks usually are composed of kin closely attached to the family through emotional bonding. Loosely knit networks are made up of casual acquaintances, many of whom have no contact with each other. Much like networks in organizations, people in family networks fulfill specific roles.

Interpersonal communication in families must frequently conquer obstacles. Some of these include generation differences, stress, nonverbal obstacles, and stereotyping. Communication with the elderly may also be challenging. Yet with a little sensitivity to the elderly's self-concepts and the encouragement of positive and meaningful discussions, this aspect of family communication can be delightfully rewarding.

Special sensitivity to interpersonal communication must prevail during a separation or divorce. During such times, challenges to self-concept abound for all parties involved, including children. Communication networks within and among families also change when a relationship dissolves. The role of intermediaries, the custody of children, and the feelings held for the other party all alter the traditional patterns of communication. Merging two families creates new interpersonal relationships, changes in territorial space, and the need for the parents to have the time and privacy to develop their own relationship.

OPPORTUNITIES FOR FURTHER LEARNING

ATKIN, E. and E. RUBIN, *Part-Time Father*. New York: Vanguard, 1976.

ATLAS, S. L., *Single Parenting*. Englewood Cliffs, NJ: Prentice-Hall, 1981.

BECKER, G. S., *A Treatise on the Family*. Cambridge: Harvard University Press, 1981.

BERMAN, E., *The Cooperating Family*. Englewood Cliffs, NJ: Prentice-Hall, 1977.

BERNHEIM, K. F., R. R. J. LEWINE, and C. T. BEALE, *The Caring Family: Living with Chronic Mental Illness*. New York: Random House, 1982.

BRAZELTON, T. B., *On Becoming a Family*. New York: Delacorte Press, 1981.

De BEAUVOIR, S., *The Coming of Age*. New York: Putnam's, 1972.

DELLA-PIANA, G., *How to Talk with Children (and Other People)*. New York: John Wiley, 1973.

DINKMEYER, D. and G. D. McKAY, *Raising a Responsive Child*. New York: Simon & Schuster, 1973.

FISHEL, E., *Sisters*. New York: Morrow, 1979.

GALTON, L., *Don't Give up on an Aging Parent*. New York: Crown Publishers, Inc., 1975.

GINOTT, H. G., *Between Parent and Child*. New York: Avon, 1965.

GINOTT, H. G., *Between Parent and Teenager*. New York: Avon, 1969.

GREIFF, B. S., *Tradeoffs: Executive, Family and Organizational Life*. New York: Times Mirror, 1981.

GROF, S. and J. HALIFAX, *The Human Encounter with Death*. New York: Dutton, 1977.

HOWARD, J., *Families*. New York: Simon & Schuster, 1979.

KORNHABER, A. and K. L. WOODWARD, *Grandparents, Grandchildren: The Vital Connection*. New York: Doubleday, 1981.

KÜBLER-ROSS, E. and M. WARSHAW, *To Live Until We Say Good-Bye*. Englewood Cliffs, NJ: Prentice-Hall, 1978.

LOGAN, M., *Happy Endings*. Boston: Houghton Mifflin, 1979.

MEAD, M. and K. HEYMAN, *Family*. New York: MacMillan, 1965.

RICCI, I., *Mom's House, Dad's House: Making Shared Custody Work*. New York: Macmillan, 1980.

SCHIFF, H. S., *The Bereaved Parent*. New York: Crown Publishers, Inc., 1977.

SILVERSTONE, B. and H. K. HYMAN, *You and Your Aging Parent*. New York: Pantheon, 1982.

YOUNG, L., *The Fractured Family*. New York: McGraw-Hill, 1973.

chapter ten

Overcoming Frustration and Resolving Conflict

PREVIEW   *After completing this chapter, we should be able to:*

Understand frustration.
Identify the bases of frustration.
Explain how frustration is linked to self-concept.
Discuss our interpersonal environment.
Explain paraconflict.
Compare plus-plus conflict, plus-minus conflict, and minus-minus conflict situations.
Know the positive side of conflict.
Understand dysfunction.
Recognize sources and types of conflict.
Discuss common settings in which conflict can arise.
Identify strategies to resolve conflict.
Realize the role relationships play in resolving conflict.
Recognize who is at fault in a conflict.
Discuss the role of argument, power, prediction, and compromise in negotiation.

Between my sophomore and junior years of college, a lack of finances and less-than-serious interest in my studies led me to the conclusion that I should be somewhere else than inside a classroom. I withdrew from college and wound up traveling with the carnival. I would not recommend it for everyone, but for me, traveling with the carnival, with the constant stimulation of change, was exhilarating. More than anything else it involved meeting thousands of people, from grandparents to toddlers, rich people to poor people, kind people to not-so-kind people. Such a life is priceless for its experiences in human interaction.

As I began to research and write this chapter, I remembered back to a summer afternoon with the carnival. In a small town in the northeast, I watched a man and a woman approach one of the carnival games which involved paying money for the privilege of throwing three baseballs at a stack of wooden milk bottles. If you knocked down all three bottles, you won a giant stuffed animal.

As the couple approached the game, the woman stopped and began to fondle one of the large animals which had been strategically placed on the counter to attract passersby. No doubt whatsoever existed in our minds that self-concept, affection, pride, and the couple's relationship were on the line with those baseballs and the three milk bottles.

Reaching into his pocket and pulling out some bills, the man promptly slapped them on the counter. After about two dozen unsuccessful throws, the man was clearly beginning to get frustrated. The woman was becoming equally frustrated about not owning the animal and continued to stroke the furry prize with more intensity.

After ten minutes had gone by, each of the baseballs had been christened with a name. Before each attempt, the man would caress each ball, talk to it, then hurl it at the milk bottles. Sometimes one, sometimes two, but never three bottles fell from the platform.

Finally, the man reached into his other pocket and pulled out more bills. It was the last of his money. This time he slammed the money onto the counter with a force that attracted the attention of nearby carnival attendants. The woman stopped caressing the animal and stepped back a few feet with a look of tension and expectancy on her face. He continued to throw wildly, sometimes missing the bottles by feet, not inches. When he was down to the last ball, he stopped for a moment and gripped the counter. Biting his lip, he looked with equal contempt at the balls, the milk bottles, and the stuffed animal. Then he eyed the attendant, saying in a threatening tone, "I better win!"

Clutching the ball tight enough to make his hand turn pure white, he stepped back, aimed, and threw. The ball clipped the left bottle, knocking both it and the top bottle to the platform and causing the third bottle to wobble in a circle on its rim. Before anyone could determine if the bottle would fall, the attendant grabbed the stuffed animal and shoved it so hard into the man's arms that he had to step back to keep from falling. Before the man could regain his balance, the attendant leaped back and snatched all three bottles off the platform, the instant before the third bottle would have come to rest upright. Obviously frustrated but throwing his shoulder back and transferring the animal to the arms of the woman, the man eyed the attendant once more and shuffled down the crowded midway.

No one doubted that if the last ball had not knocked down the bottles, the situation could have become explosive. But the attendant, realizing that the man had spent enough on the game to pay for the animal many times over and sensing a possible confrontation, had decided to resolve the conflict himself.

The scene at the carnival had all the makings of frustration and conflict that we will talk about in this chapter. We will learn that not all conflict is resolved the way it was between the man and the attendant. Sometimes acute frustration will break out in direct physical confrontation. Other times words will either soothe or scorch the conflict. This chapter first examines the characteristics of frustration and conflict, then discusses the positive and negative sides of conflict, and finally deals with the interpersonal strategies we use to deal with conflict.

U nderstanding Frustration

Two terms frequently confused with each other are *frustration* and *conflict*. Although the title of this chapter refers to conflict, conflict cannot be discussed without understanding frustration.[1] In the most basic sense, *frustration* is an *obstacle to achieving a goal.*[2] The goal may be very basic, such as getting a drink of water to quench a thirst. Or the goal can be complex and less immediate, such as accomplishing success in a career.[3] Conflict can be defined as *the simultaneous presence of two incompatible goals.*

Bases of Frustration   Frustration is a part of life. It may affect us in a very subtle manner or it may hold major consequences.

Try communicating with someone who is extremely frustrated. When you do, you are communicating with a person who elicits all of the verbal and nonverbal cues of abnormality. Facial expressions may be tight, with teeth clenched, eyes narrowed, and brow furrowed. Hands and feet may be moving nervously out of sequence with words.[4] The messages which are sent and received even can trigger frustration in those who interact with the individual.

Frustration is based in three areas: (1) the *possibility* of satisfying needs or goals; (2) the *methods* used to satisfy needs or goals; and (3) the *ability* to satisfy needs or goals.[5]

Frustration over the Possibility of Achieving a Goal A major cause of frustration is the absolute lack of *possibility* of ever achieving an identified goal. For the man at the carnival, the seeming futility of being able to knock down three milk bottles at once was fast becoming this kind of frustration.

In some cases, this kind of frustration can be easily overcome by simply accepting the inevitable and not worrying about it. Suppose you have just found out that you can get an A in a course if you memorize the book and complete a fifty-page term paper. But there are only two weeks left in the semester. How can you accomplish all this in two weeks? Your frustration can be eliminated easily by the mere realization of the impossibility of your task.

Now let's consider the frustration of mere consequences. Assume that you have memorized the book and have worked long hours all semester to complete the fifty-page term paper. You know it's good. You put finishing touches on the paper three days before it is to be turned in to the instructor. You carefully take the paper downtown to the local typing service where the receptionist assures you the paper will be ready Wednesday morning.

"Great!" you exclaim, "I need it no later than 10:00 A.M. since the instructor will dock us a complete letter grade for the entire course if the paper is even five minutes late. She accepts absolutely no excuses."

Three days later, you arise early and head for the typing service. Just as you round the corner, you see a smoldering building and three firetrucks. Standing by the debris is the receptionist who tells you everything was lost in the fire . . . including your paper. You now have no chance of reaching your goal of an A in the course, but your frustration is much greater than had you never written the paper in the first place.

Frustration over the Methods used to Achieve a Goal The goal of the man throwing baseballs was to win the large stuffed animal for the woman. The only *method* he perceived available to him was to knock down the milk bottles. Since it was not sufficient to achieve the goal, it was extremely frustrating. He did not know that the tension would reach a level at which the attendant would "give" him the animal, or that if he played long enough he might just get lucky or become a better pitcher.

Let's consider another example. Imagine that your boyfriend is leaving for Japan for three months. He lives in Los Angeles and you live in Columbus, Ohio. You plan to fly to Los Angeles to be with him for four days before he flies to Japan. You can get to Los Angeles in about four hours by plane or three days of hard driving by car. You have made your plane reservations so that you will be with him the day he leaves and can take him to the airport. But a week before you are to leave, there is a pilots' strike which shuts down air traffic throughout the country. You cannot get to Los Angeles by plane. You must drive. If you are lucky, you will spend a few hours with your boyfriend before he leaves for Japan.

Your frustration now is not over whether you can get to Los Angeles but over the *method* you will use to get there. Even though there is no doubt about the *possibility* of your getting to Los Angeles, you are frustrated that you must spend three long days in the car.

Frustration over the Ability to Achieve a Goal The lack of *ability* to hit the milk bottles produced still a third type of frustration. Here are some other examples:

You study all semester and spend extra hours working casebook questions in your accounting course but consistently never get above a C.

Three years ago your company instituted a merit-raise program in which people who excel in reaching predetermined goals receive a merit raise. You consistently miss that raise by a few points on your productivity scale.

Every semester you enter the literary contest. Although you are highly praised for your work, you never win first prize.

Again, these frustrations are caused by the inability to achieve a goal.

Frustration: What We Make of It We can see from these examples that frustration occurs in different degrees. It is also relative. In other words, frustration is only as severe as we let it be or as it has some personal meaning for us. The lack of time it takes to memorize a book and complete a paper would not be devastating to a person who did not place a high premium on getting an A in a course.

Time A number of things influence the degree to which frustration affects us. The saying "time cures all ills" or "this, too, shall pass" can be applied to frustration. Granted, the fire at the typing service is serious, but it is more critical at the time it happens than six months later.

Mounting Frustrations Mounting frustrations can also play a part. Getting a B may not seem like much. But if it comes on top of many smaller frustrations, we might react to the B the same way we would react to an F.

People in American business who have worked with the Japanese report that their workers exercise a high degree of self-discipline and self-control. In the Matsushita Electric Company's plant, for example, there is a "Self-Control Room." Inside are two straw dummies and a supply of sticks with which to beat them. Any workers who don't feel they're up to it at the moment, may leave their post, enter the room, and flail away at the dummies. It is not their boss but themselves that they are beating into shape.

(© The Economic Press *n.d.*)

FIGURE 10-1

High self concept Sees situations as gratifying Low conflict potential	Low self concept Situations are frustrating High conflict potential

◄──────────────────────────────────►

INTERPERSONAL SITUATIONS IN ORGANIZATIONS

Frustration and Self-Concept

The ability to overcome frustration is an important step in building a positive self-concept. And our self-concepts determine how we communicate with other people (Figure 10–1).

The Vicious Circle For some people, the continued lack of success in overcoming frustration can diminish their self-confidence. As their self-confidence diminishes, they are less effective in dealing with other people. Even without realizing it, they send out signals which say, "I'm insecure." "I'm not in control." "I don't have the confidence to complete this task." That, in turn, diminishes their self-confidence. It becomes a viscious circle. Above all, frustration mounts.

People as Perceived Obstacles The people with whom we interact can also be looked upon as the causes of our frustrations. When this happens, interpersonal communication is in double jeopardy. Not only must we overcome frustration to communicate effectively with other people, but the same people, we think, may be causing our frustrations.

These situations are especially important in organizational settings. Suppose Bill has been passed over for promotion. Bill perceives his boss as being responsible for not recommending him for the promotion. A coworker, Ralph, receives the promotion instead. Bill perceives himself as being just as competent as Ralph. He also feels that Ralph prevented him from getting credit for his accomplishments. While Ralph was tooting his own horn, Bill was silent and did the job. Thus, Bill is extremely frustrated over not receiving the promotion, and his frustration is immediately reflected in his interactions with his boss and Ralph.

Our Interpersonal Environment

Interpersonal interaction contributes to our self-concept if the interaction is positive. Such contributions accumulate from the many different interactions from all of the people who make up our interpersonal environment. Interpersonal environment refers to the sum total of all our daily interactions.

It includes everyone from our family, to business associates, to club members, to the cop on the beat.

Success in our interpersonal environment is determined by how well we are able to negotiate our way through interpersonal interaction that is gratifying and satisfying. Research in communication has tended to overlook this *composite* approach to our interpersonal relationships, yet psychologists are quick to recognize the relationship of our environment as a whole—physical, economic, social, and political—to self-concept.[6]

One setting in our interpersonal environment can directly affect another setting. For example, a person may be having difficulty getting along with people at work because he and his wife are going through a divorce. Another person may be having trouble interacting on dates because she is carrying on a running battle with the dean of women at her college.

Understanding Conflict

Our dog Stormy crawls under the porch as soon as the outside temperature reaches about 80°. It is cool under the porch, somewhat damp because the pine and maple trees shade that side of the house, and Stormy is perfectly comfortable. Stormy manages to resolve a conflict between what he desires and what the environment is demanding of him. He does not communicate with anyone, never asks permission to go under the porch, and does not stop if we tell him it would be just as cool in the nearby woods. Because Stormy is an animal, albeit an intelligent one, no communication changes his determination to crawl under the porch when it begins to get warm outside.

On the other hand, when our son John gets up in the morning and the sun is shining, he automatically assumes it is warm, and decides that no jacket, no sweater, no windbreaker is necessary to protect him when walking to the bus. However, suppose his father explains that if John catches a cold and misses school and his grades fall, then his privileges may need to be curtailed. John then takes some time to consider how warm it is outside and what the consequences might be of not wearing a jacket.

Stormy's and John's approach to resolving conflict are different. Stormy resolves conflict at the basic biological level. John resolves conflict at a more developed level of understanding.

Conflict and Paraconflict Professor Brent Ruben considers it important when relating communication to conflict to distinguish between these two types of conflict.[7] The conflict John experiences is what can be called *paraconflict*—conflict that is *conceived*, whether or not the conflict actually exists. Paraconflict is conceptual and involves symbols and human interaction. Most of the conflict we confront is paraconflict.

For John, reacting to the temperature outside does not have the "purity" that it has for Stormy. Stormy could care less about what other people think or what other people say about the environment. He makes his decisions on the reality of the environment. John, on the other hand, takes the messages from his father, processes them, integrates them with his own test of the outside temperature, and makes a decision. Both conflict in the pure sense (Stormy's view), and conflict as conceived (John's view), are essential to human interaction.

When conflict does arise, it is caused by a combination of choices which psychologist Kurt Lewin first categorized as plus-plus, plus-minus, and minus-minus.[8] The categories have also been labeled approach-approach, approach-avoidance, avoidance-avoidance.

Plus-Plus Conflicts Plus-plus or approach-approach conflicts are typically the easiest to resolve. They normally produce the least strain and resolving them does not seriously affect our self-concepts. In everyday life some plus-plus conflicts could include the following examples:

> You win $10,000 tax-free and cannot decide whether to spend the money on a new car, or take a world cruise.
>
> The person you have been dating for over a year, and with whom you have fallen madly in love, asks you to marry her. You cannot decide whether to honeymoon in Paris or Rome.
>
> You have a chance to attend the Texas-Oklahoma game or go sailing in the Gulf.
>
> You enjoy playing Space Invaders but are fighting the conflict of needing to use your eyes and hands simultaneously while keeping your gaze affixed to the screen.

These examples have included needing and being unable to choose between two incompatible needs or goals. Some of the major sources of plus-plus conflicts are: "(1) that time is limited, (2) that the individual's energy is limited, (3) that various material and social resources are limited, (4) that the individual cannot be in widely separated places at the same time, and (5) that different activities require the use of the same parts of the body."[9]

Although, as we said, plus-plus conflicts do not "normally" cause problems, there are exceptions. These occur when the plus-plus conflicts have what we conceive are long-range and serious consequences. You have money to invest in the stock market and your broker has recommended two stocks with significant growth potential. Although you feel positive about the stocks, and are fortunate to have the money to invest, the decision is serious. What if you choose the wrong stock and it does poorly? Now you worry about whether to sell the stock with the poor showing and invest in the other stock or wait to see if your stock will rally. By the end of the week you are so hassled about your decision that you throw up your hands in despair, sell all your stocks, and put your money in a savings account at the local bank.

Plus-Minus Conflicts "Taking the good with the bad." "Through thick and thin." "Bitter sweet." Each of these statements is a cliche for plus-minus conflicts. Plus-minus or approach-avoidance conflicts require us to approach a positive goal but simultaneously acquire something negative. The following examples show plus-minus conflicts:

> You are excited about a new car and can borrow the money but must pay a high interest rate.
> You are in love with someone but must incur your parents' wrath to be with the person.
> You have been accepted into graduate school but to attend you must quit your job.
> You need an A to bring up your grade-point average but do not want a course in Basketweaving 101 to appear on your transcript.

Under the extreme stress of severe plus-minus conflict, an individual's moods may change considerably, even within a short period of time. You may be in conversation with the person and notice changes in listening behavior and speech patterns. When the person is concentrating on the plus side of the conflict he or she is positive, expresses considerable optimism, listens attentively, and participates in interaction that is positive and gratifying. The next moment the person can become withdrawn, maintain little eye contact, and exhibit abnormal speech patterns.

Minus-Minus Conflicts Minus-minus or avoidance-avoidance conflicts can be some of the most serious. In these situations, we face two conflicting goals, both of which are undesirable. We face few alternatives except removing one of the conflicts or removing ourselves. People facing minus-minus conflicts are traditionally under considerable stress and their communication reflects this stress.

In a figurative sense an extreme minus-minus conflict is like running from a train on a railroad bridge; staying on the bridge has equal consequences to jumping hundreds of feet to the river below. Either way you lose . . . terminally. The man throwing baseballs at the wooden milk bottles was experiencing a series of minus conflicts. He could not hit the bottles. He had invested so much money he could not justify stopping. He could not satisfy the woman's need. He was afraid of humiliation if he walked away from the game. All of the conflicts were simultaneous, all were interrelated; he was "trapped" in the minus-minus conflicts.

In a war setting a soldier may face the conflict between getting killed in combat or being labeled a coward as a deserter; choosing the latter may elicit the same end result as getting killed in combat. While facing the minus-minus conflict, severe anxiety can result.

We face minus-minus conflicts in our interactions with other people. For example, imagine that you are an accountant in a corporate board meeting held to determine specifications for a new addition to the corporate headquarters. The company president is absolutely determined to include solar heating. You have determined that solar heating is simply not a practical investment at this time in your region of the country. If you agree to solar heating, the costs will run into millions of dollars and place the company in the red. If you disagree with the company president, you will lose his favor and forfeit your annual bonus. If the company goes into the red, the president may decide it is time for a new accountant. To use the old cliche: "You are damned if you do and damned if you don't."

Another type of minus-minus conflict can occur during arguments. You and two other people are discussing an issue when the two other people begin to argue. If you side with one person, you lose the friendship of the other. You decide that the best alternative is to withdraw from the minus-minus encounter and leave the room.

Combinations of Conflicts Even though we have separated the different conflicts into three categories, keep in mind that combinations of conflicts can occur and that it may become difficult to determine exactly *which* conflict is causing a problem or how different conflicts relate to each other. Add to this degrees of frustration from a variety of sources, and we begin to see how complex behavior becomes, and how dynamic and ever changing our communication patterns must be to deal with life's varied conflicts.

The Positive Side of Conflict

Not all conflict is bad. We need a certain amount of conflict to develop strength and maturity. Interestingly enough, when we think positively about people whom we might call "self-made persons," "sturdy stock," "salt of the earth," we are talking about people who have experienced considerable conflict. The self-made person who worked up from the bottom of a company or went from rags to riches undoubtedly learned how to deal with frustration and conflict.

Adversity has the effect of eliciting talents, which in prosperous circumstances would have lain dormant.

Horace

Brent Ruben aptly points out that while conflict may be "associated with feelings of stress and pain," it is an essential element of learning, creativity, and biological and psychological growth.[10] He reminds us that "a great many instances of conflict conceived to be dysfunctional because they are uncomfortable in the short run would be judged profitable"[11] in the long run.

From the time we are born we are in conflict with our environment. Overcoming this conflict meets its first test when we are able to satisfy basic needs such as food and warmth. These two basic needs continue into adulthood, taking on the form of providing for a "roof over our heads" and "putting food on the table."

At the same time that we are in conflict with our environment, we are, in our formative years, in conflict with our parents' control of that environment. An infant who wants to play in the deep end of the swimming pool may be stopped to prevent the child's drowning. The conflict of wanting and being stopped is necessary for the child's survival.

When we grow older, our life-style changes can cause the same conflicts with our environment. Sometimes we must adapt to cultural changes as well. I remember traveling with the carnival through Pennsylvania in midsummer. Towns such as New Holland, Lancaster, Bird In Hand, and Marietta were on our route. Because these towns were in the heart of the Pennsylvania agricultural region, passing through them meant interacting with people whose culture was deep in the rural traditions of the area. Many were of Pennsylvania Dutch ancestry. Later in the month we moved to the more mountainous parts of the state, where our route included such towns as Williamsport, Lock Haven, and State College. Further west we visited towns which had their roots in both the coal-mining and the steel industry of Pennsylvania. Towns such as Altoona, Johnstown, and Pittsburgh became part of our itinerary. From there we moved towards Ohio and West Virginia to Youngstown, Stubenville, Fairmount, and Morgantown.

Our adjusting to the locale and interacting with the people of the industrial areas of western Pennsylvania, Ohio, and West Virginia was in contrast to our experiences with the people of the Pennsylvania Dutch country and the agricultural regions of southeastern Pennsylvania. For one, life styles were different. In the agricultural areas, for example, attending a fair or carnival meant above all the opportunity to interact with friends and neighbors, not with the people who traveled with the carnival. The food was different, too. Church suppers in southeastern Pennsylvania gave way to the onion-and-pepper–covered hot sausage which was a favorite fare in the steel regions. Despite these differences, each change became easier and easier for us. Different people, different towns, different foods—all contributed to easing our ability to adapt to our new environments. Conflicts, whether real or conceived, were easier to resolve with each new experience.

Later, when I attended college in South Dakota, I came in contact with a number of Indians whose heritage dated back to such people as Red Cloud and Sitting Bull. Again, I found that communicating with these individuals meant resolving conflicts between their cultural background and my own. While visiting the Sioux and Crow Indian reservations, I thought about the differences that existed a hundred years earlier when the conflicts were often resolved through violent and destructive confrontations.

Dysfunction: The Negative Side of Conflict

Not all conflict produces positive results. When we reach a point at which we cannot adequately resolve the conflict or overcome frustration between what we want and what we can obtain, dysfunction results.[12] Dysfunction is *a disorder of a bodily system.*

Although we could argue that some dysfunction takes place any time unresolved conflict occurs, the term is more closely associated with abnormal behavior. The ability to recognize and to correct dysfunction in ourselves and others is important to good interpersonal communication. People such as counselors and psychiatrists are trained at correcting severe dysfunction. Most of the time the dysfunction is less serious and we must call on our own abilities.

Interpersonal Conflict

Even though conflict and frustration may be necessary for development, most of us work towards resolving the conflict or overcoming the frustration as soon as possible.

Recognizing the Conflict Source The first step in working towards resolving conflict, either in yourself or in others, is to understand the *source* of the conflict.[13] Stop and consider four possible sources of conflict: (1) an individual; (2) a group; (3) an organization; or (4) society. Reacting to one when the conflict really originates with another or not identifying the conflict is a step in the wrong direction.

For example, assume that Professor Kingsfield is part of a college committee charged with limiting the rowdyism that has been occurring outside the campus union building. Every night individuals stand on chairs and benches and deliver speeches. Heckling, chanting, booing, and an occasional fight are all part of the activity. It has reached the point that the dean of the college has formed a committee to solve the problem of rowdyism and Kingsfield must chair the committee.

After three weeks' work, Kingsfield finds that the committee is going nowhere. Of the five other people who serve on the committee, one group of three members argues constantly with the other two. One member, whom we call Professor Lowell, disagrees with the need to have a committee in the first place and reacts negatively to everything other people say. At the same time, Lowell does not want to oppose the college dean because he comes up for tenure next semester and is worried about being at odds with the college administration.

Finally, after the fourth week, when tempers have become short and no solution appears in sight, Kingsfield tells the dean that the committee is deadlocked and that he would like to be relieved of the assignment. The committee is embroiled in constant conflict and Kingsfield has no way to resolve their differences or solve the problem.

What went wrong? Kingsfield tried every means possible, everything he knew about good interpersonal communication and leading a small group towards its goal.

The problem was not being able to identify all of the *sources* of conflict.

Individual-Based Conflicts

Conflicts can be individual based. Professor Lowell, who constantly argued, had ideas opposed to those of the other members of the group. These differences need to be isolated and dealt with—for example, Lowell's tactic of shouting down other members of the committee who disagree with him. By Kingsfield's showing some of the positive points brought forth by the other members and how these may have been closely linked to Lowell's ideas, he might have resolved an individual-based conflict.

Group-Based Conflicts

Second, the group itself also caused conflict in this example. Three members who formed a liasion with each other became pitted against the remaining two members of the group.

Organization-Based Conflicts

The organization, in this case the college, was adding to the conflict. The college's traditional hands-off posture from anything political was seen as being sacrificed when the college administration acted to prohibit political gatherings and political speeches.

Society-Based Conflicts

Finally, society-based conflicts were present. In our democratic society, in which free speech is one of the basic rights, curtailment of the political gatherings was seen as contrary to society's basic principles of law.

As leader of the group, Kingsfield faced a whole series of conflicts. There is little doubt that regardless of what actions he took, the decision would have been unpopular. Faced with a real situation similar to the example, ask yourself what actions you might have taken, working through the group, to solve the problem.

Recognizing Conflict Type

As important as it is to recognize the source of the conflict, it is equally important to recognize the type of conflict. Ask yourself if the conflict is plus-plus, plus-minus, minus-minus, or a combination of these. Once you identify the source and the type of conflict, you can attempt to work towards a resolution.

Using our example of Kingsfield's committee we can see that different types of conflicts existed. Professor Lowell faced a minus-

minus conflict. Lowell saw stopping the rally as being against basic beliefs about society and not stopping them as going against the wishes of the college administration. The former made him look bad among his fellow professors who also strongly supported free speech. The latter made him feel he would endanger getting tenure if he took a public stand against the college dean.

Perhaps if Kingsfield had recognized Lowell's minus-minus dilemma, he could have recommended that Lowell withdraw from the committee. At the same time, Lowell may have looked upon his conflict as plus-minus. Plus because here was a chance to support free speech by blocking the administration's attempt to stop it. Minus because his opposition to the administration would affect his getting tenure.

When dealing with conflict situations, be sure another person perceives the conflict the same way you do. Unless Kingsfield understood how Lowell felt about the conflict, his communication to Lowell might have worsened, not lessened, the conflict.

Interpersonal Conflict Strategies

If we were to describe all of the things we have learned so far about interpersonal communication which could apply to conflict resolution, we would use such terms as empathy, understanding, appreciation, dialogue, listening, and other terms that describe communication as a dynamic, two-way sharing process.

Overcoming Frustration and Resolving Conflict

Identifying Strategies Although we could wish for a certain "ideal" that would fit every situation, research has shown us that we use many different strategies in attempting to resolve conflict. Researchers Mary Anne Fitzpatrick and Jeff Winke examined the strategies for resolving conflict used by 269 undergraduate college students.[14] They found that five strategies predominated. The five categories and the representative tactics identified by Fitzpatrick and Winke are:

MANIPULATION

Be especially sweet, charming, helpful and pleasant before bringing up the subject of disagreement.

Act so nice that he/she later cannot refuse when I ask him/her for my own way.

Make this person believe that he/she is doing me a favor by giving in.

NON-NEGOTIATION

Refuse to discuss or even listen to the subject unless he/she gives in.

Keep repeating my point of view until he/she gives in.

Argue until this person changes his/her mind.

EMOTIONAL APPEAL

Appeal to this person's love and affection for me.

Promise to be more loving in the future.

Get angry and demand that he/she give in.

PERSONAL REJECTION

Withhold affection and act cold until he/she gives in.

Ignore him/her.

Make the other person jealous by pretending to lose interest in him/her.

EMPATHIC UNDERSTANDING

Discuss what would happen if we each accepted the other's point of view.

Talk about why we do not agree.

Hold mutual talks without argument.[15]

Using Strategies Although we must be careful not to generalize over all college students or situations, the results of Fitzpatrick's and Winke's research do show some interesting trends.

Level of Involvement Along with determining specific categories of conflict strategies, Fitzpatrick and Winke examined how *involved* people were in a given relationship with another person and if this level of involvement would determine the conflict strategy. For instance, they examined various types of relationships or degrees of relationships from "married," through "exclusively involved," "seriously involved," "casually involved."[16] They determined that students "who are casually involved with one another frequently utilize either *manipulation* or *non-negotiation* tactics to resolve their interpersonal conflicts. The casually involved resort *less* often to either *emotional appeals* or *empathetic understanding* in settling their differences."[17]

Additional analysis of their data suggested that married people employ still different strategies. The researchers found that the fifty-four married people in the study tended to "utilize *more emotional appeals* and *more personal rejection* than any other relational group."[18] Marrieds employed *less empathetic understanding* than either the "exclusively" or the "seriously involved."[19]

Sex The results of Fitzpatrick's and Winke's research when examining strategies among same- and opposite-sex friends showed that "while males were much *more* likely to engage in non-negotiation tactics with their best friends, females were *more* likely to resolve their difficulties by *personal rejection, empathic understanding,* or *emotional appeal* tactics with their same-sex best friend."[20] No significant differences between strategies emerged among opposite-sex friends.[21]

Factors Affecting Strategy Use What caused the results of the research to turn out the way they did? For the answer to this question, the researchers turned to explanations evolving from conflict theorists. These theorists suggest that the amount of risk involved in a relationship will determine the conflict strategy.[22] When relationships are strong and the relational bond is close, couples are not so worried about breaking or weakening the relationship, so they can disagree using less-tactful strategies. In relationships in which the bonds are less strong, cohesiveness is important and the tendency to use more tactful, conflict-avoiding strategies becomes important.

Fitzpatrick and Winke suggest that males favoring non-negotiation strategies "may represent a move toward control."[23] They point out that "the specific tactics employed in the strategy of non-negotiation suggest that the issue of dominance is highly salient (meaning important or conspicuous) in male friendships."[24]

However, Fitzpatrick and Winke contend that females' strategies are based on their greater social acuity (meaning keenness or sharpness).[25] *Empathy* is the foundation of the chosen strategy:

> To devalue a friend, a female needs to know what matters most to her. To appeal to a friend's emotions, a female needs to select those appeals that would be most effective with a given individual. Finally, to understand a friend, a female needs to take into account the viewpoint of her friend. The dimension underlying these strategies is empathy. Females use this empathy to gain compliance from their best friends.[26]

Two considerations are important in interpersonal strategies. First, do not consider a given strategy as being good or bad. Empathetic understanding may sound like a positive goal, but as we just learned, it can be a basis for other strategies, such as appealing to one's emotions, manipulations, or non-negotiation, which may or may not be positive depending on how they are used and how they are perceived by the parties involved in the conflict. The famous General George Patton was known for having great empathy and understanding for his enemies . . . so he could destroy them.

At the same time we should not go through life being cynical. Unless we assume the best, not the worst, in people, we will have little chance of living in an atmosphere of anything *but* conflict. We often underuse or even underestimate the importance and effectiveness of "positive" empathetic understanding in resolving conflicts.

Combinations of Strategies Although we have separated interpersonal strategies based on a given research approach, keep in mind that different strategies can be employed simultaneously. Our separating them here is to help us identify them, not to suggest that they work independently of each other. For example, appealing to the "emotions" of another person means "understanding" something about that person.

Conflict Settings

If the man at the carnival had not had the stuffed animal in his arms by the time the third bottle ended upright, we might predict that to resolve the conflict, he would have taken a very direct strategy. The setting or situation in which a conflict occurs can determine the type and amount of the conflict.

This becomes obvious by examining what happens in a high-growth corporation. Industries and businesses which are undergoing rapid expansion have the potential for serious conflicts to develop among personnel.[27] For example, growth itself results only after the percentage of inflation is met. If inflation is at 8 percent, then growth takes place when the company grows at a faster rate than 8 percent. Such growth must be accomplished by other means than just raising prices 8 percent and keeping productivity at the same level. Growth beyond inflation is achieved, for example, by adding staff, bringing in automation, and training current employees in new methods of productivity. All of these things, however, mean rapid change, and change can result in conflict. More people can mean more relationships, more chance for disagreement, more chance for communication breakdowns. Automation can signify fear of losing one's job. Retraining can suggest that the old way is not good enough. New challenges, new risks of failure add to the tension.

With the increased growth rate, planning time is reduced. "Long-range" planning can mean what we will do six months from now. Deadlines are forced with less time to meet them. Pressures increase. The pace can only be withstood by young, energetic, extremely aggressive people. Conflicts over seniority develop. Workers must adapt to new workers and new relationships at a heightened pace. Transfers are rampant. Responsibilities are shifted. Friendships are few and of short duration.

Nonverbal factors associated with territorial space add to the tension. Offices are smaller. Partitions are added. Walls in one place today may be someplace else next month. Locations of mailboxes, file cabinets, and extension telephones all change.

Group discussions and collaborations take on a strained atmosphere. Pressure and conflicting schedules mean that not everyone can attend meetings. Those that can are frustrated and tense.

As productivity demands increase, the multiple growth rates become the norm and the tension and pressure become commonplace. Numbness sets in and problems go unnoticed in the rush to profits. The minus-minus conflicts multiply.

Without taking our company to its explosive conclusion, we can see how a given setting can create conflict.

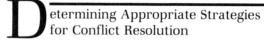

Determining Appropriate Strategies for Conflict Resolution

Just as settings and situations can affect the amount of conflict, so can they determine appropriate strategies to resolve conflict. For example, even though police officers may be trained in negotiation and crisis intervention in which the use of firearms is a last resort, most officers also know that some situations exist when nothing but a firearm can resolve a conflict.

In organizations, families, and other settings, conflicts are resolved through many different strategies and combinations of strategies. Suppose two employees argue about the different ways to get a job done. The controversy has reached the point at which a supervisor must make a decision how to resolve the conflict. What strategy will the supervisor employ? Perhaps the two employees get along well but are just stuck on resolving this particular problem. The supervisor calls the two together. A discussion takes place in which the supervisor is a mediator, and the two employees share their ideas and resolve the conflict.

On the other hand, suppose the supervisor knows that bringing the two together for a discussion will only make matters worse. The supervisor thus lets each employee explain his or her position, and then the supervisor makes the decision. The supervisor's decision is nonnegotiable, and the workers move on to their next task.

The decision to enter into a nonnegotiable decision-making process takes place in courtrooms everyday. Lawyers may have worked long hours trying to bring two parties to an agreement, but when a settlement is out of the question and the case goes to court, the judge's decision is final. The conflict can only be resolved by having a third person, the judge, make a decision that is considered binding.

Equally important to whether or not a given strategy might work is knowing how all of the parties involved in the conflict conceive it. For example, even though a police officer may determine that a criminal needing to be subdued can be talked out of holding two hostages, the criminal may have a different idea and conceive of the situation as much more serious, much more intense.

The Role of Relationships

We talked about couples' in strong relationships being more direct with each other and not as concerned about the cohesiveness of the relationship. This may work fine as long as everyone sees the relationships the same. Difficulty arises, however, when one of the parties misjudges the cohesiveness of the relationship.

Let us examine a situation in which we can apply this concept. While attending a college in California, Russel and Michelle have been dating for almost two years. At school they spend most of their free time together and psychologically have progressed through "bonding" to the point that each considers their relationship strong and stable. Each feels free to state what he or she feels, even differences of opinion. Each can handle the emotional appeals, the refusal to negotiate, especially when one or the other is very opinionated. On occasion they may argue strenuously but with little consequence since each is committed to the other.

Near the end of the semester, the pressures on both Russel and Michelle increase. Both are facing graduation and final examinations. Both want to attend graduate school. One day Michelle receives a graduate school acceptance to study in Ohio. She shares it excitedly with her friends who are full of congratulations. When Russel and Michelle are having lunch a few days later, they begin to argue over one of the concepts they have studied in their organizational communication class and which will appear on the final exam. The argument becomes more intense and then, without warning, Russel says:

> "You're coming on so strong I can't even talk with you."
> "What do you mean?" asks Michelle.
> "You act like you are shoving the idea down my throat!"
> "I am not. I just think this is the way the idea should be interpreted. What are you getting so bent out of shape about?"

Michelle is puzzled by Russel's behavior. Later when they have the time to talk things out, Russel explains his feelings about their relationship. He feels that with the acceptance to graduate school, their relationship is fast coming to an end. The problem is compounded because they have been studying for exams and have not had time to see each other and talk things out. As a result, Russel interpreted Michelle's comments about the concept on the final exam to be insensitive, dogmatic, uncaring.

As we look at what is happening between Michelle and Russel, we can see that they are looking at their relationship in different ways. Michelle perceived the strong bond to still exist between them. As a result, not worried about the cohesiveness of their relationship, she felt comfortable with a communication pattern she had gradually adopted over the past two years. Arguing about something they studied in class was not threatening but was very natural.

All of a sudden, however, Russel sees their relationship as much less intimate and close than it had been in the past. Psychologically, he has already placed Michelle thousands of miles away in Ohio. The pattern of communication Michelle was using was not, in Russel's eyes, sensitive to a relationship that had little cohesiveness.

Misjudging how another person perceives a relationship can be a problem in resolving conflicts. Add to this the fact that in families and close relationships, a strong pattern of communication may have set in and may be recurring, and we can see how interpersonal communication and using the wrong strategy to resolve interpersonal conflicts can worsen, not lessen, the conflict. Keep this in mind the next time you are dealing with another person in an adversary relationship, regardless of how insignificant the conflict may seem, whether you are in a social situation, a family setting, or at work.

Ask yourself what strategies are being employed and what strategies are appropriate, given the level of the relationship, the situation, and the context in which interpersonal interaction is taking place.

"It'll be awhile before they try to steal
another one of our accounts!"

Recognizing Who is at Fault

Many times conflicts are stress-producing experiences. When our self-concepts are at stake, we guard our actions and decisions in an effort to retain our self-esteems. Criticism, especially negative criticism, elicits psychological defenses which can further block our communication. Our ego involvement with an issue may prevent us from seeing both sides of a question. All of these factors interrelate and can cloud our perceptions of who is at fault in a conflict, who is perpetuating and prolonging the conflict, and who is working hardest to solve the conflict. The more important the issue over which the conflict rests, the more important the outcome, the more we protect our self-esteems.

Unless we are able to openly and objectively consider who is at fault in a conflict, resolving it may be difficult. Even then, we may be so dissatisfied with the solution that we accept it but will not live with it. Typical reactions are: "I will go along to the movie but do not expect me to sit there and enjoy it." "I need to make a living so I will agree to the contract but do not ever ask me to support the goals of this union again." "Go ahead, decorate the room any way you want, but do not expect me to live in it."

Research has suggested some interesting reactions to conflict situations. For example, a study by Alan Sillars which examined conflicts between college roommates found that when one roommate feels the other roommate is responsible for the conflict, the conflict seems much more stable and enduring, less open to resolution.[28]

> *In lovers' quarrels, the party that loves most is always most willing to acknowledge the greater fault.*
>
> *Scott*

When one roommate accepts more responsibility for the conflict, that same roommate sees the presence of what we can call "integrative" strategies—self-disclosure, problem solving—as opposed to strategies which involve avoiding or ignoring the other person. Expressed verbally the roommate might say: "I realize I am at fault, and therefore the conflict can be resolved by getting together and working out the problem."

When the roommate sees the other person as responsible for the conflict, he or she blames the partner for avoiding him or her. "My roommate is at fault and instead of talking to me and solving the problem, she is avoiding me."

When roommates do get together and solve their problems instead of avoiding each other, each feels more positive towards the partner.

Looking within ourselves as the cause of problems is not easy. It becomes even more difficult in conflict situations, the very place where introspection may be the most beneficial. Not only are strategies important to conflict resolution, but recognizing and admitting who is at fault play equally important roles.

Negotiation

Negotiation as a means of resolving conflict is gaining more and more attention. Not that negotiation has not been present before. Although not as sophisticated as it is today, negotiation has been present since our ancestors fought over scraps of meat, wood to keep fires burning, or water to feed cattle.

Overcoming Frustration and Resolving Conflict

Today, through the attention of the mass media, we hear about negotiation in every walk of life. A prison riot is negotiated between the police and the prisoners. A labor contract is hammered out in a locked room in which parties have agreed to stay at the bargaining table until an agreement is reached. A secretary gets a pay raise after negotiating with a supervisor.

All of these examples involved some form of conflict resolution: resolution between the conflicting needs and goals of the negotiating parties.[29]

The Role of Argument   A good negotiator understands the fine points of arguing. Argumentation is the "blood" of the negotiating body. Argumentation itself is a form of mini-conflict, and although it may seem strange to use a conflict-producing device to resolve conflict, such is negotiation. In its most effective form, argumentation means that parties in a negotiation will offer each other alternatives and then argue about the basic merits of each. Knowing how to handle interpersonal communication under argumentative conditions is a prerequisite to determining what both parties will eventually agree to. The key is to be *critical* of each others' positions but at the same time to be *cooperative*.[30] Being too critical may be construed as being uncooperative. When that happens, negotiations may break off.

The give and take of argument has its foundation in interpersonal communication. Both parties, through interaction, explore all of the possible alternatives to a negotiated settlement. Gradually, through this exploration, they move towards a mutually agreed-upon settlement.

The Role of Power   We learned about the basis of power in the chapter on organizational communication and applied it again in our chapter on communication in the family. Here we apply it to negotiation. Each party has power, despite what might be inferred by their respective titles. Professional negotiator Herbert A. Cohen states succinctly: "Power is based on perception. If you think you've got power, you've got it. If you think you don't have it, even if you've got it, you don't have it."[31]

A secretary negotiating for a raise has power over her boss, who realizes that if the secretary is dissatisfied her work will suffer, which will in turn reflect negatively on the boss. On the other hand, if the secretary lets work suffer too much, the boss will fire her; thus, the balance of power is reinstated. On the other hand, although the boss may have the power to fire the secretary, the secretary has the power to quit. Finding a new secretary may be much more costly than giving the secretary a raise. The negotiation can go on and on.

Though we tend to think in terms of dollars as the object of the negotiation, our example points out other commodities as well. Worker satisfaction with the outcome of the agreement is one of the commodities being bargained, even though it may not be stated. Even communication itself is a commodity, both in amount and content. The manner and content of one party's reaction to the other party's offer will determine subsequent communication patterns.

The Role of Prediction   Along with keeping power relationships in perspective, negotiators operate in an atmosphere of prediction.[32] Each statement and offer, each reply and counteroffer, is made with the prediction and expectation of what the other party's reaction will be.

If you plan to go see a professor about a grade, you naturally stop first—at least most of the time you stop first—to consider the reaction of the professor. You ask: "What will the professor think of me for challenging the grade?" "Will challenging this grade reflect negatively on future evaluations?" In each case you try to predict the reaction of the professor.

The professor in turn listens to you and predicts your reactions. The professor may be asking such questions as: "Will the student be discouraged from learning if I do not grant her request?" "Will the student drop the course if I do not change his grade?"

Each party predicts the reaction of the other party. The communication pattern which takes place reflects these predictive qualities.

As the negotiations continue, each party plays a cat-and-mouse game of self-disclosure, telling the other party just enough to get a reaction to try to predict with accuracy what the next reaction will be to the next proposal.

At the same time, each party is careful "not to lay all the cards on the table." Most of us do not walk into a car dealer and say "This is my best offer." We negotiate; we do not tell the salesperson what our best offer is until we know more about what the salesperson's best offer is. Then we gently give and take our positions using such information as the cost of options, the wholesale price, the dealer-preparation charges. We explore and probe for more information to try to determine profit margins and how far the salesperson will go before we look at each other and say, "This is the best offer I can make," even if, in reality, that may not be the case.

The Role of Compromise   If argument is the blood of negotiation, then compromise is the heartbeat. We have learned about the sharing process in communication: how fields of experience between individuals must overlap for effective communication to take place. Nowhere is this more true, nowhere is it more readily applied to communication, than in negotiation.

As communication is a dynamic, ever-changing process of interaction, so is negotiation. In negotiation, the fields of experience between the two parties become their respective alternatives to resolving the issue. Before an agreement is reached, be it a labor negotiation, a family feud, a lovers' quarrel, each party will explore the other party's alternatives.

Somewhere between each party's final position, the bottom line, the point beyond which one cannot go, and the position each would most like to have if he or she had his or her own way, is a host of alternatives. These alternatives are the fields of experience each party shares. Using power, prediction, and argument, they reach a final compromise.

It is perhaps fitting that we end our discussion of interpersonal communicaton talking about negotiation. Negotiation embodies everything we have discussed in this book, including the sharing of ideas, the importance of self-concept, listening skills, the use of language, nonverbal factors, the relationships among people, communication skills in small groups, and the application of these concepts to such settings as organizations and the family.

Life itself is a process of continual negotiation. We negotiate from the time we are born; we begin to interact with our environment, and then we face the challenges of interaction with other people which determine our success in social relationships and society.

I hope that as you negotiate life, this book will be a tool to make that negotiation more meaningful, gratifying, and fulfilling. Refer to it often. Consider and reconsider its contents. But above all, practice good interpersonal communication and apply that practice as a responsible citizen in society.

SUMMARY

We began talking about conflict by first examining its relationship to frustration. Frustration is a difficulty in fulfilling a need or goal. We learned that the causes of frustration are the *possibility* of fulfilling that need or goal, the *method* employed, and the *ability* to achieve fulfillment. The ability to overcome frustration is closely tied to our self-concept. If we continually experience frustration in overcoming obstacles, our self-esteem can suffer. If our self-esteem suffers too much, this will interfere with our ability to succeed. Thus, in extreme situations a vicious circle can develop in which frustration builds on low self-esteem and low self-esteem builds frustration.

Conflict is defined as the simultaneous presence of two incompatible needs or goals. We determined the difference between pure conflict, conflict of action concerning the realities of our environment, and paraconflict, based on how we conceive of conflict, and the role that symbols and human interaction play in paraconflict.

The different types of conflict we discussed were plus-plus conflicts, plus-minus conflicts, minus-minus conflicts, and combinations of these. At the same time, we discussed the positive side of conflict. Conflict in a theoretical sense is an essential element of learning and creativity, as well as biological and psychological growth. On the negative side, when we cannot handle conflict successfully, we dysfunction.

To resolve interpersonal conflict, it is important to recognize the source of the conflict, which can be society, an organization, a group, or an individual. In discussing strategies to resolve interpersonal conflict, we examined the strategy of manipulation, the strategy of nonnegotiation, the strategy of emotional appeal, the strategy of personal rejection, and the strategy of empathic understanding.

Often the setting or situation determines the amount of conflict which may be present. As an example we examined the conflict-producing atmospheres of high-growth companies. We also examined how the appropriate strategy for resolving a conflict is determined by different situations.

An obstacle to conflict resolution in relationships, and sometimes the cause of making the conflict worse, is for one party to misjudge the level of the relationship. Similarly, not recognizing or admitting each party's responsibility for a conflict can hinder a solution.

We concluded our discussion by learning about negotiation. Negotiation embodies all of the concepts of interpersonal communication we have discussed throughout this book. Argument is the "blood" of the negotiating body and is in itself a form of miniconflict used to resolve larger conflicts. Power, prediction, and compromise also play important parts in negotiation.

OPPORTUNITIES FOR FURTHER LEARNING

COFFIN, R. A., *The Negotiator: A Manual for Winners*. New York: AMACOM, 1973.

De CECCO, J. P. and A. K. RICHARDS, *Growing Pains: Uses of School Conflict*. New York: Aberdeen Press, 1974.

FILLEY, A. C., *Interpersonal Conflict Resolution*. Glenview, IL: Scott, Foresman, 1975.

FROST, J. H. and W. WILMONT, *Interpersonal Conflict*. Dubuque, IA: Wm. C. Brown Company Publishers, 1978.

HOWARD, H. H., *Divorce Mediation: A Rational Alternative to the Adversary System*. New York: Universe Books, 1980.

JANDT, F. and M. HARE, *Instruction in Conflict Resolution*. Speech Communication Association (ERIC), 1976.

JANIS, I.L., *Decision Making: A Psychological Analysis of Conflict, Choice, and Commitment*. New York: Free Press, 1977.

MONTAGU, A., *The Nature of Human Aggression*. New York: Oxford University Press, 1976.

NIERENBERG, G. I., *Fundamentals of Negotiating*. New York: Hawthorn, 1973.

PERLMAN, S., *Students Versus Parents*. Cambridge, MA: Howard A. Doyle Publishing Company, 1969.

RUBIN, J. Z., *The Social Psychology of Bargaining and Negotiation*. New York: Academic Press, 1975.

SEMLAK, W. D., *Conflict Resolving Communication: A Skill Development Approach*. Prospect Heights, IL: Waveland Press, Inc., 1982.

SMITH, C. G., ed., *Conflict Resolution: Contributions of the Behavioral Sciences*. Notre Dame, IN: University of Notre Dame Press, 1971.

STRAUSS, A. L., *Negotiations: Varieties, Contexts, Processes, and Social Order*. San Francisco: Jossey-Bass, 1978.

Glossary

Abdicrat: A submissive person. His or her control need is best fulfilled by being controlled, not by controlling others.

Abstract: Words and sentences that are more complex.

Accenting: Nonverbal messages which highlight certain words or phrases we express verbally.

Adaptors: Body movements which help us to orient ourselves or to adapt to our environment; used more when we are alone.

Adult state: The ego state of the well-adjusted person, the rational thinker.

Affection: An interpersonal need that is much more emotional than inclusion or control and may include love, infatuation, and intimacy.

Anchoring: The need for touching behavior later in life.

Argumentative analyses: Messages that, through argument, insight, or presentation of information, dispute a solution.

Assertive: Asking for what you want, telling people how you feel.

Attitudes: Subparts and support mechanisms for values; more narrowly defined than values. See also *Values*.

Autocrat: A person whose decisions may be dogmatic, based on that person's insecurity to maintain control.

Avoiding: The fourth stage in the coming-apart process of a relationship, during which the two people avoid the unpleasantness and pain of seeing each other.

Batons: Movements which account for or emphasize a particular word or phrase.

Beliefs: Our personal feelings; can be either basic beliefs, those which are not easily changed, have been positively reinforced over time, and of which we do not seek continual confirmation; or peripheral beliefs, which are not absolute.

Bogeys: Untrue rumors which create fear or lower morale in an organization.

Bonding: The last stage in the coming-together process of a relationship; signifies that commitments have been formally contracted.

Brainstorming: Interpersonal interaction, usually in small groups, with the objective of generating as many ideas into the discussion as possible.

Breadth: The number of different topics of information exchanged between individuals. See also *Depth.*

Bridges: Persons responsible for linking the gap between groups.

Bypass statements: Statements that do not say what we mean; we do not verbalize desired behavior.

Child state: The ego state in which we act silly, "let ourselves go," and react much as a child would react.

Circles of experience: A way to examine relationships by which we view our different levels of information, from our innermost thoughts and feelings to our thoughts we don't mind revealing, such as our favorite colors.

Circumscribing: The second stage in the coming-apart process of a relationship, during which two people avoid interaction that discusses the relationship.

Clarification: Positive feedback that says, "What you are saying is important to me, and I want to be able to understand it."

Classical approach: An orientation to management in which the emphasis is placed on an "organization chart"; strong emphasis on downward communication.

Closely knit network: In family communication, those people outside of the family unit with whom at least one member of the family is related.

Cohabitant relationship: Both in verbal and nonverbal communication, a relationship in which interaction plays a small role; there is little commitment from both partners to the relationship itself.

Communication model: A stop-action picture of the communicative process that enables us to look at communication from different perspectives.

Concrete: Words and sentences that are simple and direct.

Conflict: The simultaneous presence of two incompatible goals.

Connotation: The meaning of a word that is less precise and explicit than its denotation.

Contractive: A mode of speech that we frequently use when we are attempting to initiate "contact" or gain the attention of another person.

Control: An interpersonal need that encompasses a range of behavior that varies from strong or total control of others to no control.

Conversative: A mode of speech in which our language styles approach human interaction.

Deictic movements: Pointing to an object, place, or event.

Delayed feedback: Response to information received which is not instantaneous; differentiates mass communication from intrapersonal and interpersonal communication.

Democrat: An individual who has the ability to understand the feelings and desires of others and to, whenever possible, make decisions which take those feelings into consideration.

Denotation: A precise or explicit meaning of a word.

Depth: The degree of intimacy and information exchanged between individuals.

Descriptive: A mode of speech in which words appear in a definite sequence which tells a story or directs someone to do something; the same as directive.

Differentiating: The first stage in the coming-apart process of a relationship, during which the persons involved talk more about what they do not share than what they do share.

Directive: A mode of speech in which words appear in a definitive sequence which tells a story or directs someone to do something; the same as descriptive.

Downward communication: Formal communication that flows from management down to employees.

Dysfunction: A disorder of a bodily system, often produced by the inadequate resolution of conflict or by not overcoming frustration between what we want and what we can obtain.

Ectomorph: A body type best described as tall and skinny.

Ego-defense mechanism: Means we use to keep our self-concept, guard our self-confidence, and protect our egos.

Ego states: Different self-concepts which we possess and relate to at any given time; consist of the adult state, parent state, and child state.

Elaborative: A mode of speech in which language tackles the task of moving from one concept to another, much in the way paragraphs are used in a book.

Emblems: Movements which can be substitutes for words.

Empathize: To enter mentally and with emotion into the feelings of another person; a form of positive feedback.

Endomorph: A body type characterized as being short and fat.

Entry phase: An initial phase of interpersonal interaction in which communication is somewhat structured.

Evaluation: Positive feedback which is normally objective and free from personal emotion or biased opinion, and is separated from the person with whom we are talking.

Ever-ready expressor: A person whose face "says it first"—that is, is very expressive at the slightest reaction to emotion or any other stimulus.

Exit phase: The third and final phase of the developmental process of interpersonal interaction, during which the people involved might make a decision as to whether or not to continue their relationship.

Experimenting: The second stage in the coming-together process of a relationship during which people exchange basic information about each other.

Expressions of disunity: Messages showing disagreement or rejection.

Expressions of personal involvement: Messages relating personal experience, affection, commitment, or personal dilemma.

Expressions of unity: Messages showing agreement or acceptance.

External networks: Communication networks which carry information beyond the confines of the employees or people who make up the organization (i.e., communication channels with the news media).

Family: An organized system of interaction based on changing relationships between people who may live together.

Feedback: Information received back in response to information you verbally or nonverbally imparted.

Feeler: An emotional, sensitive person who likes emotional involvement with people and may lead a more carefree life than the thinker.

Fields of experience: Personal experiences which are common references that aid in processing both intrapersonal and interpersonal communication.

Firm pattern: Communication within a family designed to keep order and stability; one member of the family has control over other family members.

Formal networks: Communication networks operationally defined by organization charts, appointed committees, and other identifiable characteristics which are known by management and employees.

Frustration: An obstacle to achieving a goal.

Gatekeeper: Anyone or anything controlling the flow of information via a mass medium. A gatekeeper can expand or shrink our informational environment.

Goal listening: Beginning to establish listening goals for ourselves.

Grapevines: Informal communication networks which have become synonymous with carrying rumors.

Heterophily: Dissimilarities between two people which play a role in communication patterns; the people's fields of experience do not overlap.

Homestretchers: Rumors which anticipate something.

Homophily: That point at which two people communicating have things in common with each other; their fields of experience overlap.

Horizontal communication: Communication between people at similar levels of responsibility within an organization.

Human-relations approach: In organizational theory, running a company in a democratic way, putting the stress on everyone's being satisfied.

Human-resources approach: An organizational theory which recognizes that individuals within the company have talents which can be nutured to increase their productivity and improve their effectiveness.

Ideographs: Movements which sketch the path or direction of thought.

Illustrators: Movements such as hand gestures which compliment what we say.

Impression management: Choosing to present ourselves in a certain way to another person, verbally or nonverbally.

Impulsive: A mode of speech that is characterized by short utterances without the need for complex language structure.

Inclusion: An interpersonal need to belong, participate, to be acknowledged.

Informal networks: Communication networks which operate outside of the established and identifiable channels in organizations.

Initiating: The beginning stage of any relationship, whether it lasts a lifetime or a few minutes; the first contact with another.

Integrating: The fourth stage in the coming-together process of a relationship, when the people involved and those around them begin to view themselves more as partners than as individuals; they have a commitment to interaction.

Intensifying: The third stage in the coming-together process of a relationship, during which more personal information is exchanged and nonverbal information plays a larger role.

Internal networks: Communication, either formal or informal, that operates within an organization.

Interpersonal communication: Encoding information, communicating it verbally or nonverbally to another person, and receiving information back in return.

Intrapersonal communication: Communication within ourselves.

Intuitor: An imaginative individual, but one who can also be impatient with people who do not immediately see the value or lack of it in something or someone.

Isolates: Persons most removed from the decision process.

Kinetographs: Movements which depict bodily action or some nonhuman physical action.

Language intensity: Expressing strong opinions and emotional involvement with an issue.

Language style: The use of different words and the respective arrangement of those words.

Leadership: Influential behavior accepted by group members; it moves a group towards its recognized goal and/or maintains the cohesiveness of the group.

Leaking: Unauthorized communication in which an employee takes a grievance or complaint to the public or the press. See also *Whistle blowing.*

Liaisons: The "linkers" of information in a communication network, both in transmitting and receiving information between groups.

Loosely knit network: In family communication, those people who have limited emotional involvement and contact with family members.

Mass communication: Communication in which the presence of a mass medium helps carry the message between a sender and a receiver, the message is controlled by a gatekeeper, the sender and receiver are not in close proximity to each other, the sender and receiver are limited in the number of sensory channels they can use to process the information, and feedback is delayed.

Memory: A form of intrapersonal communication that retrieves and encodes information stored in our brains.

Mesomorph: A body type best described as muscular and athletic and physically fit.

Minus-minus conflicts: Serious conflicts that require us to face two conflicting goals, both of which are undesirable.

Modes of speech: The ways words are joined together in particular patterns to accomplish different communication goals.

Mutual gaze: The action and contact of two people's eyes, usually in an intense conversation.

Negative stroking: Verbal or nonverbal communication that makes us feel intimidated, hurt, and uncomfortable.

Nonliaisons: Group members who do not have contact with other groups.

Open pattern: Communication within a family that allows the family to function in an open atmosphere of discussion, working towards each individual's autonomy and needs, while not sacrificing the interdependence or cohesiveness of the family unit.

Opinion leader: A person who influences another person's decisions, attitudes, and behavior; a person whose judgment we trust and who we seek for advice.

Orderless pattern: Communication within a family in which each member of the family is given as much freedom as possible to seek out his or her strengths and communicate feelings to other family members.

Orthodox relationship: The traditional relationship in which each partner functions in the "we" state with little individuality.

Overpersonal: A person who may be overbearing in social relationships.

Paraconflict: Conflict that is conceived, whether or not it actually exists.

Paralanguage: The way we use the sound of our voices to utter words; includes voice quality, resonance, and tempo.

Parent state: The ego state in which we tend to be very directive in our communication and behavior, much as a parent reacting to a young child.

Personal: A person who has satisfactory relationships centering around affection.

Personal phase: The second phase of the developmental process of interpersonal interaction, during which discussion might stress more personal issues, such as our attitudes and beliefs.

Personal space: Area surrounding us that is concerned with psychological traits rather than the physical structures of territorial space; influences the way we communicate with others.

Phatic communications: Messages showing superficial interest; often joking or accommodating.

Physical noise: Sounds which may interrupt the communication process.

Physiognomy: The mostly unscientific study of the face as an indicator of personality types.

Pictographs: Early wall etchings on the insides of caves and temples. Also movements which draw a picture in the air of the shape of the referent.

Pipe dreams: Rumors which can best be described as wishful thinking.

Plus-minus conflicts: Conflicts which require us to approach a positive goal but simultaneously acquire something negative.

Plus-plus conflicts: Those conflicts which are the easiest to resolve and produce the least strain; resolving them will not seriously affect our self-concept.

Problem-solving groups: Small groups which seek solutions to problems, either by implementing those solutions or recommending them.

Procedural communications: Messages dealing with problem-solving methods, criteria for making decisions, clarity of wording, or comments on the experimental situation.

Referent: An image in our minds to which we refer when we encounter a word or symbol (flower = symbol; rose = referent).

Revealers: People whose emotions show readily on their faces.

Rhythmic movements: Movements which depict the rhythm or pacing of an event.

Rumors: Sometimes difficult-to-confirm information passed through informal channels of communication.

Selective disclosure: Choosing which information we tell other people about ourselves, dependent on how well we know the people.

Selective exposure: Choosing to come in contact with communication from others we perceive to possess certain beliefs, frequently similar to our own.

Selective perception: Hearing and consequently perceiving what is many times determined by our preconceived notions about someone or something.

Selective retention: Retaining or remembering only that communication which we perceive as important to us or with which we agree.

Self-concept: The way we feel about ourselves.

Self-disclosure: Divulging information about ourselves, our values, our attitudes, and our beliefs to see how other people are reacting to our self-concept.

Semantic noise: A misunderstanding of the meanings of words, which may interrupt the communication process.

Semantics: The science of meanings, originating from the Greek words for *significant* and *sign*.

Sensing: Using all of our senses to absorb everything we can about the person talking to us.

Sensor: An individual who likes to absorb the things around her or him using all of the senses.

Sequential structure: The independence of messages in sequence to one another.

Sharing relationship: A relationship in which sharing takes place between individuals, but in which each individual retains a great deal of autonomy in his or her life.

Solutions: Messages which recommend courses of action or state policies for guiding action.

Source credibility: How much we respect, believe in, and accept the sender of communication.

Spatial movements: Movements which depict spatial relationships.

Stagnating: The third stage in the coming-apart process of a relationship during which the two people begin to feel uncomfortable with each other and conversations are most likely unpleasant.

Stereotyping: Prejudging a person on the basis of prejudices attributed to groups or individuals.

Stroking: The supportive process for our egos, which can consist of both verbal and nonverbal communication; something many of us seek in everyday life to confirm what we say and do; can be in the form of negative stroking.

Substitute expressors: People who show different facial expressions than what they are feeling.

Supportive analyses: Messages which, through argument, insight, or presentation of information, confirm a solution.

Switching listening styles: Changes in the way we process messages by using four basic cognitive or mental switches: agree, disagree, think, or question.

Systems approach: An organizational theory that states that people and divisions within organizations are functionally dependent and interrelated to each other.

Task-oriented groups: Small groups which set out to accomplish specific goals.

Terminating: The last stage in the coming-apart process of a relationship in which the verbal and nonverbal rituals signal the end of the relationship.

Territorial space: Area around us that is defined by physical boundaries and that affects the way we communicate with others.

T-groups: Encounter groups which engage in primarily intensive communicative experiences; generally consist of well-functioning individuals who are seeking greater competence in their ability to experience life.

Therapeutic groups: Groups that bring people together for the purpose of enhancing their abilities to deal with others, and with life in general.

Thinker: A person who is deliberate in thought and action, is businesslike, and lives a highly structured life.

Transaction: The sending, receiving, and sending back of information to the sender as a form of feedback.

Underpersonal: A person who relates very superficially to others.

Upward communication: Formal communication that flows from employee upward to management.

Value hierarchy: The ranking of one's individual values.

Values: Broad-based qualities of the individual that are held as important and that affect behavior.

Verbal immediacy: The degree with which we associate ourselves with a message; the amount we aproach or avoid a topic.

Wedge drivers: Rumors which divide or relay untrue and damaging information.

Whistle blowing: External communication that management does not control; "leaking."

Withholders: People who keep feelings from appearing on their faces.

N otes

INTRODUCTION

1. Our electronic age, however, challenges this assumption daily.
2. J. D. Robinson, "The Paradox of Communications in an Information Society" (speech delivered before the American Advertising Federation, Washington, D.C., June 11, 1979).
3. Ibid.

CHAPTER 1

1. "Pigeon Talk," *Time*, February 11, 1980, p. 53.
2. "Apes Use no Language," *Newsweek*, December 31, 1979, p. 66.
3. Ibid.
4. S. L. Tubbs and S. Moss, *Human Communication: An Interpersonal Perspective* (New York: Random House, Inc., 1974), p. 6.
5. K. E. Andersen, *Introduction to Communication Theory and Practice* (Menlo Park, Calif.: Cummings Publishing Company, 1972), p. 8.
6. W. Schramm, "The Nature of Communication between Humans," *The Process and Effects of Mass Communication*, rev. ed., ed W. Schramm and D. F. Roberts (Urbana: University of Illinois Press, 1971), p. 8. Schramm posited the "sharing" emphasis of communication in the first edition of *The Process and Effects of Mass Communication*, published in 1954.

7. In the context of conflict, see: B. D. Ruben, "Communication and Conflict: A System-Theoretic Perspective," *The Quarterly Journal of Speech*, 64 (1978), 202–10.

8. Reporting the work of University of California scientists J. Ruesch and A. R. Priestwood in J. Gibson, "Understanding People: Biggest Worries Vary with Worrier's Age, Finances, and Health," *Indianapolis Star*, July 6, 1980.

9. D. Barnlund, *Interpersonal Communication: Survey and Studies* (Boston: Houghton Mifflin, 1968), p. 1.

10. F. D. Jandt, "Why Interpersonal Communication? Round II," *Human Communication Research*, 1 (Winter 1974), p. 37.

11. The term is not exclusively that of the domain of interpersonal communication. It frequently appears in mass communication reporter-source relationships.

12. G. R. Miller, "The Current Status of Theory and Research in Interpersonal Communication," *Human Communication Research*, 4 (Winter 1978), 164–78.

13. See: Ibid. Note: For a perspective on the rules approach to interpersonal communication see: W. A. Donahue, D. P. Cushman, and R. F. Nofsinger, Jr., "Creating and Confronting Social Order: A Comparison of Rules Perspectives," *The Western Journal of Speech Communication*, 44 (Winter 1980), 5–19.

14. C. R. Berger and R. J. Calabrese, "Some Explorations in Initial Interaction and Beyond: Toward a Developmental Theory of Interpersonal Communication," *Human Communication Research*, 1 (Winter 1975), 99–112.

15. For example, Miller, "Status of Theory and Research," p. 167–170.

16. For example, see Miller's discussion in "Status of Theory and Research," pp. 170–74.

17. W. Schultz's theories, specifically FIRO (Fundamental Interpersonal Relations Orientation) theory, can be found in W. Schultz, *FIRO: A Three-Dimensional Theory of Interpersonal Behavior* (New York: Holt, Rinehart and Winston, 1958); *The Three-Dimensional Underworld* (Palo Alto: Science and Behavior Books, 1966); *Here Comes Everybody* (New York: Harper and Row Publishers, Inc., 1973); *Elements of Encounter* (New York: Bantam Books, Inc., 1975); *Leaders of Schools* (LaJolla, Calif.: University Associates, 1977). See also: Stephen W. Littlejohn, *Theories of Human Communication* (Columbus, Ohio: Charles E. Merrill Publishing Company, 1978), pp. 212–17.

18. Schultz, *FIRO*, p. 22; Littlejohn, *Human Communication*, p. 213.

19. Schultz, FIRO, p. 23; Littlejohn, *Human Communication*, p. 214.

20. Ibid.

CHAPTER 2

1. The account is from the Economics Press, Inc., Fairfield, N.J.

2. Adapted from, among others, L. Thomas, *A Manual for the Differential Value Profile* (Ann Arbor: Educational Service Company, 1966), p. 6. All the authors recognize the contributions of Rokeach to the development of theoretical constructs associated with values, attitudes, and beliefs, as they affect the individual's self-concept. See, for example: M. Rokeach, *Beliefs, Attitudes, and Values: A Theory of Organization and Change* (San Francisco: Jossey-Bass, Inc., Publishers, 1969); M. Rokeach, *The Nature of Human Values* (New York: The Free Press, 1973); J. R. Bittner, "A Comparison and Analysis of the Value Profiles of a State vs. State Supported College" (unpublished honor's thesis, Dakota Wesleyan University, 1967).

3. Thomas, *A Manual for the Differential Value Profile*.

4. Thomas's approach, espoused by others under different terms, is to look at

values as existing at various distances from the person's "self." In short, some values are more important than others.

5. See, for example: J. McGuire, "The Nature of Attitudes and Attitude Change," in *The Handbook of Social Psychology, vol. 3*, eds. G. Lindzey and E. Aronson (Reading, Mass.: Addison-Wesley Publishing Co., Inc., 1969), pp. 136–314.

6. In an effort to make the concept of beliefs meaningful to the student taking his or her first course in interpersonal communication, I have deliberately grouped beliefs into broader categories than advanced courses in other disciplines might apply. For example, Rokeach breaks beliefs into various belief structures upon which there are varying degrees of consensus. Primitive beliefs with unanimous consensus are the first order, followed by primitive beliefs with zero consensus, authority beliefs, derived beliefs, and inconsequential beliefs. An example of the first would be: I attend (name of school). An example of inconsequential beliefs would be "I do not like candy with nuts in it." The former are the most difficult to change, the latter the easiest. See, for example, Rokeach, *Beliefs, Attitudes, and Values*, pp. 26–29.

7. Rokeach's approach is to see the belief system (which includes beliefs, attitudes, and values) as central to the self-concept. The individual is faced with numerous opportunities for incongruity to exist. See Rokeach, *The Nature of Human Values*.

8. Conditions about self, terminal value systems, instrument value systems, attitude system, attitude, cognitions about one's own behavior, cognitions about significant others' attitudes, cognitions about significant others' values or needs, cognitions about significant others' behavior, cognitions about behavior of nonsocial objects, are areas Rokeach sees as potential areas for contradictory relations within one belief system. Source: Rokeach, *Beliefs, Attitudes, and Values*.

9. *Stroking* is based on a number of concepts related to transactional analysis. Eric Berne's work in this area and the more popularized works of Thomas Harris are most familiar to communication scholars. Sources include: T. Harris, *I'm OK—You're OK* (New York: Harper and Row Publishers, Inc., 1969); E. Berne, *Games People Play* (New York: Grove Press, 1964).

10. See, for example: P. H. Wright, "Toward a Theory of Friendship Based on a Conception of Self," *Human Communication Research*, 4 (1974), 196–207. In reviewing research on "Self and its Attitudes," Wright points out:

> The person's concern for the well-being and worth of the entity identified as self manifests itself in four ways. These behavioral tendencies form a major motivational link between the person's conception of self and his/her interactions with the environment.
>
> First, the person behaves in ways that maintain and, when necessary, reaffirm his/her sense of uniqueness or individuality (Fromkin, 1970, 1972).
>
> Second, the person behaves in ways that define and continually reaffirm those self-attributes that are important in terms of their evaluative implications for the self as an entity (Secord & Backman, 1965; Bailey, Finney, & Helm, 1975).
>
> Third, in situations encouraging or compelling self-evaluation, the person tends to evaluate his/her self and its attributes in a positive or self-enhancing manner (Jones, 1973).
>
> Fourth, the person is oriented to some degree to changes in his/her self-attributes in the direction of positive elaboration and growth (Sherwood, 1970).

Source: Wright, "Friendship Based on a Conception of Self," p. 198. Specific references cited by Wright include: H. I. Fromkin, *Journal of Personality and*

Social Psychology, 16 (1970), 521–29; H. I. Fromkin, *Journal of Experimental Research in Personality*, 6 (1972), 178–85; P. F. Secord and C. W. Backman, *Progress in Experimental Personality Research, vol. 2* (New York: Academic Press, 1965), 91–125; R. C. Bailey, P. Finney, and B. Helm, *Journal of Social Psychology*, 96 (1975), 237–43; S. C. Jones, *Psychological Bulletin*, 79 (1973), 185–99; J. J. Sherwood, *Personality*, 1 (1970), 41–63.

11. Wright conceptualizes this concept succinctly:

> There is a distinction between the behaving person and the behaving person's conception of his/her self. The person develops a conception of his/her self as an identifiable entity through a lifetime of experience and behavior that are localized in a body that is physically distinct and continuously present. This omnipresent reference point called self includes a sense of physical distinctiveness, unity, continuity, uniqueness, and some degree of initiative or casual power.

> The active, dynamic agent in individual behavior is the person as a whole, not the self. The self, being a conception held by the behaving person has no impetus or energy of its own. However, the person is responsive to his/her conception of self, and having such a conception has important motivational consequences. Because the entity identified as self is such a stable reference point for experience and behavior, the self becomes closely associated with the rewards and punishments and the good and bad fortune of the behaving person. Out of this association, probably very early in life, the person develops a tendency to assess the well-being and evaluate the worth of the entity identified as self. The importance of this concern for the well-being and worth of the self cannot be overemphasized; it is the motivational bridge between the person's conception of self and the involvement of that self in his/her behavior, self-attributions, and social relationships.

Source: Wright, "Friendship Based on a Conception of Self," p. 197.

12. For example, see: E. Berne, *Transactional Analysis in Psychotherapy* (New York: Grove Press, 1974); E. Berne, *The Structure and Dynamics of Organizations and Groups* (Philadelphia: J. B. Lippincott Company, 1963).

13. See, for example: E. Goffman, *Encounters: Two Studies in the Sociology of Interaction* (Indianapolis: The Bobbs Merrill Co., Inc., 1961). Goffman has devised a complex analysis scheme to explain his approach to human interaction. It includes breaking down human interaction into *frame analysis;* the basic element of interpersonal communication is a *frame* and a series of frames is a *strip.* An initial *encounter* is a face engagement. Goffman places considerable importance on the "story-telling" aspect of a relationship in which self-disclosure (discussed later in this chapter) is a form of story telling. This story-telling process is what actually determines the self in the context of a given relationship.

14. Not overdramatically, although certainly this is possible. Discussing the weather possesses the qualities of specific actors in a given scene. In other words, in understanding Goffman, the reader should not be overly taken by the analogy to drama to the point of seeing every encounter as "overdramatized."

15. J. C. Horn, "Measuring Shyness, The 12-Inch Difference," *Psychology Today*, 13 (1979), 102. Reporting the work of B. Carducci and A. Webber (*Psychological Reports*, Vol. 44). The shyness test is Philip Zimbardo's "Stanford Survey of Shyness."

16. For general background on self-disclosure see, for example: P. C. Cozby, "Self-Disclosure: A Literature Review," *Psychological Bulletin*, 79 (1973), 73–91; G. Egan, *Encounter: Group Processes for Interpersonal Growth* (Belmont, Calif.: Brooks/Cole Publishing Co., 1970), pp. 234–38; L. B. Rosenfeld, "Self Disclosure Avoidance: Why Am I Afraid to Tell You Who I Am," *Communication Monographs* 46 (1979), 63–74; S. J. Gilbert and G. G. Whiteneck, "Toward a

Multidimensional Approach to the Study of Self-Disclosure," *Human Communication Research*, 2 (1976), 347–55, S. M. Jourard and P. E. Jaffe, "Influence of an Interviewer's Behavior on the Self Disclosure Behavior of Interviewees," *Journal of Counseling Psychology*, 17 (1970), 252–57; W. B. Pearce and S. M. Sharp, "Self-Disclosing Communication," *Journal of Communication*, 23 (1973), 409–25; M. Worthy, A. L. Gary, and G. M. Kahn, "Self Disclosure as an Exchange Process," *Journal of Personality and Social Psychology*, 13 (1969), 59–63.

17. Harris, *I'm OK, You're OK*.

18. C. Rogers, *On Becoming a Person* (Boston: Houghton-Mifflin, 1961), p. 344. Cited in S. W. Littlejohn, *Theories of Human Communication* (Columbus, Ohio: Charles E. Merrill Publishing Company, 1978), p. 224.

19. J. Powell, *Why Am I Afraid to Tell You Who I Am?* (Niles, Ill.: Argus Communications, 1969).

20. See, for example: W. Schultz: *FIRO: A Three-Dimensional Theory of Interpersonal Behavior* (New York: Holt, Rinehart and Winston, 1958). Also see citations in note 17 from Chapter 1.

21. G. R. Miller, "The Current Status of Theory and Research in Interpersonal Communication," *Human Communication Research*, 4 (Winter 1978), 164–78.

22. S. J. Gilbert and G. G. Whiteneck, "Toward a Multidimensional Approach to the Study of Self Disclosure," *Human Communication Research*, 2 (1976), 347–55.

23. Ibid.

24. S. J. Gilbert and D. Horenstein, "The Communication of Self-Disclosure: Level Versus Valence," *Human Communication Research*, 1 (1975), 316–22. Also citing:

   P. M. Blau, *Exchange and Power in Social Life* (New York: John Wiley & Sons, Inc., 1964); S. J. Gilbert, "A Study of the Effects of Self-Disclosure on Interpersonal Attraction and Trust as a Function of Situational Appropriateness and the Self Esteem of the Recipient," unpublished doctoral dissertation, Department of Speech Communication, The University of Kansas, 1972.

   Other related sources to a multidimensional approach to self-disclosure include: L. R. Wheeless and J. Grotz, "Conceptualization and Measurement of Reported Self-Disclosure," *Human Communication Research*, 2 (1976), 338–46; J. C. McCroskey, V. Richmond, J. R. Daly, and R. L. Falcione, "Studies of the Relationship Between Communication Apprehension and Self-Esteem," *Human Communication Research*, 2 (1977), 270–77; W. B. Pearce, S. M. Sharp, P. H. Wright, and K. M. Slama, "Affection and Reciprocity in Self Disclosing Communication," *Human Communication Research*, 1 (1974), 5–14; L. R. Wheeless, "Self-Disclosure and Interpersonal Solidarity: Measurement, Validation, and Relationships," *Human Communication Research*, 3 (Fall 1976), 48–60; S. J. Gilbert, "Effects of Unanticipated Self-Disclosure on Recipients of Varying Levels of Self-Esteem: A Research Note," *Human Communication Research*, 3 (Summer 1977), 368–70; L. R. Wheeless and J. Grotz, "The Measurement of Trust and its Relationship to Self Disclosure," *Human Communication Research*, 3 (1977), 250–56.

CHAPTER 3

1. Perhaps because of the difficulty in measuring some of those skills: R. A. Palmatier and George McNinch, "Source of Gains in Listening Skill: Experimental or Pre-Test Experience?" *The Journal of Communication*, 22 (March 1972), 70–76. Palmatier and McNinch succinctly stated over a decade ago:

Listening is a primary communication skill, and there is little disagreement among teachers and psychologists concerning the importance of listening in human learning. Even though the importance of listening ability is acknowledged, the ". . . research attack on the existence and nature of listening ability and on ways of learning and improving it has been sporadic, atomistic, and inconclusive." This same prevailing attitude prompted Dixon to comment that ". . . despite listening's preeminence as a communication skill, the evidence extant on listening reveals it to be the most neglected of the language arts."

Data are available showing that listening skills can be enhanced through specific instruction, and that a positive correlation usually exists between school achievement and listening or listening and specific study skills. However, research has not yet determined the specific relationships between significant growth in listening and growth in other academic areas. To date, research evidence is also still inconclusive as to whether boys or girls are the better listeners. Evidence on the role of intelligence as a predictor of listening ability is also lacking. The literature further fails to unequivocally recommend a strong measurement instrument for evaluating general or specific listening skills. (p. 70–71; notes omitted).

See also: T. Devine, "A Suggested Approach to Controlled Research in Language—Thinking Relationships," *Journal of Research and Development in Education* (1969), 82–86; N. Dixon, "Listening: Most Neglected of the Language Arts," *Elementary English*, 41 (1964), 285–88; M. K. Hollow, "Listening Comprehension at the Intermediate Grade Level," *Elementary School Journal*, 56 (1955) 185–61; C. Kelley, "An Investigation of the Construct Validity of Two Commercially Published Listening Tests," *Speech Monographs*, 32 (1965), 139–43; S. Lundsteen, "Teaching Abilities in Critical Listening in Fifth and Sixth Grades" (doctoral thesis, University of California, Berkeley, 1963); D. Russell, "A Conspectus of Recent Research on Listening Abilities," *Elementary English*, 41 (1964), 262–67; S. Weintraub, "What Research Says to the Reading Teacher: Listening Comprehension," *Reading Teacher*, 20 (1967), 639–47; C. Winter, "Listening and Learning," *Elementary English*, 43 (1966), 569–72.

2. R. W. Norton and L. S. Pettegrew, "Attentiveness as a Style of Communication: A Structural Analysis," *Communication Monographs*, 46 (1979), 13–26; P. Baken, ed., *Attention: An Enduring Problem in Psychology* (New York: D. Van Nostrand Company, 1966); D. Norman, *Memory and Attention* (New York: John Wiley & Sons, Inc., 1976); C. M. Rossiter, Jr., "Sex of the Speaker, Sex of the Listener, and Listening Comprehension," *The Journal of Communication*, 22 (1972), 64–69.

3. See, for example: A Mulac and M. J. Rudde, "Effects of Selected American Regional Dialects upon Regional Audience Members," *Communication Monographs*, 44 (1977), 185–95; M. Cheyne, "Stereotyped Reactions to Speakers with Scottish and English Regional Accents," *British Journal of Social and Clinical Psychology*, 9 (1970), 77–79; H. Giles, "Ethnocentrism and the Evaluation of Accented Speech," *British Journal of Social and Clinical Psychology*, 10 (1971), 187–89; B. Arthur, D. Farrar, and G. Bradford, "Evaluation Reactions of College Students to Dialectal Differences in the English of Mexican Americans," *Language and Speech*, 17 (1974), 255–70; R. E. Callary, "Status Perception Through Syntax," *Language and Speech*, 17 (1974), 187–92; B. L. Brown, W. J. Strong, and A. L. Rencher, "Perceptions of Personality from Speech: Effects of Manipulations of Acoustical Parameters," *Journal of the Acoustical Society of America*, 54 (1973), 29–35; H. S. Cairns, C. E. Cairns, and F. Williams, "Some Theoretical Considerations of Articulation Substitution Phenomena," *Language and Speech*, 17 (1974), 160–73.

4. The concept has been widely researched by McCroskey and others. See in particular: J. C. McCroskey, "Scales for the Measurement of Ethos," *Speech Monographs*, 33 (1966), 65–72; D. K. Berlo, J. B. Lemert, and R. Mertz, "Dimen-

sions for Evaluating the Acceptability of Message Sources," *Public Opinion Quarterly*, 22 (1969), 563–76.

5. L. D. Lovrien, "Navajo and Caucasian Mothers' Differing Perceptions of Behavior," *Psychology Today*, 13 (1979), 40.

6. See, for example: T. A. McCain and M. G. Ross, "Cognitive Switching: A Behavioral Trace of Human Information Processing for Television Newscasts," *Human Communication Research*, 5 (1979), 121–29.

7. A more general perspective of Mok's adaptation is found in: D. Lynch, "Getting 'in Sync' with the Customer," *Sales and Marketing Management*, 124 (1980), 42–46.

8. See: J. G. Delia, R. A. Clark, and D. E. Switzer, "The Content of Informal Conversations as a Function of Interactants' Interpersonal Cognitive Complexity," *Communication Monographs*, 46 (1979), 272–81.

9. For a perspective on the measurement of perceived effectiveness of an interpersonal encounter see: M. L. Hecht, "The Conceptualization and Measurement of Interpersonal Communication Satisfaction," *Human Communication Research*, 4 (1978), 253–58.

CHAPTER 4

1. For a philosophically based discussion of the importance of language in the evolution of communication, see: J. Flory, "Language, Communication, and the Enlightenment Idea of Progress," *Central States Speech Journal*, 26 (1975), 253–58. Flory discusses the contributions of Rousseau, Turgot, Condillac, Court de Gebelin, and Condorcet. Flory notes: "Each discussed the use of language and communication as a measure of progress of people. And each demonstrated progress at work in the development of language throughout time." (p. 253)

2. U. Bellugi, "Learning the Language," in *Language Concepts and Processes*, ed. Joseph A. DeVito (Englewood Cliffs, N.J.: Prentice-Hall, Inc., 1973), pp. 110–20.

3. F. L. Johnson, "Communicative Purpose in Children's Referential Language," *Communication Monographs*, 47 (1980), 46–55.

4. D. Atkinson Gorcyca, W. R. Kennan, and M. G. Stitch, "Discrimination of the Language Behavior of College- and Middle-Aged Encoders," *Communication Quarterly*, 27 (1979), 38–43.

5. W. P. Robinson, "Functions of Language," in *Messages: A Reader in Human Communication* (2nd ed.), ed. J. M. Civikly (New York: Random House, Inc., 1977), pp. 83–89; specifically, see pp. 84–85. In some situations, even bilingual communication operates: Nancy J. de la Zerda, "Tentative Report on Code-Switching among Mexican Americans" (paper presented at the meeting of the Speech Communication Association, San Antonio, Texas, December 1979).

6. See also: Robinson, "Functions of Language," pp. 87–88.

7. Especially helpful in researching material on language variables were: A. Bochner, "On Taking Ourselves Seriously: An Analysis of Some Persistent Problems and Promising Directions in Interpersonal Research," *Human Communication Research*, 4 (1978), 179–91; J. J. Bradac, J. A. Courtright, and J. W. Bowers, "Three Language Variables in Communication Research: Intensity, Immediacy, and Diversity," *Human Communication Research*, 5 (1979), 257–69; B. S. Greenberg, "The Effects of Language Intensity Modification on Perceived Verbal Aggressiveness," *Communication Monographs*, 43 (1976), 130–40; H. T. Hurt, M. D. Scott, and J. C. McCroskey, *Communication in the Classroom* (Reading, Mass.: Addison-Wesley Publishing Co., Inc., 1978); S. T. Jones, M. Burgoon, and D. Stewart, "Toward a Message-Centered Theory of Persuasion:

Three Empirical Investigations of Language Intensity," *Human Communication Research*, 3 (1975), 240–56; W. J. McEwen and B. S. Greenberg, "The Effects of Message Intensity on Receiver Evaluations of Source, Message and Topic," *Journal of Communication*, 20 (1970), 340–50; A. Mulac, "Effects of Obscene Language Upon Three Dimensions of Listener Attitude," *Communication Monographs*, 43 (1976), 300–307; R. E. Nofsinger, Jr., "On Answering Questions Indirectly: Some Rules in the Grammar of Doing Conversation," *Human Communication Research*, 2 (1976), 170–80; N. L. Reinsch, "Figurative Language and Source Credibility: A Preliminary Investigation and Reconceptualization," *Human Communication Research*, 2 (1974), 75–80; K. A. Andersen, *Introduction to Communication Theory and Practice* (Menlo Park, Calif.: Cummings Publishing Company, 1972).

8. Hurt, Scott, and McCroskey, *Communication in the Classroom*, pp. 76–77. See also. W. G. Shamo and J. R. Bittner, "Information Recall as a Function of Language Style" (paper presented at the meeting of the International Communication Association, Phoenix, Arizona, April 1971).

9. See, for example: M. Burgoon and L. J. Chase, "The Effects of Differential Linguistic Patterns in Messages Attempting to Induce Resistance to Persuasion," *Speech Monographs*, 40 (1973), 1–7; M. Burgoon and G. R. Miller, "Prior Attitude and Language Intensity as Predictors of Message Style and Attitude Change Following Counterattitudinal Advocacy," *Journal of Personality and Social Psychology*, 20 (1971), 240–53; C. W. Carmichael and G. L. Cronkhite, "Frustration and Language Intensity," *Speech Monographs*, 32 (1965), 107–11; see also sources cited in note 7.

10. C. E. Osgood and E. G. Walker, "Motivation and Language Behavior: A Content Analysis of Suicide Notes," *Journal of Abnormal and Social Psychology*, 59 (1959), 58–67.

11. For example: G. R. Miller and J. Basehart, "Source Trustworthiness, Opinionated Statements, and Responses to Persuasive Communications," *Speech Monographs*, 36 (1969), 1–7.

12. The arena for research in the area of language intensity is defined by Bradac, Courtright, and Bowers, "Three Language Variables," pp. 258–62, who state the following generalizations developing from investigations into language intensity:

> (1) cognitive stress is inversely related to the language intensity of sources; (2) language intensity is directly related to receivers' attributions of internality of sources; (3) obscenity is inversely related to the amount of attitude change produced by messages (at least when the source is male); (4) obscenity is inversely related to post communication ratings of source competence; (5) language intensity of a nonobscene type in attitudinally discrepant messages is inversely related to amount of attitude change produced by a subsequent persuasive attack of moderate intensity; (6) for highly aroused receivers (at least when the basis for an arousal is irrelevant to the message), language intensity is inversely related to attitude change; (7) language intensity and initial receiver agreement with the proposition of a message interact in the proposition of attitude reinforcement or change in such a way that intensity enhances the effect of attitudinally congruent but inhibits the effect of attitudinally discrepant messages; (8) language intensity in an initial message which supports receiver attitudes is inversely related to amount of attitude change produced by a subsequent persuasive attack of moderate intensity; (9) language intensity and initial source credibility interact in the production of attitude change in such a way that intensity enhances the effect of credible but inhibits the effect of less credible sources; (10) the relationship between initial source credibility, intensity, and attitude change is strengthened when receivers are high in need for approval; (11) language intensity and "maleness" interact in the production of attitude change in such a way that intensity (of a nonobscene type) enhances the effect of male but inhibits the effect of

female sources; (12) language intensity and target participation in encoding are positively related to attitude change; (13) language intensity and initial agreement with the proposition of the message interact in the production of receiver attributions in such a way that intensity in congruent messages enhances but in discrepant messages inhibits attributions of source similarity.

13. Bradac, Courtright, and Bowers, "Three Language Variables," p. 262.

14. Ibid.

15. Ibid. Citing as examples: R. Conville, "Linguistic Nonimmediacy and Communicators' Anxiety," *Journal of Psychology*, 35 (1974), 1107–14.

16. Bradac, Courtright, and Bowers, "Three Language Variables," p. 262.

17. R. P. Hart, "Absolutism and Situation: *Prolegomena* to a Rhetorical Biography of Richard M. Nixon," *Communication Monographs*, 43 (1976), 204–28.

18. Bradac, Courtright, and Bowers list the following generalizations associated with results of research in verbal immediacy:

> (1) positive affect on the part of a source toward the topics of a message is directly related to verbal immediacy; (2) cognitive stress on the part of a source is inversely related to verbal immediacy; (3) verbal immediacy is directly related to receiver attributions of positiveness of source affect; (4) verbal immediacy is directly related to receiver judgments of source competence; (5) verbal immediacy is directly related to receiver judgments of source character; (6) verbal immediacy interacts with initial receiver agreement with the proposition of the message in the production of receiver attributions in such a way that immediacy in congruent messages enhances but in discrepant messages inhibits attributions of source similarity.

19. When viewed as the degree of lexical diversity an individual employs. Lexical diversity is defined as the "manifest range of a source's vocabulary." (Bradac, Courtright, and Bowers, "Three Language Variables," p. 262).

20. K. Andersen, *Introduction to Communication Theory and Practice* (Menlo Park, Calif.: Cummings Publishing Company, 1972), pp. 141–42. Andersen approaches humor as a "strategy of interpersonal style."

21. Ibid.

22. Ibid.

23. Ibid.

24. Refer especially to generalizations 3, 4, and 5 discussed by Bradac, Courtright, and Bowers as cited previously in note 12.

25. Adapted from: F. Williams and R. C. Naremore, "On the Functional Analysis of Social Class Difference in Modes of Speech," *Speech Monographs*, 36 (1969), 77–102. Also discussed in F. Williams, "Language and Communication," in *Communication and Behavior*, eds. G. J. Hanneman and W. J. McEwen (Reading, Mass.: Addison-Wesley Publishing Co., Inc., 1975).

26. B. Bernstein, *Class Codes and Control* (London: Routledge & Kegan Paul, 1971). As discussed by Williams in *Communication and Behavior*, p. 73.

27. Ibid.

CHAPTER 5

1. Knapp classifies the functions as: repeating, contradicting, substituting, complementing, accenting, and regulating. Source: M. L. Knapp, *Nonverbal Communication in Human Interaction* (New York: Holt, Rinehart and Winston, 1978), pp. 20–25. Barker uses the terms repeating, substituting, complementing, deceiving/revealing, and regulating. Source: L. Barker, *Communication*

(Englewood Cliffs, N.J.: Prentice-Hall, Inc., 1981) pp. 72–74. See also: P. Ekman, "Communication through Nonverbal Behavior: A Source of Information about an Interpersonal Relationship," in *Affect, Cognition and Personality*, eds. S. S. Tompkins and C. E. Izard (New York: Springer-Verlag New York, Inc., 1965).

2. S. J. Ramsey, "Prison Codes," *Journal of Communication*, 26 (1976), 39. Additional perspectives can be found in: J. K. Heston and P. A. Gardner, "A Study of Personal Spacing and Desk Arrangement in a Learning Environment" (paper presented at the annual meeting of the International Communication Association, Atlanta, April 1972); A. Hare and R. Bales, "Seating Position and Small Group Interaction," *Sociometry*, 26 (1963), 480–86; G. McBride, "Theories of Animal Spacing: The Role of Flight, Fight, and Social Distance," in *Behavior and Environment*, ed. A. H. Esser (New York: Plenum Press, 1971), pp. 53–68; M. L. Patterson, S. Mullens, and J. Romano, "Compensatory Reactions to Spacial Intrusion," *Sociometry*, 34 (1971), 114–21.

3. For a review of research on personal space and a discussion of the developing theory of personal space and violations, see: J. K. Burgoon and S. B. Jones, "Toward a Theory of Personal Space Expectations and Their Violations," *Human Communication Research*, 2 (1976), 131–46.

4. K. B. Little, "Personal Space," *Journal of Experimental Social Psychology*, 1 (1965), 237–47; F. N. Willis, "Initial Speaking Distance as a Function of the Speaker's Relationship," *Psychonomic Science*, 5 (1966), 221–22; G. W. Evans and R. B. Howard, "Personal Space," *Psychological Bulletin*, 80 (1973), 334–44; J. Gullahorn, "Distance and Friendship as Factors in the Gross Interaction Matrix," *Sociometry*, 15 (1952), 123–34.

5. N. Russo, "Connotation of Seating Arrangements," *Cornell Journal of Social Relations*, 2 (1967), 37–44.

6. See, for example: D. M. Pedersen, "Developmental Trends in Personal Space," *Journal of Psychology*, 83 (1973), 3–9; R. F. Priest and J. Sawyer, "Proximity and Peership: Bases of Balance in Interpersonal Attraction," *The American Journal of Sociology*, 72 (1967), 633–49.

7. See, for example: D. F. Lott and R. Sommer, "Seating Arrangements and Status," *Journal of Personality and Social Psychology*, 7 (1967), 90–94; A. Mehrabian and M. Williams, "Nonverbal Concomitants of Perceived and Intended Persuasiveness," *Journal of Personality and Social Psychology*, 13 (1969), 37–58; G. A. Norum, N. J. Russo, and R. Sommer, "Seating Patterns and Group Tasks," *Psychology in the Schools*, 4 (1967), 3.

8. As with evaluations: R. Sommer, "Spatial Parameters in Naturalistic Social Research," in *Behavior and Environment*, ed. A. H. Esser (New York: Plenum Press, 1971); W. Leipold, "Psychological Distance in a Dyadic Interview" (unpublished doctoral dissertation, University of North Dakota, 1963).

9. See, for example: D. Byrne and J. A. Buehler, "A Note on the Influence of Propinquity upon Acquaintanceships," *Journal of Abnormal and Social Psychology*, 51 (1955) 147–148; R. Sommer, *Personal Space: The Behavioral Basis of Design* (Englewood Cliffs, N.J.: Prentice-Hall, Inc., 1969); H. Rosenfeld, "Effect of Approval-Seeking Induction on Interpersonal Proximity," *Psychological Reports*, 17 (1965), 120–22.

10. Results of research are less clear when the sex variable is involved. Also, research is scant on the effects of the women's movement and the presence of additional women in the professional workforce. See also: G. W. Evans and R. B. Howard, "Personal Space," *Psychological Bulletin*, 80 (1973), 334–44; T. Rosegrant, "The Relationship of Race and Sex on Proxemic Behavior and Source Credibility" (paper presented at the International Communication Association Convention, Montreal, April 1973).

11. E. T. Hall, *The Hidden Dimension* (New York: Doubleday & Co., Inc., 1966); S. A. Jones, "Comparative Proxemics Analysis of Dyadic Interaction in Selected Subcultures of New York City," *Journal of Social Psychology*, 84 (1971), 35–44; O. M. Watson and T. D. Graves, "Quantitative Research in Proxemic Behavior," *American Anthropologist*, 68 (1968), 971–85; O. M. Watson, *Proxemic Behavior: A Cross-Cultural Study* (The Hague: Mouton, 1970); R. F. Forston and C. U. Larson, "The Dynamics of Space: An Experimental Study in Proxemic Behavior among Latin Americans and North Americans," *Journal of Communication*, 18 (1968), 109–16; H. G. Triandis, E. Davis, and S. Takezawa, "Some Determinants of Social Distance Among American, German and Japanese Students," *Journal of Personality and Social Psychology*, 2 (1965), 540–51.

12. E. T. Hall, *The Silent Language* (New York: Doubleday & Co., Inc., 1959).

13. For example, see: J. Fast, *Body Language* (New York: M. Evans and Company, 1970); R. Sommer, "Studies in Personal Space," *Sociometry*, 22 (1959), 247–60.

14. P. Ekman, "Movements with Precise Meanings," *Journal of Communication*, 26 (Summer 1976), 14–26; P. Ekman, R. Sorenson, and W. V. Friesen, "Hand Movements," *Journal of Communication*, 22 (Summer 1972), 353–74.

15. Ekman, 19. Other discussions of emblems can be found in: P. Ekman and W. V. Friesen, *Unmasking the Face* (Englewood Cliffs, N.J.: Prentice-Hall, Inc., 1975); P. Ekman and W. V. Friesen, "Constants Across Cultures in the Face and Emotion," *Journal of Personality and Social Psychology*, 17 (1971), 124–29; P. Ekman and W. V. Freisen, "The Repertoire of Nonverbal Behavior: Categories, Origin, Usage and Coding," *Semiotica*, 1 (1969), 49–98.

16. See, for example: Ekman and Friesen, "Hand Movements," pp. 358–59 and 367–69.

17. Ekman and Friesen, "Hand Movements," p. 360. Also: D. Efron, *Gesture and Environment*, current ed. (New York: King's Crown, 1941).

18. See: Efron, *Gesture and Environment*.

19. M. L. Knapp, *Nonverbal Communication in Human Interaction* (New York: Holt, Rinehart and Winston, 1978), p. 399.

20. See, for example: A. Brandt, "Face Reading: The Persistence of Physiognomy," *Psychology Today*, 14 (December 1980), 90–96.

21. M. Knapp, *Nonverbal Communication in Human Interaction*, 2nd ed. (New York: Holt, Rinehart and Winston, 1978), p. 265.

22. Adapted from: Ekman and Friesen, *Unmasking the Face*. Cited in Knapp, *Nonverbal Communication*, p. 267–68.

23. See, for example: J. D. Boucher and P. Ekman, "Facial Areas and Emotional Information," *Journal of Comunication*, 25 (Spring 1975), 21–28.

24. As discussed in: H. T. Hurt, M. D. Scott, and J. C. McCroskey, *Communication in the Classroom* (Reading, Mass.: Addison-Wesley Publishing Co., Inc., 1978), p. 10.

25. Discussion of research on visual behavior and social interaction can be found in: P. C. Ellsworth and L. M. Ludwig, "Visual Behavior in Social Interaction," *Journal of Communication*, 22 (December, 1972), 375–403. Included in Ellsworth and Ludwig's research are discussions of individual differences, sex differences, personality differences, observer awareness of visual behavior, regulatory function, information-seeking function, interactive influence, visual behavior as a source of attribution, visual behavior in relation to interpersonal attraction and involvement, visual behavior in social psychology, cultural factors, nonverbal behavior and nonverbal cues. See also: M. Arglye and M. Cook, *Gaze and Mutual Gaze* (Cambridge, Eng.: Cambridge University Press, 1976); D. J. Cegala, A. F. Alexander, and S. Sokuvitz, "An Investigation of Eye Gaze and

its Relation to Selected Verbal Behavior," *Human Communication Research*, 5 (Winter 1979), 99–108; A. Kendon, "Some Functions of Gaze-Direction in Social Interaction," 26 (1967), 22–63; M. Argyle, R. Ingham, F. Alkema, and M. McCallin, "The Different Functions of Gaze," *Semiotica*, 7 (1973), 19–32.

26. As reported in the *British Journal of Social and Clinical Psychology* and cited in *Psychology Today*, 13 (October 1979), 40, 115.

27. An interesting popular discussion of the subject is found in: S. Isaaca, "The Living Touch," *Parents*, (February 1980), 58–62.

28. For a discussion of the changing patterns of nonverbal behavior between children and teachers see: H. T. Hurt, M. D. Scott, and J. C. McCroskey, *Communication in the Classroom* (Reading, Mass.: Addison-Wesley Publishing Co., Inc., 1978), 99–100.

29. T. Nguyen, R. Heslin, and M. L. Nguyen, "The Meanings of Touch: Sex Differences," *Journal of Communication*, 25 (Fall 1975), 92–103.

30. L. B. Rosenfeld, S. Kartus, and C. Ray, "Body Accessibility Revisited," *Journal of Communication*, 26 (Summer 1976), 27–30.

31. Ibid., 30.

32. S. M. Jourard, *Disclosing Man to Himself* (New York: Van Nostrand Reinhold Company, 1968); see also: R. Shuter, "A Field Study of Nonverbal Communication in Germany, Italy, and the United States," *Communication Monographs*, 44 (November 1977), 298–305.

33. R. Heslin and D. Boss, "Nonverbal Boundary Behavior at Airports," unpublished paper, Purdue University, 1976. Cited in: C. M. Rinck, F. N. Willis, Jr., and L. M. Dean, "Interpersonal Touch among Residents of Homes for the Elderly," *Journal of Communication*, 30 (Spring 1980), 44–47.

34. For a perspective on time (pauses) in regulating conversation see: O. Robbins, S. Devoe, and M. Wiener, "Social Patterns of Turn-Taking: Nonverbal Regulators," *Journal of Communication*, 28 (Summer 1978) 38–46. In comparisons between children of working-class and middle-class workers, Robbins, Devoe, and Wiener found (pp. 42–43):

   1. Working-class speakers emit unfilled pauses, . . . in significantly greater absolute numbers than do middle-class speakers.
   2. Middle-class speakers emit filled pauses significantly more often and in significantly greater absolute numbers than do working-class speakers.

Additional perspectives can be found in: J. V. Jensen, "Communicative Functions of Silence," *ETC*, 30 (1973), 249–57; and T. J. Bruneau, "Communicative Silences: Forms and Functions," *Journal of Communication*, 23 (1973), 17–46.

CHAPTER 6

1. The author gratefully acknowledges the work of such researchers as Altman, Taylor, and Knapp in conceptualizing the organization of this chapter. See, for example: M. L. Knapp, *Social Intercourse* (Boston, Mass.: Allyn & Bacon, Inc., 1978); I. Altman and D. A. Taylor, *Social Penetration: The Development of Interpersonal Relationships* (New York: Holt, Rinehart & Winston, 1973). Other valuable sources and information appear where indicated in the notes and in the *Opportunities for Further Learning* section.

2. See, for example: G. R. Miller, "The Current Status of Theory and Research in Interpersonal Communication," *Human Communication Research*, 4 (Winter 1978), 164–76. Representative research on stages in the development of relationships can be seen in such works as: C. R. Berger and R. J. Calabrese, "Some

Explorations in Initial Interaction and Beyond: Toward a Developmental Theory of Interpersonal Communication," *Human Communication Research*, 1 (1975), 99–112.

3. Both Altman's and Knapp's portrayals of this concept can also be studied. In this book the author chose to deviate from the pictorial representations presented by these authors to reflect the concept of dyadic communication and the growing together of two individual's personal agendas. See: Knapp, *Social Intercourse*, p. 12.

4. As discussed earlier under the label of homophily.

5. An example of the "goodbye" stage is found in: M. L. Knapp, R. P. Hart, G. W. Friedrich, and G. M. Shulman, "The Rhetoric of Goodbye: Vebal and Nonverbal Correlates of Human Leave-Taking," *Speech Monographs*, 40 (August 1973), 182–98; see also: L. A. Baxter, "Relationship Disengagement: A Process View" (paper presented to the annual meeting of the Speech Communication Association, New York, 1980); L. A. Baxter, "Relationship Closeness, Relational Intention, and Disengagement Strategies" (paper presented to the annual meeting of the Speech Communication Association, San Antonio, Texas, 1979); L. A. Baxter, "Self-Reported Disengagement Strategies in Friendship Relationships" (paper presented to the annual meeting of the Western Speech Communication Association, 1979); L. A. Baxter, "Relationship Disengagement Behavior as a Function of Perceived Mutuality of the Desire to End and Attributed Cause of the Relationship Demise" (paper presented to the annual meeting of the Western Speech Communication Association, 1980); M. L. Knapp, D. Ellis, and B. Williams, "Perceptions of Communication Behavior Associated with Relationship Terminology" (paper presented to the annual meeting of the Speech Communication Association, San Antonio, Texas, 1979).

6. See: Knapp, *Social Intercourse*, pp. 13, 17–28. The author has used Knapp's interaction stages as a means of analyzing the hypothetical relationship discussed in the text. Other scholars have used different terms and even different stages of interaction than those discussed by Knapp. Also, the application of the hypothetical example is arbitrary and makes no pretense of classifying the various stages of interaction in the same way that Knapp or others might choose.

7. The examples are taken from: W. Boroson and R. Boroson, "First Meetings," *Glamour*, 78 (1980), 96.

8. Knapp, *Social Intercourse*, p. 21.

9. A perspective on relational types can be seen in: M. A. Fitzpatrick and J. Indvik, "What You See May Not Be What You Have" (unpublished paper, Communication Research Center, Department of Communication Arts, University of Wisconsin, Madison, 1980). This paper was an important source for developing the conceptual framework for this section of the chapter.

10. The relationship may have begun as orthodox.

11. D. Morris, *Intimate Behavior* (New York: Random House, Inc., 1971), pp. 71–101. Cited in: M. L. Knapp, *Nonverbal Communication in Human Interaction*, 2nd ed. (New York: Holt, Rinehart & Winston, 1978), p. 252.

12. Another perspective can be seen in: F. L. Johnson and E. Aries, "Close Friendship in Adulthood: Conversational Content between Same-Sex Friends" (paper presented to the annual meeting of the Speech Communication Association, New York, 1980).

13. Ibid.

14. See, for example: D. S. Prentice, "The Effects of Trust-Destroying Communication on Verbal Fluency in the Small Group," *Speech Monographs*, 42 (November 1975), 262–70. Applied to group communication, see: D. G. Leathers, "The

Process Effects of Trust-Destroying Behavior in the Small Group," *Speech Monographs,* 37 (1970), 180–87.

15. See, for example: J. J. Bradac, L. A. Hosman, and C. H. Tardy, "Reciprocal Disclosures and Language Intensity: Attributional Consequences," *Communication Monographs,* 45 (March 1978), 1–17; L. A. Baxter, "Self-Disclosure as a Relationship Disengagement Strategy," *Human Communication Research,* 5 (1970), 215–22; M. Prisbell and J. F. Andersen, "The Importance of Perceived Homophily, Uncertainty Reduction, Feeling Good, Safety, and Self-Disclosure in Interpersonal Relationships" (paper presented at the annual meeting of the Speech Communication Association, San Antonio, Texas, 1979).

16. A perspective on the psychological and clinical foundations of the unwritten contract in a relationship is offered by Dr. Kenneth R. Mitchell, a former Menninger Foundation staff member, and is reported in: K. R. Mitchell, "Secret Marriage Contract," *Cosmopolitan,* 187 (August 1979), 263.

17. R. Shuter, "An Exploratory Study of Initial Interaction in Interracial and Intraracial Dyads" (unpublished paper), Marquette University, n.d.).

CHAPTER 7

1. Group size and its effects on discussion are treated in: L. Barker, D. J. Cegala, R. J. Kibler, and K. J. Wahlers, *Groups in Process: An Introduction to Small Group Communication* (Englewood Cliffs, N.J.: Prentice-Hall, Inc., 1979), pp. 172–74.

2. Further discussion of the characteristics of small groups can be found in: D. Cartwright and A. Zander, eds., *Group Dynamics: Research and Theory* (New York: Harper & Row Publishers, Inc., 1968).

3. See the discussion of the developmental perspective on interpersonal communication discussed in Chapter 1. Specifically, see the reference to the article: G. R. Miller, "The Current Status of Theory and Research in Interpersonal Communication," *Human Communication Research,* 4 (Winter 1978), 164–78.

4. The study of small-group interaction has taken many approaches in recent scholarly inquiry. One of the fruitful areas of research has been the discussion of Markov chain analysis. Cartwright and Zander's statement in *Group Dynamics* (p. 48) on the characteristics of small groups notes:

> (a) they engage in frequent interaction; (b) they define themselves as members; (c) they are defined by others as belonging to the group; (d) they share norms concerning matters of common interest; (e) they participate in a system of interlocking roles; (f) they identify with one another as a result of having set up the same model—object or ideals in their super-ego; (g) they find the group to be rewarding; (h) they pursue promotively interdependent goals; (i) they have a collective perception of their unity; (j) they tend to act in a unitary manner toward the environment.

Also cited in S. Littlejohn, *Theories of Human Communication* (Columbus, Ohio: Charles E. Merrill Publishing Company, 1978), p. 255.

5. Adapted from G. M. Phillips and E. C. Erickson, *Interpersonal Dynamics in the Small Group* (New York: Random House, Inc., 1970). Also discussed in Barker, Cegala, Kibler, and Wahlers, *Groups in Process,* pp. 11–12.

6. As opposed to groups which meet to recommend policy.

7. As with any group, research has developed various approaches to examining group interaction. In some circles, criticism has evolved over the approaches and results of this research. Thus, even though our discussion here is general, the critical reader or researcher may want to investigate such works as: E. G. Borman, "The Paradox and Promise of Small Group Research," *Speech*

Monographs, 37 (1970), 211–17; C. D. Mortensen, "The Status of Small Group Research," *Quarterly Journal of Speech*, 56 (1970), 304–9; C. E. Larson, "Speech Communications Research on Small Groups," *Speech Teacher (Communication Education)*, 20 (1971), 89–107; B. A. Fisher and L. Hawes, "An Interact System Model: Generating a Grounded Theory of Small Groups," *Quarterly Journal of Speech*, 57 (1971), 444–53; D. Gouran, "Group Communication: Perspectives and Priorities for Future Research," *Quarterly Journal of Speech*, 59 (1973), 22–29.

8. For agendas in task-oriented research see, for example: E. A. Mabry, "Exploratory Analysis of a Development Model for Task-Oriented Small Groups," *Human Communication Research*, 2 (1975), 66–74. Early work by Bales addressed the foundations of the problem many researchers have drawn upon: R. F. Bales, "Interaction Process Analysis," (Reading, Mass: Addison-Wesley Publishing Co., Inc., 1950); R. F. Bales, "The Equilibrium Problem in Small Groups," in *Working Paper in the Theory of Action*, eds. T. Parsons, R. F. Bales, and E. Shils (New York: The Free Press, 1953), pp. 111–61.

9. For a detailed look at the phenomenon of brainstorming, see: F. M. Jablin and L. Sussman, "An Exploration of Communication and Productivity in Real Brainstorming Groups," *Human Communication Research*, 4 (1978), 329–36. In subjecting twenty-four four-person groups to multiple-discriminant analysis Jablin and Sussman indicated results that suggested that "persons who are high producers of ideas perceive themselves as high status group members and are less apprehensive as communicators than those persons low in productivity." (p. 229)

10. An important source for this section of the book is: B. A. Fisher and W. S. Werbel, "Communication in the T-Group and the Therapy Group: An Interaction Analysis of the Group Process" (paper presented at the annual meeting of the Speech Communication Association, San Antonio, Texas, 1979).

11. W. S. Werbel, D. G. Ellis, and B. A. Fisher, "A Comparative Morphology of Groups: A Systems Perspective" (paper presented to the annual meeting of the International Communication Association, New Orleans, Louisiana, 1974). Cited in Fisher and Werbel, "Communication in the T-Group and the Therapy Group," pp. 3–4.

12. Fisher and Werbel, "Communication in the T-Group and the Therapy Group," p. 4.

13. E. Polster and M. Polster, *Gestalt Therapy Integrated: Contours of Theory and Practice.* (New York: Vintage Press, 1974). Also: J. B. Clark and S. A. Culbert, "Mutually Therapeutic Perception and Self-Awareness in a T-Group," *Journal of Applied Behavioral Science*, 1 (1965), 180–94.

14. Fisher and Werbel, "Communication in the T-Group and the Therapy Group," p. 5. Also: I. Yalom, *The Theory and Practice of Group Psychotherapy* (New York: Basic Books, 1975). Cited in Fisher and Werbel.

15. Fisher and Werbel, "Communication in the T-Group and the Therapy Group," p. 6.

16. Ibid.

17. T. S. Saine, L. S. Schulman, and L. C. Emerson, "The Effects of Group Size on the Structure of Interaction in Problem-Solving Groups," *The Southern Speech Communication Journal*, 39 (1974), 337.

18. Research on sequential interaction has been conducted in a variety of settings, many employing Markov chain models. See: D. G. Ellis, "Relational Control in Two Group Systems," *Communication Monographs*, 46 (August 1979), 154–66; L. C. Hawes and J. M. Foley, "A Markov Analysis of Interview Communication," *Speech Monographs*, 40 (1973), 208–19; D. G. Ellis and B. Aubrey Fisher, "Phases

of Conflict in Small Group Development: A Markov Analysis," *Human Communication Research*, 1 (1975), 195–212; D. E. Hewes, "Finite Stochastic Modeling of Communication Processes: An Introduction and Some Basic Readings," *Human Communication Research*, 1 (1975), 271–83.

19. Jablin and Sussman, "An Exploration of Communication and Productivity," p. 329.

20. P. Hayes Bradley, "Power, Status, and Upward Communication in Small Decision-Making Groups," *Communication Monographs*, 45 (March 1978), 34.

21. Ibid. See also: D. Cartwright and A. Zander, "The Structural Properties of Groups: Introduction," in *Group Dynamics*, 3rd ed., eds. D. Cartwright and A. Zander (New York: Harper & Row Publishers, Inc., 1968). Cartwright and Zander note: "Although these two (status and power) tend to be associated, we cannot be sure in all studies whether reported effects on behavior are due to the person's location in a power structure or to his rank on some dimension such as prestige or importance" (as cited in Bradley, "Power, Status, and Upward Communication," p. 34).

22. A. R. Cohen, "Upward Communication in Experimentally Created Hierarchies," *Human Relations*, 11 (1958), 41–43. As cited by Bradley, pp. 33–34.

23. Ibid. See also the work of W. H. Read, "Upward Communication in Industrial Hierarchies," *Human Relations*, 15 (1962), 3–15.

24. R. Lippit, N. Polansky, F. Redl, and S. Rosen, "The Dynamics of Power," *Human Relations*, 5 (1952), 37–64; cited by Bradley. Other research in this area includes: J. Thibaut, "An Experimental Study of the Cohesiveness of Underprivileged Groups," *Human Relations*, 3 (1950), 271–78; H. H. Kelley, "Communication in Experimentally Created Hierarchies," *Human Relations*, 4 (1951), 39–56; W. H. Read, "Upward Communication in Industrial Hierarchies," *Human Relations*, 15 (1962), 3–21; J. I. Hurwitz, A. Zander, and B. Hymovitch, "Some Effects of Power on the Relations among Group Members," in *Group Dynamics*, 2nd ed., eds. D. Cartwright and A. Zander (New York: Harper & Row Publishers, Inc., 1960).

25. Although we use the word *authority*, the word *power* also comes into play. Some researchers distinguish between the two, viewing power as the exercise of control regardless of whether it is inherent by given status or rank. In our discussion here, we have chosen to use the word authority to mean the exercise of control, regardless of whether that control is given to the individual voluntarily or is seized by the individual.

26. An even more refined way of examining conflict is to subdivide it between *interrole* conflict and *intrarole* conflict. The first would apply to the just-cited example in the text of cutting personnel from a losing division. Intrarole conflict exists within the individual and is on a more personal basis; an example would be a man who finds himself wanting to be an executive based on his upbringing and training but who marries a professional woman who expects him to stay home and take care of the house. She makes much more money than he does. From his own executive perspective, his staying home makes good business sense but is difficult to understand from a personal standpoint. See, for example: T. R. Sarbin and V. L. Allen, "Role Theory," in *The Handbook of Social Psychology*, 2nd ed., eds. G. Lindzey and E. Aronson (Reading, Mass.: Addison-Wesley Publishing Co., 1969). Also discussed in Barker *et al.*, pp. 165–66.

27. See, for example: D. S. Prentice, "The Effects of Trust-Destroying Communication on Verbal Fluency in the Small Group," *Speech Monographs*, 42 (1975), 262–70; J. Gibb, "Defensive Communication," *Journal of Communication*, 11 (1961), 141–48; M. Deutch, "Trust and Suspicion," *Journal of Conflict Resolution*, 2 (1958), 265–79; D. G. Leathers, "The Process Effects of Trust-Destroying

Behavior in the Small Group," *Speech Monographs*, 37 (1970), 180–87; D. G. Leathers, "Process Disruption and Measurement in Small Group Communication," *Quarterly Journal of Speech*, 55 (1969), 299, which states that when disruptive statements are introduced into a discussion, participants "stopped discussing ideas and started attacking each other. They stopped seeking ideas from other discussants and became aggressively committed to their own ideas." Also cited in Prentice, "The Effects of Trust-Destroying Communication," p. 263.

28. See: W. T. Rogers and S. E. Jones, "Effects of Dominance Tendencies on Floor Holding and Interruption Behavior in Dyadic Interaction," *Human Communication Research*, 1 (Winter 1975), 113–22; L. B. Rosenfeld and G. D. Fowler, "Personality, Sex, and Leadership Style," *Communication Monographs*, 43 (November 1976), 318–24.

29. T. J. Saine, L. S. Schulman, and L. C. Emerson, "The Effects of Group Size on the Structure of Interaction in Problem-Solving Groups," *The Southern Speech Communication Journal*, 39 (Summer 1974), 335–36. The quotation states a confirmed hypothesis as reflected in the results of research reported in the article. See also: J. E. Baird, Jr., "A Comparison of Distributional and Sequential Structure in Cooperative and Competitive Group Discussions," *Speech Monographs*, 41 (August 1974), 226–32.

30. G. Sorensen and J. C. McCroskey, "The Prediction of Interaction Behavior in Small Groups: Zero History vs. Intact Groups," *Communication Monographs*, 44 (March 1977), 73–80.

31. Barker, Cegala, Kibler, and Wahlers, *Groups in Process*, p. 226. Additional perspectives can be found in: C. W. Downs and T. Pickett, "An Analysis of the Effects of Nine Leadership-Group Compatibility Contingencies upon Productivity and Member Satisfaction," *Communication Monographs*, 44 (August 1977), 220–30; V. J. Lashbrook, "Leadership Emergence and Source Valence: Concepts in Support of Interaction Theory and Measurement," *Human Communication Research*, 1 (Summer 1975), 308–15. Lashbrook identified three variables providing reasonably accurate classifications of leaders and nonleaders: task attraction, extroversion, and character. The labels were consistent with various dimensions, some from source-credibility research.

32. J. T. Wood, "Leading in Purposive Discussions: A Study of Adaptive Behavior," *Communication Monographs*, 44 (June 1977), 152–65.

33. A perspective on the various combinations of groups and leaders as tested in laboratory settings can be seen in: Downs and Pickett, "An Analysis of the Effects of Nine Leadership-Compatibility Contingencies." Additional perspectives can be found in: D. G. Ellis, "Relational Control in Two Group Systems," *Communication Monographs*, 46 (August 1979), 154–66; T. Hill, "An Experimental Study of the Relationship between Opinionated Leadership and Small Group Consensus," *Communication Monographs*, 43 (August 1976), 246–57; J. A. Courtright, "A Laboratory Investigation of Groupthink," *Communication Monographs*, 45 (August 1978), 229–46; J. Yerby, "Attitude, Task, and Sex Composition as Variables Affecting Female Leadership in Small Problem-Solving Groups," *Speech Monographs*, 42 (June 1975), 160–68; V. P. Richmond, "The Relationship Between Opinion Leadership and Information Acquisition," *Human Communication Research*, 4 (Fall 1977), 37–43; E. E. McDowell, "An Investigation of Sex Roles, Dimensions of Interpersonal Attraction and Communication Behavior in a Small Group Communication Exercise" (paper presented to the annual meeting of the Speech Communication Association, San Antonio, Texas, November 1979); L. L. Putnam, "Preference for Procedural Order in Task-Oriented Small Groups," *Communication Monographs*, 46 (August 1979), 193–218; G. Philipsen, A. Mulac, and D. Dietrich, "The Effects of

Social Interaction on Group Idea Generation," *Communication Monographs*, 46 (June 1979), 119–25; E. G. Bormann, J. Pratt, and L. Putnam, "Power, Authority, and Sex: Male Responses to Female Leadership," *Communication Monographs*, 45 (June 1978), 119–55; D. L. Krueger, "A Stochastic Analysis of Communication Development in Self-Analytic Groups," *Human Communication Research*, 313–24; E. A. Mabry, "An Instrument for Assessing Content Themes in Group Interaction," *Speech Monographs*, 42 (November 1975), 291–97; R. L. Heath, "Variability in Value System Priorities as Decision-Making Adaptation to Situational Differences," *Communication Monographs*, 43 (November 1976), 325–33; R. Y. Hirokawa, "A Comparative Analysis of Communication Patterns within Effective and Ineffective Decision-Making Groups" (paper presented to the annual meeting of the Speech Communication Association, San Antonio, Texas, November 1979).

CHAPTER 8

1. M. S. Hanna, "Speech Communication Training Needs in the Business Community," *Central States Speech Journal*, 28 (Fall 1978), 163–72.

2. More detailed discussions of various approaches to management are available in a number of works on organizational communication. A review of research in the field of organizational communication can be found in: G. M. Goldhaber, M. P. Yates, D. T. Porter, and R. Lesniak, "Organizational Communication: 1978," *Human Communication Research*, 5 (Fall 1978), 76–96; M. L. Lewis, H. W. Cummings, and L. W. Long, "Communication in Organizations: A Functional Perspective with Research Priorities for the 1980's (paper presented to the annual meeting of the Speech Communication Association, San Antonio, Texas, 1979).

3. Not all examples of the classical approach are this extreme. Moreover, it is difficult to clearly separate a distinct management approach and literally apply it to all areas of corporate operation. Some managers are more "classical" than others; some corporations are more "classical" than others. Management approaches are often reflected in a management philosophy, as opposed to the behavior of every individual or even most of the individuals making management decisions. Those making significant contributions to the classical approach to management include: C. Barnard, *The Functions of the Executive* (Cambridge, Mass.: Harvard University Press, 1938); H. Fayol, *General and Industrial Management*, trans. C. Storrs (London: Sir Issac Pitman and Sons, 1949); L. Gulick and L. Urwick, *Papers on the Science of Administration* (New York: Institute of Public Administration, 1937); J. D. Mooney and A. C. Reiley, *Onward Industry* (New York: Harper and Bros., 1931); F. Taylor, *Principles of Scientific Management* (New York: Harper & Row Publishers, Inc., 1919); M. Weber, *The Theory of Social and Economic Organizations*, trans. A. M. Henderson and T. Parsons, ed. T. Parsons (New York: Oxford University Press, 1947).

4. The human-relations approach to management actually gained attention in the 1930s based upon a series of studies conducted at the Hawthorne plant of the Western Electric Company in Chicago. When working conditions grew worse but management reportedly paid more attention to the workers, productivity increased. The research was conducted under the direction of Elton Mayo at Harvard and was reported in: F. Roethlisberger and W. Dickson, *Management and the Worker* (Cambridge, Mass.: Harvard University Press, 1939). More recent analysis of the results suggests less emphasis on management's attention to the employees as the basis for productivity increases. Others contributing to the human-relations aproach include: L. Cock and J. R. P. French, "Overcoming Resistance to Change," *Human Relations*, 1 (1948), 512–32; M. Dalton, "Conflicts

Between Staff and Line Managerial Officers," *American Sociological Review* (June 1950), 342–51; W. B. Given, *Bottom-Up Management* (New York: Harper and Bros., 1949); W. F. Whyte, *Human Relations in the Restaurant Industry* (New York: McGraw-Hill Book Company, 1948). Others critical of the human-relations approach include: F. Herzberg, "One More Time: How Do You Motivate Employees?" *Harvard Business Review*, 46 (January–February 1968), 53–62; E. Huse and J. Bowditch, *Behavior in Organizations* (Reading, Mass: Addison-Wesley Publishing Co., Inc., 1973); H. M. F. Rush, "The World of Work and the Behavioral Sciences: A Perspective and an Overview," in *Contemporary Readings in Organizational Behavior*, ed. F. Luthans (New York: McGraw-Hill Book Company, 1972), pp. 58–69.

5. See, for example: R. Miles, "Keeping Informed—Human Relations or Human Resources?" *Harvard Business Review*, 43 (July–August 1965), 148–63.

6. "Corporate Communications," *Wichita Business* (1981), 31–35.

7. Adapted from: D. Katz and R. Kahn, *The Social Psychology of Organizations* (New York: John Wiley & Sons, Inc., 1966), pp. 239–43.

8. Adapted from Katz and Kahn, *The Social Psychology of Organizations*, p. 245.

9. J. W. Koehler and G. Huber, "Effects of Upward Communication on Managerial Decision Making" (paper presented to the annual meeting of the International Communication Association, New Orleans, 1974).

10. "Corporate Communications," *Wichita Business* (1981), 31–35.

11. Ibid.

12. J. D. Robinson III, "The Paradox of Communication in an Information Society" (speech delivered before the American Advertising Federation, Washington, D.C., June 11, 1979).

13. See, for example: L. P. Stewart, "'Whistle Blowing': Implications for Organizational Communication," *Journal of Communication*, 30 (Autumn 1980), 90–101; J. E. Grunig, "Accuracy of Communication from an External Public to Employees in a Formal Organization," *Human Communication Research*, 5 (Fall 1978), 40–53.

14. Especially helpful in the section on rumor and grapevine were: R. Rowan, "Where Did that Rumor Come From," *Fortune* (August 13, 1979), 130–31.

15. Ibid.

16. K. Davis, "Care and Cultivation of the Corporate Grapevine," *Dun's Review*, 102 (July 1973), 46.

17. D. MacDonald, "Communication Roles and Communication Networks in a Formal Organization," *Human Communication Research*, 2 (Summer 1976), 365–75. See also K. H. Roberts and C. A. O'Reilly III, "Organizations as Communication Structures: An Empirical Approach," *Human Communication Research*, 4 (Summer 1978), 283–93.

18. A good basis for discussion of the variable can be found in: R. A. Emerson, "Power-Dependence Relations," *American Sociological Review*, 27 (1962), 31–41; ed. D. Cartwright, *Studies in Social Power* (Ann Arbor: University of Michigan, 1959).

19. Adapted from: J. French and B. Raven, "The Bases of Social Power," in *Studies in Social Power*, ed. D. Cartwright (Ann Arbor: University of Michigan, 1959), pp. 118–49.

20. R. E. Jones, "Your Interview—Be Prepared!!" *ASCUS 80* (Madison, Wis.: ASCUS, 1980), 23. (#9 changed by author of this text to read his "or her.")

21. F. S. Endicott as reported in "Making the Most of Your Job Interview," *ASCUS 80* (Madison, Wis.: ASCUS, 1980).

22. Ibid.

CHAPTER 9

1. Much of the research on family communication has its roots in sociology and psychology, although new attention is being paid to inquiries which study families from a communication perspective. Data gathered when researchers actually lived with a family have proved potentially valuable.

2. A sociological framework for this approach can be found in the work of Hill. See, for example: R. Hill and D. A. Hansen, "The Identification of Conceptual Frameworks Utilized in Family Study," *Marriage and Family Living*, 22 (1960), 299–311. Additional perspectives from a communication standpoint, especially as family interaction is viewed as a developmental process, is reviewed by Miller. See: G. Miller, "The Current Status of Theory and Research in Interpersonal Communication," *Human Communication Research*, 4 (Winter 1978), 164–78.

3. As conceptualized by Bochner in A. P. Bochner, "Conceptual Frontiers in the Study of Communication in Families: An Introduction to the Literature," *Human Communication Research*, 2 (Summer 1976), 381–97. Citing: E. Bott, *Family and Social Network: Roles, Norms, and External Relationships in Ordinary Urban Families* (New York: The Free Press, 1971); R. D. Hess and G. Handel, *Family Worlds: A Psychological Approach to Family Life* (Chicago: University of Chicago Press, 1959); D. Kantor and W. Lehr, *Inside the Family: Toward a Theory of Family Process* (San Francisco: Jossey-Bass, Inc., Publishers, 1975); A. Koestler, *The Act of Creation* (New York: Macmillan, Inc., 1964); S. Minuchin, *Families and Family Therapy* (Cambridge, Mass: Harvard University Press, 1974); L. Wynne, I. Rychkoff, J. Day, and S. Hirsch, "Pseudo-Mutuality in the Family Relations of Schizophrenia," *Psychiatry*, 21 (1958), 205–20. Bochner's article and a related paper presented at the Speech Communication Association's postdoctoral conference on general systems approaches to human-communication research held at Purdue University in 1975 are some of the best reviews of the literature appearing in communication journals. The author acknowledges their importance in providing directions for research and the writing of this chapter.

4. The work of Kantor and Lehr (*Inside the Family*) applies here, as does the research originating in the organizational literature. When compared to organizational communication, different managerial approaches and thus different communication patterns are represented in: C. Barnard, *The Functions of the Executive* (Cambridge, Mass.: Harvard University Press, 1938); F. Herzberg, "One More Time: How Do You Motivate Employees?" *Harvard Business Review*, 46 (January–February 1968), 53–62; R. Miles, "Keeping Informed—Human Relations or Human Resources?" *Harvard Business Review*, 43 (July–August 1965), 148–63. Although we can use the perspective of organizational communication and administrative behavior to begin developing hypotheses for family communication, the precise application of organizational constructs to family communication remains risky, although it is a fruitful area for speculation and more systematic inquiry.

5. H. L. Lennard and A. Bernstein, *Patterns in Human Interaction* (San Francisco: Jossey-Bass, Inc., Publishers, 1969).

6. Adapted from J. French and B. Raven, "The Basis of Social Power," in *Studies in Social Power* ed. D. Cartwright (Ann Arbor: University of Michigan, 1959), 118–49. Related works on power and family interaction include: D. H. Olson and C. Rabunsky, "Validity of Four Measures of Family Power," *Journal of Marriage and the Family*, 34 (1972), 224–34; C. Safilios-Rothchild, "The Study of Family Power Structure: A Review 1960–1969," *Journal of Marriage and the Family*, 32 (1970), 539–52; J. L. Turk, "Power as the Achievement of Ends: A Problematic Approach in Family and Small Group Research," *Family Process*,

13 (1974), 39–52; J. L. Turk and N. W. Bell, "Measuring Power in Families," *Journal of Marriage and the Family*, 34 (1972), 215–23.

7. As reflected in: E. Bett, *Family and Social Networks: Roles, Norms, and External Relationships in Ordinary Urban Families* (New York: The Free Press, 1971); R. V. Speck, and C. L. Attneave, *Family Networks* (New York: Random House, Inc., 1973).

8. Interesting popular perspectives on the generation gap are found in: T. I. Rubin, "Bring Back the Generation Gap," *Ladies Home Journal* (September 1974), 33; T. Griffith, "Party of One: The Generation that Won," *Atlantic*, 243 (May 1979), 22, 26.

9. As reported in: "Morris Massey: Values and the Workplace," *The New York Times*, October 12, 1980.

10. H. T. Hurt, M. D. Scott, J. C. McCroskey, *Communication in the Classroom* (Reading, Mass.: Addison-Wesley Publishing Co., Inc., 1978), p. 105.

11. Examples include: B. S. Monfils, "The Aged as Subculture: A Pilot Study of Verbal Interaction Patterns" (paper presented at the annual meeting of the Speech Communication Association, San Antonio, Texas, 1979); A. J. de Long, "Environments for the Elderly," *Journal of Communication*, 24 (1974), 101–11; M. J. Graney and E. E. Graney, "Communications Activity Substitutions in Aging," *Journal of Communication*, 24 (1974), 88–95; H. J. Oyer and E. J. Oyer, "Communication with Older People: Basic Considerations," in *Aging and Communication*, eds. H. J. Oyer and E. J. Oyer (Baltimore: University Park Press, 1976), pp. 10–12.

12. E. R. Mahoney, "The Processual Characteristics of Self Conception," *The Sociological Quarterly*, 14 (1973), 517–33.

13. R. Cohn, "The Effect of Employment Status Change on Self-Attitudes," *Social Psychology*, 41 (1978), 81–93; J. Champoux, "Work, Central Life Interests, and Self-Concept," *Pacific Sociological Review*, 21 (1978), 209–20.

14. E. Palmore and C. Luikart, "Health and Social Factors Related to Life Satisfaction," *Journal of Health and Social Behavior*, 13 (1972), 68–80.

15. Although the *quality* of that communication is vitally important. K. Connor, E. Powers, and G. Bultena, "Social Interaction and Life Satisfaction: An Empirical Assessment of Late-Life Patterns," *Journal of Gerontology*, 34 (1979), 116–21.

16. The following sources were especially helpful in preparing this section of the chapter: S. Kalter, *Instant Parent* (New York: A & W Publishers, Inc., 1979); C. Berman, *Making It as a Stepparent* (New York: Doubleday & Company, Inc.); L. A. Westoff, *The Second Time Around* (New York: The Viking Press, 1977); H. Thomson, *The Successful Stepparent* (New York: Harper and Row, 1966); J. Noble and W. Noble, *How to Live with Other People's Children* (New York: Hawthorn Books, Inc., 1977); S. Gettleman, and J. Markowitz, *The Courage to Divorce* (New York: Simon and Schuster, 1974).

CHAPTER 10

1. Frustration's role in conflict is documented from such fields as social psychology. In recent years, sometimes through criticism of Freud's work, it has become vogue to dismiss the "frustration" factor as part of conflict. I find, however, that such dismissals are mostly semantic and result because early work in psychology considered frustration the all-encompassing basis of conflict. Between different disciplines and different perspectives, the use of the word frustration has become more finely tuned and has caused us to divide and subdivide concepts to the point that confusion has resulted. Although in this chapter the term frustration is used frequently when discussing conflict, it

does not reflect a lack of sensitivity to more recent distinctions which have appropriately called for caution when using the term frustration in the all-encompassing sense. See, for example: H. W. Simons, "Persuasion in Social Conflicts: A Critique of Prevailing Conceptions and a Framework for Future Research," *Speech Monographs*, 39 (November 1972), 228–47. See especially the critique of speech communication texts reflected in footnote 15 (p. 230) where Simon points out:

> Conflict is assumed to arise from the individual's paranoid response to frustration, not from the reality of the situation or the intransigence of others. To resolve or reduce conflict, the authors suggest that the group (the "system" in this case) employ "therapeutic measures" with the "deviant" as a way of socializing him. Absent from consideration is even the remote possibility that the nonconformist may have real grievances which are willfully and unjustly thwarted by others.

The argument, of course, is not with frustration per se, but with the use of frustration in the *paranoid* sense. Simon aptly points out in his article additional areas he feels have not been open to the kind of distinction and definition of terms appropriate to the discussion of conflict from a communication perspective. General perspectives on the relationship of communication to conflict can be found in such works as: T. J. Saine, "Perceiving Communication Conflict," *Speech Monographs*, 41 (March 1974), 49–52 (where the review of pertinent literature is discussed); D. W. Johnson, "Communication and the Inducement of Cooperative Behavior in Conflicts: A Critical Review," *Speech Monographs*, 41 (March 1974), 63–78.

2. Different definitions of frustration are put forth in various basic works in psychology and psychology-related disciplines. To examine the relationship to abnormal behavior see: Goodstein, L. D. and J. F. Calhoun, *Understanding Abnormal Behavior* (Reading, Mass: Addison Wesley Publishing Co., 1982).

3. Immediacy is a relative term. Many times with long-range goals, immediacy may be determined by the age of the individual. The older one gets, the more immediate the need, the more serious an obstacle to fulfilling that need; thus, the more frustration the obstacle may cause. Also, the term *need* is often interchanged with the word *goal* when discussing frustration and conflict. I have used *goal* for consistency.

4. Some of the same symptoms are associated with hyperactivity.

5. As discussed in various sources including B. R. Sappenfield, *Personality Dynamics* (New York: Alfred A. Knopf, Inc., 1959).

6. Self-concept applied to interpersonal communication stresses the need for a normally functioning self-concept as a requirement for effective and mutually satisfying interpersonal interaction.

7. B. D. Ruben, "Communication and Conflict: A System-Theoretic Perspective," *The Quarterly Journal of Speech*, 64 (1978), 209.

8. Also termed approach-approach, approach-avoidance, avoidance-avoidance.

9. An early discussion of such sources can be found in: B. R. Sappenfield, *Personality Dynamics* (New York: Alfred A. Knopf, Inc., 1935), p. 98.

10. Ruben, "Communication and Conflict," p. 209. Ruben also points out that actual conflict may not be necessary; our simply thinking it exists can play a part in our decisions. He states:

> As one may conceive of one's self to be in a dysfunctional conflict state when one is not, from the perspective of a system-in-adaptation, similarly it is possible for an individual or a multi-individual system to be in conflict when the persons involved have not so conceptualized the situation. For the individual or the species, the consequences of disease and epidemic are experienced quite apart from

whether they are identified, conceptualized, and labeled; we were as susceptible to the deleterious effects of smoking prior to research and the Surgeon General's dictum, as after. And, of course, the reverse situation may also obtain, as when one conceives of one's self as unsuited or incapable of a particular environmental demand, when in fact the concerns are unfounded. (p. 209)

11. Ibid.

12. A perspective on perceived communication conflict can be seen in the introductory discussion of Saine's article: T. J. Saine, "Perceiving Communication Conflict," *Communication Monographs* 41 (March 1974), 49–52.

13. J. Kelly, *Organizational Behavior* (Homewood, Ill.: Richard D. Irwin, Inc., and The Dorsey Press, 1969), pp. 500–5.

14. M. A. Fitzpatrick and J. Winke, "You Always Hurt the One You Love: Strategies and Tactics in Interpersonal Conflict," *Communication Research*, 1 (1975), 222–39.

15. Ibid., Table 1, p. 7.

16. Ibid., p. 8. In footnote 36 Fitzpatrick and Winke point out that:

> Since only 14 subjects indicated that they were engaged, this category was collapsed with what we called "exclusively involved." Thus, there were 54 married, 65 exclusively involved, 78 seriously involved, and 72 casually involved with their opposite sex others in this study. (italics added)

17. Ibid., italics added.

18. Ibid., italics added.

19. Ibid., italics added.

20. Ibid., italics added.

21. Ibid., p. 10.

22. Ibid. Citing: J. T. Tedeschi, *The Social Influence Process* (New York: Aldine Publishing Co., 1972).

23. Ibid., p. 11.

24. Ibid.

25. Ibid. Also citing: M. L. Hoffman, "Sex Differences in Empathy and Related Behaviors," *Psychological Bulletin*, 84 (1977), 712–22.

26. Ibid., p. 11.

27. As discussed in L. Marquit, "Work in the Fast Lane," *Northeast Training News*, (June 1978), 12–13, 18.

28. A. L. Sillars, "Attributions and Communication in Roommate Conflicts," *Communication Monographs*, 47 (August 1980), 180–200.

29. The approach to conflict discussed here is adapted from a communication-argumentation orientation as presented in: N. A. Reiches and H. B. Harral, "Argument in Negotiation: A Theoretical and Empirical Approach," *Speech Monographs*, 41 (March 1974), 36–48. Reiches and Harral point out (quoting Patchen) that "most theories of bargaining do not give direct and explicit attention to the process of interaction between the parties." Citing: M. Patchen, "Models of Cooperation and Conflict: A Critical Review," *Journal of Conflict Resolution*, 14 (1970), 392. Using an extension of Sawyer and Guetzkow's work, Reiches and Harral see "negotiation interaction" most usefully recognized as argumentation . . ." (Ibid., p. 36). Citing: J. Sawyer and H. Guetzkow, "Bargaining and Negotiation in International Relations," in *International Behavior: A Social Psychological Analysis*, ed. Herbert C. Kelman (New York: Holt, Rinehart and Winston, 1965), p. 479.

30. Ibid., p. 39, and pointing to: Douglas Ehninger, "Argumentation as Method: Its

Nature, Its Limitations and Its Uses," *Speech Monographs*, 37 (1970), 101–10. Reiches and Harral, "Argument in Negotiations," p. 39, note:

> In Douglas Ehninger's terms, they are engaged in a critical and cooperative investigation. Particularly fitting this view of negotiation, Ehninger claims that argument encompasses those situations in which mutually exclusive, or non-contenable, positions present themselves. Both arguers present their perspectives on the issue, and both may examine, probe, and correct the other's view points. Hence they product a dialectic, moving toward mutually acceptable conclusions.

31. R. Zemke, "Using Power to Negotiate: Everyone Can Do It—Successfully," *Training/HRD* (February 1980), 29–30.
32. Reiches and Harral, "Argumentation in Negotiation, p. 39. An additional perspective can be found in: W. A. Donohue, "An Empirical Framework for Examining Negotiation Processes and Outcomes," *Communication Monographs*, 45 (August 1978), 247–57.

Index

U

Underpersonal, 31, 322
Undersocial, 28
University of California at Los
　　Angeles (UCLA), 234
Upward communication, 233, 322
Urwick, L., 340
Ury, W., 256
Utah, Brigham Young University, 62

V

Value hierarchy, 322
Values, 322
Vaughan, F., 67
Verbal immediacy, 119, 322
Vermont, dialects, 108
Villard, K.L., 191
Virginia, Winchester, 128
Vocabulary, 120
Voice, 157–58

W

Wahlers, K.J., 336, 339
Wakefield, B., 91
Walker, E.G., 330
Walsh, R.N., 67

Warshaw, M., 287
Washington state, 274;
　　University of Puget Sound, 84
Watson, O.M., 333
Weaver, C.H., 91
Webber, A., 326
Weber, M., 340
Wedge drivers, 322
Weick, K., 257
Weinberg, S.B., 91, 220
Weinhold, B., 33
Weintraub, S., 328
Werbel, W.S., 337
Westoff, L.A., 343
West Virginia, 140, 299;
　　dialects, 108
Wheeless, L.R., 327
Whipple, L.J., 191
Whistle blowing, 235, 322
Whiteneck, G.G., 326
Whyte, W.F., 341
Whyte, W.H., Jr., 257
Wiener, M., 334
Williams, B., 335
Wiliams, F., 328, 331
Williams, M., 332
Willis, F.N., 332, 334
Wilmont, W., 314
Wilson, E.D., 33
Winke, J., 303, 345

Winn, W.J., 256
Withholders, 322
Wolvin, C., 91
Wood, J.T., 125, 339
Woodward, K.L., 287
Words, see Language
Worthy, M., 327
Wright, D.W., 221
Wright, P.H., 325, 327
Wydro, K., 257
Wynne, L., 342

Y

Yalom, I., 337
Yates, M.P., 340
Yglesias, H., 67
Young, L., 287

Z

Zakas, S., 165
Zander, A., 336, 338
Zemke, R., 346
Zimbardo, P.G., 67, 326
Zunin, L., 191
Zunin, N., 191